THE LIFE AND SONGS OF STEPHEN FOSTER

THE LIFE AND SONGS OF STEPHEN FOSTER

A Revealing Portrait of the Forgotten Man behind "Swanee River," "Beautiful Dreamer," and "My Old Kentucky Home"

JoAnne O'Connell

ROWMAN & LITTLEFIELD
Lanham • Boulder • New York • London

Published by Rowman & Littlefield
A wholly owned subsidary of The Rowman & Littlefield Publishing Group, Inc.
4501 Forbes Boulevard, Suite 200, Lanham, Maryland 20706
www.rowman.com

Unit A, Whitacre Mews, 26-34 Stannary Street, London SE11 4AB

British Library Cataloguing in Publication Information Available

Library of Congress Cataloging-in-Publication Data

Names: O'Connell, JoAnne, 1950–
Title: The life and songs of Stephen Foster : a revealing portrait of the forgotten man behind Swanee River, Beautiful dreamer, and My old Kentucky home / JoAnne O'Connell.
Description: Lanham : Rowman & Littlefield, 2016. | Includes bibliographical references and index.
Identifiers: LCCN 2016011230 | ISBN 9781442253865 (hardcover : alk. paper)
Subjects: LCSH: Foster, Stephen Collins, 1826–1864. | Composers—United States—Biography. | Popular music—United States—To 1901—History and criticism.
Classification: LCC ML410.F78 O3 2016 | DDC 782.42164092—dc23 LC record available at http://lccn.loc.gov/2016011230

Printed in the United States of America

To the memory of my mother, the last of the "piano girls"

And for Daniel and Kathryn

CONTENTS

ILLUSTRATIONS

Following page 202

1. Stephen's parents, Eliza Clayland and William Barclay Foster, posed for a daguerreotype in their later middle years. Courtesy of the Foster Hall Collection, Center for American Music, University of Pittsburgh.
2. White Cottage, the Foster family home where Stephen Foster was born a few miles east of Pittsburgh. It was foreclosed when he was a just toddler. Courtesy of the Foster Hall Collection, Center for American Music, University of Pittsburgh.
3. The Federal Hill mansion in Bardstown, Kentucky, long associated with "My Old Kentucky Home," was built by a cousin of Stephen Foster's father's. The composer's sister Charlotte received a marriage proposal from one of the owner's sons. My Old Kentucky Home State Park, with permission from the Kentucky Department of Parks, Tourism, Arts, and Heritage Cabinet, Frankfort, KY.
4. Sheet music cover features Thomas Dartmouth Rice performing the Jim Crow–style dance he originated in the early 1830s in the cities on the Ohio River. His twisted body is modeled after a handicapped, black man, but his leg and feet appear to be imitating a jig-like dance step. American Minstrel Show Collection, 1823–1947, courtesy of the Harvard Theatre Collection, Houghton Library, Cambridge, MA.

5. Brother William, as the Fosters' adopted oldest son was known, became vice president of the Pennsylvania Railroad and was more a father figure than a brother to Stephen. Courtesy of the Foster Hall Collection, Center for American Music, University of Pittsburgh.

6. Stephen's sister Ann Eliza married the Reverend Edward Y. Buchanan, brother of the future President of the United States. Courtesy of the Foster Hall Collection, Center for American Music, University of Pittsburgh.

7. Map from 1855 showing Pittsburgh at the point between the Allegheny River to the north, the Monongahela River to the south, and the Ohio River going west. On the northern shore of the Allegheny River is Allegheny City, where Stephen Foster grew to adulthood. Courtesy of the Archives Service Center, University of Pittsburgh Library System.

8. When the African American musician Frank Johnson performed in Allegheny City in 1842, his black band members were attacked and Mayor William B. Foster came to their rescue. Lithograph by Alfred M. Hoffy, Arch Street Gallery, Philadelphia, 1846. With permission of the Historical Society of Pennsylvania, Philadelphia, PA.

9. Henry Kleber, a classically trained German musician living in Allegheny near the Fosters, taught Stephen music theory and encouraged him to write songs. Courtesy of the Foster Hall Collection, Center for American Music, University of Pittsburgh.

10. Framed daguerreotype of Stephen Foster looking a bit rough around the edges, revealing the scar he carried on his cheek, the result of an accident or a street brawl. Courtesy of the Foster Hall Collection, Center for American Music, University of Pittsburgh.

11. While he went away to fight in the Mexican-American War, Dunning Foster left his brother Stephen in charge of the bookkeeping at his Cincinnati business. Courtesy of the Foster Hall Collection, Center for American Music, University of Pittsburgh.

12. No. 4 Cassilly's Row on the Cincinnati waterfront, where Stephen Foster worked as a bookkeeper at Irwin & Foster, his brother's business. The building is identified by the first awning on the left side, closest to the Ohio River. Fontayne-Porter daguerreotype, *Panorama of 1848 Cincinnati*, plate 2, with permis-

sion of the Cincinnati Public Library, Hamilton County, Genealogy and History Division.

13. Marion Foster, Stephen and Jane's only child, appearing quite ladylike in a long gown. Courtesy of the Foster Hall Collection, Center for American Music, University of Pittsburgh.

14. Martin Delany studied medicine under Stephen Foster's father-in-law, before he became one of the first black men to attend Harvard Medical School. Courtesy of the Schomburg Center for Research in Black Culture, New York Public Library Digital Collections.

15. Henry Foster held a clerkship in Washington, D.C., when he lobbied unsuccessfully to secure an appointment for his brother Stephen at West Point. Courtesy of the Foster Hall Collection, Center for American Music, University of Pittsburgh.

16. In top hat, long coat tails, and baton, the minstrel Edwin P. Christy projected an impressive image, refined enough to attract the ladies. American Minstrel Show Collection, 1823–1847. Courtesy of the Harvard Theatre Collection, Houghton Library, Cambridge, MA.

17. Foster's "Old Folks at Home" was originally published with the minstrel's name Edwin P. Christy on the cover as the song's composer. Published by Firth, Pond & Co., New York. Courtesy of the Foster Hall Collection, Center for American Music, University of Pittsburgh.

18. The minstrel Charles White was the king of sentimental minstrelsy. His stage characters, like this artist holding a painter's palette, portrayed African Americans as decent, refined men. American Minstrel Show Collection, 1823–1947, courtesy of the Harvard Theatre Collection, Houghton Library, Cambridge, MA.

19. Fashionable brick row house still standing at 601 Bloomfield Street in Hoboken, New Jersey. Stephen Foster lived there with his wife and daughter when he wrote "I Dream of Jeanie with the Light Brown Hair."

20. Before Stephen's publisher Firth, Pond and Company moved to Broadway, their music business was housed in a revolutionary-era building at Franklin Square. Courtesy of the Foster Hall Collection, Center for American Music, University of Pittsburgh.

21. James Buchanan was a politically valuable in-law after his younger brother Edward married Stephen Foster's sister Ann Eliza. Brady daguerreotype, courtesy of the Library of Congress, Prints and Photographs Division, Washington, DC.
22. Stephen Foster is well-dressed and optimistic as he poses for a professional photo in 1859, the year before he moved to New York. Courtesy of the Foster Hall Collection, Center for American Music, University of Pittsburgh.
23. Stephen Foster's brother Morrison was closest to the composer, until his Copperhead politics during the Civil War threatened the relationship. Courtesy of the Foster Hall Collection, Center for American Music, University of Pittsburgh.
24. Clement L. Vallandigham, the leader of the Copperheads, became a close friend of Morrison Foster and his wife after they moved to Cleveland, Ohio. Courtesy of the Library of Congress, Prints and Photographs Division, Washington, DC.
25. 1844 cartoon "Political Cock Fighters" showing presidential candidates Clay and Polk battling it out as fighting roosters in the ring, while Daniel Webster wages his "best chowders on the Kentucky Rooster." Courtesy of the Library of Congress, Cartoon Prints, American Division, Washington, DC.
26. Copperheads were Northern Democrats who sympathized with the South and favored peace at any price. Courtesy of the Library of Congress, Prints and Photographs Division, Washington, DC.
27. Henrietta Foster taught her young brother Stephen basic music theory at her farmhouse in Youngstown, Ohio. Her second husband, Major Jesse Thornton, appears in Union blue. Courtesy of the Foster Hall Collection, Center for American Music, University of Pittsburgh.
28. Stephen Foster's large brown eyes are glowing but sad in this often reproduced picture of the composer, with his coat unbuttoned and his bowtie slightly askew. Courtesy of the Foster Hall Collection, Center for American Music, University of Pittsburgh.
29. Stephen Foster poses in New York with his soldier-lyricist George Cooper (the man on the right), who was identified as "the left wing of the song factory." Courtesy of the Foster Hall Collection, Center for American Music, University of Pittsburgh.

30. Sheet music cover featuring New York lyricist George Cooper. After Stephen's death, Cooper teamed up with several different composers to write the words for variety, operetta, and vaudeville songs. Courtesy of the Houghton Theater Library, Digital Collection, Harvard University, Cambridge, MA.

31. Map from 1860 showing Lower Manhattan, where Stephen Foster spent the final year of his life in a hotel room at the corner of Bayard Street and the Bowery, a few blocks from the notorious slum Five Points. Courtesy of the Library of Congress, Geography and Map Division, Washington, DC.

32. The famous comic singer Tony Pastor worked as a minstrel and a clown before he became known as the Father of Vaudeville, and Stephen Foster wrote a song for him. Courtesy of the Billy Rose Theatre Collection, the New York Public Library for the Performing Arts.

33. Andrew Carnegie in 1861. The future steel magnate was suspected of having more than a professional interest in Jane Foster when he gave her a job in one of his telegraph offices. Courtesy of the Library of Congress, Prints and Photographs Division, Washington, DC.

34. Drawing of the interior of a New York concert saloon on Houston Street, showing a variety act being performed on the stage while waiter girls serve alcoholic beverages. Courtesy of the New York Public Library.

35. Laura Keene, the British-born theatrical manager, starred at Ford's Theatre on the night Lincoln was assassinated, but she also staged lavish musical spectacles. Albumen silver print by Charles DeForest Fredricks, c. 1863, with permission from the National Portrait Gallery, Smithsonian Institution, Washington, DC, and Art Source, New York, NY.

36. Actor Charles W. Couldock, a friend of Morrison Foster, onstage with his talented daughter. Eliza Couldock appeared in *The Seven Sisters* on the night Stephen and Jane watched the show at Laura Keene's Theater. Courtesy of the Foster Hall Collection, Center for American Music, University of Pittsburgh.

37. The surviving Foster siblings posed for a picture after Stephen Foster's death in January, 1864: clockwise, left to right, Henry Foster, Morrison Foster, Henrietta Thornton, and Ann Eliza Bu-

ACKNOWLEDGMENTS

In a project that has spanned more than a decade, acknowledgements must be extended over space and time. My deepest gratitude goes to the University of Pittsburgh's Stephen Foster Memorial and Center for American Music and to Deane L. Root, curator of the museum, who first introduced me to the idea that a new study of Foster was warranted. I would also like to thank Kathryn Miller Haines, assistant curator at the same museum, for opening up the treasure trove of documents in the Foster Hall Collection, where I accessed hundreds of letters, journals, song sheets, and miscellaneous artifacts that made this study possible. In addition, I would like to thank Edward Muller, Peter Karsten, Van Beck Hall, and Richard Ostreicher from the History Department at the University of Pittsburgh, exemplary historians who understood and encouraged the interdisciplinary nature of my research.

The librarians, curators, and preservationists who care for and maintain the archives that provide the building blocks for this biography can never be complimented enough. I want to thank the dedicated personnel at the Mifflin County Historical Society in Lewistown, Pennsylvania; the Performing Arts Library at Lincoln Center, New York; the Pennsylvania Room at the Oakland branch of the Carnegie Public Library in Pittsburgh; the New York City Public Library; and many others. I would also like to make special mention of Harvard's Houghton Library Reading Room in Cambridge, Massachusetts, where the special collections librarian Elizabeth Falsey afforded me the pleasure of rummaging through boxes of playbills, memorabilia, and songsters from the Harvard Theater Collection.

For illustrating this book and making the story visually appealing, I would like to credit the Foster Hall Collection at the University of Pittsburgh for images of Stephen Foster and his family. Other photos, artwork, maps, and song sheets that appear in the book were provided by the Historical Society of Pennsylvania; the National Portrait Gallery at the Smithsonian in Washington, D.C.; the Library of Congress; the Cincinnati Public Library, Genealogy and History Division, Hamilton County; the Archives Service Center at the University of Pittsburgh Library System; the Schonburg Center for Research in Black Culture at the New York Public Library; IBDb (Internet Broadway Database); the American Memory Collections of Sheet Music from the Library of Congress, and many others. I am also indebted to databases of newspapers such as the *New York Times*, which have made their historic collections available to researchers around the globe.

The wonderful portrait of Stephen Foster that appears on the cover is taken from the sentimental painting known as *Beautiful Dreamer* by Howard Chandler Christy. I located this huge canvas while touring the museum at the Stephen Foster Folk Culture Center State Park in White Springs, Florida, where the original hangs on the wall. I am grateful to park service specialist Andrea Thomas for permission to use it on the cover of my book.

Not to be forgotten are the writers, historians, musicologists, independent scholars, and other curious men and women on whose ideas I have built many of my arguments. Although their names are too numerous to mention here, no such list would be complete without mentioning musicologist Charles Hamm, whose *Yesterdays* is still the most comprehensive, readable, and insightful history of American song in print. Books and articles about nineteenth-century history, economics, politics, and society that I used to fashion Foster's background story can be found in the lengthy bibliography at the back of this book.

Finally, I am deeply indebted to my publisher, Rowman & Littlefield, and their former senior acquisitions editor Bennett Graff, who offered the contract that allowed me to bring my work to the public. I would also like to thank Rowman & Littlefield's acquiring editor for music Natalie Mandziuk, who, among other things, held my hand throughout to ensure we got across the finish line; series editor June

Sawyers for her advice and encouragement; former assistant editor Monica Savaglia for many contributions; and senior production editor Kellie Hagan, who handled the crucial final stage of the book's production.

Of course, I want to thank friends and family, including Daniel, Kathryn, John, Debra, and Barbara, who listened to me talk about the Fosters for years when the composer and his family became my family, and for supporting me in my continued dedication to the project.

In an acknowledgement of this nature, I cannot fail to mention Pittsburgh, Pennsylvania, Stephen Foster's hometown, where I lived for eight years, enchanted by the same hills, valleys, and rivers that touched the heart of the composer. The city that glows at night and looks best when viewed from the lofty heights of Mt. Washington was endemic to Foster's spirit and music and became intertwined with my being as well. Although the factories and smokestacks are no longer visible, reminders of the past can be seen in the many century-old brick buildings still standing, gracefully defying their age. The White Cottage, where Foster was born, stands on Penn Avenue with its reconfigured architecture and has been converted into an apartment building. Only a plaque notifies the public that this was the famous composer's birthplace. Allegheny Town, where Stephen grew to manhood, is today known as the Northside of Pittsburgh, but the green commons where the composer walked hand in hand with his daughter Marion still survive. Reproductions of the paddle steamers that carried Foster to and from Cincinnati still ply the famous waterways, where even now it is possible to book a seat and fall into a reverie of long ago.

STEPHEN COLLINS FOSTER LIFE EVENTS

1807 William Barclay Foster of Virginia marries Eliza Clayland Tomlinson of Maryland in Chambersburg, Pennsylvania, and settles in Pittsburgh, Pennsylvania. They start a large family.

1814 William Barclay Foster purchases a farm, a few miles east of Pittsburgh, on which he constructs the family home, White Cottage, on land bordering the Allegheny River. He also lays out a town named Lawrenceville and donates land for the construction of the Allegheny Arsenal.

1815 After their baby son dies, William and Eliza Foster adopt an eight-year-old boy and name him William B. Foster Jr., after the dead child.

1815 William Barclay Foster spends his own fortune to send military supplies to Andrew Jackson in New Orleans and is not reimbursed by the government.

1826 The White Cottage is foreclosed by the Bank of the United States, but the Fosters remain in the house for several additional years. William Foster Jr. leaves home to start his career building canals.

1826 Stephen Collins Foster, the ninth child of William and Eliza Foster, is born on July 4th at the White Cottage. His older living siblings are William Barclay Jr., Charlotte Susanna, Ann Eliza, Henry Baldwin, Henrietta Angelica, Dunning McNair, and Morrison Foster.

1828 The musically talented Charlotte Susanna Foster travels to Kentucky to visit relatives.

1829 The Fosters' last child, James Clayland, is born. Charlotte dies at the age of nineteen in Louisville, Kentucky.

1830 James Clayland dies at fifteen months old. Around this year, the Fosters move out of the White Cottage into a series of boarding-houses in Pittsburgh.

1832 Eliza Foster moves to Harmony, Pennsylvania, with Stephen and four of her children. William Barclay Foster remains working in Pittsburgh with his son Dunning.

1833 William Barclay Foster and his family move to a house in Allegheny Town, Pennsylvania, across the river and northeast of Pitts-burgh.

1833 Ann Eliza Foster marries the Reverend Edward Young Buchanan, brother of the future president of the United States, James Buchanan.

1833 Eliza Foster takes Stephen and his sister Henrietta to visit Eliza's half brothers in Augusta, Kentucky.

1833 Stephen, at the age of seven, walks into Smith and Mellor's Music Store in Pittsburgh and astounds everyone when he plays "Hail Columbia" on the flageolet.

1834 An African American bound servant named Kitty "with up-wards of three years to serve" moves into the Foster house.

1835 William Foster Jr. is transferred to work on the canals in Youngstown, Ohio, where he buys farmland intending to build a house for the Fosters.

1835 The neighborhood children and nine-year-old Stephen per-form minstrel songs in a carriage house in Allegheny, singing "Jump Jim Crow" and "Zip Coon."

1836 Eliza Foster moves to a boardinghouse in Youngstown, Ohio, with her sons Stephen and Morrison.

1837 Henrietta Foster marries Thomas Wick and settles in Young-stown, and Stephen visits his sister frequently. William Foster Jr. mar-ries Thomas's sister Mary Wick.

1838 William Foster Jr.'s wife Mary dies and he leaves Youngstown. The Fosters settle back in Allegheny and become financially dependent on their adopted son, who will become very successful with the rail-roads.

1840 William Foster Jr. puts Stephen in school at the Towanda Academy in central Pennsylvania and later transfers his brother to the Athens Academy at Tioga Point.

1841 Stephen writes his first composition, "The Tioga Waltz," and performs it at the Athens Academy graduation ceremony. Stephen abruptly leaves the school.

1841 Stephen enrolls at Jefferson College in Canonsburg, Pennsylvania, and stays one week.

1841 William B. Foster Sr. applies for bankruptcy under the new national bankruptcy law.

1841 Stephen and his parents move into a house in Allegheny purchased by William Foster Jr. Stephen stays at home and studies with the German musician Henry Kleber.

1842 William B. Foster Sr. is elected mayor of Allegheny City.

1842 Henrietta's husband Thomas Wick dies and William Foster Jr. remarries a widow from a wealthy New York family.

1843 William Foster Jr. builds a large new house for the Fosters at 605 Union Avenue in Allegheny City, which will become their permanent home.

1843 Frank Johnson's African American band performs in Allegheny City and the musicians are attacked by white mobs. Stephen's father defends the musicians.

1844 George Willig of Philadelphia brings out Stephen's first published composition, "Open Thy Lattice, Love."

1845 Stephen composes the minstrel songs "Lou'siana Belle" and "Old Uncle Ned" for the "Knights of the Square Table," a neighborhood music club.

1846 Stephen takes a job at McCormick's Cotton Mill in Allegheny. He applies to be admitted to West Point and is turned down.

1846 Stephen moves to Cincinnati to work as a bookkeeper at his brother Dunning's business along the Ohio River.

1847 Dunning goes off to fight in the Mexican-American War, and Stephen starts handing out original compositions to minstrel performers in Cincinnati to sing on the stage.

1847 W. C. Peters of Cincinnati publishes "Oh! Susanna" and several other Foster titles.

1848 Stephen composes a unique minstrel song "Nelly Was a Lady" that depicts African Americans as human beings with feelings.

1849 Stephen signs a royalty-paying contract with the New York music publishers Firth, Pond and Company.

1850 Stephen returns to Pittsburgh and marries Jane McDowell at the Trinity Episcopal Church in Allegheny. They move into the house on Union Avenue with all the Fosters.

1851 Stephen and Jane's daughter, Marion Foster, is born on April 18.

1851 Stephen spends time with his abolitionist, poet friend Charles Shiras and writes "Old Folks at Home." He allows the minstrel performer Edwin P. Christy to put his name on the sheet music cover as composer.

1852 Stephen takes a trip down the Mississippi River to New Orleans, where from the deck of the boat, he watches slaves working in the fields.

1853 Stephen composes "My Old Kentucky Home, Good Night!" and collaborates with Charles Shiras on a musical play that is performed in Pittsburgh.

1854 Charles Shiras dies and Edwin Christy retires from the stage. Minstrelsy becomes more insulting toward African Americans and Stephen abandons the minstrel genre altogether. He devotes his talents to writing parlor songs.

1854 Stephen moves to New York alone to work on the *Social Orchestra*. His wife and daughter join him in a row house in Hoboken, New Jersey, where he writes "Jeanie with the Light Brown Hair."

1855 Stephen moves back home to Allegheny City; his parents Eliza and William Foster die.

1856 Stephen composes campaign songs to help his sister's brother-in-law James Buchanan win the presidency.

1857 William Foster Jr. sells the Allegheny house while Stephen sells the royalty rights to all his songs. Stephen, Jane, and Marion move into boardinghouses.

1858 Stephen neglects his songwriting for nights out drinking. On a trip to Cincinnati, he spends the night serenading and carousing.

1860 Morrison Foster marries and moves to Cleveland, where he joins the Copperheads. William Foster Jr., dies, and Stephen and his family move to New York City.

1861 The Civil War begins. Foster contacts new publishers in New York but they pay no royalties. Jane Foster moves to Greensburg, Pennsylvania, where she works in a telegraph office relaying war news.

1862 Stephen writes Civil War songs that he dedicates to Abraham Lincoln and becomes estranged from his politically conservative family. He begins to discover a new direction in his songwriting.

1863 Stephen collaborates with a young lyricist named George Cooper, and together they write variety and music hall style songs. Stephen composes the music for a song performed by Tony Pastor, the father of vaudeville.

1864 Stephen suffers an accidental or self-inflicted injury in his hotel room on the Bowery. He is taken to Belleview Hospital, where he dies three days later on January 13, 1864.

INTRODUCTION

At one time, nearly every American knew the name Stephen Collins Foster and could sing along with the choruses of his best-loved songs, melodies immediately recognizable by their nicknames, like "Swanee River" and "Doo-dah!" Not today. I recently walked into a music store, an actual brick-and-mortar building where sheet music could still be purchased along with electronic keyboards and guitars and power amplifiers. When I asked the young woman assisting me if she recognized the composer's name, she answered with a blank expression. Men and women who grew up before the civil rights movement sang Foster's songs in schools and around campfires or heard the familiar refrains as background music in their favorite films. Indeed, his melodies swirled around in the recesses of the mind like cultural DNA, ready to provide a comforting blanket of nostalgia and security—so much a part of Americana that they were conflated with folk music.

For more than a century, the man who wrote the state songs of Florida and Kentucky was a towering figure in American music, until his once-revered plantation songs were subjected to allegations of racism and nobody would dare perform them. Songs not disparaged as racist like "Beautiful Dreamer" and "Jeanie with the Light Brown Hair" were lost to the new generation for other reasons. During the rock 'n' roll era, they sounded too sweet, the music not jarring enough, and the words were too sentimental for modern tastes. Still, Foster's most famous melodies continue to pop up again and again, even if only as historical markers of the past. In the award-winning film *The King's*

Speech the stammering king of Great Britain learns to overcome his handicap by singing to the tune of Foster's "Old Folks at Home," and every May on Derby Day "My Old Kentucky Home" is broadcast to millions of Americans in their living rooms, where some people still know the words and sing along.

Very little is understood about the man who wrote the songs that captured the American spirit and were hummed and whistled by people at all points on the social spectrum. Foster kept no personal journal, and what few letters he wrote when he was away from home were destroyed or lost by his family. He was a difficult man to know. One acquaintance wrote the following of the world-famous composer: "He would walk, talk, eat and drink with you, and yet always seem distant. . . . Whether it was a natural bashfulness, or a voluntary reserve, I cannot say, but those who knew him most intimately were never familiar."[1] Stephen Foster's family was also protective of his image and purposely created a smokescreen to obfuscate the facts surrounding his life and, later, his mysterious death.

Few people realized that the man who wrote about canebrakes and cotton was actually a Northerner from Pittsburgh, Pennsylvania, who never, as an adult, stepped below the Mason-Dixon line. When he wrote "Way down upon de Swanee River . . . Sadly I roam," the composer of "Old Folks at Home" was not recalling a muddy river in northern Florida, but rather one of the three rivers of his hometown, the Monongahela, the Allegheny, or the Ohio. His songs about roaming "far from home" actually derived from personal memories of a youth spent traipsing from town to town in the cold, hilly lands of western Pennsylvania and Ohio, not in the sun drenched, flat terrain of the South, dotted with cabins and wild flowers. The real Foster grew up surrounded by mountains embedded with coal that was dug out to fuel Pittsburgh's burgeoning factories, where deafening machines spit out black puffs of smoke against darkly burnished skies. Early biographers who speculated that Foster must have visited the South to write so knowingly about cotton did not understand that he learned about the white fluffy fibers in Pittsburgh, which boasted cotton mills as big as its iron manufacturing plants long before the city produced steel. Although the cotton mills are long gone, Stephen's hometown still contains reminders of his lost world in the hills and valleys of the cityscape and along the rivers he traveled frequently.

One problem confronting Foster's legacy is that while the composer was known to feel sympathy for the oppressed and to express that sympathy in his songs, he never openly avowed the antislavery cause. But even if he could not stand up to his conservative family and express his sentiments openly, his songs did, and that is what matters. His greatest plantation songs, like "Oh Boys, Carry Me 'Long" and "My Old Kentucky Home," were based on antislavery antecedents and carried messages of sympathy in words that were often camouflaged in slave dialect. Foster's inability to speak out against slavery was not that unusual at the time. Most Northerners, in fact, were like Foster—defiantly pro-Union and sympathetic to the plight of the slaves, yet with insufficient backbone to oppose the institution. He was in good company. Many men more courageous and politically astute, including President Lincoln, hemmed and hawed and appeared to stay on the fence about slavery for a very long time.

With Foster, it is best to deal with intentions, rather than with external communications, because he left no formal record of his true feelings on politics. Perhaps because his goal was to become the premier writer of America's songs, he thought it best to publicly steer clear of politics. The only time his music made an overt political statement was when he wrote campaign songs for President James Buchanan, but the songs may have stemmed from familial obligation, since Buchanan's brother was married to Stephen's sister and the Fosters relied on Democratic political connections to survive.

When the Civil War broke out, Stephen's older brother Morrison joined the radical pro-Southern wing of the Democratic Party that attacked President Lincoln and urged an immediate end to the war. Although many biographers concluded that Stephen held the same opinions as Morrison, the brothers were completely different. While Morrison was promoting Copperhead ideology and peace at any price, Stephen was writing war songs that encouraged men to fight for the Union to the bitter end. He was comfortable with subterfuge and ambiguity, for the minstrel stage had a history of conveying messages behind the burnt cork. If he could not openly oppose his family, he expressed his true feelings in the words to his songs.

To all outward appearances, Foster looked like a man who vacillated and changed his opinions and politics on a whim. Sometimes his actions are baffling, at other times infuriating. After stating his intention to become the best minstrel songwriter, he abruptly changed course and decided not to write minstrel songs at all. During the Civil War, he wrote and dedicated songs to Abraham Lincoln, yet four years prior to that, he had written campaign songs for the anti-abolitionist James Buchanan. And three years before that, when he was close friends with an abolitionist, he wrote songs that were sympathetic to the slaves and carried antislavery messages. He often gave the impression of being contradictory—one minstrel called him a "vacillating skunk"—but Foster was a conflicted man, forever fighting personal instincts opposed to those of his family. He even wavered back and forth on the style of music he would choose for his life's work, before finally deciding to abandon minstrelsy. His ambivalence and vacillation are terribly frustrating, but may have been the only way he could function and survive, since he was unwilling and unable to make a formal break with his family.

Although few performers today are comfortable singing Foster's plantation songs, at one time some people believed their sentimentality made them instruments of compassion in the antislavery crusade. When the antislavery *Uncle Tom's Cabin* was played on the stage, Foster's plantation songs were included and when the Fisk Jubilee Singers gave concerts of spirituals throughout the North and in Europe after the Civil War, they included Foster on their programs. Frederick Douglass did not like minstrel shows, but he did like plantation songs, because, he said, "they awaken the sympathies for the slave, in which anti-slavery principles take root, grow and flourish."[2] Douglass wrote, "It would seem almost absurd to say it, considering the use that has been made of them, that we have allies in the Ethiopian songs. . . . They are heart songs, and the finest feelings of human nature are expressed in them. 'Lucy Neal,' 'Old Kentucky Home,' and 'Uncle Ned,' can make the heart sad as well as merry, and can call forth a tear as well as a smile."[3]

Seven years before the outbreak of the Civil War, Foster's sympathetic minstrelsy was replaced by a raucous denigrating brand and he abandoned the genre altogether. Unfortunately, even if Foster stopped writing for the minstrel stage when it was timely to do so, it is all too easy for the present generation to ignore him, especially if his legacy is defined solely by plantation songs. It is essential to see that he earned the designation "father of American music" not for any one genre, but because his oeuvre was all-encompassing, far-reaching, and long-lasting. Foster wrote more than two hundred songs in different genres, and his legacy needs to be reassessed and appreciated in light of his total contribution to American music. He wrote sentimental songs for the ladies, war songs for the Union Army, mourning songs for the bereaved, religious hymns that were fun to sing, and parlor music for amateur performers. He even wrote a musical play that paved the way for Broadway.

Foster renounced the antebellum music style soon after he moved into Lower Manhattan at the beginning of the Civil War, when he began writing songs for the new variety stages that were popping up all around him, precursors to vaudeville. When the mood of the nation changed at the onset of the war, musical needs changed, too, as soldiers on furlough rushed to hear songs that made them laugh. Variety music was earthy and lively, custom-tailored to the ambiance of the concert saloons and music halls that rose up while minstrelsy declined. To create the new music, Foster joined forces with a young Union soldier who wrote the comic lighthearted lyrics the new genre demanded. Unfortunately, his critics and biographers scorned his efforts, and lumped his best theatrical songs like "If You've Only Got a Moustache" and "Mr. and Mrs. Brown" together with all his New York productions and labeled them "potboilers." The critics claimed he lost his muse in his final years, because they did not appreciate that his new musical style was a choice that led him into the future of popular song.

Stephen Foster was America's first professional songwriter. When copyrights and new technologies in printing and transportation turned music into a viable business option, he was the first man to try, and for a while succeed, at earning his living solely from writing songs, rather than from publishing or performing them. In writing songs that satisfied the needs of the people, he established a model for professional song composers in the future. Popular music reaches into the soul of the generation for which it is written, making men and women more responsive to their feelings as it helps them work out issues and deal with trying situations. In the antebellum years, Foster's songs of nostalgia helped a nation undergoing change come to terms with those transitions, and during the Civil War, when people needed to laugh to relieve unbearable stress, his comic songs helped them laugh. Other composers wrote popular songs before Foster, but none touched the hearts of so many, nor did their songs provide comfort and enjoyment to people

from all classes, genders, and races. Foster's songs lived on because
they served a vital function in their society, but they would not have
survived had his genius for melody not kept people singing them over
and over again.

When I first began to investigate Foster, I was curious about his
relationship to minstrelsy, but after years of study I concluded that his
broad creative imagination transcended both the limited minstrel genre
and the antebellum parlor songs. I began researching Foster at the
University of Pittsburgh under the direction of Deane L. Root, Curator
of the Stephen Foster Memorial Museum and Director of the Center
for American Music. Dr. Root first introduced me to the idea that what
little we know about the composer is "as much myth as fact" and that
more investigation into his life and works was warranted.[4] I took up the
challenge convinced that no matter how racist some of Foster's plantation songs appear today, the father of American music should be studied and understood, rather than shunted aside and forgotten. Once
engrossed in the research process, however, I learned that unraveling
the real Foster beneath layers of misrepresentation would not be an
easy task.

The official Foster archives in Pittsburgh contained few letters in the
composer's handwriting, although thousands of documents and memorabilia by family members and supporting actors in his life drama were
carefully catalogued, filed, and stored. Morrison Foster appointed himself keeper and protector of the Stephen Foster legacy immediately
after his brother's death, and then, by his own admission, consigned
hundreds of family letters, and perhaps some by Stephen himself, to the
flame. Concerned with protecting his brother's image from allegations
of alcoholism and dissipation, Morrison preserved only documents that
he thought significant and, with the exception of his songs, left little for
the biographer to investigate that would provide clues to the inner man.
Years later, when Morrison published the short biography *My Brother
Stephen* at the end of the nineteenth century, he avoided any topic that
might prove controversial and produced a hazy sketch of the composer
as he wanted him to be seen.

While it is not unusual for families to destroy the correspondence of
famous relatives to protect their reputations, with Stephen Foster the
task was done only too well. To counter the scarcity of personal records,
I turned to the historical record and researched the world in which he

lived, struggled, and died. I studied song sheets, newspapers, marriage and death records, and, of course, the history of Pittsburgh and the nation as a whole during the composer's life. The economy needed investigation, too, because Foster's generation endured excruciating economic hardships as they rode the waves of a fickle economy that offered no safety nets or laws to protect the poor. For details about his last years, where the only documents to survive are dated reminiscences provided by friends and acquaintances who knew him when he lived on the Bowery, I looked for answers in New York's theatrical scene during the Civil War.

Perhaps the point to consider is that Foster was not a static composer, and his reputation should not be defined by any one genre. Whatever he wrote, he was creating what the public and his publishers wanted. He was dynamic and changed his music to suit the times. More importantly, each new genre he touched was a step on a continuum that led to the next stage in popular music. His parlor songs like "Jeanie with the Light Brown Hair" set a standard for generations of popular songwriters to follow. His great plantation songs established a model of hybridity that can be seen in all the later African-infused genres, from jazz, through rock and roll, to rap. His songs for the variety stage left a footprint for vaudeville, and his musical spectacle established a model for musical comedy. Even his hymns established a blueprint for religious music crafted on the popular-song model.

Foster moved out of the antebellum mold and ventured into new and exciting musical styles in the last years of his life, but for decades, the critics denigrated his New York songs and refused to see that he was purposely venturing into new territory. Even today, they associate him mainly with his plantation songs, thereby limiting and misinforming his legacy. Foster's life was tragic. His family did not understand him. Performers and publishers took advantage of him and laughed at his naivety. They paid him almost nothing for his songs yet scorned him for his inability to demand more money for his genius. Foster may have appeared misdirected at crucial moments in his life, incapable of taking a position and sticking to it, but he was a man swept up in changing times and ideas. He was sensitive to the needs of the people and filled with compassion for the human suffering he saw all around him, which he assuaged with his songs. For this and many other reasons, his memory should not be neglected, nor should his songs or his life be relegated to a footnote in musical history.

I

PIONEER ELITES

William Barclay Foster spared no expense entertaining friends and neighbors on the tree-shaded grounds behind his rambling, white, cottage-style farmhouse. He mingled freely with his guests, chatting amiably as he replenished their glasses and escorted them around his estate at the edge of the town he had founded a dozen years earlier a few miles east of Pittsburgh. A haven from the belching smokestacks on the western horizon, the normally quiet Lawrenceville echoed that day with the sound of a cannon fired repeatedly and the laughter of joyous, if slightly inebriated, celebrants. While extravagant demonstrations on the nation's birthday were not unusual in the first part of the nineteenth century, the 1826 Fourth of July was the Jubilee, a commemoration of fifty years of liberty, and everyone anticipated a spectacular occasion. Liquor flowed and toasts were raised again and again to honor the founding fathers, whose wizened portraits were propped up on picnic tables for everyone to see.[1]

The men and women at William Foster's outdoor party were pioneer settlers of western Pennsylvania or their descendants, spirited folk who thanked heaven for their rights as freeholders to till the thousands of acres that had fallen almost gratuitously into their laps. When they tipped their glasses to the image of George Washington, staring out at them from one end of a long wooden table, they felt especially grateful. Not only was Washington the father of their country, but Pittsburghers also regarded the first president as the father of their city. At just twenty-one years of age, George had made a daring trip on horseback in freezing temperatures to the land, then claimed by the French, determining it was worth fighting for. When he returned the next year with a contingent of soldiers, he inadvertently kicked off a global war that ended with British control of most of North America, including the area that would be known as Pittsburgh.

Years later, a legend grew up that the young Washington, while traveling back to Virginia, had fallen off his raft into the icy Allegheny and pulled himself out onto the very ground now claimed by the Fosters. William, of course, knew the story and enjoyed telling it. Sometimes, he would strike a pose imitating Washington holding a map of the land at the forks in one hand above his head, while maneuvering his 6' 3" body onto the frozen riverbank; then he would point to the exact spot where the great man was "cast on the night of December 28, 1753 and nearly frozen."[2] William was indeed proud of his homestead and its history. His property extended all the way to the southern edge of the Allegheny and included the shoreline made sacred by the founding father.

If William drank a bit too much on this particular holiday, he needed no excuse. Alcohol was produced and consumed freely in western Pennsylvania, ever since the area's first settlers learned they could turn their wheat and rye into whiskey and carry it across the mountains on horseback to eager buyers in the East.[3] William was more excited than usual, however, for on this July 4th he was awaiting the arrival of a new addition to his already overextended Foster clan. As the partygoers congratulated their host on the birth of a child on such an important day, little did they know that this holiday was destined to be special in several ways and that those who witnessed it would speak many years later about what they considered a miraculous occurrence. The miracle, as everyone viewed it, was the near simultaneous demise of the nation's two surviving founding fathers, eighty-two-year-old Thomas Jefferson and ninety-year-old John Adams, who passed peacefully from this earth within hours of each other on the famous Fourth. Jefferson went first, followed by the elder Adams, but the survivor did not know it. Adams's last words, feebly uttered in little more than a whisper, were "Thomas Jefferson survives!"[4]

Had William Foster's wife Eliza known of the deaths of the founding fathers, she would have been too occupied to mull over their departure. While partygoers laughed boisterously a short distance from her window, Eliza lay inside her house confined to her bed in the sweltering heat of midsummer. Birthing was nothing new to the woman who had suffered through labor pains eight times, but bringing forth a new life in her then "advanced" thirty-eight years, well within earshot of the holiday barbecue revelers in her back yard, was a novel experience. From her bed, she could hear the garbled words of patriotic speeches, their messages drowned out in lively strains of Scots-Irish tunes played on squeaky fiddles. At noon precisely, the cannon from the nearby arsenal boomed an especially loud "national salute" while a band played a patriotic hymn—probably "Hail, Columbia"—and a short time later Eliza welcomed her ninth child into the world. When she finally dozed to sleep, calm in the knowledge that the baby boy born at 12:30 that afternoon was both strong and healthy, William and his guests lifted their glasses to honor the little tot who had indeed come into the world on the Fourth of July.[5]

News of the deaths of Adams and Jefferson reached the Fosters in Pittsburgh several days later—the telegraph would not be invented for another twenty years—and relatives immediately encouraged the mother to consider the names of the deceased luminaries and call her boy "Jefferson or Adams and no other name."[6] But Eliza preferred to name him after the ten-year-old son her girlhood friend Sarah Lowry Collins had only recently consigned to the grave. She called her newborn Stephen Collins Foster. When the child grew to be a man, he would himself be known as a founding father—the father of American music—and the fact that he had been born on the Fourth of July would be considered nearly as miraculous as the passing of the two founding fathers on the same day.

Eliza Foster was a young bride on November 28, 1807, the day she first set eyes on what was then the backwoods town of Pittsburgh. Starting out from Philadelphia, she and her new husband William covered three hundred miles in two weeks by a combination of horseback and coach, since many of the snow covered roads were not yet wide enough to accommodate stages or wagons and the land was mountainous. In Eliza's own words:

> Not having the present advantages of canal or turnpike or railroad, the journey was slow and monotonous and it was not until the fourteenth day . . . of her staging in an uncomfortable coach, that she hailed with delight the dingy town of Pittsburgh, her future

home. . . . It was an evening, when weary and faint with fatigue, the writer was conducted, or rather borne, into the hospitable mansion of her husband's partner . . . a dwelling in the center of the town where she was kindly received and treated by the family. After resting and changing from traveling apparel into other garments, she was shown into an apartment below stairs where blazed in all its brilliancy a coal fire.[7]

If Eliza felt disappointed with the "dingy town of Pittsburgh," she remained mute on the topic. The United States Census for 1800 claimed that Pittsburgh housed its population of less than 1,600 in four hundred roughly constructed edifices. Only a few years before Eliza settled into the western lands, black and brown bears and packs of howling wolves ran through the wooded terrain and scared the human populations. Now, the sounds of domestication were evident in the clanging of the bells the cattle and horses wore around their necks and in the cackling of the crows as they attacked the farmers' newly planted corn. In spite of the primitive environment, Eliza enthusiastically referred to herself as a "young and joyous bride" when she arrived in the city she would call home for the next nearly fifty years.

Born Eliza Clayland Tomlinson in 1788 in Wilmington, Delaware, the mother of the future composer was orphaned a few years later when her own mother Ann died and her father took a new wife and moved to Kentucky. Eliza went to live with her mother's family, the Claylands, in Baltimore, Maryland, a thriving port city that boasted all the cultural attractions a young woman could desire. Many of the Claylands were proud and well-off Episcopalians who had sailed into the Chesapeake from England in 1670, and Eliza's cousins on the Eastern Shore of Maryland owned slaves and ran a large plantation next door to the one where the famed abolitionist Frederick Douglass grew up before making his escape to freedom.[8]

Eliza's family on her father's side may have seemed less exalted than the Claylands at first glance, for Joseph Tomlinson, Eliza's father, was a saddle maker by trade. Nonetheless, they were accomplished people in their own right. Eliza's half brothers John and Joseph Tomlinson from her father's second marriage were born and bred in Augusta, Kentucky, where John became a physician and Joseph, the president of a college. The most illustrious of Eliza's relatives was undoubtedly the Philadelphia inventor of steam engines, Oliver Evans, who was related through marriage on Eliza's father's side. Evans surprised everyone when he built a compact cylinder engine that used high-pressure steam and easily outpaced the competition's larger, low-pressure models. After Evans married Eliza's Aunt Sarah, a sister of Joseph Tomlinson, the orphaned Eliza spent months at Aunt Sarah and Uncle Oliver's home on Race Street in Philadelphia. While visiting there in 1805, she witnessed the workings of her uncle's fantastical steam engine called the "Orukter Amphibolos" when spellbound crowds formed along the road to watch the thirty-foot contraption on wheels move cumbersomely, yet independently, down the road toward the Schuylkill River. Originally designed to dredge sandbars, her uncle's novel steam engine changed travel and life in the cities of the Midwest forever when it was adapted to river boats, enabling them to move effortlessly and poetically along the Mississippi.[9]

It was on one of her usual visits to the home of Uncle Oliver and Aunt Sarah that Eliza met her future husband, William Barclay Foster. The "short, good looking, blue-eyed" young man had stopped in Philadelphia to transact business, but soon found himself involved in the ever more intricate transaction of courting.[10] Eliza was of average height but full-figured, and her luxuriant brown hair only complemented her intense dark eyes. When William offered marriage, the nineteen-year-old Eliza accepted readily, even if it did mean being transplanted to a town far to the west that had only eleven years earlier been made safe for settlers. At the Battle of Fallen Timbers in 1794, less than forty years after the land was relinquished by the French, the hot-tempered captain "Mad Anthony" Wayne decisively defeated the Indians and opened up the Ohio valley, including Pittsburgh, to the permanent settlement of whites.[11]

William Barclay Foster traced his roots to the Scots-Irish Presbyterians who migrated to America in the early eighteenth century and ultimately found their way into southwestern Pennsylvania. Forging pathways through the Appalachians, they brought their music and songs with them. Neither Scots nor Irishmen, they were a peculiar product, natives of Scotland who had left their homeland to settle in war-torn Northern Ireland, where they had been invited to restore Protestant rule. In Ulster, however, they suffered discrimination after the Anglicans outlawed Presbyterian ministers and proved little more welcoming than the Catholics. Then they looked across the ocean to William

Penn's religiously tolerant colony, where the pacifist Quakers needed tough fighters to handle the Indian menace on their western border and welcomed them into Pennsylvania.[12]

William's paternal grandfather, Alexander Foster, was one of the spirited men who left Londonderry in Ireland around 1725 to settle in Philadelphia. Some years later, Alexander's son James, William's father, moved further south to Virginia, where William Barclay Foster was born in 1779. James fought in the American Revolution and, at the end of the war, moved with his family and other Scots-Irish settlers into Washington County, Pennsylvania, just below Pittsburgh. When Foster came of age, he was drawn to the new town twenty miles to the north, a hilly region already dominated by men and women of similar ethnicity who had moved in earlier from Maryland and Virginia. An early nineteenth-century engraving of Londonderry depicting a waterway with trees on bluffs overlooking the harbor bears a striking resemblance to early portraits of Pittsburgh and may account in part for the attraction the land held for its newest immigrants.[13]

When he proposed marriage to Eliza Clayland Tomlinson, William Barclay Foster was already in partnership with Ebenezer Denny, a merchant and later Pittsburgh's first mayor. Denny had hired William to run his general store, but soon decided to make the younger man a partner tasked with keeping the store well stocked with merchandise from the East. William's job, similar to that of import-exporter, involved bringing such Western products as whiskey, flour, and furs, down the Mississippi River to New Orleans, where they would be exchanged for slave-produced goods. Once traded, items like coffee and sugar were loaded with other merchandise onto ocean-going vessels that made their way around Florida and Cuba up the eastern Atlantic coast. After rounding Florida, where pirates once nearly captured William and his replenished boat, he sailed to Philadelphia and New York, where he sold or exchanged the goods from New Orleans for manufactured products that Pittsburghers greatly needed. Morrison Foster, one of Stephen Foster's brothers, described the rugged work their father engaged in "about twice a year" when he was still a young man:[14] "It was their custom at that time, the beginning of this century, to load flat boats with the products of the neighboring country—furs, peltries, whiskey, flour, etc., and float them down the Ohio and Mississippi Rivers to New Orleans, where the goods were exchanged for sugar, coffee, etc."[15]

Although a daguerreotype of William and Eliza Foster shows a man in his late middle years attired in a neat gentleman's suit, the younger William, when he was not courting, would have dressed in the stereotypical pioneer woodsman's uniform: a raccoon or beaver cap; leather breaches; and a fringed, rough, outer jacket—probably with a rifle swung across his chest. The transport business during Pittsburgh's pioneer days was rough and physically demanding. Getting goods downriver out of Pittsburgh was fairly easy because flatboats could travel south and west on the natural currents of the Ohio and Mississippi Rivers, but the boat trip upriver before the invention of steam power was all but impossible. Boatmen were often required to push long wooden poles down into the river sludge to force the flatboats up the Mississippi. For this reason, most of the downriver boats were broken up after they reached their destination in New Orleans, and the wood used for house construction. Knowing this, William avoided the rivers on his return trip. Instead, he weighed down the backs of sturdy horses with his eastern goods, and rode or walked along side of the animals all the way to Pittsburgh. The trip was dangerous and William was known to bring armed guards with him when his homeward journey took him through the woods of Tennessee, Mississippi, and western Virginia, where Indians and highwaymen seemed to lurk in every shadow.[16]

William Foster probably regaled the wide-eyed Eliza with accounts of his daring escapades and scrapes with death, stories that impressed the nineteen-year-old as both dangerous and romantic. Obviously, the adventures enhanced the reputation of the western man who came courting and induced Eliza to accept his proposal. To win her hand, William had to convince the bride-to-be and her family that he was strong enough, smart enough, and brave enough to earn a living on the frontier. He had to demonstrate that he could provide comfortably for a wife and the many children that would come their way and that he was honorable and reliable.

Eliza and William did not marry until they reached Chambersburg, Pennsylvania, a town situated almost half way between Philadelphia and Pittsburgh in the Blue Mountains, and Eliza had to trust that William would in fact marry her. No woman would want to share the fate of the fictional Charlotte Temple from the novel of the same name, who was abandoned by her confidence man lover and died unwed in childbirth.[17] Of course, Eliza had complete faith in William. She also had friends and relatives in Chambersburg to protect her honor and the minister who married the couple was David Denny, a relative of William's partner Ebenezer Denny. If anything went amiss, word would get back to Pittsburgh.[18]

Still, Eliza took a risk of another kind when she left the East Coast for uncharted and uncultured lands in the West. Would she be happy far from the world she had known? William was honorable and hard-working, and his family tree was pedigreed. He could read and write, handle the books in a business, and dabble in politics. His father and uncle, both educated men, were trustees and founders of Jefferson College at Canonsburg, Pennsylvania, a school situated twenty miles to the south of Pittsburgh. Still, the decision to marry a man and move with him to a backwoods town where civilization had only recently planted recognizable markers would have been a momentous one. Perhaps the fact that Eliza was an orphan for most of her young years and was dependent on the kindness of aunts and uncles made the decision easier. She had been brought up in the cultured environment of Baltimore and Philadelphia, where she associated with friends and family of kindred spirit, and now she would be leaving all that behind to move hundreds of miles into the raw hinterland.

Fortunately, Pittsburgh was growing and advancing rapidly. If the town offered only the bare necessities of life when Eliza first moved there, all that changed within the decade. Music teachers, piano sellers, theaters, museums, concert and lecture halls—all the amenities considered essential for a cultivated lifestyle—were listed in the town's directory and could be found on many a street corner. A few years after Eliza and William settled in, the population reached nearly 5,000. Most of the town's earliest houses were built of wood, but structures of greater endurance popped up overnight, constructed from the whitish brick taken from the recently dismantled Fort Pitt, which was no longer deemed necessary to guard the triangular land bounded by the three rivers. Street numbers were yet to be affixed to many of the houses, but the town's increasing prosperity was evident in the many new industries that were sprouting up everywhere. The first iron foundry had been established before Eliza's arrival, and a few years later Pittsburgh had a court, a market house, a bank, and five churches for the pious. By 1816, when Pittsburgh officially became a city, the lowlands between the Allegheny and Monongahela rivers were covered with private residences, businesses, and factories, and streets were laid out and named for the local elites.[19]

Like many young people of their generation, Eliza and William were drawn to the western frontier by the "unbounded opportunity" that seemed to await them in the thousands of acres of unclaimed land. In a day and age when wealth was measured in land acquisition, William was buying up as much of the green commodity as he could and reselling it for a profit. Success seemed easy to achieve at first, and within a few years of settling, the couple were on their way to realizing the western migrant's dream. They were living in their own comfortable house at the corner of Sixth Street and Cherry Alley in downtown Pittsburgh, and their family was enlarging with Eliza producing offspring at fairly regular intervals.

The Fosters' first child, born in 1808, was a girl named Ann Eliza who lived less than two months. In December 1809, a second daughter named Charlotte Susanna was joyously welcomed into the family. Two years later in January 1812, Eliza gave birth to yet another girl whom she named Ann Eliza, after the first-born daughter who had died. A son born in May 1814 and appropriately named William Barclay Foster lived only ten months. Soon afterward, however, the Fosters took a little boy of about eight years of age into their home and honored him with the name of their dead son. Little is known about the paternity of the adopted boy, although he may have been the illegitimate son of the senior William.[20] He had the same shimmering red-gold hair as the eldest daughter Charlotte, and since Eliza was a brunette, her husband was probably fair-haired.[21] In any event, the child was brought up in the Foster home as their own, while Eliza continued to produce children for another fifteen years: Henry Baldwin in March 1816; Henrietta Angelica in September 1818; Dunning McNair in January 1821; Morrison in June 1823; Stephen Collins, born July 4, 1826; and a boy named James Clayland in February 1829.

The nation was still at war with Great Britain when William purchased a sizable piece of land, turned it into a town, and named it after a war hero. On April 5, 1814, William purchased a 121-acre farm from Alexander Hill a few miles northeast of Pittsburgh on which he planned to build a large house for his growing family. Romantic and visionary, he decided before he began construction that he would lay out a town and call it Fosterville. Instead, the new town William founded on the south side of the Allegheny River became Lawrenceville after he hastily renamed it in honor of Captain James Lawrence, the American sea captain who had been mortally wounded the previous year while defending his ship from British attack. The thirty-year-old captain was immortalized for his dying words "Don't give up the ship!" but naming the town after the sea captain was only the first of William's patriotic gestures.[22]

In the last years of the War of 1812, when anxiety over British invasion ran high, a place was needed in Western Pennsylvania to manufacture and store arms, and William Foster was only too happy to do his part. A few weeks after he bought Alexander Hill's farm, he sold the government thirty acres of it for $12,000, a phenomenal amount of money in those days, and had the dual satisfaction of making a handsome profit at the same time he was rewarded with a surge of patriotic pride. Work began immediately on the Allegheny Arsenal, and when completed, it resembled a medieval stone fortress with a tower one-hundred-twenty feet high and forty feet square at its base. The arsenal served the area for many years as an arms and ammunitions factory, a storage facility, and a supply center for the troops, and during the Civil War it contributed to the Union's victory. To show the dead were not forgotten, officials set aside several acres of William's land for the poignantly titled "Lawrenceville Burying Ground," which was designated a final resting place for those who had given their lives in the recent war, although veterans from other wars were interred there over time.[23]

William Foster was understandably proud of the part he played in creating the arsenal. In 1816, one year after the war with Britain ended, the patriarch, his chest puffed up, had the honor of escorting James Monroe around the grounds while he demonstrated that his little town could play a big part in America's history. Ann Eliza Foster, the second daughter, recalled "the day on which Pa rode out with President[-elect] Monroe, when he visited the Arsenal. . . . Pa was sitting in the midst of the uniforms and officials by which His Excellency was surrounded."[24]

Even before construction began on the arsenal, William Foster began planning the family home that would be known as the "White Cottage." Clearly, with his family increasing every few years, he needed the extra space, but the sprawling house facing the Allegheny River offered, in addition, serenity, natural beauty, and status. In winter, the front yard was blanketed in snow, but in the summer, the wooded terrain became a canvas of immense greenery and shade. Benjamin Henry Latrobe, the man who later built the Capitol in Washington, had already been commissioned to design the Allegheny Arsenal when William offered him the opportunity to design his family residence as well. Latrobe had come to Pittsburgh a few years earlier to build steamboats, but when his boat models failed to work on the western rivers, he welcomed the contract to design the White Cottage.[25] The soon-to-be-renowned architect set the Foster house on four acres in the middle of a "grove of forest trees" facing Penn Street, as Penn Avenue was then known, high enough on "a beautiful knoll" to command "a view up and down the river for miles."[26]

The main building of the White Cottage measured fifty feet across the front, and contained four rooms on one floor and a center hall. A two-story wing of three or four rooms stretched to the east, and large, coal-burning fireplaces were built into the corners of each of the four rooms on the main floor. The home was designed to look like a cottage, deceptively larger on the inside than it appeared on the outside, a style popular in the Jacksonian era when understatement was preferred to the ostentatious architecture later generations used to flaunt the owner's status. The exterior was painted a bright white to offset its deep green shutters, and the grounds in fact constituted a small working farm. A smokehouse, a sturdy barn for the cows, a stable for the horses, and rustic pens for the pigs were neatly lined up in the back of the house. Tucked below the ground, the Foster property's stone spring house was cooled in the summer months by running water from an overhead stream, and kept "pails of frothing milk," freshly drawn from the cows, cold until offered to thirsty visitors or sold to neighbors. The White Cottage was completed in 1815, and Henry Baldwin became the first Foster child to be born there the following March.[27]

As soon as they moved into the new house, Eliza and William Foster entered into the social milieu of the first families of Pittsburgh. They attended dinners, picnics, weddings, and funerals with the men and women whose names today stand out on the city's street signs or show up in the names of neighboring townships and counties. These pioneer elites were united by blood and marriage and formed a close-knit coterie that found strength in the similarity of their backgrounds and often their politics. As Eliza explained, "The O'Haras, the Butlers, the Dennys, the Collins's, the Nevilles, the Ormsby's, the Wilkins's, the Kirkpatricks, the Addisons, the Craigs, etc. were one voice in state affairs and gave the same tone to every opinion. . . . There was none to make them afraid."[28] These proud families also lived in the most lavish dwellings in town.[29] James O'Hara, reportedly the richest man in Pittsburgh, was a neighbor of the Fosters on Penn Street, as was John Woods, whose father laid out the original plan for the city. Woods was a prominent attorney who had handled land sales for the heirs of William Penn, the founder of Pennsylvania.[30] He lived in a large brick home and his yard, a mass of "orchards and grassy slopes, hoary old trees, shrubbery and flower gardens," backed up to the Allegheny River.[31] Eliza's stories about the family's interaction with these important men and women of the city were carefully preserved and passed on to her son Stephen, who learned early on to equate the images of the refined lifestyles of long ago with a birthright and a marker he should himself strive to achieve.

Membership in the elite class of Pittsburgh had its own peculiar qualifying standards. Although many families had connections with the seaboard elites, Eastern connections were not a requirement. Upper class westerners were often first generation self-made men, tough fighters with Scots-Irish ancestry, who had conquered—not inherited—their wealth and status, and who fought anyone who threatened to usurp their newly acquired dominance.[32] This select group consisted of merchants, lawyers, businessmen, large landowners, and men with military and political standing. Most had made money in real estate speculations, which kept the town's many lawyers busy handling questionable land titles. Although these men had impressive material acquisitions, wealth was not the major factor qualifying a man for upper class status in Pittsburgh. Two qualifications for elite membership were by birthright and could not be purchased: The upper class had to be able to truthfully claim that they were descended from or closely associated with the region's early settlers. And more importantly, they had to be able to claim descent from a Revolutionary War officer.[33]

The Fosters had the necessary qualifications, according to these last two criteria. William Foster qualified as an original settler since moving to Pittsburgh in 1799 and going into partnership with Ebenezer Denny, one of Pittsburgh's most prominent residents. But William also qualified by blood connections to Revolutionary War officers. Samuel Jones wrote in *Pittsburgh in the Year 1826* that, while the city's first families had to be "related to a revolutionary officer," they could compensate for their "deficiency" in Revolutionary ancestry by "unrol[ing] their deeds, or those of their ancestors to boundless tracks of land in the country or to lots in town."[34] William Foster, of course, was a large landholder in the first quarter of the century, a man who could roll out the titles to his splendid country acreage or his numerous city building lots, or he could show off Lawrenceville, the town he had built—but he did not have to.

Both William and Eliza Foster had ancestors who had served in the Revolutionary War, in some cases as officers directly under the command of George Washington. William's father, James Foster, belonged to the Liberty Company of Londonderry Volunteers, a band of Scots-Irish fighters, and later joined a Virginia regiment that was present at the siege of Yorktown and the surrender of Cornwallis. Another ancestor, Reverend William Foster, was a 1764 graduate of the College of New Jersey, today Princeton. As pastor of the Presbyterian Church in Chester County, Pennsylvania, he recruited soldiers for the Continental Army by riding from town to town, rounding up men and personally forcing them to enlist.[35] On Eliza Foster's side, two of her uncles from the Clayland family died in service to their new country and a third was praised personally by George Washington for his conduct at the Battle of Brandywine. Thus Eliza and William and all their children, including Stephen Foster, belonged to the elites of Pittsburgh through their ancestral bloodlines to Revolutionary War officers.

When Eliza reached middle age, she wrote a journal-like re-creation of her life at the White Cottage, basing her facts on a combination of memory, personal notes, and preserved newspaper clippings. She wrote in the third person "for the benefit of her children" in a fiction-like style and changed the names of the people and places she knew. Her son Morrison Foster, years after his mother's death, gathered the pages together and hand copied them. Because Eliza was concerned with identifying with the elites and because how one spends leisure time was and is an indicator of status, her journal describes in great detail the varied recreational activities the Fosters shared with Pittsburgh's best families in the first decades of the nineteenth century. Her memories may have improved with time, but it is also likely that her early married life was in fact happy. Although Eliza recorded sorrowful tales of funerals and failed courtships, she more often regaled the reader with stories of glittering entertainments at the fashionable homes of the elites, where, she insisted, "Parties, theatricals, and balls were the order of the day."[36] If Eliza appeared overly sensitive to the issue of social status, she can be forgiven, because by the time she sat down to write her life story she had lost much of it.

In one vignette, Eliza described how the officers from the arsenal staged and rehearsed amateur theatrical performances in her parlor at the White Cottage, where the parts of the ladies were taken by the "junior gentlemen" and the tickets were given out free of charge, but selectively. The shows were not only "a source of amusement but also of improvement," and, as she explained, "Many evenings were made enjoyable with a little wine and a great deal of nonsense." In another vignette Eliza described a Fourth of July party in 1818, which the elites turned into a three-day celebration at three different locations. On July 3rd, Eliza attended a party at the Allegheny Arsenal with her uncle, Major Clayland, who was "treated with so much friendship by General Washington" at the Battle of Brandywine. On the Fourth, "gaily and fashionably dressed ladies and gentlemen," including a "Miss Fulton" of steamboat fame, boarded the steam propelled *Shamrock* at the wharf in Pittsburgh and traveled up the Allegheny River to celebrate a pleasant day of alfresco feasting and dancing at John Wilkins's "beautiful farm" Pine Creek.[37]

> The ladies were handed to the shore. A dressing room made of limbs topped from large trees was prepared, ready for their reception. In a short time, the whole company assembled together. At one, the company dined on cold ham, cold tongue, broiled chicken, plenty of sweet corn, and cold pies, custards and tarts, and sweetmeats. After a merry dinner, the gentlemen led the ladies to a level shade where they danced to the delightful music of the band attached to Colonel Constance's regiment.[38]

The next evening the celebration continued at the Fosters' boat house on the Allegheny River, where the guests enjoyed the strains of music that resounded from the floating river barge where "a fleet of musicians" played for anyone within earshot.[39]

Another journal entry offered a vivid description of a lavish, indoor dinner party at the handsomely decorated home of the mother of the boy after whom Stephen Collins Foster was named. Sarah Lowry Collins, the "daughter of a wealthy land and slave holder of Maryland," was

married to Thomas Collins, "a leading lawyer who had been educated in
the best circles of a flourishing eastern city." Like Eliza herself, she had
met her future husband while visiting an out-of-town aunt. After Sarah
accepted the marriage proposal from the prosperous Collins widower,
the couple moved to Lawrenceville where they built an impressive
house near the Fosters. The Collins parlor showcased a grand harp in
its bay window and the walls were graced by portraits of their four
daughters by Thomas Sully—early in his career, the yet-to-be-famous
artist had crossed the mountains from Philadelphia to Pittsburgh in
search of paying commissions. Alongside the Sully canvases were portraits of Jefferson, Napoleon, and Lafayette, and when the elderly
French general visited Pittsburgh in 1825, the Collins daughters
dressed in their finest and attended a ball held in his honor.[40]

Eliza preserved many stories in her journal, and in some of her
vignettes, she relayed a moral to her story. The tragic tale of George
Ross, the handsome twenty-year-old son of Senator James Ross, addressed the question of whether it was possible or even wise to attempt
to breach the walls to upper class society. When George became infatuated with a girl Eliza referred to as Evelyn Watson, the senator, whose
name is commemorated in Pittsburgh's Ross Street and Ross Township,
sent his son on a lengthy journey out of the country for the purpose of
forgetting her. Several years later, just as George was returning home,
he learned of Evelyn's premature death and was himself drowned
when, shaken by grief, he attempted to cross the turbulent waters of
Turtle Creek, just east of Pittsburgh, on horseback. The basic outline of
the story is true because George Ross's death by drowning was reported
in the February 16, 1814 edition of *The Mercury*.[41]

Apparently, George's pompous father did not think Evelyn was good
enough to marry his son, and Eliza speculated on what would have
improved Evelyn's chances, had she lived, of being accepted by the old
senator. Evelyn Watson's father had money and her uncle had served as
the pastor of the First Reformed Presbyterian Church of Pittsburgh for
decades. Her three brothers became successful men—a doctor, a lawyer, and a preacher—yet Senator Ross remained adamantly opposed to
the marriage. Perhaps Eliza was thinking about her own daughters
when she suggested, between the lines, that a young woman from a
less-exalted social set could find acceptance if she received a proper
education. "Her father was at fault," Eliza wrote about Senator Ross.

"He should have sent her far away to school. . . . But that did not suit his views. Some old gentlemen think it is the ruin of a young girl to send her to boarding school." Eliza seemed to suggest that Evelyn Watson might have broken the society's rigid class boundaries had she been sent to a boarding school, where she would have acquired training in the feminine accomplishments, "the kind of training that would suit the circle."[42]

Eliza may have been looking for justification for the time and money she spent on her own daughters' education. Indeed, whenever she could afford to do so, Eliza sent her girls to specialty schools in the East or to local academies to acquire the marks of culture that made a girl acceptable in the best social circles. Her ambition for her daughters was "that they should have the advantages of an education in the aristocratic tradition in which she herself had been brought up."[43] Charlotte and Ann Eliza began their training in the admired feminine accomplishments, which included music, painting, dancing, and languages, at a local girls' school run by a Mrs. Brevost. This inspiring lady, reportedly the daughter of a French gentleman who had lost his money and land after the defeat of Napoleon, ran a select "Boarding and Day School for Young Ladies on Second Street, between Market and Wood Streets" in downtown Pittsburgh. At one time Mrs. Brevost employed William Evens, the town's foremost music teacher, and Charlotte Foster became his student. A native of England, he opened his first school in "Pennsylvania's smokehouse" at the corner of First and Wood Street in 1811 and taught everything from voice to wind and bowed instruments, to organ composition, for which he charged $1.50 to $3.00 per quarter. He taught in the Pittsburgh area for nearly fifteen years until his death in 1854, and he was most successful at attracting a female clientele. Stephen Foster was not identified as one of his many students.[44]

After Charlotte completed Mrs. Brevost's demanding program, Eliza sent her to St. Joseph's Academy in far-off Emmitsburg, Maryland, on the eastern side of the Allegheny Mountains.[45] Not quite twelve years old in 1821, she set out on a fatiguing stage ride with her father and two friends, Ann and Mary Cassilly, to study and board at the Catholic school founded by the "saintly Elizabeth Seton." That Eliza knew the school mistress from years before when she was a young girl in Baltimore gave the mother some comfort, but did nothing to ease her daughter's disquiet. The distance from home was great and Charlotte's letters reveal that she was homesick. "I rise early," she confided to her mother in November of 1821, "and I sometimes fancy myself at home with sister Ann Eliza, skipping along the Lane. . . . The tears sometimes for a moment fill my eyes, but I brush them away, for everyone looks so sweetly and kindly on me here."[46] Eliza Foster read her daughter's letters carefully, but she never doubted that sending her off to school was in Charlotte's best interest.

The following year, Eliza entertained the thought of sending her second daughter Ann Eliza to Troy, New York, where Emma Willard conducted a famous female seminary with courses as academically challenging as those reserved for young men.[47] In the end she decided not to send the ten-year-old away, but finances may have been the real reason to keep the more reserved younger daughter at home. Two girls at boarding school at the same time would have been prohibitive. The third daughter, Henrietta Angelica, had to acquire "accomplishments" on her own because she came of age when the Fosters had little money to pay for costly schooling at a private seminary. Henrietta learned to play the piano and the guitar, and to sing the sentimental songs of her day from her mother, an older sister, or an outside source. Since she was closer in age to Stephen and he spent more of his youth around her, it was Henrietta's sweet songs that most influenced the boy composer growing up.

Clearly, Eliza Foster was the motivating influence, the matriarch of the genteel arts, who determined that her daughters, when compared with the young ladies of the East, would never be embarrassed by a lack of accomplishments. William Foster acceded to the whims of his wife, for Eliza was the cultural arbiter in her home, and a gentleman would never contradict his wife in matters of domestic concerns. Eliza's husband was comfortable with the rougher edges of life. What William really felt about his daughters' devotion to keyboard skills may be summed up in a newspaper clipping from the *National Intelligencer* that he pasted in his scrapbook and kept for twenty years:

> Music is, doubtless, a delightful accomplishment, it "hath charms to soothe the savage breast, soften dull rocks," and so forth. . . . But, I would humbly submit to the young ladies of this precocious, intellectual and highly accomplished generation, that all the sounds which are producible from a piano are not Music! Oh! Is it not a torture to "sit with sad civility" and listen to that disease (excuse the bull) called

> a popular song? Why, the thing is more contagious than the cholera.
> Every amateur catches a popular tune; and one has to listen to it for
> the thousand and first time, varied only by the blunders and affecta-
> tion of the player. Oh! Parents! Why will ye . . . make your daughters
> learn music as a *mantrap*, whether they have the organ developed on
> their pericrania [*sic*] or not? Oh! Satan, what a sad blunderer you
> were to kill Job's daughters! Why did you not teach them to play on
> the piano, and sing "Come Rest in This Bosom!" Your business
> would have been done at once, you wily fiend. Job could not have
> stood it—he would have cursed and died. [48]

William must have found the article hilarious, especially because
"Come Rest in This Bosom" by Thomas Moore was one of Charlotte's
favorite performance pieces. In the evening, when the family gathered
in the parlor to put on their little concerts, Charlotte played and sang
her sweet sentimental airs, and her father listened, even if the songs he
enjoyed were "in a lighter vein and could hardly be listed among the
classics." No matter how many times his children laughed when
William sang his favorite "ribald old tune" about an "agreeable" milk-
maid named Dorothy Draggletail, or a ditty called "The Three Rogues,"
he never attempted to impose his less refined tastes in music on his
daughters. [49]

Eliza may have been unusual for a Pittsburgh mother in her insis-
tence that her daughters become devotees and practitioners of the arts.
Not all the western women of her generation approved of the so-called
"female accomplishments." Some considered them elitist and the more
envious voiced a preference to see the daughters of the well-to-do families give up what they considered "idle habits" for more productive
work. One friend of Eliza quipped, "I should like to see Mrs. Neville's
or Mrs. Wilkins's pretty daughters at the spinning wheel." [50] Eliza paid
no attention. She raised her daughters in the refined traditions of the
East, which meant hours devoted to musical practice. Even when she
did not have a piano of her own, Ann Eliza went "every day to Mrs.
Malory to practice on her piano," and Mr. Malory said the thirteen-
year-old "plays and sings better than any person of her age." [51]

Still, chores had to be done around the house, and in Pittsburgh
where slavery was outlawed, the Fosters, who associated manual labor
only with a lack of wealth, employed bound servants—black, white, and
of mixed race. One conspicuous bound servant in Foster family lore was

Olivia Pise, or "Lieve" as she was called, the product of an African mother and a white French father who escaped from her homeland after the Haitians overthrew their French masters in a violent revolution. The older children remembered "Lieve" carrying cold milk from the ice house at the White Cottage to serve guests, but Foster legend claimed the West Indian girl played a more influential role in the young composer's development, when she brought the six-year-old Stephen to her church of "shouting colored folk" and introduced him to the plaintive motifs he later incorporated into two of his best-loved plantation songs.[52]

A less influential bound servant was a white child named Tom Hunter, born in 1818 in the White Cottage, where his mother lived and did domestic chores after her soldier husband committed suicide. It is hard to imagine that Tom was bound at birth to labor for the Fosters in the free state of Pennsylvania, but he was. His birth was carefully noted in the family Bible along with the birthdays of the Foster children, and when Tom had "a tooth ache that swelled his jaw," Eliza "sent for the doctor and nursed him for two days." Supposedly Tom left the Fosters when he turned sixteen and traveled to the far West, but he probably left long before then, when the Fosters became destitute and could no longer care for him.[53]

When Stephen was still a toddler, the genteel lifestyle that Eliza recorded in her journal, wherein the labor was done by bound servants, her daughters sang sentimental songs, and her home was a source of pride and serene happiness, came swiftly and abruptly to an end. Yet impressions of the White Cottage and the culture of refinement were firmly planted as seedlings in the young boy's psyche, even if he could not recall the particular events, parties, balls, or carriage rides that Eliza wrote about so descriptively in her journal for her children to enjoy. In subsequent years, when the family's finances were in a permanent state of decline, and in adulthood, when Stephen struggled to make his own way in a highly competitive world, he would write songs that longed for a past that was always markedly better than the present.

2

FORECLOSURE AND THE DEATH OF CHARLOTTE

William Barclay Foster, and his wife Eliza, if she knew, must have put on brave faces during the Fourth of July celebration when they welcomed the birth of their newest son and toasted the health of the nation with their neighbors. Unbeknown to most of the people at the party was the fact that the beloved White Cottage had been foreclosed a few months earlier on May 6, 1826, and the party's host was "at the end of his resources." The Bank of the United States, the privately owned national bank in Philadelphia, built to last forever in stone and marble, foreclosed on all of Foster's property in the southern half of Lawrenceville, including the house and its land on the river, leaving him only a few parcels near the arsenal. William and his family were allowed to remain at 3600 Penn Avenue for at least three years longer, having made some arrangement to rent it from the bank or perhaps from the new owner, but on September 6, 1827, the house with its four bucolic acres passed into the hands of Malcolm Leech, "a prosperous wholesale grocer of Pittsburgh," who paid the bargain price of $4,000. [1]

The exact date the Fosters moved out is not known, but toward the end of 1829, or perhaps sooner, they were living in a rented house on Water Street in what had once been an exclusive neighborhood in downtown Pittsburgh, until the smoke from the city's new industries drove the wealthier residents further east to places like Lawrenceville. William Foster was perplexed to think that the year Pittsburgh began to work its way out of the depression, his own fortunes were on the decline. New houses were going up everywhere at the end of the decade, once bridges opened up the landmasses on the northern side of the Allegheny River, and turnpikes made it easier and quicker for people from the East to move west. Many of Pittsburgh's new residents turned to manufacturing to make their wealth, but such opportunities did not present themselves to William who was past the age of fifty, had just lost his home, and no longer found life to be an upward adventure.

William Foster is often blamed for the debacle that resulted in the foreclosure of the White Cottage and the decline in the family's comfort and security. In middle age, in pleading letters to his oldest son, he comes across as a whiny dependent man who has lost all confidence in his ability to provide for his family. Yet in his younger years, fortune smiled on William, particularly when he formed partnerships with successful men like Ebenezer Denny and Anthony Beelen, and when his many real estate investments were climbing. When he attempted businesses on his own, William was not so fortunate. His "Iron Works" on Grant's Hill lasted less than a year and when he became the manager of the Pittsburgh and Greensburg Turnpike, a company that operated stages and wagons between Pittsburgh and Philadelphia, he ended up embroiled in legal battles with the owners. Without passing judgment on his business sense, it is fair to say that William was frequently hit by the unpredictable antebellum economy that guaranteed recurring panics and depressions and provided no safety nets. But he was also a visionary betting on chimerical schemes, seeing what he wanted to see rather than the harsh realities of life.[2]

In the last year of the War of 1812, William decided to personally foot the bill to send a boatful of military supplies to Andrew Jackson. To some, this example of extreme patriotism suggested a quixotic man who put his country's security before that of his family. But William may have believed that the security of his family depended on the future security of the nation. However one interprets this generous act, the story of his contribution to Jackson's victory at New Orleans reveals a great deal about the temperament of Stephen Foster's father. The senior William can be viewed as trusting, idealistic, and patriotic, or as a man who was prone to making impetuous, impassioned decisions. When the young nation went to war, William Foster with feverish exuberance selflessly put his own fortune at risk to ensure that General Jackson would have the supplies he needed to whip the British.[3]

William Foster was Quartermaster and Commissary of the United States Army in 1814 when "urgent orders came to Pittsburgh to send forward clothing, blankets, guns and ammunition to the relief of Jackson's army."[4] Since no money came with the orders and the federal government was unable or unwilling to guarantee payment, the Pittsburgh manufacturers demanded personal assurances that they would be paid if they were to produce the goods. According to his son Morrison, "with his own money and upon his own personal credit," William procured "the necessary supplies" and became personally indebted because the Pittsburgh manufacturers had no confidence that the government would pay them back. When they insisted on personal notes in lieu of the Army's official guarantee, "the distracted commissary immediately gave them."[5]

In late November 1814, William Foster stood by and watched as the manufacturers loaded a forty-five ton steamboat aptly named *Enterprise* with various supplies and "munitions from the North Side Army Ordnance."[6] The boat's interior compartments were stuffed with thousands of items that would be needed to sustain the army—1,000 camp kettles, 1,000 pairs of shoes, 500 blankets and 500 wool overalls, along with 1,000 eighteen-pound and 1,000 twelve-pound cannon balls. On December 1, 1814, Captain Henry Miller Shreve sailed from Pittsburgh with his valuable cargo, reportedly calling out, "I'll get there before the British, or sink this boat." Two weeks later he docked at New Orleans.[7] After unloading the goods, Andrew Jackson ordered Shreve to transport some women and children out of harm's way before he "was engaged in the battle of the 8th of January, serving at the sixth gun of the American Batteries."[8] The day proved glorious for the Americans and one of humiliation, defeat, and great loss of life for the British.

Of course, the Battle of New Orleans proved not so glorious for at least one American who, after the war ended, tried without success to get back his money. The government reimbursed William Foster for some of his expenditures, but left him $2,704.90 short. "Congress refused to approve certain sums advanced, contending that Mr. Foster had paid for the goods with his own notes on his own responsibility and that reimbursing him for losses sustained by reason of the depreciation of treasury notes would establish a dangerous precedent." Judge Walker of the U.S. Court of Pittsburgh in 1823 heard the case and gave his opinion: "Terminate as this cause may [be] Mr. Foster has established for himself a character for zeal, patriotism, generosity, and fidelity which cannot be forgotten; and has placed a laurel on his brow that will never fade." The Jury turned a verdict in favor of William Foster but the judgment was never paid, nor would the "laurel on his brow" pay the family's ever-mounting debts. [9]

William's inability to satisfy his claim against the government marked the beginning of the Fosters' financial decline, but his devotion to Jackson was not the only factor. Failures and bankruptcies on the national level wreaked havoc on the Fosters' finances. For several years after the end of the war, business transactions and land purchases in Pittsburgh were off the charts, encouraged by "credit buying and paper money." Business was booming and Pennsylvania authorized the opening of forty-one new banks, each of which issued its own notes to satisfy the buying frenzy. The easy credit resulted in out-of-control land speculation, until the Second Bank of the United States ordered the resumption of specie payments and called in its loans to the state banks. William Foster's troubles then became insurmountable. Caught in the fragile chain link of debtors and creditors, he could not come up with the payment when the Bank called in his personal loans and mortgages, because men who owed him money were having their own loans called in at the same time. [10]

Of course, had William been less patriotic and cared less about the success of General Jackson, or had the government repaid him for all his generosity, he would have had a larger reserve to fall back on while he and his family rode out the hard times. Instead, he was caught in the maelstrom. Part of the problem could be blamed on the vengeance of the British. Pittsburgh manufacturing had boomed during the War of 1812, but no sooner had the battles ceased, than jealous British manufacturers decided to nip their American competitors in the bud. They dumped tons of British-made products onto American docks at such low prices that the local manufacturers could not compete. Steam engine factories that were the pride of Pittsburgh almost disappeared, as did glass works. In fact, most of the industries limped along and to the dazed spectators who walked the now-empty streets, "the city seemed dying." [11]

What started as the Panic of 1819 soon evolved into a major depression that lasted nearly a decade and caused immense personal suffering. The Fosters lost most of their properties, but those who maintained theirs could neither rent nor sell as people packed up and left the city that had been doubling its population each previous decade. Signs in the windows read "To Let—For Sale," but there were neither renters nor buyers. One newspaper editor exclaimed in amazement, "There are now more buildings than families; in old times there were two families to a house, now there seem two houses to a family." In some ways the Fosters were more fortunate than the families with no property to relinquish. Those without property to offset their debts went to debtors' prisons, which swallowed rich and poor alike. An editor with ironic satisfaction quipped, "For the most part, the men who inhabit our jails were lately among our best livers." During the summer of 1819, 115 persons were imprisoned for debt, most of whom owed less than ten dollars. One man was jailed for owing eighteen cents. [12]

A common reaction to the depression was to "Damn the Banks and the Witch that begot them," and to join anti-bank political parties. The Bank of the United States, the Eastern behemoth that held mortgages on most of the land in the West, became especially culpable when it called in its loans to the local banks and forced them to foreclose on their own customers. Men like Foster, who lost their homes and their dreams, cursed the institution until their dying day and over the next decade formed the backbone of Andrew Jackson's new Democratic Party. At the end of the 1820s, the depression had run its course and most of Pittsburgh returned to normal. For some, however, the scars ran too deep for financial well-being to be restored. William was not able to recover from the losses he had endured over the previous decade, nor could he duplicate the security and lifestyle his family had known. [13]

The prospect of returning happiness for the Fosters soon became even more unlikely. In the wake of the loss of the White Cottage and their wealth, the family experienced a succession of personal tragedies of the gravest order. In May 1828, the Fosters' beautiful daughter Charlotte boarded the *Waverly* and sailed first to Cincinnati, Ohio, and from there to Kentucky, where she planned on visiting and staying with relatives of her father. In the late autumn of the following year, the nineteen-year-old Charlotte died in Louisville. The death of their eldest living daughter, followed only months later by the loss of the Fosters' youngest baby boy to an unnamed childhood disease, devastated the family. Eliza Foster suffered especially from the traumas and sank into a deep depression from which she emerged only after resigning herself "to the will of that omniscient power," God's divinely ordained plans for her future.[14]

Although Stephen had little if any memory of his dead sister, he read the carefully preserved letters by the musically gifted Charlotte, and his mother Eliza spoke with a heartbreaking poignancy of her golden-haired daughter who played the piano and the harp expertly, and sang the sad sentimental songs that were so much appreciated by her generation. In her journal, Eliza shared a precious memory of the musical performance given by the nine-year-old girl when a Mrs. Feibiger visited the Fosters at the White Cottage and asked Charlotte to sing and play for her on the piano:

> "Come, Charlotte," said Mrs. Feibiger, "before I ride, sing and play some of those favorite little airs of yours." Charlotte lifted her soft, blue eyes and looked sweetly at Mrs. Feibiger. She did not whine, nor look affected, nor did she undertake to excuse herself by saying she had a cold or other such reprehensible device, but walked modestly to the piano, and seating herself, played and sang "There's Nothing True but Heaven" in a manner that touched the feelings and moved the hearts of all present.[15]

Charlotte was just eighteen when she traveled down the Ohio River, chaperoned by Henry Baldwin and his wife, close friends of her mother and father. Her oldest brother William, who was established financially, in all likelihood paid for her passage because she asked him to, and when her father dropped her off at the boat, he told her if she needed extra money to ask Mr. Baldwin, who, Charlotte was assured, would be reimbursed. The travelers arrived in Cincinnati on a "Friday night at 8 o'clock" on May 16, 1828, and Charlotte and the Baldwins took lodgings "at Watson's, a most splendid hotel."[16] Mrs. Feibiger, the woman who had listened to Charlotte play the piano as a child, immediately sent a carriage to bring her to her own elegant house in the city, where Charlotte was feted at "concerts and balls" and shown off to the best families. She dazzled everyone and wrote home confidently to her mother, "I never enjoyed myself more."[17] At one social outing, she devoured "strawberries in abundance, danced to the piano once or twice, [and spent] the rest of the time promenading."[18] At the lavish home of a Mrs. Kilgore, she met a musically inclined young lady from Virginia who had "one of the sweetest voices" and Charlotte taught her to sing "I'd be a Butterfly" because, she wrote teasingly, "she is not much larger than the insect itself and the song is apropos." Charlotte was a social success and wrote home coquettishly to her mother, "Remember me to all the gentlemen who inquire about me."[19]

The girl from Pittsburgh, who was "accustomed to see houses look black" from the city's smoke, was delighted with Cincinnati and thought it "the most beautiful city in the Western country." Yet by the middle of June, Charlotte left the fair city behind when her father's cousin Joshua Barclay escorted her by boat to his house in Louisville, where she again met "ladies of the first respectability" and attended rounds of parties at the homes of elites like the Clays of Kentucky, where she "danced every set." In spite of a heavy calendar of social obligations, Charlotte could not resist the temptation of harp lessons and assured her parents that the money would be well spent. "I only intend to take a few weeks' lessons and the money I have will pay for it. I would much rather do without some gagew [*sic*] and make a little improvement." She was especially taken by the Barclay piano, which "is a delightful one," and wrote home, "Between it and the harp I almost live on musick [*sic*]." After only three or four lessons on the harp, she could play Thomas Moore's "Come Rest in This Bosom," "Flow on those Shining Rivers," and "I Have Loved Thee."[20]

Charlotte was having a wonderful time in Louisville, but in late June, 1828, her father worried that the "extreme heat of the weather" would endanger her health and he urged her to "descend the river at least as far as Cincinnati." He added, "Your ma is not in good health" and closed with the admonition, "Do not, my dear child, delay one day in leaving Louisville on any account whatever."[21] A week later Charlotte responded to her father's importuning letter with a headstrong and willful reply that Louisville was very hot indeed, but so what? As to her mother's health, she wrote dismissively, "I should feel very solicitous about thy Dear Mother if I did not think it was a sickness she is troubled with every two years."[22] Charlotte was correct on one account. Eliza was several months pregnant with her tenth and last child, a boy named James who would be born the following February.

In spite of his frequent letters urging her to leave Kentucky, the hapless William was no match for his shrewd daughter. Charlotte had the upper hand and decided to negotiate the terms of her return by assuring her father that if he could only provide her with a piano, "home would be the happiest place on earth to me." Since learning that her older brother had received a salary increase, she asked, "Could not brother William affect you to get one? Mr. Valtz [the piano dealer] will trust you for a year and if at that time it cannot be paid for let him take it back."[23] But as soon as the deal was struck, Charlotte navigated her way, not to Pittsburgh, but to the nearby Pearce home, also in Louisville, where William Prather, the brother of her friends Julia and Matilda, courted her "almost every day." Charlotte was very impressed by the Pearce lifestyle, which made her think of the lost comforts of the White Cottage. "I think a Kentucky farmer's life is very happy, those who are rich and have their negroes and overseers as Mrs. Pearce has . . . . It reminded me of the happy times I used to spend in the country at home."[24]

Charlotte's importuning demands for a piano paid off in August 1828, when her brother William had a "handsome and well-tuned" one shipped to the Fosters.[25] She thanked him, saying "I am sure it will hasten my return home,[26] but with no permanent house in Pittsburgh to come home to, she made no promises and insisted on negotiating further. When Charlotte learned that her father had accepted a position as Collector of Tolls for the Pittsburgh-Blairsville Canal,[27] she implied there would be no homecoming without a new house, then boldly asked her brother "to tell me how it is with Pa's appointment if he is to have a house built in Allegheny Town this fall or not 'til spring and if he receives any pay yet . . . . These are questions I do not like to ask him but which would be very satisfactory for me to know."[28]

Instead of giving Charlotte a date for a new house to be constructed, the senior William warned her against remaining in Louisville "during the summer and fall," where "the season of fever and ague has now arrived" and added, "Dear little Stephen was very unwell a few days ago, the mosquitos being very troublesome at our house."[29] Perhaps he hoped that concern over her baby brother would bring her home, although no one yet understood the dangers wrought by the innocuous looking creatures that swarmed around stagnant water beds and canals, and carried the deadly strains of malaria and yellow fever to unsuspecting victims.[30]

Charlotte heeded her father's warnings only to the extent of moving sixty miles inland to Federal Hill, a plantation house in Bardstown,

Kentucky, a location she described as "one of the healthiest places in the world."[31] Senator John Rowan, or Judge Rowan, as he was known in the family correspondence, was another relative from the Barclay side. Ten years earlier, he had built the large, brick, Federal-style mansion that became "The Old Kentucky Home" shrine and named it in honor of the new Federalist Party. He lived there with his daughters Ann, Josephine, and Eliza and two of his three sons, Atkinson Hill Rowan (the middle son) and John (the youngest).[32] The Rowan girls were eager to meet the vivacious Charlotte, and it was they who insisted that their father pick up their cousin in Louisville, and bring her by carriage to Federal Hill. The plan was for Charlotte to stay in Bardstown until November, when the judge would personally take her back to Pittsburgh. Instead, Charlotte left Bardstown after only three weeks and returned to her Barclay cousins with the excuse that she "missed her friends in Louisville."[33]

Charlotte had been away from home almost five months, and despite numerous invitations to dances and supper parties hosted by the Kentucky elite, there were as yet no marriage proposals. A friend of Charlotte's warned her that she had "overstayed" her visit and was "turning out a coquette" and her parents' friends in Pittsburgh hinted at the same thing. In a letter dated October 4, 1828, Eliza Foster informed her daughter of the rumors: "Mr. Baldwin told Mr. Foster the other day you were the Belle of Louisville. Now is the time to bring her home, said he, as much as to say before her vallue [*sic*] is lessen'd."[34] But more was going on in the way of marriage prospects than Eliza knew. On October 18, 1828, Charlotte wrote her mother from Louisville and explained why she had left Bardstown so abruptly. She said she had received a marriage proposal from one of the Rowan sons, probably Atkinson Hill, but felt obliged to refuse.

> I will tell you a secret about my late visit to Federal Hill. I told you Mr. R[owan] had two sons at home, the eldest is about 25 a lawyer very clever and generally considered handsome. Now it must remain between you and I if I tell you he wish'd me to engage myself to him but as usual I could not love him and would not do him or myself the injustice to make promises I was not inclined to perform. You may conclude I was glad to get to Louisville again. I suppose he would think I might be glad to get the son of a Senator of the United States and so distinguished a man as [his father] John Rowan, but I cannot

let considerations of this kind influence me when my happiness for
life depends upon it. [35]

It was from this letter written in confidence that the legend developed
in the Foster family and continued at Federal Hill that Charlotte received a proposal from John Rowan, the youngest son of Judge Rowan.
It is more likely that Atkinson Hill Rowan proffered the marriage proposal. Charlotte described the mystery suitor as "the eldest son at
home" and the judge's eldest son William Lytle was already married
and no longer living at home. Charlotte also said the man in question
was "about 25 a lawyer" and the only Rowan who fit that description
was Atkinson Hill, who was born in 1803, making him exactly twenty-
five when he met Charlotte and already practicing law. John Rowan was
twenty-one and Charlotte only mentioned him in connection with her
younger sister Ann Eliza, whose favorite was "our cousin John (Rowan).
He is one that few girls could see and not admire." But Charlotte
mentioned Atkinson Hill many times in her letters and he followed her
to Louisville on more than one occasion. [36]

It is not too difficult to figure out what was going on in Charlotte's
head and heart. She would have felt embarrassed and uncomfortable
staying around Federal Hill after she refused the young man's proposal,
even if she felt justified in her decision. She admitted he was clever,
handsome, and from a superior family, but she was not in love with him.
Speculating that she could end up "an old maid," she queried, "is it not
better to be one than married without loving?" Charlotte seemed drawn
to the lively lifestyle of the Southern elites, but she may also have had
her heart set on someone in Louisville, a man such as William Prather.
"When I speak of the Pallace [sic] I mean Mr. Prather's. It is so call'd
and they the Royal Family." [37] A legend developed that Charlotte received and accepted a marriage proposal from William Prather, but
that, like the story about the young John Rowan, is not substantiated by
the family letters. Still, Mr. Prather's attentions—one friend wrote to
Charlotte that "Mr. P. is still devoted"—might have influenced her to
turn down the Rowan proposal and wait around hoping Mr. Prather
would pop the question. [38]

Clearly, Charlotte was torn. She admitted that while "a great deal of
flirtation" was going on, there were "very few who I could be serious in
a flirtation with." Then she reiterated a thought that passed through her

mind several times: "I am too hard to please, when I consider I have neither wealth nor beauty but let the consequences be what it [sic] may I cannot help it. I suppose the end will be I shall be an old maid."[39]

Charlotte finally did come home in November, arriving in plenty of time to help Eliza with the birth of the baby James on February 3, 1829. She remained in Pittsburgh to care for the family, while Ann Eliza traded places and went to stay with the Barclay cousins in Louisville. But Charlotte was not happy at home, where finances were still in disarray, a new baby was demanding to be fed, and chores had to be done. She pined for the carefree, sunny days she spent at parties with her friends and relatives in Kentucky and contrasted them with the miserable dark smoky days in Pittsburgh. For that reason, when Matilda Prather invited her and Ann Eliza to attend her wedding in May, she snatched the first opportunity to board a packet boat and arrived in Louisville the third week in May, in time for the nuptials.[40] At Matilda's wedding dinner, Charlotte had the attentions of William Prather and men whose names could be found on the registrar of the Kentucky elite, but she did not receive a second request for her hand in marriage.[41] Instead, some of the rich families asked her for introductions to Pittsburgh's wealthy Collins daughters, and although the weather plantation owner William Croghan called on Charlotte he did not call again.

On June 1, 1829, Charlotte informed her parents that she wanted to return home.[42] Her letter crossed one her father wrote saying "we wish you and Ann Eliza to come home . . . if Mrs. Barclay's situation will permit."[43] Sally Barclay, the wife of William Foster's cousin Joshua Barclay, was pregnant with her second daughter and Charlotte was expected to watch over her and assist with the birth. Tragically, when Charlotte was ready to come home, she found she had waited too long. After the Barclay baby Georgiana was born, the mother and the newborn took ill, and William Foster advised his daughter to remain in Louisville to nurse them back to health. On June 11, 1829 William Foster wrote Charlotte and Ann Eliza with a decision he would regret for the rest of his life:

> In my last letter I desired you both to come home on the *Pennsylvania* when she returned. Since that time your mother and I have concluded that it is best for Charlotte to remain for the present with Mrs. Barclay and Ann Eliza will come home either in the *Pennsylvania*, or in company with Miss Prather when she goes to Balti-

more . . . . We have many reasons for this arrangement which can be better explained when we see you. [44]

The "many reasons" for leaving Charlotte in Kentucky to care for the sick Barclays were never explained nor was the responsibility for her subsequent death openly acknowledged. [45] William's decision was based in part on the culture's belief in the role of women as nurses and caregivers, and on the generation's appalling ignorance of the pathology of germs and disease. Charlotte responded dutifully to her father's letter on June 22. She would remain in Kentucky as her parents requested, and Ann Eliza, who "is getting tired of company," would travel home on the *Pennsylvania*, if possible.

Sometime that summer, after she had returned to Pittsburgh, Ann Eliza wrote Charlotte that when the family asks "Stevie" why his sister does not come home, her baby brother always says, "Sister Charlotte down the ribber, 'tuck in the mud." [46] By August 1829, Charlotte must have felt both figuratively and literally stuck in some kind of muck. Throughout the summer, she remained in Louisville nursing Sally Barclay, who became increasingly ill, as did her infant daughter. [47] When her Rowan cousins requested her presence at Federal Hill, Charlotte found it difficult to leave the Barclays. Judge Rowan "says they have a grudge at me for not coming up to Federal Hill, that it was as much to say I have been there once and that is enough." Apparently she did acquiesce and paid the family one more visit, probably at the behest of her parents, who encouraged her to see if she could reignite the spark that Atkinson Hill had once felt. After visiting her would-be suitor, however, Charlotte indicated that his sentiments toward her had changed and were nothing more than "passing compliment":

> You and my father's kind advice in a letter I received at Bardstown with regard to a certain person I try to abide by, but I think you have mistaken his politeness in thinking it anything more than passing compliment, for my own part I do not look upon him as anything more than a friend and am very certain he is that as well as the rest of the family, since my return from Bardstown. [48]

If Charlotte entertained hopes about a romance with William Prather, that notion evaporated, too. Prather stopped at the Foster house in Pittsburgh sometime late in the summer of 1829 while escorting his sister Julia to Mrs. Turnbull's, a private female academy, in Baltimore. Although Foster legend has it that William Prather stopped in Pittsburgh to ask for Charlotte's hand in marriage, Charlotte never indicated that in her correspondence and it never happened. Apparently, the mysterious Mr. Prather did show up with his sister Julia at the Foster house where the younger William met him, but in his letter to Charlotte he reserved comment. He said only that he did not have "the pleasure of becoming acquainted with him (Prather) as well as he should."[49] Perhaps William sensed Prather had no serious intentions regarding his sister, and he wanted to spare Charlotte's feelings. Or, the wealthy, stuffy Kentuckian might have been shocked to see the level of poverty to which the Fosters had sunk. Even if they were still occupying the White Cottage, by this date they would have been packing.

By August 1829, Charlotte very much wanted to leave Kentucky but feared her boat would get "'tuck in the mud," as her baby brother Stephen explained her dilemma. With water levels low that summer, Charlotte worried she would not make it all the way back to Pittsburgh, even though the younger William stressed that her "fears in relation to the canal are unfounded" since the boats were "in successful operation . . . between Pittsburgh and Blairsville." He also told her not to worry about the situation at home: "Father commenced his duties as collector about three weeks since and attends very little to electioneering."[50] The senior William corroborated the story, saying he had opened an "office on the 10th of August in Allegheny Town" and was "duly employed ever since." But then he backed off, noting that further east "the earth was parched." "Don't leave," the father advised, "until the water will admit the largest and most comfortable boats to come with safety to Pittsburgh."[51]

Charlotte wanted her brother William, the only knight in shining armor among all the beaux, to come to Louisville to pick her up, which he said he would do, although he could not give a definite date. Nonetheless, Charlotte was delighted at the prospect. She had not been out since the eldest Barclay daughter "had been ill with bilious fever [yellow fever] and I have attended her, who is now quite well." Then she admitted that Kentucky "has not been as healthy this summer as last . . . . The weather has been extremely warm and we had a great deal of rain."[52] The letter is eerily prescient of lines in Stephen Foster's "Oh! Susanna:" "It rained all night the other day, the weather it was dry." The senselessness of it all! Did Stephen read the letter and become inspired to write those words as a paean to the memory of his lost sister Charlotte Susanna? It rained in Louisville yet the weather was so dry in Pittsburgh that the river was too low to bring the boats up.

The letter Charlotte wrote to her brother William on September 4, 1829 was probably the last she wrote in her brief life. In it she acknowledged that all the dances and promenades; all the musical displays, the sheet music purchases, and the harp lessons; all the time, effort, and money spent developing accomplishments did not guarantee a girl a marriage proposal from a man she wanted to marry. As Alexis de Tocqueville would note in his famous book a few years later, Americans were inordinately concerned with money. To William she wrote with eyes wide open:

> I expect you begin to think it is almost time I was out of the way and in a house of my own but I beg you will not be thinking there is any prospect of the kind, for I really and candidly think you will have the pleasure of my company many years yet as Miss Foster, either the gentlemen are very hard to please as I am some times. When I reflect seriously upon the subject I come to the conclusion I certainly must be an old maid for anyone who is worth having can find girls enough who possess both riches and beauty, the most powerful attractions neither of which I possess. The conclusion must be I must remain as I am or be more humble in my expectations.[53]

Then she asked him "to let me have some of the one thing needful," money.

By the time William received Charlotte's letter, his sister's fate was sealed. The tiny invisible microbes that no one even knew existed invaded Charlotte's body, now made frail from sitting up night after night with the sick Barclays. The following month, on October 13, 1829, George W. Barclay, Joshua Barclay's brother, sent frantic messages, one by steam packet and another by horse messenger, to Pittsburgh, telling the Fosters that their daughter was deathly ill and they had better come to Louisville at once.[54] Although Charlotte had nursed the sick Barclays back to health, no one in the Barclay family was able to save Charlotte. William and Eliza decided not to travel themselves, and instead put daughter Ann Eliza on the steamboat *Sylph* to Kentucky, praying she would be able to restore the health of the beautiful and much-loved

Charlotte.[55] Eliza was still nursing the six-month-old baby James, but why her father did not accompany Ann Eliza is too sorrowful to fathom. Charlotte died on October 20, 1829, before her sister reached Louisville, but her memory is enshrined in Foster legend as the accomplished nineteenth century "piano girl" whose idealized life and death inspired Stephen to write some of the most beautiful parlor songs in the sentimental tradition.[56]

In two tear-stained letters written in November, 1829, Atkinson Hill Rowan, the man who had wanted to marry Charlotte and was with her when she died, responded to Ann Eliza's request for a description of her sister's passing.[57] In the "age of the beautiful death,"[58] recording Charlotte's last moments was more than a way of sentimentalizing her loss and mitigating the pain of the bereaved family. The details were meant to ensure the living that the loved one's death had been "triumphant" and that she would be welcomed into the realm of the eternal.[59] Atkinson Hill Rowan informed the Fosters that Charlotte became "more tranquil" as she neared the end, and "about an hour before day, when all were silent, she sang a song preserving with much melody and great accuracy, every note." The bereaved lover attributed Charlotte's demise to "a deep melancholy, not perceivable when she was in health," but which exhibited itself "in the wild, plaintive and touchingly tender songs which she always sang," even on her deathbed.[60]

Charlotte Foster was laid to rest in Louisville in a cemetery plot reserved for the Bullitt family, friends of the Barclays. Just seven months later, the Fosters' fifteen-month-old baby boy, referred to by his father as the "sweet fellow," died in May 1830. Eliza, not surprisingly, succumbed to a debilitating grief after the loss of her daughter, her infant son, and her home all within a few years. On May 14, 1832, she apologized to her son William for not writing more than one letter in the preceding two years: "there was the weak and tremulous state I was left in after the death of your ever to be lamented sister Charlotte and equally interesting little brother James, that my body has only recovered strength, since my mind was restored to that tranquility which [comes from] a perfect reconciliation to the will of that omniscient power which regulates and rules . . . all my gone by days are nothing but a dream, the song of joy, the delightful cottage, and the sound of the deep-toned instrument still come dancing on in the arrear of memory . . . but now I have little to ask . . . all is well that God in his mercy sends me."[61]

3

ALL UP AND DOWN THE WHOLE CREATION

In the wake of the death of the two Foster children and the family's precipitous financial decline, William Foster put his plans on hold for building a new house to replace the White Cottage. In lieu of the promised permanency of a new home, the Fosters began an itinerant existence that shuffled them between rented rooms and houses, or accommodating relatives, for nearly ten years. They stayed in touch with some of their old friends, but they rarely received invitations to dine with the elites after they settled into the nebulous social space best described as "genteel poverty." Although they managed to maintain the high cultural standards of the top families, the Fosters' economic displacement was still traumatic, especially for Stephen, who experienced the family's misfortunes during his most impressionable childhood years. The songs he would write as an adult about wandering, loss, separation, and home seemed eerily foreshadowed in the historical events of his early life.

During these tenuous years of transition and readjustment, the family uprooted frequently, and when the situation demanded it, they broke up and lived separately just to survive, with the youngest children residing with their mother. William Foster usually remained in Pittsburgh where he worked from a rented, downtown office space and tried to keep an eye out for business opportunities. His son Dunning, who early on demonstrated an interest in business, stayed with his father and proved "very useful" handling secretarial jobs and doing "errands" in town.[1] Whenever finances permitted, the senior William rented a house that the entire family could share, but they just as quickly dispersed and moved on when the money ran out.

Sometime in 1832, Eliza Foster and four of her children, Henrietta, Morrison, Stephen, and Henry, moved to Harmony, Pennsylvania, a 6,000-acre village thirty miles north of Pittsburgh that had been established as a haven for celibate religious thinkers. After the Harmonists moved out, Dr. Muller, a friend of the Fosters, opened a "manual training school for boys" a few miles to the south in Zelienople, where sixteen-year-old Henry learned the skills that would help him advance in the industrializing world. The Foster's oldest living daughter was staying in Meadville, Pennsylvania, ninety miles north of Pittsburgh, at the home of a Jane Buchanan Yates, whose brothers were the politically ambitious James Buchanan and the much younger, spiritually minded Edward. Ann Eliza was already of courting age and Edward Young Buchanan was paying close attention.

Eliza saw her son "Henry frequently in the evenings" and soon asked Ann Eliza to join them to make the family as nearly complete as possible.[2] Besides missing her daughter's company, Eliza needed her to homeschool Morrison and Stephen. The serious Ann Eliza showed up in Harmony with a full program of study for her two younger brothers. She even asked her father in Pittsburgh to send her "Plutarch's Lives and the two first volumes of Hume's History [of England]," which she said "I wish partly for the children." She probably wanted them for herself. Ann Eliza enjoyed heavy reading material and anything to do with religion appealed to her. She also asked for a large Bible that "belongs to George Buchanan," Edward and James's father, who, she said, was not "long for this world."[3] Her tutoring services were needed because Eliza had already taken the boys out of the local school, offering the excuse that "the weather was so intensely warm and their walk [to school] was long." A more plausible explanation was the high cost of formal schooling.[4]

Eliza found a short-lived tranquility in the tiny village, where, far from the bustle and smoke of Pittsburgh, she took solitary walks on tree-shaded pathways near her house and learned to accept her many losses as the will of God. But Harmony was never home to Eliza. The house they occupied had served as a summer cottage for the Fosters in better days and the family remained broken up with Dunning and his father still living in Pittsburgh. But William Foster was making every effort to gather his family together and in June 1832, he announced that their "new house in Allegheny is to be finished in October."[5] The state may have provided the home as a perk for his new position with the Canal Commission, but however it came to them, by January 1833, the Fosters were living together as a family in the house he had promised Charlotte he would build nearly five years earlier.[6]

The Fosters' new house was one of approximately a half dozen they bought, built, or rented in what was then called Allegheny Town, on the northern shore of the Allegheny River opposite Lawrenceville. The new neighborhood was attractive in its own way, however. It had large, open, green spaces and its distance from the "smoke and coal dust" of Pittsburgh had caused fine residences to pop up and its population to triple in the previous decade.[7] As were nearly all the houses they subsequently occupied, this one was near the river. In fact, most of the houses and farms in Allegheny were constructed so close to the river that the residents could count on "being flooded out" each spring. During one of these river risings, a young Stephen Foster watched in amazement as his older brothers Henry and Dunning rowed out into the tumultuous waters to rescue a dog that clung to the roof of a small dog house as it bounced up and down on the waves. Growing up in a neighborhood bordered by a river, the young composer heard the sounds and felt the movement of the water every day and learned to incorporate the experience into his greatest songs.[8]

Four months after the Fosters moved into their new house, the friendship between Ann Eliza and Edward Buchanan that began at the home of Edward's sister in Meadville blossomed into something more.[9] The couple became romantically involved after Edward returned to Allegheny Town, where his parents had once lived, to study for the ministry at the Episcopal Institute on Western Avenue, and Ann Eliza attended classes with him and proved to be a very zealous student. The young people took their marriage vows on April 9, 1833, at "Christ's Church (Allegheny Town) in the presence of all our family, and with a very respectable collection of friends and acquaintances." The oldest son William, ever considerate of the needs of his adoptive family, sent a generous gift of fifty dollars to pay for proper clothing for the bride. Soon after the wedding, the newlyweds returned to Meadville where Reverend Buchanan began his career as a preacher.[10]

With Ann Eliza married and out of the house, the senior William wanted to find employment for his two older sons, Henry and Dunning, and asked his son William if he could find either of them a position "as a rod bearer on the canal." He said he wanted to see his boys "both go to business this spring [as] I can't keep them together," and he worried as any father would who had no means of ensuring his sons' futures.[11] Eliza Foster dealt with financial pressures in her own way. Needing a break from her husband's complaints about money and life's injustices, she decided to make a little escapade away from Allegheny, a practice she would follow for the rest of her life. One month after daughter Ann Eliza's wedding, she ushered Morrison off to Meadville to stay with Ann Eliza and her new husband and left Dunning to work in Pittsburgh "in Mr. Hogan's bookstore." Henry remained with his father in Allegheny, where "an elderly widow woman" was found to keep house for them "until ma returns."[12] Then Eliza packed up seven-year old Stephen and fifteen-year old Henrietta and left in the middle of May for an extended visit with her two half-brothers in Kentucky. John Tomlinson, a successful physician, and Joseph Tomlinson, a college president, paid the boat passage for all three Fosters, as was expected.

After drifting four nights at a sleepy pace, the packet boat carrying Eliza, Henrietta, and Stephen arrived at Augusta, Kentucky, on the bank of the Ohio River at eleven o'clock at night. They stayed three weeks, but the visit proved ill-timed when Eliza's half-brother Joseph, along with young Stephen, came down with either a bout of fever or cholera.[13] Writing to her brother Morrison in 1883, the then-elderly Ann Eliza referenced a letter she had written fifty years earlier when she was a young bride in Meadville. "I do not find any allusions to Stevy in any [of the old letters] but one from Meadville, of the date of June 18, 1833, in which I say he had gone with Ma & Etty [Henrietta] to Augusta, Ky, to visit our half uncle Tomlinson, & that he had been attacked by cholera, as had also Uncle Joseph, but that both were happily recovered."[14] This is the only suggestion in the family correspondence that Stephen had been afflicted with the deadly disease, but in 1833 a cholera epidemic devastated Bardstown, Kentucky, taking the life of Atkinson Hill Rowan, the young man who had loved Charlotte Foster, and Bardstown was about 125 miles southwest of Augusta. It is also possible that Stephen contracted something before he left home, because several sources said cholera hit Pittsburgh in 1833, which would have given Eliza reason enough to leave the city when she did.[15]

Whatever illness afflicted "Stevy," Eliza and the children left Augusta as soon as they could and traveled northwest on the Ohio to Cincinnati, where they stayed with the Cassillys, friends of the Fosters who would entertain the young composer when he returned to the city fourteen years later. From Cincinnati, they boarded another boat and traveled one-hundred miles in a southwesterly direction until they reached Louisville on the opposite bank of the river. Eliza may have wanted to pay a visit to the gravesite of her beloved Charlotte, whose remains were still buried in Louisville in the Bullitt family cemetery. Some scholars have even suggested that on this trip she made her way to Bardstown where she introduced Stephen to her husband's cousins at Federal Hill, but the idea is unlikely.[16] Wherever Eliza and her children stopped in Kentucky, she did not stay long. Painful memories tore at her heart—reminders of what might have been, and the three Fosters boarded a steamboat, once again paid for by her brothers, and arrived back in Allegheny the first week in July.

Around this time, either before or after the trip to Kentucky, Stephen first demonstrated his remarkable musical talents to the public. He was about seven years of age when his mother took him into Smith & Mellor's Music Store in downtown Pittsburgh, where he had a chance to see and touch the shiny new musical instruments on display in the showroom. One that caught his eye was a "flageolet," a nineteenth-century woodwind similar to the recorder or flute, which produced a soft, gentle tone in a two-octave range. Stephen astounded everyone within earshot that day in 1833 when he lifted the instrument from the counter, examined it for a few minutes, and gave an impeccable impromptu performance of "Hail, Columbia in perfect time and accent." Morrison Foster described the incident:

> At the age of seven, he [Stephen] accidentally took up a flageolet in the music store of Smith & Mellor, in Pittsburgh, and in a few minutes he had so mastered its stops and sounds that he played Hail, Columbia in perfect time and accent. He had never before handled either a flageolet or flute. It was not long after this that he learned, unaided, to play beautifully on the flute.[17]

Eliza already knew her son was blessed with a gift for music. At the age of two he plucked out tunes on his sister Ann Eliza's guitar that he called his "ittly pizani," and Eliza may have brought him to Smith & Mellor's to get a professional assessment of Stephen's budding talents. One of the partners in the store was William C. Peters, who years earlier had been a music teacher to the older Foster daughters. Eliza knew him and respected his opinion, but whether the man who later published "Oh! Susanna" was in the store that day to witness Stephen's remarkable exhibition has not been determined. Peters opened a second music store in Louisville in 1829, but he still traveled back and forth between the two cities to check on sales in his Pittsburgh store and to give concerts on Penn Street. He also kept a "Musical Repository" at No. 19 Market Street in Pittsburgh where he warehoused "Splendid Piano Fortes" for immediate sale and built custom pianos to order.

In May 1834, little more than a year after moving into the first Allegheny house, the Fosters moved again, this time to a riverfront, frame house they rented for "125 Dollars" opposite "Smokey Island."[18] Later that summer, when cholera again threatened Pittsburgh, they relocated to a house in "a very pleasant and healthy spot on the bank of the Ohio," a safe distance from the epidemic.[19] The year was hard on the William. He had held on to the toll collector position for as long as he could, but in June he quit, explaining to his oldest son that the annual salary of $420 was insufficient to support the family. He said he needed "an average of 1227.00 per annum" just to survive and feared being "dismissed from service for using public money." With a family pressed for food and clothing, the funds staring him in the face were too great a temptation.[20]

After resigning from the government position, he dabbled in any venture that came his way, including making "small trade about the coal pits" and pursuing claims against people and businesses that owed him money.[21] He even sued his good friend Henry Baldwin, the man who had escorted Charlotte to Cincinnati, for $3,000.[22] William was frequently on the road, chasing after old debts or offering his services on a case-by-case basis to settle land claims for people in far-off states, but neither activity provided him with a steady supply of cash. When he became desperate, he sold his one remaining property on the Allegheny River to the town of Lawrenceville, which transformed it into a public market and boat landing.[23]

The summer of 1834 also found a new influence in the Foster household. In July of that year, Sarah Collins, after whose son Stephen had been named, "made a present of an excellent coloured girl, with upwards of three years to serve." Kitty moved in with the Fosters and took over the more onerous household chores from Eliza, whose fingers were "so stiff they will not follow her ideas, and her sight fails a little."[24] Exactly how much influence this African American servant had on Stephen's music can only be estimated. Two years after his impromptu performance of the staid "Hail, Columbia" at Smith & Mellor's Music Store, and a year after Kitty moved in, the nine-year-old took part in a minstrel show the children put on in a backyard in Allegheny. Morrison Foster, with the help of his brothers and friends, had fixed up a neighbor's carriage house into a theater, where they performed the amateur shows "three times a week." Parents, siblings, and neighbors made up the audience, applauding wildly whenever little Stephen walked on the stage in an oversized ragged coat and began dancing and singing "Jump Jim Crow," the song on "everybody's tongue."[25] Morrison Foster described the children's show in which Stephen made his debut as the "star performer":

> When he was nine years old a thespian company was formed, composed of boys of neighbor families, Robinsons, Cuddys, Kellys and Fosters. The Theatre was fitted up in a carriage house. All were stockholders except Stephen. He was regarded as a star performer, and was guaranteed a certain sum weekly. It was a very small sum, but it was sufficient to mark his superiority over the rest of the company. "Zip Coon," "Long-tailed Blue," "Coal-Black Rose" and "Jim Crow" were the only Ethiopian songs then known. His performance of these was so inimitable and true to nature, that, child as he was, he was greeted with uproarious applause, and called back again and again every night the company gave an entertainment, which was three times a week.[26]

When Stephen sang "My Long Tail Blue," he dressed in his father's best, blue, broadcloth coat, and strutted about the stage, moving his little arms and legs in time with the lively music. The jacket was cut short in the front, as was the style in the 1830s, but in the back the two swallowtails hung low to the ground on the boy's slight body. The children charged a small fee, but Stephen earned more money than the rest of the boys for his "inimitable" interpretations of the popular minstrel ditties. Morrison said his brother was a wonderful mimic and that his performances were outstanding, leading one to believe that he must have seen some live minstrels to put on such a good show.[27]

Minstrel performers had been performing in the smoky city ever since the early 1830s, when a young, white man named Thomas Dartmouth Rice donned a wooly wig, smeared his face with grease and burnt cork, and stepped out on a stage in the guise of a black plantation bumpkin named Jim Crow. Rice claimed he modeled his famous song persona after a disabled African American stable hand he came across in Cincinnati who was singing "in an unmistakable dialect" the soon-to-be-famous refrain: "Turn about an' wheel about an' do jis so, An' ebery time I turn about I jump Jim Crow."[28] After expropriating the words to the song, Rice set them to a lively country song white Americans would appreciate and then developed dance steps to go along with it, modeled on the black man's contorted body movements.[29] Although the genesis of the Jim Crow song is replete with contradiction and myth, Edward Le Roy Rice, the minstrel's son, claimed that his father next boarded a boat to Pittsburgh, where he met a black porter named Cuff working at Griffith's Hotel on Wood Street, who supplied the tattered clothing that completed the farcical creation.

The story goes that Rice walked onto the stage in Cuff's "old coat forlornly dilapidated, with a pair of shoes composed equally of patches and places for patches on his feet, and a coarse straw hat in a melancholy condition." He was greeted "with a thunder of applause," followed by uproarious laughter. At the end of the act, Cuff needed his clothes to get back to work on the waterfront. After being ignored by Rice who was bowing repeatedly to his adoring fans, the black man, in a comical state of undress, stepped out from behind the curtain and implored the minstrel in front of the audience, "Massa Rice, gi'me nigga's hat—nigga's coat—nigga's shoes—gi'me niggas's t'ings—Steam boat's comin'!" That brought the house down.[30]

If much of Rice's story sounds like public relations fluff, the reader can still glean some basic facts. Minstrelsy originated along the Ohio River in Cincinnati, Louisville, or Pittsburgh, or in a combination of these cities, depending on who tells the story. Rice's son claimed his father debuted in Pittsburgh on "an unpretending structure, rudely built of boards, and of moderate proportions sufficient, nevertheless, to satisfy the taste and secure the comfort" of the men who gravitated to the shows.[31] No matter the city, the important thing to remember is that Rice had the entrepreneurial instinct to grasp the attraction "Jim Crow" had for the working-class men who were becoming a major presence in the industrializing cities. Factory workers, iron forgers, glassmakers, and mechanics all but demanded an entertainment of their own, and that entertainment was minstrelsy.

According to his son, Thomas Dartmouth Rice remained in Pittsburgh for two years. Then he moved onto stages in Philadelphia, Washington, and Baltimore before he opened at New York's Bowery Theater on November 12, 1832, where he was an immediate sensation.[32] Rice was neither the first white man nor the first American to dazzle audiences with a face covered in burnt cork, but he became known as "Daddy Rice," the creator of blackface entertainment, because he "gave the first entertainment in which a blackface performer was not only the main actor, but the entire act."[33] George Washington Dixon impersonated blacks in New York in 1827 when he sang "Coal Black Rose" and "My Long Tail Blue," and became known for a stage persona he created named "Zip Coon," a fictional, black, urban dweller who was the polar opposite of the countrified Jim Crow. Zip wore fancy city clothes, a long-tailed blue cutaway jacket like the one nine-year-old Stephen borrowed from his father, and a monocle over one eye. But despite his sartorial improvement over Jim Crow's patched clothing, he was a comical character. When he tried to use big words, malapropisms came out of his mouth, and the elegance of his stylish clothes only emphasized the inelegance of the person wearing them. The minstrel songs Stephen Foster sang as a child in the neighbor's converted carriage house were the songs Thomas Dartmouth Rice and George Washington Dixon had made famous.

As a child, Stephen, along with tens of thousands of adults, was captivated by the music, the dance—indeed the whole incongruous mix—of race, class, and ethnic identities that made up minstrelsy. Try to imagine a white man from New York singing hillbilly tunes while his feet move feverishly to a fast-paced country tune like "Turkey in the Straw."[34] The hillbilly music to which he dances is played on fiddles and banjos and the dancing man has blackened his face and covered his head with a "wooly" wig in a grotesque imitation of a man of African descent. Whether he wears a straw hat and patched clothing as the Jim

Crow character or comes to the stage as the exaggerated urban Zip Coon, he enunciates his words in an exaggerated plantation dialect and smiles broadly at an audience of mostly Northern white mechanics, factory workers, craftsmen, butchers, and firemen. The entertainer had to be a strong singer and an adept dancer, as well as a very seasoned comic, because the image is so preposterous as to demand a suspension of disbelief to be believable at all.

When not distracted by costumes, dialect, and offensive vocabulary, the country music sound comes through and emphasizes the incongruity of the show. In spite of the references to the slave South, the music was based mainly on Anglo-American oral tradition songs of the Appalachian Mountains that the early settlers carried with them as they moved west across America. But the show was infused with African American elements as well, especially in rhythm and dance movements. The boatmen on the Ohio River played "mountain" tunes on their fiddles when they docked in Pittsburgh, Cincinnati, and Louisville, the cities where minstrelsy originated, and free blacks sometimes played the fiddle music on these river boats. Newspaper accounts from the early 1830s say Thomas Rice brought his Jim Crow show as far north on the rivers as upstate New York and Pennsylvania.[35]

The Jim Crow song that originated along the Ohio River absorbed elements from dance music in the Midwestern river towns, where "jigs were sung often as ditties on their own account." When the British travel writer Frances Trollope attended a ball in Cincinnati in 1832, around the same time and in the same city Rice claimed he first heard the "Jim Crow" refrain, she noted that Americans employed a "caller" who shouted out the directions to the couples on the dance floor so they would know what movements or turns to make. Trollope said "the figures are called from the orchestra in English" to the dancers, with phrases like "all round, chasse, four open back again, etc." In the refrain for "Jump Jim Crow," the singer calls out "Wheel about and turn about and do jis so," which sounds like a "caller" giving directions to the dancers for the movements they are supposed to make next.[36]

"Jump Jim Crow" and the other minstrel songs Stephen sang as a child performer were neither refined nor polite. The words were written in a faux black dialect that marked the song character as comical and illiterate, which would not have appealed to Eliza Foster's sensibilities. The verses were rambling, nonsensical, and contradictory, depicting disorder rather than an orderly sequence of events, and when sold as sheet music, the publishers of such songs featured a simple piano accompaniment and chorus and grotesque images on the cover.[37]

Morrison Foster, who was Stephen's senior by three years, was old enough in the early 1830s to have seen and appreciated Daddy Rice when he came to Pittsburgh. He knew all his popular songs and decades later entertained his own children with songs "made famous by minstrel man, T. D. Rice." Even if Stephen were too young to have seen Rice's show and to have absorbed anything from watching it—although little children do learn dance steps and perform in recitals while still in kindergarten—many other minstrel performers came to town after Rice left for the East, and Stephen and Morrison might have watched their shows. But Stephen could have learned the lyrics to the songs from a comic songster, a booklet that contained the words without the music to the most popular blackface songs. Songsters were reasonably priced, and following the performance, minstrel entertainers sold them in the lobby to customers who were walking out humming or whistling the tunes. In January 1837, the year after he appeared in the children's minstrel show, ten-year-old Stephen wrote his father who was working in Pittsburgh: "I wish you to send me a commic [sic] songster for you promised to." He added that he would also like to have "a pensyl" or "the money to by [sic] Black ink," but admitted that if he had his "whistle I would be so taken with it I do not think I would write at all." He mailed the letter from a small town in Ohio where the Fosters' itinerary brought them next.[38]

4

SCHOOLDAYS IN BROTHER WILLIAM'S SUNSHINE

In the summer of 1835, William Foster Jr., the family's adopted, oldest son, was transferred to Youngstown, Ohio, to direct the construction of a canal line that would transport the village's ample coal supplies to energy-hungry industrialists in the East. The senior William followed after him and immediately became mesmerized by the acres of green, rolling pastureland just sixty miles northwest of Pittsburgh. In spite of his devastating losses in real estate, the older man still grew giddy at the prospect of making his fortune in land and convinced the younger William to look around for a farm to buy in Youngstown to which all the Fosters could move. The father was down on his luck. He had just returned from Washington where his request to be reimbursed for the money he spent outfitting General Jackson was again denied.[1] He was overwhelmed by his problems and knew not what to do. That winter he closed up the Allegheny house and sent Eliza, Morrison, and Stephen to board at a Mrs. Squires in Youngstown, while he stayed with Henrietta in the Pittsburgh home of Eliza's relative George Evans. Henrietta, however, was bored and lonesome and wrote her mother that she was "homesick when I see any person from Youngstown particularly." She urged her father repeatedly to move the entire family to the village where Brother William (as he was affectionately known in the family) had settled, and in March, 1836, William agreed to put the latest "Allegheny Town property" on the market.

In truth, Henrietta missed more than her mother and brothers when she wrote that she was "homesick." Pressured by his father, the younger William had bought a large stretch of land in Youngstown, adjacent to a farm owned by the Wick family, where he planned to build a farmhouse for the Fosters. Henrietta visited her brother as often as she could, and on one of her visits, she met the neighbor's son Thomas Wick and fell in love. The couple married on October 20, 1836, and Henrietta moved in with her in-laws until they could find a farm of their own.

As fate would have it, Cupid's arrow struck Brother William at the same time, but he was not so lucky. He fell in love with Thomas's lovely, younger sister Mary Wick, whose frail body was being devastated by tuberculosis. Mary tried to be optimistic and ignored the signs of her declining health. In June 1836 she reassured her fiancé, "my health remains much the same . . . . I spend my time practicing on the piano, some I devote to my friends, and some in performing domestic duties."[2] But after Mary traveled to Pittsburgh in September to purchase her wedding dress, she returned looking unwell and Henrietta wrote her brother to come as soon as he could. William, who was working in another state, hurried back to Youngstown at the end of 1837 and married Mary. A few months later, while he was again away at a job site, a letter arrived by courier to inform him that his bride of only a few months had died on January 8, 1838.[3] William returned to Ohio briefly for the funeral, but then went back to Kentucky to bury his grief in hard work.

Mary's death came the year after a massive new depression threw the economy into a devastating downturn from which the Fosters and the nation suffered for nearly five years. After Andrew Jackson closed down the Bank of the United States that had foreclosed on the senior William's home a decade earlier, the institution in retaliation called in its loans to the smaller banks and caused thousands to lose their homes and farms. But William never blamed the bad times on his hero Jackson. While "the silk stockings gentry are damning Jackson for killing their savior God Moloch," William cried, "the country . . . damns all the Banks and hurrahs for Jackson."[4] Stephen's mother also complained about hard times, but she was annoyed that not everyone suffered equally. To her eldest son she wrote enviously, "Pittsburgh looks very dull as to business in Market Street, but yet one would not suppose business to be going down when they see the elegant coaches with silver trappings on the splendid horses by which they are drawn." Eliza's tastes were simpler. As she explained, "I am truly thankful that I have shoes to put on my feet without having earned them by the swet [sic] of my brow."[5]

From the start of the Depression of 1837 until the end of the decade, Eliza and William moved back and forth between Allegheny Town and Youngstown, staying with relatives or boarding, but they never became permanent residents of Ohio as the senior William had envisioned. After the death of his wife, the younger William abandoned thoughts of building a farmhouse in Youngstown, and while his father continued to study real estate prices, he eventually decided he was too old to start a new venture. In the spring of 1838, the Fosters were all living together in Allegheny, when Henry Foster informed his brother William, "We are like many of our neighbours, pretty hard run, but will not complain."[6]

Eliza Foster, during these uncertain times, remained active, taking to the road to care for her daughters when they were expecting. In May 1836, she left Stephen in the care of Mrs. Squires in Youngstown to travel to Lancaster County, Pennsylvania, where Ann Eliza's husband had the previous year "taken charge of two congregations, his health being quite restored."[7] She went to assist her daughter with the birth of her second child, a girl poignantly named Charlotte. Ann Eliza's first child, a boy born in 1834, was conveniently named James in honor of both her dead baby brother and her politically active brother-in-law James Buchanan.[8] The trip east took four days and involved riding the scary, nearly vertical, portage railroad, a precarious string of railway cars whose steam engines propelled Eliza over the Allegheny Mountains on ten incline planes, five on each side, four cars at a time.[9] On her way home, she visited girlhood friends "from the eastern shore of Maryland" now living in Philadelphia, where she toured the government mint "in full operation." There she had the exhilarating experience of holding gold bullion ("French money") in her hand, which, she joked, was "too heavy to keep."[10]

The following summer, in August 1837, Eliza traveled to Youngstown to help Henrietta with the birth of a black-haired, blue-eyed baby girl named Mary, after her sickly sister-in-law. Eliza brought Stephen with her and deposited him at the farm of her husband's elderly Uncle John Struthers in Poland, Ohio, seven miles south of Youngstown, while she nursed her daughter back to health.[11] After six weeks, Eliza and Stephen were back in Allegheny with all the Fosters, but the next summer they rented out the Allegheny house and moved in with Uncle Struthers, who borrowed money to make his old farmstead comfortable for the family that paid him two dollars per week for room and board.[12] Stephen loved spending summers with his septuagenarian great uncle, an old-time settler and Indian fighter who entertained the boy with stories of hunting "'coons and opossums," but shuffling back and forth between two states at such an early age must have formed in him an image of home as a perpetual-motion machine.

Fortunately for the Fosters, just as the senior William's health and earning capacities waned, the younger William's star began to rise. The patriarch of the family was nearly sixty years of age and had lost the use of his right hand when the Fosters came to depend on the success of the younger William for their financial well-being. A widower with no children of his own, he lavished money and gifts on his brothers and sisters and impecunious parents (for which he received meager expressions of thanks) and became more of a father figure than a sibling to Stephen, who was nearly twenty years younger. Brother William had "assumed the mantle of responsibility" while still in his teens and continued to provide for the Fosters until Eliza and William died nearly thirty years later.[13]

Young William began his career in canal building in April 1826, only a year after the great Erie had been completed and a few months before Stephen was born. When an engineer named Nathan Roberts from the New York Canal System came to Pittsburgh to build a canal to the Kiskiminetas River, the senior William invited him to dinner at the White Cottage and introduced him to his impressive son. "Suppose you let your son go with us, Mr. Foster, and learn to be an engineer," suggested the enterprising Mr. Roberts, and the father was only too happy to oblige.[14] Initially apprenticed as an "axeman," William hacked away tirelessly at the earth in Kentucky and Pennsylvania, carving out the manmade waterways that would improve trade, speed up transportation, and tie the nation together. He worked for years without complaint under dangerous and uncomfortable conditions, toiling away in the mud and sludge on rainy spring days and in the summer when fatal diseases were apt to strike.[15] One "dreary, wet Sunday" he spent the entire day confined to a "good capacious and water proof" tent but reassured his family that "we live rather comfortably [and] the fare is rather coarse but wholesome."[16] William worked for twenty years on the canals systems, becoming chief engineer, until they became obsolete and he transferred to a successful career with the Pennsylvania Railroad, where he eventually became vice president.[17]

For much of the 1830s, financial worries and failures so eroded the senior William's confidence that the role of caretaker and provider was taken over by the younger man. As his son's earning capabilities quickly outstripped his own, the father turned to the son for advice on financial and business decisions, and more and more directly asked for money. All the Fosters—mother, father, sisters, and brothers—readily asked Brother William for handouts, and acted like his generosity was payment for a debt. The younger William was, after all, an illegitimate child who had been taken into the family at an early age and brought up, trained, and educated through William and Eliza's beneficence. As the older man's economic situation deteriorated, he schemed to find solutions, and when none was forthcoming, he inevitably turned to his son William. It is true that the Foster boys often borrowed from one another, securing their debts with promissory notes, but the only one who actually had anything to give during the hard decade of the 1830s was Brother William. If Stephen Foster, throughout his life, continued the habit of importuning relatives for money, it was one he learned early on by example.

Sometimes the senior William manipulated his son through threats of dire repercussions for the entire family if his requests for money were not met. One time he cajoled William into giving him "300 Dollars to prevent any unpleasant situation." Another time, he asked for two hundred dollars and revealed an unwonted prejudice: "I beg that you will not disappoint me. I have no other resource, unless I throw myself on the mercy of the Jew brokers here."[18] When the younger William was promoted with an increase in salary, the father rejoiced and demanded to know "what your pay will be," anticipating that a portion would go directly toward the family's expenses.[19] In all fairness, it should be noted that the senior William used his political connections to secure appointments that propelled his son's career forward, but that does not mean he did not take undue advantage of the younger man's generosity.

When he needed capital to launch a business, the senior William turned to his son for the funds. After Henry Foster lost his job at the start of the Depression of 1837, the father envisioned opening a general store that he and Henry would run together, and convinced William to become the major backer in the venture. But by the time the store got off the ground, the economic downturn was in full force, nobody had any money, and the partners were "selling goods at cost."[20] After that store failed, William convinced his obliging son to invest in a second store, which went the way of the first before the enthusiastic father realized that sales were being made with promissory notes, not cash.[21] That proved to be the clincher! The younger William then advised Henry to get out of the general store business once and for all, and when his brother-in-law Thomas Wick asked for money for yet another store, "William [junior] refused to have anything to do with business here with Thomas Wick or anyone else."[22] By the end of the decade he walked away from all the business schemes concocted by his father or anyone else in the family.[23]

As luck would have it, just as William was learning to say no to his importuning family, his father found himself deeply in debt with creditors hot on his back. William and Eliza were living in Youngstown when they packed up and rushed back to Pittsburgh after learning that land they owned east of the city "in Wilkins and Plumb Townships" was to be offered for "sale by the Sheriff."[24] William did not want his property auctioned off, but he also worried that with land values cut in half, a sale at auction might not bring enough to cover his debts. His friend "Sam'l P. Darlington" had been "shut up [in jail] by the Sheriff and God only knows how many more" for not being able to satisfy their creditors, and he asked himself, "Will I share their fate?" William was "in debt some five or six hundred dollars to different persons, a considerable part of which had been sued." Therefore, when one of his creditors "proposed a compromise," William Foster hurried back to settle accounts.[25]

By 1840, nearly all the Foster children had established their independence. Henrietta and Ann Eliza were married with families of their own and the boys were either settled in business or on their way to becoming so. Morrison had started his career in a steam engine factory owned by Eliza's cousin Cadwallader Evans, who taught him to "to be an accountant, and also mathematics."[26] Next, he transferred to one of the oldest cotton establishments in Pittsburgh, where "Mr. McCormick one of the partners took a great fancy for him."[27] After one year, McCormick opened a factory of his own in Allegheny and hired Morrison, who was as "steady in his office as an old man,"[28] to work for him. Morrison remained at McCormick's Cotton Mill for nearly twenty years. Dunning Foster, who had gotten his business experience early on working for his father, spent much of his time in Cincinnati clerking on the Ohio River boats and would soon form a successful partnership in a related business on the river.[29] Henry Foster, who had studied at the vocational school in Harmony, was not yet settled, but business opportunities frequently came his way through his father's personal and professional connections.[30] William Jr., of course, was already very successful and had recently received an executive promotion on the canal lines. That left only thirteen-year-old Stephen for his parents to worry about.

William knew he had to find a suitable home for his adolescent son. He and Eliza could board with the "widow lady" Mrs. Paul at her house on Second Street in Pittsburgh near the Monongahela River, but the situation would not work for an active teenager.[31] For years Stephen had found a haven from responsibility at his sister's new farm in Youngstown, a present from her father-in-law Henry Wick. In the fall, he roamed the woodlands behind the farmhouse imitating wild birds with his flute and he chased after his two nieces, ten years his junior. In Henrietta's parlor, he heard the sentimental songs Charlotte had played in the White Cottage plus some Henrietta had recently learned, like "My Hopes Are Departed Forever," which inspired Stephen years later to write his own song with a similar title.[32] She also accompanied her young brother on the piano while he played his flute and, most likely, taught him the rudiments of the keyboard, since years before she taught him "all the simple chords [on her guitar] that his eager little hands could manage."[33] In the summer, Stephen returned to his Great Uncle Struthers's farm, where he "never appears to have the least inclination to leave." Apparently, Struthers put no restrictions on the boy, letting him "do as he pleases with the horses and cattle, which makes him the greatest man on the ground!" Uncle Struthers also appreciated Stephen's musical talents and early on predicted he "would be something famous if he lived to be a man."[34]

Whatever fate intended, William and Eliza wanted Stephen to devote his energies to acquiring an education, and as usual, they turned to their son William for help. It is not surprising that the Fosters worried about his education, for their youngest had a history of being unable or unwilling "to stick to school," even though the record shows some schools agreed with him. At the age of five, Stephen and Morrison attended "an infant school taught by a Mrs. Harvey," but when asked to recite the alphabet, Stephen bounded out of the classroom "with a yell like that of a Comanche Indian," and ran a mile and a half to his home. The next year Stephen must have settled down because Eliza wrote, "The little children go to school with quite as happy faces as though the world had no thorns in it." After the Fosters moved to Allegheny, Stephen enrolled in the Allegheny Academy under the direction of his father's friend Joseph Stockton and did not have any noticeable problems.[35] The school was attended by students from the best families, and Morrison Foster described Stockton as "a perfect tutor. He was learned, he was firm, he was amiable, and he was thorough and practical," attributes that may have appealed more to Morrison than to Stephen, who kept a special place in his heart for the headmaster's assistant John Kelly. The Irishman had "a genial disposition and out of school played ball and prisoner's base with the boys, and excelled in many athletic exercise," while "in school he required rigid attention to business."[36]

Stephen may have likened most schoolmasters to Thomas Gradgrind, a fictional character from Charles Dickens's 1854 novel *Hard Times*, after which the adult Foster would write a song with a similar title. No student of his had "ever seen a face in the moon; . . . had ever learnt the silly jingle, Twinkle, twinkle, little star," for Gradgrind taught only practical subjects and no child was allowed to wonder. Dickens acknowledged an ongoing struggle between the head and the heart, and of course Dickens's schoolmaster ignored the heart, causing his students much unhappiness. Years later Stephen wrote a poem entitled "Old Schoolmaster," which a group of Kelly's former students read aloud at a banquet held in the teacher's honor. Apparently Kelly was the one schoolmaster who did not remind him of Dickens's "man of facts and calculations."[37]

On January 12, 1840, the senior William, after reflecting on Stephen's erratic school attendance, confided with a sigh of relief to son Morrison, "We have concluded to let Stephen go with William who will put him to school at the Academy at Towanda where William's office and headquarters are. I think it an excellent chance for the dear little fellow to get an education."[38] The previous year, two years after losing his wife, William had moved to the small town of Towanda in central Pennsylvania, where he was appointed principal engineer for a canal line that would run along the Susquehanna River and connect Pennsylvania to New York. As soon as he could, the accommodating young man took time out from his busy schedule to comply with the wishes of his adoptive parents and see that Stephen was settled into school.[39]

The roads were covered in heavy snows when the younger William arrived on January 14 in Youngstown, Ohio, to pick up his baby brother. After the excited teenager was bundled up in heavy blankets, William threw in a hot brick to keep the boy's legs and feet warm, and the pair set off in a horse-drawn sleigh toward Pittsburgh whence they would commence the three-hundred-mile journey to the Towanda Academy. The sleigh followed the old stage road through Bedford to Harrisburg, gliding smoothly over mounds of snow that would have been impassable with conventional wheels. They stopped in Harrisburg, the state's capital, where Stephen visited the House of Representatives and met with their father's friend, Governor Porter. In spite of the distance and the cold, "to Stephen the journey was a joyous adventure, and remained with him all his life as a beautiful memory to which he often referred with delight."[40]

Towanda, Pennsylvania was situated on a hilly tract of land bordering the Susquehanna River, with streets oriented toward the river bank. Originally a trading post where men could conduct business and swap the latest news stories, the town operated several taverns and a distillery before the courthouse was even finished. The Towanda Academy at 314 State Street was a five- year-old building in the Greek Revival style with tall, brick, Doric pilasters and "a dentil frieze and projecting cornice." The houses in the town were also constructed in the Greek Revival style, with ornate entrances and fluted ionic columns that faced directly onto the sidewalk, and the bank and the bookstore were three stories high. With fewer than seventy houses and fewer than 500 people, Towanda was small even by early nineteenth-century standards.[41] Sometime that year, Henry Foster showed up to work as a rod bearer on the canal, a temporary position Brother William had found for him, while his father pulled strings to find something better for his son in Washington.

Stephen started classes at the Towanda Academy soon after he arrived in the town, but the experience did not prove such a "joyous adventure" as had the ride through the snow to bring him there. Either he was not inspired academically, or the curriculum did not offer courses that interested him. Many years later a school chum named William Wallace Kingsbury provided his recollections of Foster's days at Towanda, where the two boys spent their time playing "truant" and "gathering wild strawberries":

> Well do I remember the inimitable Stephen C. Foster . . . . We often played truant together, rambling by shady streams or gathering wild strawberries in the meadows or pastures, removed from the sound of the old academy bell. Our mutual luxury, in which we jointly indulged in those excursions without leave was in going barefoot and wading in pools of running water . . . . His love of music was an all-absorbing passion, and his execution of the flute was the very genius of melody.[42]

It is easy to imagine Eliza learning of her boy's absences from the Academy and his lackadaisical study habits and throwing up her hands in dismay. Years later, the composer's school day antics became part of Foster folklore, and were attributed to his unique musical genius and artistic personality.[43] For his mother, however, sticking to school was a matter of developing moral stamina, a feat that called for the right role model. That Eliza wanted her stable, oldest son to be that role model was only natural, but what is surprising is that she referred to the younger William as Stephen's "father" as well: "As to Stephen," she wrote her oldest son in August 1840, "I leave everything regarding the future for him to your judgment. You are not only his brother but his Father, and I trust all his feelings will ascend to you as his patron."[44]

As Stephen's appointed "patron," William decided his young brother would leave the Towanda Academy, where he found too many distractions, and transfer to the Athens Academy at Tioga Point, fifteen miles further north. The state subsidized school was very popular with the local boys and girls, who enjoyed "four 11-week terms, each followed by a 2-week vacation," and a variety of courses including bookkeeping, for which Stephen signed up. The students found ample outdoor activities to engage their leisure hours, but the Athens Academy imposed greater restrictions and some after-school activities may have been supervised. In the winter, there were ice skating on the frozen rivers and bobsledding down the hills. Springtime offered an unspoiled countryside for

exploration, hills for climbing, and boating on the Chemung and Susquehanna Rivers. In the early mornings, the songs of meadowlarks,
orioles, and sandpipers provided a musical exchange that was interesting to a creative boy with a flute. [45]

For a modest fee, most of the Athens students boarded in the neighbors' homes, many of which were picturesque with bright white fencing
and tall trees. When Stephen started classes in the fall of 1840, he
moved into the house of a Mr. Herrick, but on November 9 he wrote
William to complain. "I have no place to study in the evenings as the
little ones at Mr. Herrick's keep such a crying and talking that it's
impossible to read." He really wanted his brother to pay Mr. Herrick for
firewood. "There is a good fire-place in my room and if you will just say
the word I will have a fire in it at nights and learn something." He
signed off, "I must stop writing as I am very cold." [46]

In spite of Stephen's carping, William must have made the right
choice for his little brother because it was at the Athens Academy that
the fourteen-year-old wrote and performed his first composition, the
"Tioga Waltz." Arranged for three or four flutes, Stephen played the
leading part himself on the evening of April 2, 1841, when the music
was presented for the first time at the April Exhibition, the school's
graduation ceremony. [47] The trustees and faculty of the Academy, along
with relatives of the students, attended the performance and responded
with much applause and even demanded an encore. Stephen dedicated
the "Tioga Waltz" to Frances Welles, one of the few females attending
the Academy and the sister of his Athens schoolmate Henry Welles.

The wealthy Welles family had relatives in high places, and one was
reportedly the founder of the Wells-Fargo Express Company. Their
large stone house on 400 acres just south of Athens was known as the
Tioga Point Farm, although the entire area between the Sayre and
South Waverly rivers was called Tioga Point. Even the Chemung River,
which flowed past the Herrick house where Stephen boarded was at
one time called the Tioga. The meeting of the rivers at Tioga Point
must have reminded Stephen of the confluence of the three rivers in
Pittsburgh, and provided him with a comforting sense of home. Morrison Foster years later described the "Tioga Waltz" as "Liquid runs and
yodeling bird-notes . . . woven into the theme Te-a-oga, the meeting of
the waters." [48]

Stephen spent many evenings at Frances's home, where she sang, played the piano, and rehearsed the heroine's parts for school plays with effectively dramatic declamations. She was, like his sisters, an accomplished young lady, with skills in acting and, of course, music. Stephen and Frances were "two temperaments akin," and the latter took the young composer "under her wing" and introduced "the shy Stephen into Athens social circles," where he became "the life of the young society of the place."[49] What his feelings were toward the seventeen-year-old Frances can only be surmised. He was several years younger and may have regarded her as an older sister. Conversely, he may have been infatuated and had a crush on his delightful grown-up schoolmate.

At her upcoming graduation ceremony, Frances was scheduled to perform a Greek dialogue, which she rehearsed at her home with Stephen, who practiced his own recitation of "Lord Ullin's Daughter," the sentimental poem of tragic love by Thomas Campbell. But Frances had more pressing matters on her mind as spring approached. Just seventeen years old, she was engaged to be married when she abruptly advanced her wedding day and decided to leave the school. She skipped her graduation performance and urged Stephen "one suspects, to provide some counter attraction on the program to assuage the instructors ire." In other words, Frances may have asked Stephen to write the "Tioga Waltz" to fill in for the absence of her Greek presentation. Stephen's choice of a waltz may have upset the "old school" Athens headmasters who could have considered the new dance scandalous, but Frances and Stephen wanted something musically innovative on the program.[50]

On April 17, 1841, Frances Welles married Charles B. Stuart, a construction engineer for the Erie Railroad then being laid across New York State. Stephen attended the wedding and at the ball following the ceremony, the "Tioga Waltz" was performed for the second time, again to much applause. The original score for Stephen's first composition has been lost. What we have today is a transcription for the piano made a half-century later from Morrison Foster's whistled version, which he published in 1896 in his biography *My Brother Stephen*. After Frances's wedding, Stephen "underwent a violent reaction" and fell into a state of depression. He complained frequently to his mother of homesickness and wrote his brother William that he was cold. "Don't pay Mr. Herrick for fire in my room," he admonished, "as I have not had any since you payed [*sic*] him last." Mostly, he begged to be allowed to leave the school.[51]

Frances's departure may have caused Stephen to relive the painful experience of his family's frequent uprooting. Only three months earlier, in January 1841, he had met Henry Welles, who probably introduced him to his sister.[52] Now his new family away from home had dissolved. Whatever the reasons for Stephen's unhappiness—and there were many excuses given—Stephen left the Athens Academy shortly after Frances's wedding. He wanted to live in Towanda with his brother or board with a young artist named Kettle. He begged his brother William, who wanted him to go back to Athens, to let him study privately with Mr. Vosberry, "a very good mathematition [*sic*]" while he lived in Towanda "as cheap as I could live in Athens that lonesome place." In return, he promised that he would "not be seen out of doors between the hours of nine & twelve A.M. and one & four P.M.," and would not touch his music until "after eight Oclock [*sic*] the evening."[53] Stephen never returned to Athens, and the fact that the Academy accidentally burned down the next year only made Foster's decision irreversible.

A few months after Stephen renounced Athens, the Fosters made one final attempt to give their youngest son a formal education. On July 20, 1841, Stephen was ushered off to Canonsburg, Pennsylvania, to enroll at Jefferson College, a school with "about two hundred and thirty students" twenty miles south of Pittsburgh. Stephen's grandfather on his father's side had been one of the original trustees of the school and Stephen said he "found among the quantity of Students . . . several of my old acquaintances," but neither the ancestral connection nor the familiar faces could convince him to stay in school.[54] One week after entering Jefferson College, he bummed a ride home with another disgruntled student. Later, he ungraciously wrote his brother William from Pittsburgh to justify his impulsive decision to leave the school:

> When I wrote to you from Canonsburg I did not tell you whether I liked the place or not (if I remember aright) but now I will take the liberty of telling you that I became more disgusted with the place as long as I stayed in it. It is not a good time to begin college in the middle of the Season as I could not get into any class for three or four days after I went there, and when I did get started into a recitation it was in irregular hours.[55]

The composer never seemed to run out of excuses for abandoning schools, but at Canonsburg he may have been stressed about not having enough money to pay the bills. Although his father paid the tuition in advance at Jefferson College, Stephen complained to his brother William of several accounts owing and said that he needed money for the little extras, such as the small fee to join a literary society "as all of the students belong to them." But more serious deficits were the boarding fees that Stephen's father did not pay and that Stephen asked his brother to pay "at the end of every month," which amounted to $8.50 plus an additional $1.25 per week for washing expenses "as I have to keep myself very clean here."[56]

Jefferson College was the last attempt that the family made at providing Stephen with a formal education. As his father said with sad resignation, "I cannot get him to stick to school."[57]

When it became apparent that formal schooling would never suit Stephen's temperament, his mother provided an informal nonstructured education, which seemed to work best for her son. Eliza encouraged him to study or at least read whatever books they had at home, and she had him copy lengthy tracts of Shakespeare, Sir Walter Scott, and Byron, which he later recited from memory. Stephen must have felt remorse about his actions and embarrassment in front of his big brother, because he told his father "he would like to be in brother William's sunshine."[58] A year later, when William asked his oldest son one last time if he could find a job for Stephen, the young man backed away from the care of his irresponsible, dreamy eyed sibling. For the rest of his life, Stephen came to feel that he lived in his successful older brother's much magnified shadow.[59]

5

AT HOME IN ALLEGHENY

Following the debacle at Jefferson College in Canonsburg, Stephen moved back with his parents, where he continued his education in a somewhat haphazard yet personally satisfying fashion. The senior Fosters were probably boarding with Mrs. Paul at her new location on Penn Street when their youngest son arrived unannounced at their door and told them he was through with school.[1] While Mrs. Paul's "fine house pleasantly arranged, good table, and a respectable neighborhood" were agreeable to William and Eliza, boarding would never do for a teenaged boy. Eliza wanted to rent an entire house where she and her husband and her unmarried children could live comfortably together, but the one available in town "whence Dunning and Morrison could board" cost a prohibitive $150 a year. Once again the younger William came to the rescue. He offered the Fosters the use of a large house he had recently acquired in what was by then called Allegheny City,[2] and on August 14, 1841, Eliza thanked him for his generous gift.[3]

Although the most cost effective way for the Fosters to live was all together under one roof, Eliza literally begged her son William to allow Stephen to "board with Ma" before she brought him to the new Allegheny house. She said it was "too lonesome without one child" at home and promised he would attend school in the day. Mostly, she seemed embarrassed that Stephen had dropped out of school after she had asked her oldest son to oversee his education in the first place, so she flattered him with the knowledge that Stephen had his regrets about not returning to Towanda when he had the chance. One month after he left Jefferson College, Eliza wrote:

> Stephen will not stay at Canonsburg. He says he has lost conseat [*sic*] of himself because he was once in his life a great fool and that was when he did not go back with brother William. He begs me to ask you to say that he must board with Ma and go to day skool [*sic*], indeed if I am in allegany [*sic*] town I shall be almost too lonesome without one child with me for if I should be ill I would be in a bad way.[4]

Whether or not William ever gave his formal approval for keeping Stephen at home, one month later they were all settled in what may have been their fourth house in Allegheny, and Eliza wrote to inform her son of their daily activities in the house he had provided:

> We have fairly settled down into the house keeping having a good girl which enables me to keep clean and comfortable as I study nothing but our comfort, which little we have I take great pleasure in attending to it. . . . Everything around our neighborhood looks natural and perfectly harmonizes with the very pleasant association of home. The Robinsons have been to see us, looking as cheerily as they could to welcome us back.[5]

The Robinsons, who lived nearby in a large, three-story, gable-roofed house on the Commons, would remain in touch with Stephen throughout his life.

The fifteen-year-old adapted well to his new situation. Although he did not go back to school, Stephen studied what he wanted, when he wanted, and with whom he wanted. He had private tutoring with a Mr. Moody, "a first rate teacher of mathematics in Pittsburgh," and he dabbled in whatever else interested him. He took language lessons with a Belgian man named Jean Herbst and became proficient in both French and German. He learned to paint, and according to Morrison Foster, became "a credible artist in water colors as an amusement." Eliza tried to convince herself and others that her youngest had changed and was more serious about his regular school courses than before. "He is not so much devoted to music as he was, other studies seem to be elevated in his opinion," she said.[6] But her husband William, who was more honest, remarked simply that Stephen's "leisure hours are all devoted to musick [*sic*], for which he possesses a strange talent."[7]

It was probably around this time that the boy with the "strange talent" took lessons in music composition and theory from Henry Kleber, a German immigrant who lived in a house on Sandusky Street in Allegheny, a few blocks from the Fosters. Kleber, who was ten years older than Stephen, had moved to Pittsburgh in 1830, where he taught at a Dr. Lacey's Seminary for Young Ladies, in addition to giving private lessons in town. His musical interests were diverse and far-flung, for he performed as a tenor soloist and concert pianist, composed dance music, and organized and directed wind bands. Later he and his brother Gus established a piano and music store in Pittsburgh, where they retailed Steinways, and published and sold sheet music, including some of Stephen's songs.[8]

Kleber may have been a hard taskmaster, or Stephen proved to be a diligent student when the subject interested him. Morrison Foster, who also took lessons from Kleber, said his younger brother "studied deeply and burned much midnight oil over the works of the masters, especially Mozart, Beethoven, and Weber" which "were his delight."[9] Whether or not the "midnight oil" was an exaggeration, the Foster family believed "that Stephen learned practically all he knew of theory from Henry Kleber, who was never too busy to help his young friend."[10] Kleber later encouraged Stephen in his desire to become a professional songwriter and was an important influence in the composer's life, even if he remained in the background.

Eliza was pleased with the progress Stephen was making in his studies at home, and she was happy just to have his company. But Stephen may have been lonely for companionship other than his mother's since Morrison started for work early in the morning, and when his father traveled, he and his mother were left alone in the house for weeks at a time. Once, when the senior William rode out to Erie, Pennsylvania, chasing after an unpaid debt, Stephen and Eliza took in a stray female "tortoise-shell collour'd cat" because, according to Eliza, they could not entice real girls who "like gay places." She insisted that even the cat "lies about the fire [in] the middle of the hearth rug" with nothing better to do than wait for Stephen to give "her all the little bits he is permitted to gather for the sake of her company."[11]

Even if Stephen felt lonely, his mother appeared to be enjoying herself for the first time in many years. A new Christ Episcopal Church "with an excellent preacher in it" had opened up nearby "on the same lot where the old house which Mr. Buchanan occupied stands," and offered "fine musick [sic], fine stoves, plenty of room, and people flocking in."[12] Mention of the new church's location was a reminder that the parents of James and Edward Buchanan had lived in Allegheny before the Fosters moved in.[13] In November 1841, with both Morrison and Stephen living at home, Eliza regaled son William with a list of her mundane household chores to impress upon him that she was an industrious and appreciative homemaker:

> You know what I am doing very well at this season, turning old clothes in[to] new ones, looking after the baking and the cooking and brushing about the house, and sometimes taking a comfortable rest in a rocking chair, by a pleasant coal fire to read the Cronicle[sic] in the forenoon, and the daily American at four o'clock in the afternoon, going to bed at nine o'clock that I may rise at six to have breakfast for Morrison who is off to his business the moment it is over, we have ever and anon a quiet and peaceable and temperate house exactly such a one as I have always been longing for.[14]

Eliza's husband kept busy, too, but four years after the Depression raged, William still did not have his finances in order. He got involved with the Washingtonians, promoting the temperance cause throughout Pittsburgh and Butler County, and seeing to it that the attendees at his meetings "signed the teetotal [sic] pledge and organized a temperance society."[15] But he had lost faith in his favorite pastime, land speculation, and in March 1841, complained, "It is almost impossible to sell real property at half of what it would have brought three years ago." Frustrated, he turned to old friends with political connections for help. Walter Forward promised that should he himself be appointed Comptroller of the Treasury, he would get William a government post and William gushed with pride, "He wants me at Washington as a companion and political advisor!!"[16] But when the offer finally came through, it was only for a clerkship in the Treasury, and William already had his eye on something bigger.

A few months earlier, "a very respectable citizen" had offered to announce William Barclay Foster "as a candidate for the office of Mayor of Allegheny City," and he eagerly accepted. Uncertain about the outcome of the race, William traveled to Washington to accept the Treasury position, but as soon as he got word that he had won the election, he turned the post over to his son Henry. William said he wanted the clerkship to provide "a foothold" for his son in Washington, "which may be permanent in case I should live or die, he can help his mother."[17] In this way Henry Foster became a government employee earning a steady annual income of $1,000 handling land claims, and his father William returned to Allegheny in January 1842 to become the city's third mayor, an office he held for two years.

William might have been too distracted to handle the duties of mayor if he were still plagued by personal debts. Fortunately, in the wake of the terrible suffering brought on by the Depression of 1837, a new bankruptcy law that brought relief to ordinary debtors was enacted on August 19, 1841, and William immediately took advantage of it.[18] No national bankruptcy law existed in the 1820s when the White Cottage went into foreclosure, when most states had their own basically ineffective insolvency laws and business failure was judged a disgrace or even a crime.[19] By the 1840s, however, business failure was judged "a random consequence of uncontrollable economic forces" and filing for bankruptcy became the "rational" way of dealing with the irrational.[20] The sad irony is that because the law protected the ordinary man, the elite creditors quickly denounced it, and President Tyler repealed it less than two years later as a concession to the rich.[21]

Stephen's idyllic situation, comforted and coddled by a loving mother at his beck and call in his older brother's house, did not continue uninterrupted. No matter how content Eliza Foster was waiting on her boys and attending to housekeeping, she always found an excuse to travel east, sometimes mingling with interesting people with political connections. In February 1842, her son William escorted her to "Washington City," where they joined her son Henry who was working at the Treasury. He showed them around town and mother and son took walks "up the Pennsylvania Avenue every afternoon to see the fashions," after which Eliza quipped, "Arch street in Philadelphia is nothing to it." She danced at a presidential levee held by President Tyler and visited "once at the Capitol." She even ran into her husband's old friend "Harmar Denney at the President's" and engaged him in "quite a long conversation."[22]

When Eliza traveled east, Stephen and Morrison remained in Allegheny with their father, and in 1842 an African American woman named Catherine Russell was hired to care for the house. Perhaps Eliza was hoping for male bonding between father and son in her absence, but the senior William had just taken on the mayor's duties, and had neither the time nor the patience to deal with the moods of an overly sensitive teenager. Much of William's job involved the tedious "witnessing [of] deeds and contracts," but the position also forced him to "witness many cases of female intoxication & prostitution" that he described as "truly lamentable." He rejoiced when "one miserable drunkard sign'd the [temperance] pledge," but William had to hold him in the county jail for twenty-four hours before he would sign.

When Eliza was away, the teenaged Stephen sometimes helped his father out with the secretarial duties relating to the mayor's position, working out of the office he kept in his front parlor. But Stephen was not interested in the work or in the problems his father handled.[23] He brightened up, however, when William brought him and Morrison to meet the great Charles Dickens who stopped in Pittsburgh at the end of March 1842 and stayed at the fancy Exchange Hotel at the corner of Penn Avenue and Sixth Street. Mayor Foster was probably present as part of the welcoming committee when Dickens visited the Arsenal in Allegheny during his visit and concluded that the city was "very beautifully situated on the Allegheny River, over which there are two bridges."[24]

That same month Stephen was introduced to Dickens, Eliza's eastern travels took her to Baltimore, where she stayed with relatives on her mother's side and "had a great time making out the Chronicles of the Clayland family . . . identify[ing] the descendants of Thomas Clayland and Susanah Seth" who had settled in Maryland from England.[25] After Baltimore, she accepted an invitation to visit her haughty cousin Mrs. Skinner at her plantation "Wood Lawn," one of "the elegant mansions along the extensive Eastern Shores of Maryland, the land of my ancestors."[26] The Skinner plantation was next door to Colonel Edward Lloyd's plantation, where the abolitionist Frederick Douglass spent several years of his youth, before escaping to freedom.[27] In his autobiography, Douglass described the Skinners and their neighbors:

The adjoining estates to Col. Lloyd's were owned and occupied by friends of his, who were as deeply interested as himself in maintaining the slave system in all its rigor. These were the Tilgmans, the Goldboroughs, the Lockermans, the Pacas, the Skinners, Gibsons, and others of lesser affluence and standing . . . . [P]ublic opinion in such a quarter . . . was not likely to be very efficient in protecting the slave from cruelty. To be a restraint upon abuses of this nature, opinion must emanate from humane and virtuous communities, and to no such opinion or influence was Col. Lloyd's plantation exposed.[28]

Henry Foster, whose office was in Washington, was close enough to ride out and visit his mother at "Wood Lawn," where he started a flirtation with the oldest Skinner daughter Salina, who had a few years on Henry.[29] In spite of the age difference, Eliza was eager to see Henry marry his wealthy distant cousin, but nothing came of it, as the lady did "not want to get married."[30]

By the end of May, Eliza was tired and longed "again to be settled at home" with her husband and younger sons. After months of traveling, she complained that her "long life" was devoted to "studying the comfort of others," but she assured her son William that when she got home she was "resolved . . . to make people walk the chalk and take some pains to make me happy."[31] But when Eliza arrived in Allegheny on May 27, 1842, she had no time to think about her own comfort. She set out immediately with Stephen for Youngstown to console her daughter Henrietta, whose husband Thomas Wick had succumbed a few days earlier to the same disease that had taken his sister Mary.[32] His death from tuberculosis did not come as a complete surprise, the disease "having lingered around and about him for more than a year."[33] Eliza spent several months comforting her daughter, and when she returned to Allegheny, she left Stephen in Youngstown with his twenty-three-year-old sister to distract her while she adjusted to her widowhood.

In her time of need, the grieving Henrietta, like the other Fosters, turned to Brother William, but her request was of a more personal nature. On July 2, 1842, in a long, self-pitying letter, she begged him to return to Youngstown, move in with her, and care for her and her young children. She said he was the only brother who was in the position to take on the responsibility, and she urged him to do so. "I should like to have some one of my brothers live with me and provide everything we needed to live on and there is none of them in a situation to do so but yourself. Oh how I wish you would give up canalling and settle in Pittsburgh with me in the way I have mentioned."[34] Her in-laws wanted her to live with them, but she described the Wicks as people of an inferior educational level. Eventually, in spite of his sympathetic feelings toward his sister, William turned her down and Henrietta, Stephen, and Henrietta's three children returned to Pittsburgh around Christmas to live with the Fosters.[35]

It was not that William was indifferent to his sister's plight. After four years of widowhood, he was finally starting to repair his own life. On September 22, 1842, the month after Henrietta pleaded with him to come and live with her, William married Elizabeth Smith Barnett, a beautiful widow with a three-year-old son, and the couple settled in a house William bought on the river in Towanda. The new Mrs. Foster came from a wealthy New York family and when she entertained, she did so lavishly in low-cut gowns that scandalized her small town neighbors. Her sister Lavinia was married to J. Edgar Thomson, a prominent executive with the Pennsylvania Railroad and later William's business associate. When Elizabeth and William visited the Fosters in Allegheny, which they did frequently, his new wife was a popular daughter-in-law, but the chatty, intimate letters between Eliza and her son disappeared after his marriage. Family lore insists, however, that the conversations continued, only the letters were lost.

In 1843 William Jr. made one final gift to ensure the comfort of his adoptive family. Not far from the home they currently occupied, he built for their use a new three-story brick house at 605 Union Avenue on land he had purchased several years earlier from the adjacent Methodist Protestant Church. The new house had a lovely view facing onto the East Common's parklike expanse of greenery near the river, and became for the Fosters their most permanent residence since the loss of the White Cottage. It was situated in the best part of town, near homes owned by the lawyer John McKnight and the wealthy banker Robert Simpson Cassatt, whose daughter Mary Cassatt became famous for painting portraits of mothers and children.[36] Brother William did not deed either of his Allegheny houses to the Fosters, but the family lived in the Union Avenue property on and off for the next twelve years. Sometimes Eliza and William paid rent to their son; at other times, they lived free of charge, but when money was especially tight, or when the family broke apart and did not need such spacious living quarters, they put the house up for rent and moved out.[37]

The Fosters adapted readily to their new home, with each member of the family finding something enchanting about it. "Pa has made a beautiful little garden and rises early every morning to dress and weed it," Eliza proudly informed her son William.[38] Stephen was delighted with the place too. He could stroll absentmindedly on the broad greenery surrounding the house while he fit lyrics to the tunes that were already forming in his head, and he could visit the pretty next-door neighbor girl Susan Pentland to try out his songs on her rosewood piano.[39] Even the Fosters' new dog enjoyed the location of the house on the Allegheny Commons, where it could romp and play, or chase and bark at the cows grazing in the summer. Eliza began friendships with many of her neighbors, and when the weather warmed, she gossiped with them behind the house while they waited for their bread to bake in the large outdoor communal ovens. Because the houses were close, the neighbors dropped in and out often, stopping by for musical evenings around the piano and chitchats by the fire.

It was in the fine new house on Union Avenue that Stephen Foster began composing in earnest. He heard music all his life, of course, but in Allegheny, with its ethnically diverse population and equally diverse music, the sounds all came together for him. The Fosters lived in a quadrant predominantly populated by Scots-Irish, Irish, and English families who played the music of their ancestors. Susan Pentland and Stephen's widowed sister Henrietta, who brought her piano with her when she stayed there with her children, played traditional parlor songs, many along the Irish model of Thomas Moore. Their father picked out racier tunes on his violin, and their neighbors scratched out Scots-Irish melodies on their fiddles in their backyards. Henry Kleber introduced Stephen to the German composers at his regular music lessons, but he could have heard their music performed at concerts in Deutschtown, Allegheny's German section. Allegheny also had more than 120 African American families, who sponsored three churches in the neighborhood where Stephen had the chance to hear African-influenced spirituals. But most importantly, the steamboat brought singers and musicians from far and wide to perform in Pittsburgh across the river, and as a teenager, Stephen had a chance to see and hear and learn from them.[40]

The British-born composer Henry Russell stopped in Pittsburgh on his American tour sometime in the middle 1840s when Morrison, and probably Stephen, saw him in concert and Morrison described him as "the best ballad singer" he ever heard.[41] Russell wrote and performed his own songs, many of which dwelled on catastrophes and anything that created high drama, but he was even more successful with his sentimental songs like "Woodman, Spare that Tree."[42] When Russell sang the song, one hysterical man with tears in his eyes jumped up from his seat and demanded to know if the tree had been saved. Russell's songs were highly emotional, but they were also operatic sounding, as he claimed to have studied with opera composers in Italy.

Family sources believe Stephen heard Henry Russell when he performed in Pittsburgh and that he "made a deep impression" on the young man and inspired him to "try great things himself."[43] For his first published compositions, Foster adapted existing poems to his own music, just the way Russell did. He used the same poets Russell used for his songs, and in one case, the same poem. For the words to "Open Thy Lattice, Love," Foster adopted the poem "Serenade" by George Pope Morris, the poet who had written the words on which Russell based his song "Woodman, Spare that Tree." Then, after Russell set the poem "The Good Time Coming" by Charles MacKay to music, Foster used the same poem for his 1846 song "There's a Good Time Coming."[44] There is little question that Russell influenced Foster. As musicologist Charles Hamm explained, Russell's style "suggests the sound of so many of Stephen Foster's songs, but it was Foster who knew Russell's songs, not vice versa."[45]

When Stephen came across the poem "Serenade" by George Pope Morris in *The New Mirror*, the poem had already been set to music by several different composers, all of whom called their compositions "Open Thy Lattice, Love." Foster probably already knew that Russell had used Morris's poetry for his "Woodman" song, which encouraged him to set "Serenade" to music, even though others had done so before. George Willig of Philadelphia published Stephen's setting of the poem in 1844, and like the other compositions, he titled it "Open Thy Lattice, Love," and then incorrectly credited it to "L. D. Foster." Stephen was just seventeen when he wrote and dedicated the song to "Miss Susan Pentland," whose piano was available to him when the Fosters did not have one of their own. Probably because of this song, a legend grew up about a romance between Susan and Stephen, but the latter's fascination was probably with her piano. Susan later married one of the boys from their Allegheny circle, and she and Stephen remained friends for life. But when the youthful composer dedicated the song to her, it was more likely evidence of that growing friendship.

Another type of music, antithetical to the sentimental genre, was fast capturing Stephen's attention and that of his young friends in the mid-1840s. Minstrel songs or "negro melodies," as they were sometimes called, belonged to Foster's generation. Young people sang them, danced to them, played them on the piano or violin, and could not get enough of them. The songs were known in Allegheny because minstrel performers visited Pittsburgh frequently during those years and Thomas Dartmouth Rice, the "Jim Crow" creator who performed in Pittsburgh more than a decade earlier, returned to the city in 1845. That was the year Rice's family claimed the famous minstrel met Stephen Foster, a credible claim since Stephen wrote his first minstrel song that same year.[46] In fact, Stephen was so enamored of minstrel music in 1845 that he turned down his sister Ann Eliza's request to write "some organ music" for her husband's church with the excuse, "I have no knowledge of that instrument." It is more likely that Stephen had no interest in religious music at the time and did not want to bother with it. He even offered to ask Mr. Mellor, the music store owner, "to lend me some music that he thinks will suit, which I will copy and send to you."[47]

In 1845, Stephen was busy with his brothers and their friends forming a club called the Knights of the Square Table, which met at the neighbors' houses to perform the new minstrel music that was all the rage. In explaining the phenomenon that was taking hold of his generation, Morrison Foster claimed, "At the time, negro melodies were very popular," a statement that is just as true today of music with African American roots. Morrison then described how Stephen first ventured into minstrel songwriting:

> In 1845, a club of young men, friends of his, met twice a week at our house to practice songs in harmony under his leadership. They were, J. Cust Blair, Andrew L. Robinson, J. Harvey Davis, Robert P. McDowell, and myself. At that time negro melodies were very popular. After we had sung over and over again all the songs then in favor, he [Stephen] proposed that he would try and make some for us

himself. His first effort was called "The Louisiana Belle." A week
after this, he produced the famous song of "Old Uncle Ned."[48]

The club thus served as a testing ground for Stephen's newest compositions. The boys invited the talented neighborhood girls to join them in
performing their favorite songs around the piano, and when they ran
out of favorites, Stephen composed new ones. "Louisiana Belle" and
"Old Uncle Ned" were some of the great songs that came out of this
practice. The experience was perfect for a novice composer. When the
club met, Stephen handed his friends a new song he had just written,
and either he or another club member played the song on the piano,
while one or two of the girls with the best voices stood up to sing. He
did not have to feel intimidated by the judgment of strangers. The
young ladies who performed his songs were well trained in the musical
arts and many were fine singers, but they were still amateurs. Even the
musically gifted ones expected to marry and confine their talent to their
own parlors. The men were not judgmental either. They considered the
gatherings no more than an evening's entertainment. The next day, they
would go about their trade or business. The only one of the charming
Knights with any serious aspirations about music was the young composer.

Stephen's first minstrel songs were written in a strong, black-style
dialect, which he probably learned from the songsters, those little books
containing the words without the music to the most popular songs. Or
he could have learned dialect from listening to African Americans in
conversation. The Fosters, when they could afford to, employed free
blacks as servants, and Stephen could have listened to them speak or to
the two black servants who worked for the neighbors, individuals who
impressed him enough to inspire two of his most famous songs, "Nelly
Bly" and "Old Black Joe." But neither Stephen nor anyone in his family
knew any of the free blacks of Allegheny on a personal or intimate level.
When and if the Fosters spoke about slavery, they spoke in hushed
voices and left no record. There were several antislavery organizations
in Allegheny, but the Fosters were not involved, even though their
house on Union Avenue was located next door to the Methodist Protestant Church where, it was reported, "Eliza Foster slipped in to join her
Methodist friends at prayer meeting" and the local abolitionist Charles
Avery stepped in on occasion to lecture.[49] Inside the sacred halls, "ex-

citing debates upon the subject of slavery" took place at special meetings where men were urged "to take a deliberate and firm stand" to
protect the "happiness of the human race."[50] The Fosters did not attend
these meetings, as they were not among the handful of men and women
in the neighborhood who were courageous and passionate enough to
speak out openly against slavery.

When Stephen was in his teens, race relations in Allegheny City
were often vicious, and the economic hardships of the late 1830s and
early 1840s only increased tensions and mob attacks. The attacks were
usually "led by unemployed whites who hoped to drive the blacks out of
the area," especially if they appeared to be making financial gains.
When the economy soured, American-born and immigrant white work-
men joined forces in Pittsburgh to shout "Down with the Niggers!" and
"Send them back to Africa where they belong!"[51] That relations between the races were degenerating in the 1830s was made evident by
the fact that when Pennsylvanians rewrote their state constitution in
1838, they took away the free black man's right to vote, a right enjoyed
for many years in Pittsburgh and in Allegheny.[52]

Just how callous white feelings were regarding blacks in Allegheny
was made indelible by the horrific experiments of one Thomas Semple,
a tanner by trade, who served as mayor of Allegheny City in 1841, just a
year before William Foster served his two terms as mayor. An African
American man who was said to have "ruthlessly killed a farmer,"
drowned when he fell through the ice of the Allegheny River while
trying to avoid capture. When his body was recovered, it was left in the
Town Hall awaiting the coroner's inspection. During the night, Semple
stole the body and, in an experiment to see if human skin could be
made into leather, brought "the corpse to his tanyard, peeled it and
tanned the skin," and later turned it into "belts, watch fobs, and razor
straps for his friends." Although a committee of irate citizens clamored
for Semple's trial on charges of inhumanity, the jury exonerated him on
the excuse that he had "merely been conducting a scientific experiment." Semple retired an honored citizen of Pittsburgh.[53]

Racism was just as virulent when the African American band leader
Frank Johnson came to perform in Allegheny City in 1843 with his ten
black musicians. The band arrived in Pittsburgh from Cincinnati on the
steamboat *Little Ben*. On Friday, May 12th, they gave a "Grand Soiree
Musicale" at Philo Hall, where they were well received by the audience.

The next Tuesday they were scheduled to perform at the Temperance Ark in Allegheny where Stephen's father, then mayor of the city, had recently held temperance rallies. Tickets for Johnson's show were twenty-five cents each and on the night of May 16, 1843, "friends of temperance and good Music" assembled inside the Ark to hear the music, while outside, white ruffians formed an intimidating mob that proceeded to attack the black musicians when they tried to leave the theater.[54] Frank Johnson must have been shocked. A few years earlier, his band had performed the same musical soirée in Philadelphia and London, without setting off a commotion.[55]

A newspaper account of the incident said the aggressors were composed of "native born subjects and sons of aristocrats," not of the "potatoe [sic] foreigners." The assertion is surprising considering that Pittsburgh in the early 1840s had a large population of Irish workers who competed with free blacks for jobs. In addition, Frank Johnson's band was performing for the temperance cause, making the Irish who relished their right to imbibe especially prone to protest. According to one contemporary article:

> During the evening, the mob on the outside of the Ark in which the Band were performing for the benefit of the temperance cause, were with some difficulty kept quiet and after the performance had closed, WM. B. Foster, Esq., the Mayor of Allegheny City, advised the members of the band to remain within the building, and he went out and appealed to the better sense of the mob in a short speech, after which he conducted a portion of the band through the crowd, the remainder intending to await the arrival of a carriage from the city.[56]

The African American musicians who managed to find seating in a carriage were carried across the river to safety in Pittsburgh, but those who got stuck in Allegheny were not so fortunate. The mob reconvened at the corner of Diamond and Federal Streets, where Mayor Foster made another speech and tried to escort the black band members through the increasingly volatile crowd. As the musicians frantically tried to reach the bridge that crossed the Allegheny River, they were assaulted "in the most brutal manner with brickbats and stones," leaving many injured and one man with a deep cut in his forehead. The next day, the newspapers reported that "the blood on the pavement near the bridge where the assault was committed stood in pools." Although the press claimed the "mob was mostly composed of boys and young men," no one could be sure who threw the stones.

Four men, all white, were brought before Mayor Foster on charges of riot and assault and held on $200 bail. Although at first it appeared that the citizens of Allegheny were determined to see color-blind justice carried out, when the rioters came to trial, the jury returned a verdict of "Not Guilty and the defendants pay the cost of the prosecution." The attack and the verdict showed that Allegheny City was not friendly to blacks, no matter how talented or professional they were. But the fact that Stephen's father put himself in danger and came to the defense of the black band when they were being attacked must have left a strong imprint on the mind and heart of the impressionable sixteen-year-old.

On a perfectly clear, dry spring day in April of 1845, the most devastating fire in Pittsburgh's history broke out and within hours destroyed one third of the city, including thousands of homes and businesses. Because the Fosters lived across the river in Allegheny, their home was not touched, but McCormick's Hope Cotton Factory kept some of its accounting books in a warehouse in Pittsburgh. Ever the dutiful employee, Morrison Foster became the hero of the day when he rushed in and saved the records before the building bulging with flammable cotton was engulfed in flame. Stephen Foster, then only eighteen, helped fight the flames that left charred skeletons of the city's buildings and the daunting smell of smoke to remind people of nature's devastating powers.[57] A few months later in August, a gas leak in the basement of the Methodist Protestant Church next to the Foster's house caused an explosion that destroyed the interior of the church and ended with the death of four people. Many of the injured and dying were carried into the Foster home, which was the house closest to the church, and Eliza assisted in caring for the unfortunates as best she could.[58]

Whether or not the burned-out landscape or the devastating explosion had an impact on the family's plans for the future, the Fosters knew they would be going their separate ways. At the beginning of 1846, the senior William, who was in Washington representing a Mr. Cochran "before the committee on claims,"[59] met with President James K. Polk, whom he described as "mighty polite entirely."[60] He was hard up for money when he accepted the offer of his old friend John H. Eaton, formerly Andrew Jackson's Secretary of War, to present his claim to Congress for the supplies he had sent to New Orleans more than thirty years earlier. The senior William had friends in high places, to be sure, but none of them could get the government to pay up, even after William paid a personal visit to the president.[61]

Stephen had his eye on Washington, too, although no employment offer surfaced. He dreamed of taking Henry's place at the Treasury after the latter expressed an interest in leaving, and confided to his sister Ann Eliza, "Henry has written home to say that he would like to change places with some person until he may have time to come to Pitts. and rest himself, and as it would be a very pleasant change I have thought of taking his place in Washington."[62] But Henry decided to keep the job, returning to Pittsburgh only long enough to marry a local girl named Mary Burgess in January 1847. He went back to Washington and stayed at the Treasury until the Whig Zachary Taylor took over the presidency and threw all the Democrats out of office in 1849. Morrison Foster no longer spent much time in the Union Avenue house either. He ventured as far south as New Orleans, "once or twice every year descending the river with large amounts of money to purchase cotton" for McCormick's factory, and found it more convenient to board when he was in town.[63] Dunning Foster was gone too, having moved to Cincinnati where he entered into a steamboat partnership that handled cargo conveyed along the Ohio River.

Since the size of the Foster family had shrunk considerably, and expenses and upkeep were high, Eliza and William decided to make the Allegheny house available for rent to another, presumably larger family. The exact date the Fosters moved out is not known, but sometime between February and November 1846, William, Eliza, and Stephen went to live "at different family boardinghouses and the St. Charles Hotel, at the corner of Wood and Third Streets."[64]

The St. Charles Hotel must have been modestly priced because the Fosters stayed there often. We can only wonder how Stephen spent his time cooped up with his family for months in a room in a house or a hotel in downtown Pittsburgh, and what effect the crowded environment had on his creative spirit.

As the year 1846 came to a close, changes were in the air for many of the Fosters. After Brother William accepted a position with the Pennsylvania Railroad and Dunning entered into a partnership in Cincinnati, Stephen appeared to be the only Foster with no plans or direction for the future. The dreamy-eyed, young man toyed with thoughts of attending West Point, the nation's military academy in upstate New York. The idea may have originated with Brother William because years earlier Eliza had asked his advice regarding Stephen's attending the school.[65] But it was Henry Foster who, by hobnobbing with the political elites in Washington, worked the hardest to get the appointment for his brother. Stephen made an application to the military academy at the end of 1845 or early in 1846, but receiving the appointment involved getting a sufficient number of very positive recommendations, a feat that was difficult for a young man with a poetic nature and a poor family. A prominent politician made the final selection from among many qualified young male applicants, or at least, male applicants with qualified and impressive family connections.[66]

About a dozen years after Stephen made his application, Ann Eliza's son Edward did get an appointment to West Point, but by that time he could offer the recommendation of his uncle James Buchanan, who was then president of the United States. Edward, who began the "cadet life" in 1859, considered soldiering the "grandest profession a man can have."[67] In contrast, it is almost comical to think of Stephen Foster applying to West Point. The fate of the "Class of 1846," as explained in the book of that title, was to meet in mortal combat as the legendary commanders of the armies of the North and the South. We have to smile when we juxtapose the name of Stephen Foster with those of Thomas "Stonewall" Jackson, Robert Anderson, and William Tecumseh Sherman, men who either attended West Point in the 1840s or graduated from the Academy in 1846, around the time Stephen made his application.[68]

Presumably Foster's temperament would not have fitted him for the daily activities of a cadet, which included rigorous academic classes, physical exercises, military drills twice a day, and marching. Of course, there was an escape that tempted most of the cadets, and would have appealed to Stephen. In 1824 an Irishman named Benny Havens opened a popular tavern about a mile south of the academy, which stayed in business for fifty years in spite of being the bane of the West Point superintendents. Thousands of cadets sneaked out at night to find "a home cooked meal, and more often than not, something a bit stronger to fortify their spirits." When Cadet Jefferson Davis was caught at the tavern, he was court-martialed, dismissed, and then reinstated.[69]

Stephen's application for West Point was passed over, and the spot given to a young man referred to in the Foster correspondence as G. McKn., an abbreviated spelling for McKnight. The recipient was obviously a relative of the wealthy lawyer neighbor of the Fosters in Allegheny, John McKnight, and even today the McKnight name marks a busy thoroughfare in Pittsburgh. But Henry Foster, writing from Washington on March 16, 1846, was not impressed and expressed surprise that the appointment went to "young McK." Dunning concurred, "I can scarcely believe it possible that there is so little justice in our Government." But then he consoled himself and Morrison with the idea that "it may result for the best, as I doubt very much whether Steve's health would have permitted him to remain at the Point, had he received the appointment."[70]

Putting aside considerations of health, if Stephen, by some fluke, had been admitted to the Academy, his name might have joined the names of other misplaced poets and artists who were accepted, only to be dismissed before graduating, including Cadet Edgar Allan Poe who spent more time imbibing at Benny Havens than studying and Cadet James McNeill Whistler, who exasperated his drawing instructors by adding a couple of mischievous boys to an engineer's rendering of a bridge.[71] We can imagine similar examples of frustrating student-professor confrontations if Foster had been accepted at West Point. What attracted him to the nation's foremost military academy is anyone's guess. He was probably drawn in by the glamour of the idea and equally inspired by a psychological drive to identify with a truly masculine vocation.

After the appointment fell through, the Fosters were desperate to find a place for their youngest son. In June 1846, Morrison got his own employer to give Stephen "a small position in Mr. McCormick's new Hope Warehouse, checking cotton bales as they were rolled up the wharf directly from the steamboats into the building."[72] Dunning thanked Morrison for the effort, adding: "I hope he may succeed, if we get Stephen comfortably situated it will be a great object gained."[73] Even before Stephen started working at the cotton mill, he spent time there, waiting around while Morrison was at work, because on September 15, 1845 he closed a letter to his sister Ann Eliza Buchanan, "I am writing amidst the bustle of the Hope ware-house you must forgive therefore my haste."[74]

Whenever Stephen stopped by McCormick's warehouse, however, he had the opportunity to see bales of cotton being unloaded on the docks in Pittsburgh. Some critics have marveled how Foster, who never spent any length of time in the South, could write so convincingly about cotton, but he did not have to go south to see cotton in the mid-nineteenth century. Stephen grew up in Allegheny when the city was home to most of Pittsburgh's cotton factories and his brother Morrison was in the cotton business for almost as long as Stephen could remember. Cotton was big business in Allegheny City, and trade with the South was a natural, everyday affair. It was little wonder that Stephen wrote convincingly about cotton in his minstrel songs. Even Andrew Carnegie, later the nation's steel king, worked in a cotton mill as a boy in Allegheny and knew the touch and feel of cotton.

The city that would later be known for steel production had a thriving cotton industry throughout the first half of the nineteenth century. When Stephen worked for McCormick, cotton was at its apex in Pittsburgh. Five large factories plus many smaller ones, mostly in Allegheny City, consumed 15,000 bales of cotton annually and produced yarns, sheeting, batting, and other cotton products amounting to $1.5 million.[75] By comparison, eleven window-glass factories at mid-century produced only $600,000 in manufactures, less than half the value of textiles; only iron greatly out-produced cotton in Pittsburgh, with forty-five iron establishments producing 6.5 million dollars' worth of iron products.[76] Although the cotton industry would suffer within a few years and eventually disappear from Pittsburgh, in the summer of 1846 cotton was still thriving, but for some reason or another Stephen left McCormick's after only a few months. The Fosters then decided that their youngest should move to Cincinnati to work for his brother doing much of the same type of work he did at the Pittsburgh factory—that is, overseeing the loading and unloading of cotton. Dunning Foster next took on the responsibility of Stephen, and in the process, opened up a whole new range of possibilities for the, up to that time, misdirected young man.

6

MUSICAL BOOKKEEPER

Sometime at the end of 1846 or the start of the new year, a shy twenty-year-old, uncertain about his future and about how best to direct his talents, boarded a packet boat that carried him to the city that claimed the title "Cultural Capital of the West." The exact date of Stephen's departure for Cincinnati is unknown, but it is possible that he waited until January to leave home, when his brother Henry returned from Washington to marry Mary Burgess of Lawrenceville and his sister Henrietta found a new mate in Jesse Thornton of Ohio. Both weddings took place in Pittsburgh and Stephen probably waited around to attend the nuptials before embarking on the 400-plus-mile trip to Cincinnati. Fortunately, river travel was quicker and far easier between the two cities than it had been when Stephen made the journey with his mother and Henrietta thirteen years earlier. Stephen's destination was Irwin & Foster, his brother Dunning's new business on Front Street at No. 4 Cassilly's Row, a low-rise, square, brick edifice named for Michael P. Cassilly's family, Eliza's old neighbors from Pittsburgh.[1] Cassilly's Row stood in full view of the city's largest steamboat landing on the majestic Ohio River, a propitious setting for Stephen to learn a trade and assume the responsibilities of middle-class manhood.

Although Dunning Foster had clerked on the Ohio River for several years prior to going into business, the man who supplied "the energy and stability" and the real experience in the partnership was his friend Archibald Irwin, whose father had started the business in the 1820s. As a successful commission merchant agency, Irwin & Foster competed with several firms along the river, all eager to fill the steamboats they represented with products the local manufacturers and suppliers wanted to bring downriver. Most of the boats handled by Dunning's firm traveled in a southerly direction, to Louisville, Nashville, Memphis, and New Orleans, although a few transferred their goods to ocean-going vessels that traveled north to Baltimore, Philadelphia, New York, and Boston.[2] Business was brisk and highly competitive, especially in the spring when the local merchants were pressured to get the recently butchered hogs to market. Although Cincinnati bragged of her cultural superiority, calling herself "Queen City" of the West, she was more widely known as "Porkopolis" for the hundreds of thousands of pigs that were slaughtered and processed there annually.

Stories abound about Stephen working on the riverfront in Cincinnati, where he saw cotton being loaded and unloaded off the boats, but less picturesque products were also loaded onto the boats to be transported on the Ohio. The cargo included various products of the unfortunate pig, including carcasses, bristles for brushes and upholstery, pigskins, bones to be turned into buttons, and lard for soap and candle making. Cincinnati, with a population of 115,000, was one of the fastest-growing cities in the Midwest precisely because of her steamboat and pork industries, and the city supplied employment to anyone willing to work in the dirty business of pork packing. Unloading bales of cotton from the South and reloading them for shipment to factories in the North was only one of the jobs the free blacks handled on the Cincinnati wharves. Dunning, of course, had more cotton business than the other commission merchants, because as soon as Irwin & Foster opened, Morrison sent his brother many contracts to haul cotton from the South to McCormick's mills in Pittsburgh and Allegheny.[3]

At first, Stephen lived with his brother Dunning at the Broadway Hotel along the Ohio River, but afterward he moved into a nearby boardinghouse run by a Jane Griffin on "tree-shaded Fourth Street in a good neighborhood."[4] He boarded just around the corner from the Cassillys who were still living on the west side of Broadway between Third and Fourth Streets where he visited often.[5] A contemporary portrait of Broadway around Fourth revealed three- and four-story, brick row houses separated by a few trees planted sporadically; a wide, cobblestoned thoroughfare filled with handsome multi-horse-drawn carriages, and gentlemen in top hats strolling the sidewalks carrying walking canes, their well-dressed ladies at their sides. Altogether, it was a delightful display of mid-century urbanity.[6] Cincinnati was a beautiful city in the late 1840s, even more so than when Charlotte Foster visited the Queen City on her way to Kentucky in 1828 and marveled that the buildings looked as if they had been "built just yesterday," because they were not covered with the black soot that was the hallmark of Pittsburgh for much of the nineteenth century. In 1843, Charles Dickens also described Cincinnati as "a beautiful city . . . with its clean houses of red and white, its well paved roads, and footways of bright tile."[7]

Stephen's working hours in Cincinnati were divided between a desk job inside Cassilly's Row and outside work on the wharves. He was responsible for seeing that the clients' merchandise was loaded on and off the boats with proper bills of lading and that the products coming from the South were recorded in a ledger book before they were received by their rightful owners. Irwin & Foster also booked passengers on the riverboats since they specialized in daily packet service from Cincinnati to Pittsburgh and Louisville. Men, women, and children had to be boarded properly and the passenger lists carefully checked, before the boats took off. In the middle of the nineteenth century, the riverboats still offered the most comfortable, dependable, time-efficient, and elegant means of transportation, in spite of the unappealing cargo that was stowed belowdecks.[8]

Cincinnati was a thriving city and the sounds and sights on the wharves would have mesmerized Stephen. "Teamsters shouted, wagons clattered on the stones, bells and whistles sounded above the work songs of the roustabouts," was one man's description of the Ohio waterfront.[9] Stephen would have seen all sorts of men and women, black and white and some in between. Haughty Southern planters, wizened river captains, black roustabouts, and buckskin-clad settlers with their eyes to the West walked briskly down the wharf, either in the direction of the riverboats or toward the nearby Cincinnati Hotel. Middle-aged matrons chaperoning young ladies in bonnets and hoop skirts followed at a slower pace behind them.[10]

Sometime in the fall of 1848, the Cincinnati photographers Fontayne and Porter set up their cameras and captured the scene that greeted Stephen every day from his place of employment on Front Street. Eight beautiful daguerreotypes, the newest way to record without pen or paintbrush, preserved images of the Second Presbyterian

Church with its spiraling clock-tower, the handsome Kilgour House where sister Charlotte stayed years before, the Bazaar made famous by the writer Frances Trollope, and the 142-foot-high observatory that "commands a fine view of the city and more particularly of the Ohio River and the Kentucky scenery beyond."[11] Stephen's workplace, the long row of buildings that made up Cassilly's Row, is also visible with some sixty steamboats afloat on the Ohio.[12]

In 1846, the year Stephen moved to the Queen City, war broke out between Mexico and the United States, and the following year Dunning Foster decided to join General Winfield Scott's forces in Mexico and leave his younger brother on his own to handle the affairs of business. On June 9, 1847, Dunning made out his will, should he die in Mexico. He left everything he possessed "to be safely invested for the benefit of our dear Mother as long as she lives, after her death to be applied to the benefit of our Father." To Stephen he willed his watch, but "the Emerald Gold ring I have left with Stephen give to Ma."[13] Next, Dunning traveled to Pittsburgh to bid farewell to his mother and father before departing for the land that was "a vague, faraway affair" to Eliza Foster. Richard Cowan and Bill Blakely, boyhood friends of the Fosters, joined Pittsburgh's Jackson Blues and set off together, reaching Mexico before Dunning did.[14] Fortunately, Morrison missed the war altogether. He had joined the Third Regiment and was accorded the rank of sergeant, but his company was somehow not called to Mexico.[15]

In the meantime, Stephen remained at Irwin & Foster's, overseeing the cargo being loaded on and off the boats and keeping records of the daily transactions, but he had plenty of time for interests more congenial to his nature. Left alone in Cincinnati from the middle of 1847 until the middle of the next year, Stephen had plenty of time to do as he pleased. Although Morrison always contended that Stephen "was a beautiful accountant and his books kept at that time are models of neatness and accuracy," Dunning's partner Archibald Irwin left no performance review of the young composer and we get the feeling that once Dunning was away fighting in Mexico, Stephen devoted more time to music than to bookkeeping.[16] He was in fact very busy writing and publishing songs during these Cincinnati years and being introduced to music publishers and minstrel performers.

Soon after moving to Cincinnati, or perhaps before, Foster renewed his acquaintance with William Cumming Peters, the Pittsburgh music store owner who had only the year before opened a store in Cincinnati. Born in England, he spent his teen years in Canada and settled in Pittsburgh about the time Stephen Foster was born. Peters's connection to the Fosters went back to the days when he had been one of Charlotte Foster's music teachers when she was a child. After teaching for a number of years, Peters opened his own music store in Pittsburgh, but left it to establish a second music store in Louisville around 1829. In 1845, he turned the Louisville store over to the management of his son Henry and, in partnership with two other sons, opened a third store in Cincinnati.[17] How and when Stephen first made contact with Peters in Cincinnati is not known. He could have reached out to him before he moved to Cincinnati, early in 1846, when he was living with his mother in a boardinghouse in downtown Pittsburgh, because on October 9, 1846, Peters and Field issued Foster's "There's a Good Time Coming," the firm's first title by Stephen Foster.

From 1846 until 1849, W. C. Peters, or a variation of that name, published songs for Stephen Foster.[18] A few months after the aspiring composer arrived in Cincinnati, Peters made an arrangement with George Willig of Philadelphia to reprint "Open Thy Lattice, Love," before he came out with "Oh! Susanna," "Louisiana Belle," and "Old Uncle Ned." Stephen had written "Old Uncle Ned" and "Louisiana Belle" in Allegheny for the amusement of his friends, but the exact lineage of every song published in Cincinnati may never be known. Stephen traveled home by packet boat from time to time, and he dedicated his parlor songs to friends in both Pittsburgh and Cincinnati. Either way, his songs were published in Cincinnati.[19]

Many of Foster's parlor songs from the 1840s had, like "Open Thy Lattice, Love," a dedication published on their title page. "There's a Good Time Coming!" copyrighted 1846 was dedicated to Mary D. Keller, a Pittsburgh girl, and the following year, Stephen composed "Where Is Thy Spirit, Mary?" which he dedicated to the same girl, by then deceased. Later in 1847 he wrote and dedicated the more light-hearted song "What Must a Fairy's Dream Be?" to another Mary, a relative of Archibald Irwin named Mary H. Irwin. When Archibald saw the song, if he did, we have to wonder if he winked or winced at what could be interpreted as an employee's dereliction of duty. In 1848, Stephen dedicated "Stay Summer's Breath" to Sophie Marshall who lived with her grandparents, the Cassillys, around the corner from Stephen in Cincinnati. Sophie's voice was beautiful and Stephen enjoyed composing at her piano and having Sophie sing the song he just completed, just as he had done at Susan Pentland's house.[20] He also spent time at the home of John B. Russell, whose lovely "dark-eyed, dark-haired daughter" Eliza played the piano "whenever Stephen stopped by for the evening."[21]

Stephen was obviously combining his composing with flirtations and social engagements, although he did not confine his dedications to the fairer sex. The romantically titled "Summer Longings," published in 1849, was dedicated to Samuel P. Thompson, "a young fellow who lived at Mrs. Griffin's boarding house" where Stephen was staying at the time.[22] In the middle of the nineteenth century such a suggestive demonstration of affection from one man to another usually signified the romanticism of the age, rather than the sexual preference of the author. Stephen also attended a classical vocal concert in Cincinnati in the spring of 1849 by the opera singer Eliza Ostinelli Biscaccianti, an acquaintance of Morrison Foster. Although the soprano was a granddaughter of the famous American composer James Hewitt and had been born in Boston, she studied in Italy and performed under the Italian sounding name Madame Biscaccianti. In a letter to Morrison, Stephen remarked that he had paid her a visit and was "as much delighted by her conversation and agreeable manner as I was subsequently by her singing at her concerts."[23]

More important than the parlor songs or the classical arias at this stage in Stephen's professional development were the minstrel songs he wrote that jumpstarted his career as a professional songwriter. In Cincinnati, Foster met live minstrels who performed regularly at the popular theaters and halls in the city, drawing in local, as well as out-of-town, folks for a full evening of entertainment. The minstrels were always looking for new material, and they recognized the unusual quality in Foster's songs, which made them an immediate success on the stage. Foster attended their shows and made his first professional contact with minstrels in the Ohio city, where a dozen blackface troupes performed in the late 1840s, including the Sable Harmonists, the Empire Minstrels, and the less-known, but ambitious, group called Campbell's Minstrels, who became known for singing Foster's "Oh! Lemuel."[24]

Stephen quickly learned how valuable these minstrel performers were in marketing his songs, and he made every effort to introduce himself and his music, but it took some time before the naive young man learned to be self-protective. Blackface entertainers would teach him much, not only about what songs to write, but also about how crafty human nature could be, especially behind the burnt cork mask. The first known public performance of a Foster composition by a minstrel performer took place on September 6, 1847, at the Eagle Ice Cream Saloon in Pittsburgh, while Foster was living in Cincinnati. The previous year, the owner of the establishment, a man named Andrews, had taken over the large hall on the second floor above the Saloon to "keep it for concertizing," and hired Nelson Kneass, formerly a singer and pianist for the Sable Harmonists, to handle the concerts. The latter quickly brought onboard Joseph Murphy, another Sable Harmonist minstrel, an accordion player named Huntley, and four new singers (George Holman and three female vocalists) who later went on the road as "The Original Kneass Opera Troupe." As the name suggests, Andrews's Saloon sold ice cream, not alcohol, but offered, in addition to musical entertainment, live models known as "tableaux vivant," who stood motionless in classical and some said sexually suggestive poses wearing just a body suit with revealing tights.[25]

Andrews attracted customers by running newspaper ads that offered "Free Concerts Every Evening" for the cost of the "Ice Cream Ticket at 12 ½ cents each." In the summer, Kneass added "Afternoon Soirees" that brought in even more customers. What seemed to attract the largest crowds was a contest for the best original minstrel song, where the customers could vote by their applause. On August 31, 1847, Andrews advertised a competition in the *Daily Commercial Journal* for a silver cup to be awarded "to the author of such original words of an Ethiopian Melody or Extravaganze [*sic*] to be set to music by the present Troupe, as shall be decided the best by the spontaneous voice of the audience at the TRIAL CONCERT, Monday evening, September 6." When Morrison Foster learned about the silver cup competition in Pittsburgh, he wrote to Stephen in Cincinnati and asked him to send a composition that he would submit in person. Stephen sent his brother "Way Down South, Whar' de Corn Grows," which Morrison entered in the contest. On the evening of September 6, 1847, Nelson Kneass sang it at the Ice Cream Saloon while he accompanied himself on the piano. According to Morrison, the audience chose Stephen's song as the winning number by its superior "applause," but the prize cup went to Mr. Holman, "the tenor singer," for his song "Wake Up Jake, or the Old Iron City."[26]

Nelson Kneass was in the practice of noting which competition song earned the loudest applause and then rushing out to copyright it in his own name. The day after Stephen's "Way Down South" was performed at the Ice Cream Saloon, Kneass hurried down to the courthouse to take credit for the song, when he ran into Morrison Foster, who was already standing before the judge taking out the copyright in Stephen's name. There was no problem because Judge Irwin was an old friend of the Fosters, and Morrison, who knew him personally, promptly informed the judge of the attempted fraud. It should be noticed that Kneass's advertisement offered the prize for the best "original words of an Ethiopian Melody . . . to be set to music by the present Troupe," and Kneass had arranged Stephen's song on the night he sang it at the Ice Cream Saloon.[27] Perhaps he thought he was justified in copyrighting his own arrangements, even if it were someone else's melody. At any rate, Kneass was very underhanded, and this occasion was not the first time he claimed ownership of a song he did not write. The famous, if macabre, "Ben Bolt" was copyrighted in 1848 by W. C. Peters of Louisville and attributed to Kneass, but the authorship is questionable.

Kneass and his company continued to perform Foster's songs at the Eagle Ice Cream Saloon even after the debacle with "Way Down South." On September 11, 1847, at the Grand Gala Concert given on their "Last Night," the program included "The Old Iron City," followed by "Away down Souf" as they spelled it, and "SUSANNA—a new song never before given to the public." Raymond Walters, in his study of Stephen's years in Cincinnati, speculated how one of Foster's most famous songs ended up debuting at the Eagle Saloon:

> Who it was that escorted Susanna from Cincinnati to Pittsburgh for her casual debut in an ice-cream saloon we can only guess. It may have been M. J. Tichenor, whose name blossomed forth in the caption title of the song when W. C. Peters published it a year later under the heading "Songs of the Sable Harmonists." Tichenor was with the Sable harmonists at the Melodeon in Cincinnati at two separate engagements in the preceding spring. When the Harmonists left for Pittsburgh in the middle of April, Tichenor may have taken a copy of the song with him, in accordance with Stephen's letter to Mr. Millet.[28]

But Stephen may also have given manuscript copies of "Oh! Susanna" to Joseph Murphy when he was performing in Cincinnati with the Sable Harmonists, at which time the composer handed him copies of "Lou'siana Belle." When Kneass hired Murphy to perform at the Eagle Saloon, the minstrel could have brought "Oh! Susanna" with him. What is apparent is that Stephen's dubious habit of giving out manuscript copies of his songs to the minstrels before they were protected by copyrights was not confined to Cincinnati. Pittsburgh and Cincinnati were culturally and geographically connected in those days by the steamboats and the river, and the minstrels traveled back and forth regularly between the cities carrying their songs, either in their heads or in manuscript or printed copies. Although William Cumming Peters was already publishing Stephen's songs in the fall of 1847, he did not go out of his way to protect the ingénue composer from the minstrel sharks. He may have even encouraged it because that way he would know a successful song before he put his money into publishing it.

Stephen often walked backstage at the Melodeon and National theaters in Cincinnati and handed out handwritten songs for the minstrels to sing that night on the stage, with "no restrictions nor permissions in regard to publishing them."[29] To William Roark, the then-current star of the Sable Harmonists, Foster gave the manuscript copy of "Uncle Ned," which became a staple with him, and he handed over "Lou'siana Bell" to Joseph Murphy, also of the Sable Harmonists, to sing in the spring of 1847. None of these transactions involved royalties for future performances, and most may not have even involved an exchange of money.[30]

Once Foster's songs were performed on the minstrel stage and proved that they were popular with the audiences, the music publishers envisioned tantalizing profits and rushed to put them into print. Foster's minstrel songs appeared in special editions promoting the performers, with or without Foster's permission. William E. Millet of New York, who was publishing a collection of songs frequently performed by the Sable Harmonists, is one of the few who asked Stephen for permission to include "Uncle Ned," "Oh! Susanna," and "Lou'siana Bell" in his anthology.[31] Most publishers paid Stephen nothing for using his songs in their special collections, nor did the minstrels pay anything when they sang his songs over and over again on the stage and filled their pockets after every show. Foster did not stop handing out unprotected compositions until several years later, when he signed an exclusive royalty based contract with a New York publishing firm that demanded that he stop.

By 1848, W. C. Peters & Company was on its way to becoming one of the largest and most powerful music publishing houses in antebellum America and, some sources believed, Peters had Foster's "Oh! Susanna" to thank.[32] Peters made a fortune on the song, to be sure, but with publishing houses in three cities, he was already very successful before "Oh! Susanna" came off his press. His music business on Fourth and Walnut Street was housed in a lavish stone building constructed "on a most extensive scale" next to "the most prominent and elegant buildings in Cincinnati." Yet history has condemned him for lining his own pockets while he gave Foster a pittance for America's most well-recognized "folk-song." Obviously, Peters could never see Foster as more than the little boy who picked up the flageolet at his store in Pittsburgh and began playing it effortlessly—a man with a talent for putting out a tune, but certainly not an ounce of business sense.[33]

Perhaps Peters treated Foster neither better nor worse than other publishers treated the trusting young man. When he volunteered "two fifty-dollar bills" as complete payment for "Oh! Susanna," the composer was happy to receive it. But there was duplicity involved, because the twenty-two-year-old appeared not to know just how successful his song had become. Stephen wrote a friend in Pittsburgh regarding its sale: "Imagine my delight in receiving one hundred dollars in cash! Though the song was not successful, yet the two fifty-dollar bills I received for it had the effect of starting me on my present vocation of song-writer."[34] The rest of the story is vague. Some historians contend that Peters made $10,000 on "Oh! Susanna," which was a huge sum at the time—enough money to enable him to establish a music publishing "empire."[35] Others argued that Peters already had a thriving conglomerate with stores in different states and that his relationship with Foster was just business as usual. At least a dozen other firms published "Oh! Susanna" without even crediting Foster as the composer, and the minstrels performed his songs over and over again, offering him a onetime payment, if that, and like the publishers, not always crediting him with authorship.

As to whether or not Peters took unfair advantage of Stephen Foster, biographer Richard D. Wetzel did not seem to think so. "There can be no doubt that Peters profited handsomely from Foster's titles in his inventory, but if Foster's payment in dollars was comparatively small, he benefited from Peters's characteristic and uncommon attention to editorial details." Wetzel seemed to think that the relationship was mutually beneficial: "It was, in Foster's own words, Peters's gift of $100 for 'Susanna' that set him on his career as a songwriter."[36] Peters also gave Foster his first taste of celebrity. He published and promoted the young man's songs, putting his name on the title page of his more refined songs, such as "Stay Summer Breath" and leaving it off the minstrel songs since Stephen initially considered the minstrel genre low class and crude, and asked Peters not to print his name on those songs. Peters, however, marketed all the songs intensely, with or without the Foster name, and his advertising was responsible for having the composer's name appear in print 122 times.[37]

> Among the other "Songs of the Sable Harmonists," consisting of "Susanna," "Uncle Ned," and "Lou'siana Belle," the latter were given without credit to the composer as Stephen then preferred. But following the title of his song composed in the musically and socially acceptable style appeared "S. C. Foster."[38]

Peters made sure there were "favorable displays of his compositions in the music stores so generally patronized by professional and amateur musicians of the city." As Raymond Walters who chronicled Foster's Cincinnati years explained, "Far from being an obscure bookkeeper who made no ripple on the Cincinnati musical waters, Stephen received quite as much local recognition as a modest young fellow in his early twenties could hope for."[39]

Finally, it was probably Peters who introduced Foster to Firth, Pond, and Company, the music publishers with whom he would maintain a profitable, long-term relationship and who taught him not to give out his manuscripts so freely. When Foster's introduction to the New York firm took place is not known, although "A Good Time Coming," the first Foster song put out by W. C. Peters, was published "in conjunction with Firth, Hall, and Pond" under the imprint Peters and Field of Cincinnati. The partnership of Firth, Pond, and Company grew out of Firth, Hall, and Pond of New York. If, as has been suggested, Peters made the arrangement "to release the writer to a New York firm," that could have been Peters's way of easing his conscience and getting rid of the young composer at the same time.[40]

The timing was right for Firth, Pond, and Company to invest in new talent. The firm was new in 1847, having organized after William Hall broke away from Firth, Hall, and Pond to start an independent company with his own son, leaving John Firth and Sylvanus Pond to establish Firth, Pond, and Company with their sons.[41] John and Sylvanus were already advanced in years, so they left the new partnership in the hands of the next generation, Thaddeus Firth and William Pond, who were young, energetic, and keenly interested in the newest musical craze, minstrelsy.[42] When they saw how successful Peters was with "Oh! Susanna," they knew they would benefit from signing with Stephen, but like Peters, they could have been more generous. They published "Nelly Was a Lady" and "My Brudder Gum" in 1848, and paid the young composer with fifty printed copies of each song.[43] Presumably Foster could sell the printed music sheets to minstrel performers, which was preferable to handing out manuscript copies for free. At least the printed copies did have a copyright printed on them.[44]

Firth, Pond, and Company may have been giving Foster a trial run. The partners were happy with his work because the next year they offered him a contract that paid a royalty of two cents on all future songs. In a letter dated September 12, 1849, written in response to a proposal made either by Stephen or his brother Morrison, Firth and Pond wrote, "We will accept the proposition therein made, viz. to allow you two cents upon every copy of your future publications issued by our house, after the expenses of publication are paid." The publishers encouraged Foster to have the minstrels perform the songs to "introduce them to the public in that way," but they warned Foster: "In order to secure the copyright exclusively for our house, it is safe to hand such persons printed copies only, for if manuscript copies are issued particularly by the author, the market will be flooded with spurious issues in a short time."[45]

Foster was already in a royalty paying contract with F. D. Benteen of Baltimore since the end of 1848, but the contract apparently did not have an exclusivity clause that would have prevented him from contracting "future songs" with Firth, Pond, and Company. F. D. Benteen published piano variations on "Oh! Susanna" as well as a "Susanna Polka" and a "Susanna Quickstep," and remained Foster's primary publisher throughout 1850. Indeed, the majority of Foster songs that came out in 1850 were published by F. D. Benteen, not by Firth, Pond, and Company. Little seems to be known about the Baltimore publisher other than that the company was short-lived. It started out as a successor of George Willig of Philadelphia and Baltimore, but by the middle 1850s was taken over by Miller & Beacham. The publishers were all connected somehow. Not only did they share plates, men who had worked for one company broke away and started their own publishing companies and kept in contact with the composers with whom they had worked. Foster's introduction to Benteen probably came through George Willig, the man who published "Open Thy Lattice, Love" in 1844.[46] F. D. Benteen of Baltimore shared plates with W. T. Mayo of New Orleans, a name that appears in conjunction with Benteen on the cover of some of Foster's songs. In 1850, Benteen published ten songs for Foster, when Firth, Pond, and Company published only six. The next year, Firth and Pond took over and published the majority of Foster's songs, as Benteen began to fade out of the picture.[47]

Before Foster became involved with Firth, Pond, and Company, editions of his songs came off the music presses without the composer's name on the title page. As explained earlier, when William C. Peters first began to publish songs by Foster, the latter may have requested that his name be left off the minstrel songs. But why it remained so with other publishers is not so clear. In March 1848, for example, Mason, Colburn & Co. issued "Uncle Ned Just issued this day, the favorite and popular Negro Melody" without mentioning Foster. The omission of Foster's name may have been at the composer's own request, as it was with Peters, but it is more likely that the publishers got hold of Foster's manuscripts from the minstrels, and then proceeded to publish them without permission from, or payment to, the composer. Some of the blame must fall on the shoulders of Stephen himself. A revealing letter written to the New York publisher William E. Millet in response to his request for permission to publish some of Foster's songs explains in part the origination of the dilemma. To Millet, Foster wrote on May 25, 1849,

> I gave manuscript copies of each of the songs "Lou'siana Belle" "Uncle Ned" & "Oh, Susanna" to several persons before I gave them to Mr. Peters for publication, but in neither instance with any permission nor *restriction* in regard to publishing them, unless contained in

a letter to Mr. Roark accompanying the m.s. of "Uncle Ned"—although of this I am doubtful. Mr. Peters has my receipt for each of the songs. The only information I can give you in regard to dates, as my memory does not serve me, must be in copying the years named on the title pages of the Cincinnati publications . . . . If I see Mr. Roark (who lives in our city) I will give you further information in regard to the letter which I wrote him. [48]

The Cincinnati bookkeeper obviously could not keep his own song records straight. He was not sure when he wrote any particular song, or what minstrel's name would be printed on the cover. But once Firth and Pond became his principal publisher, they made sure they put the Foster name on their sheet music covers, even if they featured the name or picture of the minstrel alongside of it. [49] Of course, some publishers believed they would make more money giving credit to the performer and forgetting about the composer, especially if the latter's name were less known. Consequently, minstrel songs were often published with showy lithographs of the minstrel performer or at least the minstrel's name in large print on the title page. But Stephen Foster was earning a name for himself, and since copyright protection had been extended to cover musical compositions in 1831, most music publishers wanted to include the composer's name on the title page. By 1848, publishers were "becoming increasingly sensitive to each other's property" and Firth, Pond, and Company rightfully regarded the Foster name as their property. It was a valuable commodity to which they claimed ownership and they warned the naive young man to beware of minstrel performers and music publishers who offered neither payments nor promises of royalties. [50]

Even after Foster knew enough to copyright his songs, he continued to have problems when unscrupulous minstrel performers tried to establish copyrights in their own names, pretending that they, the performers, had written the songs themselves. In addition to the subterfuge involving Nelson Kneass and "Way Down South," Foster became embroiled in a difficulty claiming ownership of "Nelly Was a Lady." [51] Before he signed the contract with Firth and Pond, he had given the minstrel Charles White a copy of "Nelly" in manuscript form, for performance purposes only, but White had the audacity to bring the song directly to Foster's own publishers and claim authorship of it. Firth, Pond, and Company, unaware of the deception, copyrighted it in

White's name in February 1849, with the title "Toll the Bell for Lovely Nell, or My Dark Virginia Bride," one of the lines of the chorus. When the song's true author became known to his New York publishers, they entered a new copyright on July 18, 1849, under the original title "Nelly Was a Lady" and the words "Written and Composed by S. C. Foster" were printed on the title page.[52]

When Stephen first moved to Cincinnati and was suddenly propelled into the arena of professional blackface entertainers, it was only natural that he would want to write for them. By the middle 1840s, minstrel shows were the most popular entertainment around, and Stephen loved seeing and hearing his songs performed by real minstrels on a real stage in Cincinnati. He delighted in watching the faces in the audience as they laughed, beat their feet in time to the music, and sang along with his words. That the minstrel shows portrayed blacks in a denigrating or negative light did not enter his mind. Later in his life, Foster succeeded in refining the minstrel genre and in the process made the songs less demeaning to African Americans. But at this early stage in his career, he just wanted to find a place where he could nurture his own talents and be paid to do so. Minstrelsy attracted tens of thousands of customers, and was growing more popular every day.

The unusual entertainment had debuted a decade earlier in the cities on the Ohio River as a one-man show that catered to the tastes of the urban masses and was on a level with circuses and freak museums. Working men loved these rough and raucous minstrel shows, for they were, like themselves, products of the Industrial Revolution. In the darkened theater, the all-male audience worked out their anxieties and felt better about their status when they laughed at the antics performed on the stage by strangely costumed white men in grease paint. Here were men even more repressed by the economic system than they were. Few women were found in the audience of these early shows, which were as misogynistic as they were racist. Minstrel skits lampooned high society, social elites, the bosses of the factories, female rights, and all the other "isms." If a female protagonist were called for in the skit, a man in drag played the part.[53]

In seeking an explanation for the strange masked entertainment, musicologists and social historians often point to class conflict as one of the crucial issues. William Mahar envisioned the minstrel stage as a place of social inversion, where class animosity finds release in make-believe, lower-class victories over the ruling elites. Alexander Saxton argued that blackface could be viewed as a safety valve for an explosive society, because the minstrel show encouraged the audience to work out their social frustrations by vicariously attacking blacks on the stage, instead of attacking their social betters in the streets. Dale Cockrell argued that a song like "Jim Crow" "promised subversion" of the exist-ing social order, in fantasy at least, for a few hours when the lights went down around the stage.[54]

Eric Lott, in his appropriately named *Love and Theft*, supported an intriguing explanation for minstrelsy's popularity, one that carries over to our present-day fascination with musical forms with black antece-dents. Lott argued that whatever else minstrelsy was doing on a social level, white Americans wholeheartedly enjoyed the entertainment. They would not pay to sit through minstrel shows night after night if racial denigration and the resolution of class antagonism were the only reasons for the productions. Lott argued that white Americans were attracted to and ultimately captivated by certain aspects of black culture and made it part of their own popular culture. Thus, in spite of the denigration of African Americans that the art form entailed, Lott argued that whites in the audience believed they were seeing and hear-ing something of authentic black music and dance on the minstrel stage, they liked what they saw and heard, and subsequently "incorporated black music styles into their own white cultures."[55] In a similar vein, W. T. Lhamon credited minstrel performer Thomas Dartmouth Rice and the "Jim Crow" song for "white fascination with blackness in the Atlan-tic world," a phenomenon that continues to this day with jazz, rhythm and blues, rock 'n' roll, rap, and hip hop.[56]

Of course, historians of blackface often disagree about the entertain-ment's function and its ultimate effect on society. Mel Watkins believed that the comic and insulting characterization of African Americans on the minstrel stage did long term damage to the image of blacks in America, to black and white relations, and to blacks themselves. He argued that "minstrelsy was advertised as a peephole view of what black people were really like. To that extent," he said, "it affected all of soci-ety because those people who didn't know blacks . . . assumed that those characterizations, those depictions, those foolish characters on stage, were real black people."[57]

The question remains, however, why African Americans were the chosen group for denigration. Why blackface and wooly wigs? Why not denigrate some other group? And why did minstrelsy burst on the scene when it did? Exactly why blacks were selected to play the underdog on the minstrel stage had much to do with the fear that infected the environment in the 1830s. Minstrelsy started and peaked during the years when slavery and blacks became an issue of intense concern to white Americans. In 1831, around the same time that Thomas Dartmouth Rice made his stage debut as Jim Crow, William Lloyd Garrison preached immediate abolition and put fear into the worker's heart that free blacks would take away jobs and socialize and possibly intermarry with their children. That same year, the slave Nat Turner led a brutal rebellion in Virginia, in which at least sixty white men, women, and children were murdered, many while still asleep in their beds. Northern workers who feared job loss and race mixing joined Southerners who feared slave uprisings and mayhem to put down the abolitionists who they believed would cause havoc, if not suppressed.[58]

Minstrelsy, which was very complex, called ethnicity into the equation, in addition to race, gender, and class. The group of people in the North with the most to fear from slave emancipation was the hundreds of thousands of Irish immigrants who poured onto America's shores in the 1840s. When they moved into American cities, they made up the core of the minstrel audience, yet they were in a constant competition with free blacks for menial jobs and felt the most threatened by abolition. John Finch, an Englishman traveling in America in 1843, noticed that "particularly the poorer class of Irish immigrants in America are greater enemies to the Negro population and greater advocates for the continuance of Negro slavery than any portion of the population in the free states."[59] Interestingly, 1843 was the very year the Virginia Minstrels debuted their three-act, large-cast, minstrel show and introduced the decade when minstrelsy became the most popular entertainment in the nation.

The fear that the Irish, or any other group, experienced had all sorts of ramifications. One response was to make African Americans into scapegoats for all the real and imagined fears of whites and to turn them into objects of ridicule on the minstrel stage. In the early minstrel shows, the stage blacks were made to appear so ridiculous they could not threaten anyone in the white audience. The rural Jim Crow character was extremely ignorant and wore patched clothing and rags. The urban Zip Coon character, on the other hand, wore fancy clothes above his station but he mispronounced and misused words. Even when the Jim Crow character took on a charismatic persona, he was given few traits that whites admired as manly virtues. Even when he outsmarted his social betters through shrewdness and cunning, he was never truly admirable. He was created for white, working-class men to laugh at, so that they could relieve stress and feel better about their situation while they looked down their noses at the stage blacks. African Americans on the minstrel stage were transformed into non-threatening caricatures.

Whatever factors contributed to the success of minstrelsy, the early shows could not have succeeded without the racism that underpinned nineteenth-century American society. Virtually everyone was a "racist," although few men or women in the nineteenth century would have used the word or thought of it as a criticism. Racism, or the belief that racial characteristics and differences denoted superiority and inferiority, was prevalent in antebellum America, and the idea was supported by professionals who claimed to have "scientific" proof. A doctor writing for the Philadelphia *Journal of Medical and Physical Sciences* in the late 1820s, when Jim Crow made his stage debut, said that the "black races are substantially different" from and inferior to "the Caucasian in mental condition, as well as in bone and nervous systems, skull dimension, and internal bodily organs," and a census report published a few years later contended that the rates of insanity and mental retardation in free blacks were many times higher than that found in enslaved blacks.[60]

America was buzzing with theories about racial differences in the 1840s when minstrelsy became the favored entertainment. "Scientific racists" like the British-born George Robbins Gliddon, who came to Pittsburgh in 1847 to lecture on ethnology, as they called the study of the origin of the races, captivated large audiences with "historical evidence" that "proved" the races were inherently unequal. Samuel George Morton collected and measured the interiors of human skulls from around the world and concluded that Caucasian skulls were the most impressive in cranial capacity, while "Negro" skulls, which he placed at the bottom, were evidence of "the lowest grade of humanity." Another "scientist" named Louis Agassiz electrified his audience in 1847 when he stated, "The brain of the Negro is that of the imperfect brain of a seven month infant in the womb of a White." Many whites supported the erroneous conclusions of these pseudo scientists who insisted that civilizations and races coexisted in a fixed hierarchy in accordance with God's plan, and "neither time, the environment, nor education could change the fixed order" of the inherent inequality of the races.[61]

Unfortunately, Stephen Foster grew to adulthood when such ideas, even among the educated, were freely bantered about. Men and women who were appalled by slavery and expressed sympathy for the slave still did not believe in the equality of the races. Some went so far as to say that all men should be treated equally before the law and even given civil rights, but they did not believe blacks and whites could live together as social equals because they did not believe all people were created equal in all respects. Many northern whites, when they came into contact with blacks, saw them only in a manner that conformed to their own prejudices. And, unfortunately, during the early years of minstrelsy, the image of African Americans projected on the stage conformed to those same twisted prejudices.

7

THE AWAKENING IN CINCINNATI

Stephen Foster lived in Cincinnati for three and a half years, and the experience left him a changed man. He had signed on with two respected publishing houses, his songs were being published and widely performed, and he knew he would earn his living as a composer. But what is more important, his music changed, too, because something he learned in Cincinnati prepared him to write his greatest plantation songs, music loved the world over like "Old Folks at Home" and "My Old Kentucky Home." For Stephen to change his minstrel songs, some outside influence must have induced the transformation. One biographer who chronicled Foster's Cincinnati years believed the rich array of music and arts in the Queen City of the West was the key to Foster's emerging musical genius.[1] Foster surely was awakened when he lived in Cincinnati, but it is unlikely that an internal transformation resulted from a sudden introduction to the city's arts, however fine and omnipresent they were.

It is more likely that the city's peculiar location on the Ohio River across from the slave state Kentucky, with its ongoing dialogue about slavery, was the real impetus for the awakening that led him to inject his songs with a message of compassion. With his brother Dunning off fighting in Mexico, Foster was left very much on his own in Cincinnati, which allowed him the freedom to open his mind and heart to more progressive ideas than he would have been privy to back home. The years he lived in Cincinnati coincided with the Mexican-American War, when some of the most intense arguments erupted over freedom versus slavery, debates that in the near future would turn into actual physical violence. Although Ohio was a free state, white Cincinnatians did not relish the idea of freed slaves moving into their city to threaten their social order and their jobs. Consequently, talk of the pros and cons of slavery abounded in Cincinnati, where Stephen had a chance to hear a variety of opinions on race and human bondage, to participate in the discussions, and to develop his own ideas, which were antithetical to those of his family.

He would have heard or read lengthy arguments about whether slaves who escaped across the river should be returned to their owners and whether slavery was just or not. He might have also heard how, ten years earlier, a white mob broke into the Cincinnati office of the abolitionist James G. Birney, smashed his press, and dumped everything into the Ohio River. Birney's case induced Salmon P. Chase, later Lincoln's treasury secretary, to get involved with the antislavery cause when he rightly concluded that anti-abolitionist mobs infringed on free speech when they attacked editors and destroyed their presses.[2] Stephen would not have missed recent reports in the papers of how Chase defended John Van Zandt who was caught trying to escort fugitive slaves to safety, and how he lost the case because the pro-Southern sentiments in Cincinnati were so strong.[3]

In spite of the unpopularity of the abolitionists in Cincinnati, the city had more stops on the Underground Railroad than elsewhere, and stories of daring escapes and secret hideaways were leaked constantly and whispered from person to person. There were safe havens and railroad stops in Pittsburgh, too, but living under his family's tight thumb, Stephen had little opportunity to learn anything about their secret activities.[4] In the city across from a slave state, however, he would have heard how slaves from Kentucky crossed the Ohio River and found temporary refuge in the cellars and attics of the abolitionists until they could be escorted to another stop on the Underground Railroad. The leader of the abolitionists in Cincinnati was a Quaker named Levi Coffin, who had moved from Indiana in 1847 and settled in the Ohio city about the same time Stephen did. At his new home near the river, Coffin held secret meetings in his parlor and paid the German owners of a livery stable to supply him with horses so he could transport the fugitives to freedom. When he hid them in his attic, his wife carried baskets of food camouflaged with "some freshly ironed garment on the top, to make it look like a basketful of clean clothes."[5]

It was while attending a meeting in Levi Coffin's parlor in Cincinnati that Harriet Beecher Stowe, the famous abolitionist writer, first heard the true story of a black woman who crossed the frozen Ohio to freedom, clutching her baby in her arms. The author later immortalized the feat in her novel *Uncle Tom's Cabin,* which used highly sentimental prose to awaken sympathy in the hearts of hundreds of thousands of Northerners.[6] Even President Lincoln acknowledged the power of the tears produced by her pen, reportedly greeting Stowe with the words, "So you're the little lady who made this big war."[7] Although the composer and the writer were in Cincinnati at the same time, they are not known to have met, yet Stephen would learn to write songs that used sentimentality in the same way, to create sympathy and compassion for the slaves.

Stowe, who came from a family of Connecticut abolitionists, lived in Cincinnati with her husband and six children the same years Stephen lived there. In 1849, after cholera devastated the city and took the life of their youngest child, the Stowes packed up their belongings and moved the family to Maine, where Harriet began working on *Uncle Tom's Cabin.* The author claimed the book was inspired by her son Charlie's death, which reminded her of the anguish slave women felt when their children were taken away in the dark of night and sold to the highest bidder.[8] In creating her fictional characters, she drew on true stories whispered to her by the free black women she employed as domestics in her Cincinnati home.

Stowe was also influenced by a new race theory conceived by Alexander Kinmont, who came to Cincinnati in the late 1830s to lecture and promote his ideas. Known as "romantic racialism," the theory left its mark not only on Stowe's sensitive portrayal of blacks in her novel, but it also affected the minstrel stage for a few years, from the late 1840s to the early 1850s, when African Americans were portrayed in a more sympathetic light. Romantic racialism offered a relatively sympathetic, if still racist, interpretation of African racial differences. Foster's generation was fascinated by race theories, but only the romantic racialists espoused the novel idea that some of the differences "peculiar to the black race" were good and valuable, even morally superior to those found in whites. Kinmont theorized that the "simplistic traits" attributed to blacks were redeeming virtues—docility, devotion, affection, and obedience were, after all, Christian virtues—which meant that slaves deserved sympathy and kindness.[9]

Even intellectuals like William Ellery Channing took note of romantic racialism. In 1840, he preached: "We are holding in bondage one of the best races of the human family. The Negro is among the mildest and gentlest of men." The black man became the perfect candidate for Christian perfection "because he carries within him, much more than we, the germs of a meek, long suffering, living virtue."[10] By associating African American traits with Christian virtue, romantic racialists created an image of blacks that, while condescending, could be construed as deserving of sympathy, and argued that a Christian people should not oppress the weak and crush the helpless. The most extreme of the romantic racialists might deny that descriptions like "childlike, affectionate, and docile" denoted inferiority, and even suggest that "the Negro was the superior race because his docility constituted the ultimate in Christian virtue."[11] Whether Foster heard of the romantic racialists is not known, but there can be little doubt that he was at least indirectly influenced by their ideas. The songs he wrote in his last year in Cincinnati show that he was looking at blacks differently and creating black song characters notable for their more sympathetic characterization.

Stephen may also have had a change of heart in Cincinnati because of what he saw with his own eyes. On the wharf, he could watch the black river workers in action, strong free men who impressed with their manliness and humanity. Mark Twain described them as "no pitiful handful of deckhands, firemen, and roustabouts, but a whole battalion of men."[12] Cincinnati had a relatively small population of African Americans, less than 3,500, but they had made positive economic advancements in the 1840s. Blacks could earn money on the riverboats and even more in the slaughterhouses, because pork packing was sufficiently undesirable that blacks were allowed to work in it. Probably the key to the success of free blacks was the unusual demographics of the city—the fact that Germans, not Irish, were the dominant immigrant group in Cincinnati. Germans held controlling interests in the pork business and German sausage makers were not prejudiced about hiring blacks as assistants. Thus the meat business, along with the steamboat trade, offered blacks job opportunities that were unique to the city.[13] And the improved economic status resulted in an improved image of

African Americans for the eyes and the ears of the impressionable young composer.

What had Foster learned in Cincinnati, where every day he came into contact with hardworking, free, urban blacks? Based on the songs he began to write toward the end of his stay in the border city, we can conclude that he gazed at these hardworking African Americans loading and unloading heavy cargo on and off the wharves and began to take notice. Watching them carrying bales of cotton from the steamboats or simply noticing their faces as they strutted with confidence about their work, Foster saw that they were not chattel, but were indeed "men." Cincinnati was probably one of the few places the adult Foster had the chance to see black men working on the waterfront, because, surprisingly, in most Northern cities by the late 1840s, blacks had been pushed out of the waterfront by the dominant Irish population. According to an 1850 table of "Negro Labor in the United States," blacks worked on the boats and levees of the port towns along the Ohio, the Missouri, and the Mississippi rivers, but few blacks in the larger cities that boasted growing Irish populations had jobs on the waterfront after the 1840s.[14]

Morrison Foster confirmed the idea, when he claimed in his biography that Stephen was influenced by the music of the black singers and musicians he saw and heard on the Cincinnati waterfront. Blacks on the levees and black firemen in the bowels of the boat sang while they worked and those who were musicians played dance music for the passengers.[15] Stephen probably had to move to Cincinnati to hear black stevedores sing in their strong, full voices while they loaded and unloaded the boats. He may have seen and heard them on the docks in Pittsburgh when he was a boy, but it is very probable that with the large number of Irish living there in the 1840s, African American waterfront workers in Stephen's native city were few in number by the time he grew to be a man.[16] Author Peter Quinn, in his novel *Banished Children of Eve*, may have had it right in his fictionalized account of Stephen Foster watching the black workers on the docks in Cincinnati:

> Sometimes, after work as a clerk in the steamboat office in Cincinnati, Stephen would go down to the docks and watch the gangs of Negroes load and unload the boats. They were men. He had never given it much thought before. Never looked at negroes with any intent of figuring out who they were, no more than he tried to distinguish the individual horses in the work teams that endlessly hauled

wagons to and from the docks. Now he watched them. When the work stopped, they stood together in a group, talking and looking over their shoulders at the white men who oversaw them. Their whole way of speaking and gesticulating changed when they were by themselves. There was a litheness to their step, an energy and grace-fulness, that they lost when the whites returned. Rhythmical, playful, high-pitched. Yet there was something sly and mocking in it, conspir-atorial. White people were unnerved by it. They were sure it was at their expense, Sambo and Cudjo making sport of their master, aping his walk or mannerisms, returning his contempt . . . . He [Foster] never spoke to anyone about the Negroes, never asserted what ob-servation had confirmed to him: these are men.[17]

Other factors that would have influenced Stephen in Cincinnati to open his heart and mind to the slavery issue were the newspapers he read when he lived there. Two newspaper editors with antislavery opinions impressed him very much and probably had an influence on his deci-sion to write songs that had a sympathetic trajectory. We know that Stephen knew these men and/or read their papers because of two things. First, when William D. Gallagher of the *Cincinnati Gazette* praised several of Foster's songs in his newspaper, Stephen wrote and dedicated a song to him. Second, in a letter to his brother Morrison, Stephen identified the *Cincinnati Chronicle*'s Edward Deering Mans-field, as "the editor whom I consider the most powerful and talented writer in the West."[18] That Stephen Foster was aware of the editors was always known. What was not acknowledged was that both men were outspoken antislavery advocates. When Stephen wrote Morrison of his admiration for Mansfield, Morrison knew nothing of the writer's anti-slavery sentiments.

In June 1847, William Gallagher gave a "nod of recognition" in his newspaper to Stephen's recently reissued "Open Thy Lattice, Love." He described it as "a sweet little melody for the Piano, just published by Mr. S. C. Foster, whose spirited air of 'A Good Time Coming' pub-lished two or three months ago, has become a decided favorite." Foster, to demonstrate his gratitude for the kind publicity notice, dedicated his new song "Lilly Ray" to the man described by Foster biographer Ray-mond Walters as "friend William D. Gallagher . . . . Poet, literary critic and public official." Although the biographer described Gallagher as "a formative influence upon letters in the Middle West comparable to that of leading New England poets and critics," he failed to notice that Gallagher was pro-labor and antislavery.[19] Yet Gallagher's poem, "A Hymn of the Day that Is Dawning," has a similar sounding title to the new Foster song that Gallagher announced in his paper, "A Good Time Coming!" Gallagher's poem announced his antislavery sentiment clearly when he hailed the day the slave shall be "at last enfranchised":

> When the master with his bondmen, For a price shall divide the soil,
> And the slave, at last enfranchised, Shall go singing to his toil . . .
> Be firm, and be united, Ye who war against the wrong!

In Gallagher's poem "The Laborer," he exhorted workingmen, "Stand Up—erect! Thou has the form and likeness of thy God!" In another poem for the oppressed entitled "Song of the Knitting Girl," the protagonist is "Never doubting the Better Day," as she sits by the fire, mechanically repeating "And I knit—I knit—I knit." (The words recall the popular "Song of the Shirt," whose female protagonist rhythmically sings the words "stitch, stitch, stitch.")

Gallagher later joined the Republican Party and supported Abraham Lincoln in the 1860 presidential election. That he might have influenced Foster to think that African Americans were men is suggested by a few lines in one of his poems:[20]

> Ha! How the fetters fall! Was this—was this a slave?
> It looks so like a man, 'tis hard to think It other than a man![21]

The other influential antislavery voice much admired by Stephen was that of Edward Deering Mansfield, editor of the *Cincinnati Chronicle* and later the *Cincinnati Weekly Atlas,* or *Daily.* Mansfield was spewing forth antislavery ideas in his newspaper from 1846 to 1849, the years when Stephen lived in Cincinnati and became mesmerized by him. Years later, Mansfield wrote:

> The *Cincinnati Chronicle* was thoroughly anti-slavery, but not Abolitionist, so called. It was a Whig paper throughout its whole career, having the confidence and support of the most influential people in the city. It never hesitated to criticize and expose the conduct of the slaveholders or the political laws which maintained them, but did not think it necessary to establish a separate party for that purpose. . . . We were utterly opposed to slavery in the day when two-thirds of the community were for it, and two-thirds of the remainder compromised with it. We . . . lived to see its entire destruction in this land of

the free, as it is called, free in fact, standing out before the world the only successful republic. [22]

If Stephen read Mansfield's *Cincinnati Chronicle* he would have been introduced to an "able and brilliant corps of contributors," including "Miss Harriet Beecher [Stowe who] published her first stories in it." Mansfield became acquainted with the Beecher family when he and the Beechers lived in Litchfield, Connecticut, and he followed the famous abolitionist family to Cincinnati. He published his articles in the *Chronicle* under the initials E. D. M., and his political philosophy was anathema to everything Morrison Foster believed in. He opposed opening up the Mexican lands to slavery, which he considered a moral wrong. He denounced both the compromiser Henry Clay and the statesman Daniel Webster for their indifference to slavery, for lacking "the moral courage to take a stand upon human rights and defend it upon the ground of moral law." [23] Mansfield, like Gallagher, became a Republican, supported Lincoln, and during the Civil War, promoted the Union war effort in lengthy *New York Times* articles. [24]

If Stephen read the newspapers of these men, or got caught up in antislavery discussions in Cincinnati, he had to be very quiet about it and never reveal his sentiments to his diehard Democratic family in Pittsburgh. Every communication thus would be coded. But he would want to express his new feelings through some media, in some way. And for Stephen, that would be through his minstrel songs into which he injected a new message of sympathy. If one were to pass judgment on the awakening of Foster's moral consciousness by analyzing his songs, it is possible to conclude that the young composer opened his eyes in Cincinnati to see beyond the racial stereotypes that regularly appeared on the minstrel stage. Before Foster moved to the Ohio city and immediately upon his arrival, he wrote minstrel songs unthinkingly—jaunty numbers that conformed to the pattern of racial denigration that the minstrels wanted. Eager to please the minstrels, he wrote songs that "were faithful to the genre" with "texts depicting blacks as simple, good natured, irresponsible creatures." These early songs contained offensive lines, but they were "stock attributes of the minstrel stage black" at the time. "Away Down South" contains the line "My lub she had a very large mouth, one corner in de norf, tudder in de souf," words which could have been easily sung by a blackface minstrel with exaggerated painted lips. Even the iconic "Oh! Susanna" is not immune to criticism for its insensitive content:

> I jumped aboard de telegraph,
> And trabbelled down de ribber,
> De lectrie fluid magnified
> And killed five hundred Nigger.

The "telegraph" was the name of a steamboat, and there were many deadly explosions on the river in those days to be sure, but the magnitude of deaths—"five hundred Nigger"—comes across as senselessly callous and cruel. Still, Foster's protagonist comes across as a human being with feelings. He has traveled all the way from Alabama to Louisiana in search of his lady love Susanna, escaping a steamship explosion, a burst engine, and a runaway horse. Susanna must have been sold south, the cruelest fate for a slave, and Foster's protagonist tells the audience that if he cannot find her in Louisiana, he will "surely die":

> I'll fall upon the ground.
> But if I do not find her,
> Dis darkie, 'ill surely die.

A change in Foster's moral compass is apparent for the first time with "Nelly Was a Lady," the song the minstrel Charles White almost stole from him. With this song, Foster made a true departure—from his insensitive characterization of blacks in his earlier minstrel songs, to compositions that carried messages of sympathy. "Nelly Was a Lady" offered the audience the image of a black man grieving over the death of his "dark Virginny bride." Since bereavement was regarded as a reverential state in the antebellum society, whites could empathize even with a black man who grieved and sang out, "Now all dem happy days am ober."[25] "Dem happy days," we presume, referred to the days when Nelly was alive, not to life under a plantation system. Calling Nelly a bride and a lady was unusual, too, because slaves could not legally marry, nor would female slaves be referred to as ladies, but the protagonist's heartfelt grief over his wife's death, which the chorus repeatedly announces with the tolling of the funeral bell, has elevated his humanity in the eyes of the audience. The dark complexioned widower in the song received the sympathy from the white audience because his grief revealed that he was a feeling human being who displayed the same sensibility as they did when their spouses died.

When Stephen began to write minstrel songs that showed sympathy for his black protagonists, his musical style changed as well. Harmonics were restricted to tonic, subdominant, and dominant in early printed versions of "Oh! Susanna," revealing a musical structure that reflected the supposed simple nature of the protagonists in his early minstrel songs.[26] Beginning with "Nelly Was a Lady," his minstrel songs offered a "more sophisticated harmonic, tonal chord progression," while maintaining simple diatonic melodies that suggest the pentatonic scale.[27] Although classified on its title page as an "Ethiopian Melody" and written in dialect, "Nelly Was a Lady" reveals a transition toward greater musical complexity and borrowings from his parlor style, including a slower tempo, chromatic passing tones, and an interesting musical setting for the words "Toll de bell."[28] Foster's next minstrel songs would continue to demonstrate sympathetic portrayals of blacks and greater musical sophistication.

By the summer of 1848 Dunning Foster had returned from Mexico in one piece, but Morrison, who managed to avoid the war, lay deathly ill in Cincinnati recovering from a fever that he contracted in his travels south to buy cotton. Earlier in the year, his boss McCormick had sent him to Tennessee to "make arrangements with one, two or three houses in Nashville to purchase . . . 10 or 1200 Bales [of cotton]."[29] Morrison, however, was only able to purchase 835 bales before a serious illness cut short his business negotiations. Too weak to travel all the way home on the riverboat, he was dropped off in Cincinnati where his mother Eliza, after racing west on a packet boat from Pittsburgh, met him on the dock. Morrison in his fragile state was gently transported to Dunning's boardinghouse where Eliza nursed him day and night. Sister Ann Eliza must have expected the worst, because her desperate letters arrived in Cincinnati regularly, urging her brother to prepare himself "for appearing in the presence of a just and Holy God." Fortunately, Morrison recovered, and in July 1848, Eliza Foster took a moment to give heartfelt thanks for the good health of her three sons in Cincinnati.[30]

Morrison may have escaped the clutches of an early death by fever, but he soon decided he would risk his life in search of gold. He wanted to join the tens of thousands of adventurous men who journeyed to California each year seeking the fast track to wealth. Fortunately, Dunning Foster, who had already fought a war in Mexico, discouraged his brother from attempting the feat. In December 1848, he wrote Morrison:

> Mr. Whim . . . of gold hunting is very good but I cannot advise you to undertake the journey and more especially as you would be obliged to go without money sufficient to give you a good start of it. I have no doubt that a young man with proper industry could make a future. I cannot doubt either but whether the experience and change of climate and perfect estrangement from every body for whom you feel any interest would compensate for the accumulation of riches to be left for others to enjoy is a question that I cannot so easily satisfy myself about. You must expect to undergo many hardships that you do not deserve of in a trip so full of uncertainty and adventure.[31]

Dunning had seen enough naive hopefuls depart his city in search of gold in the far West, only to see them return defeated and empty handed. These daring men would board a boat in Cincinnati, travel south to New Orleans, and then transfer to an ocean liner that would take them around South America to California. Alternately, they could board a boat in Cincinnati that would take them to a town like Independence, Missouri, and from there continue by land to California. Irwin & Foster chartered steamboats that carried the gold rushers to several Missouri River towns that served as "jumping-off places" for the wagon train west.[32]

Dunning convinced Morrison not to take the chance, but his most convincing argument may have been that he was not able to offer his brother "much assistance in money in case you make up your mind to go."[33] If Morrison had gone, he would have heard a familiar refrain, as the men with gold dust in their eyes trekked their way to California singing Stephen's "Oh! Susanna" like a marching song. Gold was discovered the same year that W. C. Peters published the song, and the Forty-niners adopted it and changed the words to suit their situation:

> Oh California! That's the land for me
> I'm going to Sacramento,
> With my washbowl on my knee![34]

In May 1849, cholera reached Cincinnati, and a trip to California would not have been a bad idea. The dreaded disease that killed Harriet Beecher Stowe's baby son and 8,000 others in the Ohio city would continue throughout the summer until stifled by the chilled air of autumn.[35] The afflicted suffered from diarrhea, vomiting, and agonizing cramps, and those who succumbed did so within days or even hours of the onset of symptoms. Cholera, a waterborne disease that was spread through food or water contaminated by human feces, was initially brought to America on ocean going ships, but now steamboats carried the disease west on the Ohio River, where it festered in stagnant interior waterways. Once Eliza learned of the approach of the disease, she was determined to have Stephen leave the now-frightening city and return home. Her youngest son, however, appeared unaware of the seriousness of the situation, and as late as April 27, 1849, Stephen wrote his mother, "Tell Ma she need not trouble herself about the health of Cincinnati as our weather here is very healthy, the cholera not having made its appearance."[36]

The more experienced Dunning, however, mentioned the threat of the disease six months before it appeared, when he predicted at the end of 1848 that cholera "is hourly expected." He had learned that a certain captain named "Smith . . . . a proud and worthy man ....will be here tonight a corpse, having died in a few hours."[37] The cholera also had a negative effect on business. Dunning noted that the "accounts today [of cholera] are to deter boats from leaving for New Orleans." Business, he said, was already "very much affected, also pork is declining rapidly and will go a good deal lower."[38] Eliza, naturally, was very relieved to learn that Stephen would be leaving Cincinnati and returning home to Pittsburgh that summer to attend the weddings of several old friends.

Dunning escaped the cholera epidemic, as he had escaped a heroic death in battle, but he was infected in Mexico with either tuberculosis or some tropical disease. He returned from the war emotionally wounded, too, retaining ghoulish memories of battle-inflicted deformities. At a "masqued party" held at Sophie Marshall's house in January 1849, Dunning's "character was a Mexican soldier with the last remnants of a uniform and less of a face."[39] The returning veteran was summoned to "a party almost every night," but by summer with cholera ravaging the city, fading health, and a decline in business, the good times were coming to an end. In his poor physical state, Dunning considered getting into another line of work and since Stephen had neither the talent nor inclination to take over the Cincinnati business, he decided to sell the partnership and send his younger brother home for good.

At the beginning of 1850, Stephen was back living in Allegheny City. There were many reasons for his decision to leave Cincinnati. The budding composer had already decided on a career in music and felt confident enough to pursue it, especially after signing the royalty-generating contract with Firth, Pond, and Company. William Cumming Peters had moved to Louisville to run another music business he had opened years ago. In addition, the political scene at the beginning of 1850 was turning into a bubbling cauldron. Even before the Mexican-American War ended, arguments arose about what to do with all the land that would come to the United States at the war's conclusion, and the question on everyone's lips was whether slavery would be allowed in the new territories or if the land should be preserved for free white men.

On a more personal level, Stephen may have wanted to return home because Jane McDowell, the Pittsburgh girl he began courting in Cincinnati, returned home in the middle of 1849 and he missed her. The nineteen-year-old had boarded a riverboat to Cincinnati at the beginning of the year ostensibly for a change of scenery and to become reacquainted with old friends and relatives. But Jane's hidden agenda included securing a husband, as was the case when Charlotte Foster visited the city twenty years earlier. Jane stayed with the Stewarts, a family that was not socially active, but Stephen nonetheless became a frequent visitor. In a letter to Morrison written in January 1849, Dunning discussed the girl who had just arrived in town:

> I am sorry that Jane McDowell is not with some of the young ladies that go into society, as I fear she will not have as favourable an impression of our people as she would have were she to see more of them. Mr. Stewart's family is not generally visited by people that would interest her much; however, she appears to enjoy herself very well, and does not complain in any way. She is, by the way, a very sensible and interesting young lady....They often sigh over the friends at Pittsburgh, and wish to be with them, but as yet I have not heard them set a time to go up. They say they will go up when I do, but as that is a very indefinite period, it is not very conclusive as to the time they will be in Pittsburgh.[40]

Stephen may have been the reason Jane came to Cincinnati in the first place. Whether the romance blossomed on its own or Stephen's affections were on Jane's mind before she left Pittsburgh has not been determined, nor is it known what the couple had in common, other than stories about life and friends back home. But there was evidently a strong attraction because when Jane was suddenly called back to Pittsburgh in May, Stephen followed after her and married her, but the couple did not live "happily ever after."

8

NON-COMPANIONATE MARRIAGE

Jane McDowell was the pretty, petted, and according to some, temperamental daughter of Andrew Nathan McDowell, a prominent physician of Pittsburgh. Enshrined in folklore as the living embodiment of "Jeannie with the Light Brown Hair," she was one of five girls "reared in an atmosphere of luxury" in a house on Penn Avenue in the same neighborhood and on the same street where the Fosters had built their beloved White Cottage. The McDowell home's spacious front parlor was filled with dark wood furniture and an African American servant greeted guests at the door and ushered them inside. Whereas Stephen Foster's home had been converted in his memory to a lost object when he was just a toddler, Jane McDowell had the advantage of enjoying her home and privileged lifestyle for many years.[1]

Jane was born on December 10, 1829, making her Stephen's junior by only three years. She had been acquainted with the composer long before he began courting her in Cincinnati, since the families had known each other for decades and her father was the Fosters' family doctor. Stephen appeared to be completely captivated and paid regular visits to the Stewart home (where Jane stayed in Cincinnati), but the visits ended abruptly when Dr. McDowell died suddenly on May 7, 1849, and Jane hurried back to Pittsburgh. Stephen followed after her almost immediately, making an excursion home in June, but he returned to Cincinnati to take care of business. Not until after he signed his publishing contract with Firth, Pond and Company in September did he return to Pittsburgh for good at the beginning of the year. If the couple corresponded during their separation, there are no extant love letters. Her father's unexpected death, however, must have compelled Jane to consider marriage a very serious matter. At least two of her four sisters were still without husbands, and the doctor left his widow with insufficient means to provide for them all.[2]

In February 1850, Stephen was back in Allegheny City where he at first continued the courtship casually, meeting Jane in the parlor of her own house on certain prescribed evenings. But Stephen's nightly visits suddenly took on a new urgency when a handsome new suitor showed up on the scene competing for Jane's attentions. Richard Cowan was a friend of Morrison's and a former member of the Knights of the Square Table, the boys' social club in Allegheny City. He was tall and impressive, a veteran of the Mexican-American War who still wore his military overcoat to impress the ladies. Stephen's granddaughter Jessie Welsh Rose described the competitive game that was acted out in Jane's parlor when the unexpected suitor showed up on the night that was assigned to Stephen for courting. The following story came to Rose from her grandmother Jane. She relayed it to a reporter, who published it in the *Pittsburgh Post* on July 4, 1926, on the one-hundredth anniversary of Stephen Foster's birth.

Cowan was "a lawyer, wealthy, handsome, and distinguished in appearance," according to Jessie Welsh Rose. "Mr. Foster suffered somewhat from the contrast. One evening owing to some miscalculation on Miss Jane's part, both called at Dr. McDowell's home at the same hour. Steve came first." After Cowan was escorted into the parlor, Stephen "turned his back on the pair, took up a book and read the evening through." At ten-thirty, the lawyer suitor stood up and pulled his "military broadcloth cape about him elegantly, [and] bid the forbidding back of Stephen a low sweeping 'Good Evening, Sir.'" As soon as Cowan departed, "Steve had risen, was standing by the table pale and stern as she came in. 'And now, Miss Jane, I want your answer! Is it yes? or is it no?'"[3]

Jane may have been taken aback by the impetuous nature of the proposal or she may have anticipated it, having purposely confused the evening when Cowan was to show up. Whatever the truth of the situation, Jane accepted Stephen's proposal and they were married in July 1850. Unfortunately, the marriage, which was marked by frequent quarrels, breakups, and a long separation, simply did not work. They may have been incompatible souls by nature, as family sources suggest that neither one was the other's first choice for a mate. A letter written to Morrison by a female friend in 1849 stated that Jane McDowell had been "engaged to some chap near New Lisbon," Ohio, suggesting that Jane might have encouraged Stephen's advances because her first choice had not worked out. Stephen, too, could have been a rejected lover. There was a woman named Martha Morse he visited in Pittsburgh whenever he came home to Allegheny, according to one family member. "Stephen admired her greatly, called on her and took her places, even to see his cousin Annie Evans when she was ill."[4] If a romance did in fact exist, there are no clues to why it broke up. Death did not shatter the relationship, because Martha survived, married, and had a daughter of her own who lived just outside of Pittsburgh, in Aspinwall, Pennsylvania.

Stephen may have married Jane simply because he fell in love with her, as falling in love had become a normal part of middle-class American courtship by the mid-nineteenth century. Men and women increasingly believed that love was the "whole thing" in a marriage and that "Marriage without love cannot fail to be a source of perpetual unhappiness."[5] Encouraging the legitimacy of romance were novels and magazine articles that were preoccupied with romantic love, now considered an essential to domestic harmony. The nineteenth-century concept of romantic love, however, precluded irrational passion, which, one issue of *Lady's Godey's Book* advised, should not be the overriding factor. Passion should be tempered by a sensible amount of self-control.[6]

Stephen Foster's passions were more impetuous than controlled on the day he asked Jane to marry him, but other influences were at work at the same time. One factor that could have pushed Stephen forward was that many of his friends were getting married, and in June 1849 alone, he attended three weddings in Pittsburgh. On June 5, the neighbor girl Susan Pentland married Andrew Robinson, one of Stephen's boyhood friends. Just two weeks later on June 19, Anne Robinson, Andrew's sister, married J. Cust Blair, disappointing Dunning who had had his heart set on her and subsequently never married. Finally, in that same month, Louisa Bell, a girl whose musical sounding name may have inspired Stephen several years earlier to write his popular minstrel song "Lou'siana Bell," married a man from St. Louis, Missouri.[7]

Jane probably attended these weddings with Stephen, since they belonged to the same social set, and the festive occasions may have put the young couple in the marrying mood, blinding both to the fact that they were polar opposites. If Jane were indeed the "sensible lady," Stephen appeared to be anything but sensible. Yet opposites do attract and Stephen may have been drawn to Jane's grounded practicality and sensed that he needed that leveling force in a wife. Advice manuals of the day, upon which many middle-class lovers so curiously relied, actually stressed the idea that contrasts between husband and wife in temperament were acceptable, as long as the couple shared similarities in background and interests. By following the dictates of the manuals, as many believed, the "marriage of companionship," so idealized in the nineteenth century by the American middle class, could be realized. What lovers expected from the companionate marriage was the "appreciation of each other's character and the strong sympathy and similitude of thought and feeling."[8] We can only hope that Stephen and Jane shared that conjugal "appreciation" and "sympathy" at some time in their marriage.

Why Jane accepted Stephen's rash proposal is a question that comes to mind, especially when she had another suitor who diminished him "somewhat by the contrast." Perhaps Dunning's description of Jane as "a sensible young lady" holds the answer. Cowan was eight years older than Jane and had a reputation for being a lady's man. She may not have felt confident that he would ever propose, or he might have taken too long, if he had ever gotten around to it. He was ambitious, even concerning his female conquests, and as soon as Jane married, he was busy pursuing the wealthy Annie Denny, a relation of William Foster's old partner Ebenezer Denny.[9] In all probability, Jane suspected that Cowan was not a serious contender and, since the death of her father the previous year, she felt an urgency to marry and get on with her life. Of course, a more flattering explanation for Jane's acceptance of Stephen's proposal is that she was impressed with his personal charms, along with his new and growing celebrity. His songs were selling, and what was more, people were singing them—in the theaters, in the streets—everywhere it seemed. By the summer of 1850, Stephen's fame was on the rise, and Jane may have believed she loved him.

What is certain is that the couple was not drawn together by a mutual interest in music. Before Stephen moved away to Cincinnati in 1846 and after he returned home and married, he participated in a tight knit musical group in Allegheny City, where "singing around the old square piano in the evening was the principal social diversion of all the friends of Stephen Foster and his brothers." Yet Jane's name did not appear in Stephen's musical circle, which included many women, such as the Lightner sisters, Jessie and Julia. Jessie had a deep contralto voice, and Stephen brought many of his new songs to her to sing before he sent them off to his publisher in New York. Several of Jane's sisters, of course, were musical, but when they held musical evenings in their parlor on Penn Avenue, Jane was not known to participate or to take pleasure in listening to others who did.

Stephen and Jane Foster were married by a minister from the Trinity Episcopal Church on Monday, July 22, 1850. Without a photograph, we can only guess how she appeared when she stood before the minister to take her vows. Family lore has it that Jane was very pretty, and Stephen's song immortalized one of her features, her luxuriant "light brown hair." A wedding gown pattern published in *Lady's Godey's Book* the year they married flaunted an elongated tight fitting bodice made more slender by corset stays and laces, a huge hoop skirt, and long, fitted sleeves overlaid by puffed fabric that extended to the middle of the arm. Agnes McDowell, a sister of Jane who was present at the wedding, noted in a letter to another sister who was too ill to attend, that "her wedding dress fit her beautifully. . . . [A]ll of Jane's dresses fit her beautifully, and her other garments were made quite neatly." She also noted that "Jane & Stephen F, were pretty much frightened . . . Steve quite pale. They each had to repeat some part of the ceremony after Mr. Lyman, which made it, I think rather embarrassing. Jane repeated her part in a different kind of a voice altogether from her usual tone of voice. It was owing to her strain."[10] Strain about what? Maybe the nervousness resulted from some inner voice telling her the marriage was a bad idea.

There were, of course, many reasons for nineteenth-century women and men to be nervous as their wedding day approached. Young people were warned in advice manuals to look into the character of prospective mates and to make their selections accordingly, as divorce was rarely an option. What they married was usually what they got, and women in particular were reminded that they should not try to reform their husbands. A young woman could also be nervous in anticipation of the danger that the marriage bed entailed, and Jane's generation had female friends and relatives who had died in childbirth. Marriage could indeed be a risky business for a woman, but it could be stressful for a man for other reasons. While their lives might not be directly threatened, they did have to think of their livelihoods, which needed to be secure and sufficient, because with marriage the man assumed the total financial burden of supporting his wife and any offspring that would come along at regular intervals. This last thought could have been running through Stephen's mind when he nervously took his vows.[11]

After the wedding, "on that same evening," Stephen and Jane Foster left for an extended "honeymoon" excursion to New York and Baltimore. Stephen had informed his brother William the previous week, "The trip will be on business as well as for pleasure as I wish to see my publisher as soon as possible."[12] Along the way, they visited relatives in at least three cities in Pennsylvania—Chambersburg, Mercersburg, and Paradise—and Eliza Foster's Clayland relatives in Baltimore. But the real reason for the excursion was to enable Stephen to make contact with his publishers: Firth, Pond and Company in New York and F. D. Benteen in Baltimore. At the risk of portraying him in a less-than-romantic light, it is fair to assume that the trip to New York was on Stephen's mind months before he married. He had already shown that he was a serious and industrious composer, having published a dozen successful songs the year before he married, but to ensure there was no slack in his work or that his publishers did not lose interest, he wanted to stay in contact.

Firth, Pond and Company might have even demanded that he pay them a visit in New York. The publishers were still located at No. 1 Franklin Square, in an ancient building that had been around since the time "the national capital was in New York City," but they were very successful.[13] In addition to "new and beautiful vocal and instrumental music," they sold an assortment of musical instruments, including pianofortes, guitars, flutes, trombones, fifes, bugles, and tambourines. Their flutes and guitars were advertised "of our own manufacture, of superior tone and finish," and the year Stephen visited them, they sold $80,000 in musical instruments alone.[14] It was all very exciting for Stephen, proof that his muse was thriving, and for the first time in his life he felt confident in his career choice.

On September 8, 1850, after their six-week combination honey-moon-business trip, Stephen and Jane moved into the Allegheny house, which had recently been freshened with coats of white paint on the woodwork and trim. The newlyweds joined Stephen's parents, Morrison (when he was not traveling for McCormick), and Henry and his wife Mary with their two-year-old daughter "Burgess." They also had two women servants, probably squeezed into the top floor rooms. Living space was cramped with the two additional people, but soon there was a new arrival. On April 18, 1851, exactly nine months after the wedding, Stephen and Jane Foster's only child Marion was born in the house on the East Common, and, with the extra mouth to feed, Stephen increased the board he paid his parents from five dollars to six dollars per week. But a few months later in August, Stephen, Jane, and Marion moved in with Jane's mother in Lawrenceville, where Stephen paid rent to his mother-in-law. [15]

The reason for the sudden change of residence may have been something other than overcrowding. Sometime between the end of February and April of that year, Stephen's father suffered a major, debilitating stroke that turned him into an invalid for the rest of his life. A newborn in the house would have caused too much noise and commotion for the bedridden and seriously ill man, and Jane may have preferred living with her own mother after the birth of her daughter. It is also possible that the Fosters found Jane's pride and spunk annoying. No letters exist attesting to a warm relationship between Jane and her mother-in-law Eliza. At any rate, Stephen and Jane stayed at the McDowell house until Christmas, when they returned to live with the Fosters.

The young Foster couple had many difficulties to face in addition to surviving in a crowded household on an erratic income. At the time of his stroke, William was working as a soldier's agent registering land claims, and Stephen and Morrison immediately took up the slack, doing what they could to see that the income from their father's latest venture continued coming in. Still, William's illness must have cost the Fosters lost revenues. Every little bit counted, especially since the previous year the senior William made what turned out to be his last futile claim, which at the time amounted to $5,218.60 with accrued interest, against the government. Between keeping the records for the soldiers' claims and writing songs for royalties, Stephen still had a difficult time meeting the expenses of his little family, a problem with which he struggled for the rest of his life.[16]

Stephen and Jane's marriage lasted almost fourteen years, with the couple living together on and off for the first ten years, separating when Stephen went away on business or Jane packed up her bags and walked out with Marion. But until Stephen made his final move to New York in 1860, they were never separated for more than six months, although there were numerous breakups followed by emotional reconciliations. Who or what was to blame for such a tumultuous relationship? Opposites can attract, but ultimately the very differences that attracted the couple in the first place can break them apart. If Stephen initially admired Jane's practical side and inner strength, especially when compared with his own vacillating inner core, in the end he could not stand it. And if Jane were initially drawn to Stephen's dreamy-eyed pose and impulsive decision making, she eventually grew fed up with the juvenile antics, especially when tied to a weakness for alcohol whenever life did not meet his expectations.

Stephen and Jane were products of different families and upbringings, not so much externally, as internally. Both Jane's father, Andrew McDowell, and Stephen's father, William Foster, were descended from Scots-Irishmen who migrated to Philadelphia and then moved west. Like the Fosters, the McDowells claimed an impressive lineage, with many doctors in the family, a president of a college, professors of Latin and Greek, and many connections to George Washington. Jane's father had lived in Chambersburg, Pennsylvania, the town where Eliza and William Foster were married nearly a half-century back. Her mother, Jane Denny Porter of Chambersburg, was a girlhood friend of Charlotte Foster's, and her grandfather had established an iron foundry along the Allegheny River. In the early 1830s, the McDowells moved to the growing city of Pittsburgh, where the doctor set up a successful medical practice and counted the Fosters as both friends and patients.[17] But here the similarities ended, because Andrew McDowell was a much less conventional man than William Foster. Dr. McDowell trained the black abolitionist Martin Delany in the medical arts, and the year before he died, he encouraged Delany to enter medical school in the East. While Stephen was living among conservative Democrats where no one would say or do anything to improve the lives of African Americans,

Jane's father was instrumental in sending one of the first black men to Harvard Medical School.

Martin Delany was born in Virginia in 1812 to a free mother and an enslaved father. He was born free because Virginia law assigned the status of the mother to the unborn child. When Martin was ten years old, the Delanys moved to Chambersburg, Pennsylvania, where Martin became acquainted with Dr. McDowell, probably while doing odd jobs for him around the house. One day the doctor opened the doors of his library to the young man and gave him a copy of Thomas Jefferson's *Notes on the State of Virginia*. When Delany read the book, he was shocked to learn that the founding father wrote that blacks were inferior in reasoning and beauty to whites. In July 1831, the year William Lloyd Garrison started his abolitionist newspaper, Delany took off for Pittsburgh, walking most of the way. He was immediately welcomed into the city's black antislavery society, and later moved across the river to Allegheny with his family. [18]

The McDowells moved to Pittsburgh a few years later, and Delany was soon visiting his old friend and mentor again. When he told the doctor that he wanted a career in medicine, McDowell at first discouraged him, but seeing Delany show up every morning at his door eager to learn something new in the medical arts, he took him on as a student. Delany was soon setting bones, sewing up wounds, and cupping and bleeding, and he treated cholera patients in Pittsburgh in the early 1830s when the accredited doctors ran the other way. He spent his evenings pouring over anatomy and physiology books, but when the Depression of 1837 set in, Delany gave up his studies and became a professional bleeder for the doctors in the neighborhood. In Pittsburgh's business directory for 1837, one listing following the names of the city's physicians read "Delany, Martin R. Cupping, leeching, and bleeding." [19]

Two months after Stephen and Jane married in 1850, the Fugitive Slave Act passed, demanding that whites in the North participate in the capture and return of slaves to their masters in the South. At a mass meeting held the next week in Allegheny, the mayor, several congressmen, and prominent citizens urged residents to petition the law's repeal. Martin Delany also spoke to the crowd, predicting that the law would never be repealed without "the overthrow of the Union." Delany was thirty-seven years old and he was a fighter, but he decided the best way to attack the iniquitous law was to make the most of his own life. With letters of recommendation from doctors Joseph I. Gazzam and F. Julius LeMoyne, prominent abolitionist physicians from Pittsburgh, he set out for the East to apply to medical schools. He did not carry a recommendation from Dr. McDowell, because Jane's father had died the year before. Dr. Oliver Wendell Holmes, Dean of the Faculty of the medical school at Harvard, accepted him and Delany paid for the term and started classes. But before he could complete his studies, white students protested his presence on racial grounds, and Delany returned to Pittsburgh to practice medicine without the benefit of a Harvard diploma.[20]

Stephen and Jane may have started out with different ideas about politics, but it is possible that during their courtship and during the first years of their marriage, Jane may have influenced her husband to adopt a more liberal mindset. For the daughter of Dr. Andrew McDowell certainly was brought up in a more politically liberal environment than Stephen. The favorite servant in Jane's family was a black man named Joe, later immortalized in Foster's plantation song "Old Black Joe." While Stephen's song persona is an old slave whose "head is bending low," the real Joe was a confident, free African American who chauffeured the doctor on his rounds in his handsome, custom-made carriage to attend to his patients. He was a familiar fixture at the McDowell house, and was fondly remembered for ushering nervous male suitors, carrying floral bouquets to the McDowell daughters, into the parlor. Stephen was impressed with the man enough to promise him personally that he would write a song about him, which he did long after Joe was dead. According to Stephen's granddaughter, "Old Black Joe" was the one song no one was allowed to sing in the house in later years, because the memories were too poignant and the song always brought her grandmother Jane to tears.[21]

When Jane moved into the Union Avenue house, her ideas may have collided with the conservatism of her in-laws. Not only was her family more left leaning in politics, but Jane was outspoken and independent minded. Her upbringing as the pampered daughter of a well-to-do physician did not prepare her to be the wife of a whiney, self-absorbed musician. Wifely duties included playing the soothing helpmate to a husband with problems, but Jane was never prepared to deal with the problems Stephen brought to the marriage. The antebellum society designated the wife the moral arbiter of the home, which meant that when Stephen drank excessively, as he often did, the wife was held accountable. She was supposed to keep her husband on the upright path, not through nagging, but by providing unquestioned love and devotion in a tranquil home setting. [22] Of course, the Allegheny house held too many people for it to be peaceful and the couple's fluctuating finances, along with Stephen's drinking, only aggravated the situation. When arguments broke out, the Fosters initially blamed Jane's "high temper," without looking for an explanation for the arguments. Jane was a strong remarkable woman, but in many ways she was ahead of her time. If the Fosters did not initially appreciate or understand her, they became more forgiving in later years, especially after they learned just how difficult her marriage had been. The family maintained, however, that in spite of their quarrels and separations, Stephen was always faithful to his "Jeanie with the Light Brown Hair." That may have been true as far as another woman was concerned, but alcohol and depressed moods would always draw him away. [23]

In spite of their differences, Stephen was happy for the first few years of his marriage, judging by the number of songs he wrote and the businesslike manner in which he went about composing. Records show that in July 1851, after his daughter Marion was born, he rented an office in which he installed a piano so that he could work without interruptions. [24] He had been composing on a piano owned by his sister-in-law Mary, who brought the instrument with her when she married Henry and moved into the Foster house. (When she and Henry later moved into Mary's mother's house, the piano went with them.) Stephen also began to keep a fastidious record of his song lyrics. On June 26, 1851, he made the first entry in the 200-page manuscript book he used to work out nearly all the songs he would write from that time until he moved to New York in 1860. The collection is interesting because it shows the order in which the songs were written and how the composer's ideas and poetic phrases and words evolved from one stage to the next. The book also reveals the songs that did not make it—the ideas that never found complete development. [25]

The first song Foster worked out in his manuscript book was "Laura Lee," which took up eight pages and was published by F. D. Benteen in August 1851. The difference between the initial trial and the final version shows that Foster could end up with completely different words but maintain the same idea behind them. If we dare to transfer the words to his real-life situation during the second year of his marriage, and imagine that "Laura Lee" is Jane, we see a man who is disappointed with love once reality has set in. The strain and stresses of life have altered Jane's voice, and to Stephen, it is no longer "glad and free." The following is the original verse of the song, before publication:

> When vows of love were truthful, I loved thee Laura Lee
> Ah then thy heart was youthful, Thy voice was glad and free
> Then life was in its morning, With raptures running wild
> Then with each days returning, a new born spring time smiled[26]

In the final published version, the words are different, but the sentiment is almost the same. In the first version, the "raptures running wild" of early love are gone. In the published version, both the lover and love's "happy dream" have "passed like a flitting beam":

> Why has thy merry face, Gone from my side
> Leaving each cherished place, Cheerless and void?
> Why has the happy dream, Blended with thee,
> Passed like a flitting beam, Sweet Laura Lee?[27]

Even before he finished working out "Laura Lee," Stephen began sketches in his manuscript book for two other songs that made it to press, and several others, including one about a mother and her child, which did not. Finally, on page 14 of the handwritten book, the heading reads "Way down upon de old plantation," which of course became "Way down upon de Swanee River," the first line in Foster's greatest plantation song.[28]

9

"SWANEE RIVER," E. P. CHRISTY, AND SENTIMENTAL MINSTRELSY

To many nineteenth-century men and women, "Old Folks at Home" was the ultimate testament to Stephen Foster's genius. When Firth, Pond and Company published the song in the fall of 1851, it became an immediate sensation. Newspapers reported that "Swanee River," as it was popularly known, was on everyone's lips, sung by people high and low, and music publishers had to keep their presses running day and night just to keep up with the demand. The song represented a new sentimental genre that included such titles as "Nelly Was a Lady," "Oh! Boys Carry Me 'Long," "Farewell My Lilly Dear," "Massa's in de Cold Ground," and "My Old Kentucky Home." Although these examples of a new type of minstrelsy came to be called "plantation songs," the publishers in Foster's day lumped all his songs that were sung in slave dialect together, identifying them on the cover as either "Ethiopian" or "Plantation Melodies," whether they were poignantly sentimental songs or lively minstrel tunes. Firth, Pond and Company identified "Old Folks at Home" on the title page as an "Ethiopian Melody" in very florid script, but the song is probably best described as "sentimental minstrelsy."[1]

Plantation songs like "Old Folks" were hybrids that combined the sentimental elements of the parlor songs Charlotte Foster sang decades earlier with certain characteristics of the jaunty minstrel tunes like "Oh! Susanna." Like other famous hybrids, they borrowed and combined elements selectively from their individual antecedents to make the prized product. "Old Folks," for example, had a slow-to-moderate tempo and the power to bring tears to the eyes like the sentimental parlor song, but the protagonist sings in a slave dialect when he recalls the Southern imagery of "de old plantation" and "de banjo tumming." There was something special, however, about "Old Folks at Home" and the other songs crafted along this hybrid model. All of these songs were refined enough to be welcomed in the middle-class home and even into the lady's parlor by virtue of their powerful sentimentality, which created a much desired emotional response that antebellum Americans relished in the listener.

What made the song so popular? Although there is no definitive answer for why it captured the minds and hearts of the people, it is fair to say that "Old Folks at Home" carried generations of listeners on a sentimental journey in search of the elusive home. The first line of the song, "Way Down upon the Swanee River, sadly I roam," was pregnant with meaning for men and women who wandered "all up and down de whole creation" in search of security and happiness. Many Americans in the 1850s had engaged in some sort of actual roaming, whether they were country folk seeking jobs in the city, young men with opportunities outside their village, or adventurers heading west, and the Swanee River song proved a good traveling companion, too, since rivers were the major highways. The song was particularly meaningful to the hundreds of thousands of immigrants "far from home" who came to America in the 1840s looking to start new lives after leaving their "old folks" behind. But the song was just as meaningful for the native born who could not find the sense of home they longed for in a landscape vastly altered by the changes of the modern age.

The world had indeed changed in the nineteenth century and become for many a "sad and dreary" place since the introduction of industry and all the transformations it wrought. Home in turn came to be idolized and its emphasis placed "Old Folks" in the popular category of "home songs" and made it easy to sell. Stephen may have thought that by using the word in the title he could cash in on the genre's popularity, since "Home Sweet Home," composed by Henry Bishop with lyrics by John Howard Payne, was the most popular song in America at midcentury. When the Swedish soprano Jenny Lind sang it on tour with P. T. Barnum in 1850, there was not a dry eye in the audience, and she traveled to cities in the backwoods of the nation singing to men and women who carried handkerchiefs into the concert halls. Both "Old Folks" and "Home Sweet Home" were relished because of the heightened emotions they evoked in recalling the love of home, a sentiment dear to antebellum Americans. The sentiment, in fact, was so poignant and powerful that even a slave roaming in search of home could induce the audience to well up in sentimental tears.[2]

That the greatest home or travel song was written by a man who had lost his home and spent much of his youth wandering should come as no surprise. "Roaming" and "home" were central themes in Foster's great plantation song, and the experience was understood intuitively by many in his generation for whom movement was seemingly constant and home was an unattainable quest. Foster intended alternative meanings for the key words in the song, making it possible for anyone to sing or hear "Old Folks" and interpret it in a way that was personally relevant and meaningful. The listener could interpret "roaming" and "home" at face value, or he could give these emotion-packed words less concrete meanings. "Roaming," for instance, could be an all-encompassing metaphor for an existential journey toward self-realization, the search for moral perfection, security, happiness, social standing, or even freedom. And "home" could be an actual physical structure or that sense of wholeness, belonging, and love that all people are seeking.

Similarly, the protagonist in "Old Folks" who longs for "de old plantation" is not seeking an actual slave plantation, but that elusive non-physical space "where simplicity, happiness, all the things we have left behind, exists outside of time."[3] The plantation became a metaphor for the comfort and security many experienced in their youth and, as was apparent in Foster's sentimental parlor songs, the protagonist cannot find what he seeks in the present and instead gazes backward to a time and place he can "never more behold." When their world was invaded by industry's "machine in the garden" and their nation threatened with disintegration, Americans developed a taste for nostalgic recollection of simpler days from an imaginary, rural past.[4] To satisfy their needs, Foster created sentimental songs that gazed backward and invoked images of long ago and "far away," while they carried the listener along on a soothing ride into nostalgia.[5]

Surprisingly, recent psychological studies have suggested that Foster may have been on to something with his nostalgic backward gaze. Psychological experiments by Constantine Sedikides and others conclude that all sorts of benefits accrue from what they call "nostalgizing"—from raising self-esteem and counteracting "loneliness, boredom and anxiety" to making "death less frightening." Thinking fondly on the past makes people "more optimistic and inspired about the future" and leaves them "with a stronger feeling of belonging."[6] One study that involved music shows that when a song made the participants feel nostalgic, "the more meaningful their lives seemed." Most importantly for Foster's generation, perhaps, is the idea that nostalgic recollection can help people come to terms with the changes in their lives. Some psychologists are concerned that for "nostalgizing" to be effective, a person needed to have happy childhood memories, but Foster's songs provided idealized images of a past that people could pine over even if their personal memories had not been that rosy.[7]

Foster's most popular song re-created the experience of the longed-for, pre-industrial world, a peaceful image of landscapes without smokestacks and steam engines screaming in the background. "Old Folks" is not so much about recalling actual memories, which may not have been pleasant, as about reveling in an improved vision of the past as people wanted it to be, and Foster provided all the prompts for the revel. The song's lyrics invoked the natural—flowers, birds, and bees buzzing—along with images of happy childhood days spent "on de little farm" with "de brudder" and "kind old mudder." Foster's generation used nostalgic recollection as a coping mechanism. In a society that was in flux, the "Swanee River" song provided a sentimental journey into the past, more fantastic than real, and brought comfort to people who were uncomfortable with the present.

The sentimentality in "Old Folks at Home" and other plantation songs was responsible for the satisfying experience of nostalgic recollection. A stirring, poignant image prompted by a song or a minstrel performance caused eyes to fill with tears and provided a rush of feelings, often of sympathy or empathy, but also simply of the pleasure of the sentimental. Even today, when people watch a sentimental film, they enjoy the emotion of nostalgia and the experience provides comfort. Apparently, people in Foster's generation felt better when listening to something that reminded them of the simpler days of their youth and temporarily lifted them out of their doldrums. The era put great faith in the restorative power of good memories. Dostoyevsky wrote in *The Brothers Karamazov*, "You must know there is nothing higher and stronger and more wholesome and good for life in the future than some good memory, especially a memory of childhood, of home."[8]

Of course, the images in the songs and on the minstrel stage were not real, and when the Northern workers in the audience watched a stage re-creation of life on a Southern plantation, they were not seeing the world they knew in their youth. They had never seen a real plantation, slaves, or the South, yet they equated the sunny land below the Mason-Dixon Line with a pre-industrial ideal.[9] Such phrases in "Old Folks" as "one little hut among de bushes" and "de bees a humming all round de comb" encouraged nostalgic reveries and provided temporary escape for men who walked into a deafening, smoking factory every day of their lives. But it seems safe to hypothesize that these urban workers who found comfort watching faux blacks sing and play the banjo on an imaginary plantation were also comforted by the racist images they found on the minstrel stage that elevated their own status in comparison and informed them they were not the lowest people in the abusive hierarchy established by their social betters.

To appeal to the generation that revered the past and enjoyed looking backward, antebellum artists often put "Old" in the title of their artworks. Foster started many of his sentimental songs that way, including "Old Memories," "Old Uncle Ned," "Old Dog Tray," and finally "Old Black Joe." And just as he benefited from using "Home" in the title, he must have used "Old" as a hook to attract buyers. Antebellum artists from diverse genres did the same thing. The famous publishers Currier and Ives put the word in dozens of titles of the prints they sold to the public, such as "The Old Farm Gate," a lithograph that portrays "a scene of rural peace and plenty in a by-gone day" with children playing, a cottage, and a dog.[10] Idealized scenes from the past were very fashionable in a society on the brink of change and artists like William Sidney Mount and the Hudson River painters created rural fantasies on canvass to preserve vignettes of their disappearing natural landscape.

Interestingly, these artists painted the world not as it really had been, but as they imagined it and as their customers wanted to see it. Foster did the same thing with his plantation songs, but he used Southern references to re-create his rural portrait. The difference between the painters and the composer was that the former located their idyllic settings in the New England countryside, with rustic barns and burnished golden harvests, whereas Foster placed his on a plantation in the

South with cotton and canebrakes. Yet both the New England country-side and the Southern plantation were vanishing tropes in a rapidly changing world. Industry was here to stay, and in the future pastoral images would be confined to Currier and Ives prints and minstrel stages.[11]

Even the muddy river in northern Florida that Foster chose to use in the first line of his greatest plantation song was a fantasy. He had never seen the Suwannee that rises in a swamp in Georgia and snakes its way southwest across the state of Florida to the Gulf of Mexico. His brother Morrison explained how he selected the unlikely waterway "far, far from home" when the Allegheny was just outside his front door. Stephen, he said, walked into his office one day, intensely engrossed in writing a new song for which he needed "a good name of two syllables for a Southern river." He might have added that the name would be sung with the second syllable an octave higher than the first. When Morrison suggested Yazoo and then Pee Dee, a river in South Carolina, Stephen declined both. He had already tried the latter in the first draft of his song, but decided against it, probably because a Boston publisher had put out a popular minstrel tune in 1844 called "Ole Pee Dee," and Foster was old enough to remember it. Morrison then explained that the right name turned up when he pulled an atlas from the top of his desk and pointed at the Suwanee. "That's it, that's it exactly!" Stephen exclaimed before he rushed back to draw a line through the word Pedee in his manuscript book and carefully write above it the unforgettable "Swanee."[12]

"Old Folks" was one of the composer's most successful songs, but throughout his life and even fifteen years after his death, Stephen Foster's name did not appear on the sheet music. On the title page of his most beloved plantation song, the name of a famous minstrel performer, Edwin Pearce Christy, appeared as composer. Foster was accustomed to having the name of the minstrel performer or his troupe printed on the cover, but never as composer. Even when he started working with minstrels in Cincinnati and wanted to remain anonymous, no one else's name was printed on the title page as composer. Various reasons have been suggested for Foster's decision to allow Christy to take credit for writing the song. Possibly, he was influenced by the editors of highbrow music journals who were in the habit of denigrating the minstrel genre, or he might have needed the money Christy paid him, since in 1851 he had a wife and child to support. Another possibility is that his wife or mother, or perhaps the composer himself, did not at that moment want the Foster name associated with blackface minstrelsy.

When and where Stephen and Christy were first introduced, or if they ever met in person, is not known. Stephen may have met the dapper, charismatic performer before he moved to Cincinnati, because the Christy Minstrels appeared in a concert in Pittsburgh late in October in 1846, when Stephen was boarding with his parents in the downtown section of the city. The *Pittsburgh Daily Commercial Journal* announced that the minstrel troupe would be giving a performance nearby on the third floor of the Old Odeon Theater, and the aspiring composer might have stopped by, watched the show, and introduced himself afterward. He could have brought Edwin or another minstrel one of the songs he had written for the Knights' Club and initiated the relationship that way. Another possibility is that Stephen met Christy later, on one of his travels to the East, perhaps on his honeymoon trip in 1850 when he visited his publishers in New York and Baltimore.[13] This is a good possibility because Foster's first songs with the Christy name on the title page—"Dolly Day," "Gwine to Run All Night," and "Angelina Baker"—were all published in Baltimore by F. D. Benteen, who was the first to designate them "Plantation Melodies."[14]

But whether or not they met personally, Stephen and Christy had already established a working relationship a few months before Stephen married and set off for New York. In his first extant letter to the minstrel dated February 23, 1850, Stephen enclosed copies of two of his latest songs and apologized "that the title-page had been ordered, and probably cut before I was informed of your desire that your name should not be used in connection with other bands." He then promised Christy to "have a new title page cut bearing the name of your band alone."[15] "Gwine to Run All Night" and "Dolly Day" were published with the words "Christy and Campbell Minstrels" on the top of the page, but the name "New Orleans Serenaders" was printed on the bottom. Foster's next song "Angelina Baker" came out "As sung by the Christy Minstrels," with no other name on the title page. (Later, Foster authorized the publisher to reissue "Gwine to Run All Night" with only the Christy name.)

Edwin P. Christy was a self-made entertainer with a true showman's talent. He was born in 1815 to a poor family in Philadelphia and spent his youth as a circus performer. Later, he played banjo and tambourine in local bar rooms and hotels in and around Buffalo until he had developed his technique sufficiently to organize and perform in his Christy Minstrels. In 1846 the new troupe opened in New York City at Mechanic's Hall on lower Broadway, having been fortunate enough to secure the space when the Ethiopian Serenaders left for a European tour and vacated the performance hall. The next year, Christy Minstrels had not only filled the void but had surpassed in popularity all the other minstrel troupes in the city. Christy was the dignified master of ceremony or "interlocutor," who sang sentimental plantation songs in a sweet voiced tenor, usually in burnt cork makeup, and bantered jokes back and forth with his appropriately named end men, "Brudder Tambo" and "Brudder Bones." He was surrounded by blackface minstrels who made up his chorus and played the fiddle, bones, tambourine, and banjo, or performed dances and comedic skits associated with the South.[16]

Christy put on a spectacular show that attracted a better clientele than the competition, and he drew crowds wherever he went. His ads read "organized in 1842, the Oldest Established Band in the World," although he was probably not the first to offer a full evening of entertainment with three acts, intermissions, and dozens of minstrels dancing and singing at once.[17] Most scholars believe the Virginia Minstrels initiated the first, large-cast, blackface productions in 1843, but Christy, whose performances were more refined and featured more sentimental songs, became "the unchallenged leader of his profession" and ended up leasing Mechanics Hall for a nearly ten-year run on Broadway.[18] While Stephen's songs were recognized far and wide, the Foster name was comparatively unknown, and he was thrilled to be in a working relationship with the famous minstrel. In a letter to Christy written on June 12, 1851 from Allegheny City, Stephen took great care in setting out the details of what would serve as an informal contract between the performer and the composer. The letter reveals the bare outlines of their future relationship.

Dear Sir:

I have just received a letter from Messrs. Firth, Pond & Co. stating that they have copy-righted a new song of mine ("Oh! Boys, carry me 'long") but will not be able to issue it for some little time yet owning to other engagements. This will give me time to send you the m.s. and allow you the privilege of singing it for at least two weeks, and probably a month before it is issued, or before any other band gets it (unless they catch it up from you.) If you will send me 10$ immediately for this privilege I pledge myself, as a gentleman of the old school, to give you the m.s. I have written to F. P. & Co. not to publish till they hear from me again. This song is sure to become popular, as I have taken great pains with it. If you accept my proposition I will make it a point to notify you hereafter when I have a new song and send you the m.s. on the same terms, reserving to myself in all cases the exclusive privilege of publishing. Thus it will become notorious that your band brings out all the new songs. You can state in the papers that the song was composed expressly for you. I make this proposition because I am sure of the song's popularity.[19]

Stephen had offered to supply the minstrel with fresh manuscripts at least two weeks before they were published, and he was grateful for the publicity that association with the big minstrel star practically guaranteed. He would send Christy copies of his newest songs to study, rehearse, and perform before they went to press and before "any other band" had the opportunity to debut them. Later, Christy paid Foster ten or fifteen dollars to be identified as the song's main performer and the words "As Sung by E. P. Christy" or "the Christy's Minstrels" were printed on the title pages. The Christy name appears as performer on the earliest editions of "Nelly Was a Lady," "Nelly Bly," "My Brother Gum," "Dolcy Jones," "Oh! Lemuel," "Dolly Day," "Angelina Baker," "Farewell, My Lilly Dear," "Massa's in de Cold Ground," "Old Dog Tray," and "Ellen Bayne."

Surprisingly, Christy's name does not appear on the title page of the very sympathetic "Oh! Boys, Carry Me 'Long." Apparently, in this case, the minstrel's ten dollars only purchased the privilege of singing the song before it was entered for copyright on June 24, 1851. Four days earlier, Stephen had given careful instructions to Christy about how the song should be sung, in a "pathetic, not a comic style."

Your favor of the 12th inst., inclosing ten dollars for the first privilege of singing "Oh! boys, carry me 'long" is received. Accept my thanks.

Herewith, I send you the m.s. according to agreement. I am not certain that you use a piano in your band; but I have arranged an accompaniment for that instrument at a venture. If you have a tenor voice in the company that can sing up to "g" with ease (which is probable) it will be better to sing the song in the key of "g." Thus you will not carry the bass voice quite so low. I hope that you will preserve the harmony in the chorus just as I have written it, and practice the song well before you bring it out. It is especially necessary that the person who sings the verses should know all the words perfectly, as the least hesitation in the singing will damn any song—but this you of course know as well as myself. Remember it should be sung in a pathetic, not a comic style. You will find the last three verses on another page of this letter. I regret that it is too late to have the name of your band on the title page, but I will endeavor to place it (alone) on future songs, and will cheerfully do anything else in my humble way to advance your interest.[20]

How much Foster's songs owed their success to being identified with Christy can only be estimated. There can be no doubt that having Christy perform the songs was beneficial, but publishing "Old Folks at Home" with the words "WRITTEN AND COMPOSED BY E. P. CHRISTY" on the title page was a poorly conceived decision.[21] Remorse and guilt plagued Stephen soon after because it was his own idea to sell Christy the right to be identified as the song's composer. As he later explained, it was his "intention" to omit his name from his "Ethiopian songs, owing to the prejudice against them by some," which, he thought, "might injure my reputation as a writer of another style of music."[22] To the real composer's dismay, "Old Folks at Home" became an immediate success with every class of people and continued to be published throughout Foster's life with the wrong name on the cover. Firth, Pond and Company knew who wrote the song and paid royalties to the right man, and over time they made sure the public knew the truth by ensuring that newspaper advertisements for any new Foster songs contained the headline, as "Composed by Stephen C. Foster, the author of Old Folks at Home." *The Musical World and New York Musical Times* also stood by him, informing their readers that "S. C. Foster is the author. . . . E. P. Christy probably bought the song and the right to be considered its author at the same time . . . but such things always come out sooner or later."[23]

A year after the ink was dry on the sheet music, Stephen continued to experience angst over his error in judgment because, as an artist, he needed to have his talents recognized. On May 25, 1852, he tried to rectify the situation when he wrote Christy a letter that is so business-like and straightforward that it sounds as if it were the handiwork of Morrison or another brother. With a determination in his voice that was unusual for the composer, he informed Christy that he had "concluded to reinstate my name on my songs and to pursue the Ethiopian business without fear or shame."[24]

> E. P. Christy, Esq.
> Dear Sir:
>   As I once intimated to you, I had the intention of omitting my name on my Ethiopian songs, owing to the prejudice against them by some, which might injure my reputation as a writer of another style of music, but I find that by my efforts I have done a great deal to build up a taste for the Ethiopian songs among refined people by making the words suitable to their taste, instead of the trashy and really offensive words which belong to some songs of that order. Therefore I have concluded to reinstate my name on my songs and to pursue the Ethiopian business without fear or shame and lend all my energies to making the business live; at the same time that I will wish to establish my name as the best Ethiopian song-writer. But I am not encouraged in undertaking this so long as "Old Folks at Home" stares me in the face with another's name on it. As it was at my own solicitation that you allowed your name to be placed on the song, I hope that the above reasons will be sufficient explanation for my desire to place my own name on it as author and composer, while at the same time I wish to leave the name of your band on the title page. This is a little matter of pride in myself which it will certainly be to your interest to encourage. On the receipt of your free consent to this proposition, I will if you wish, willingly refund you the money which you paid me on that song, though it may have been sent me for other considerations than the one in question, and I promise in addition to write you an opening chorus in my best style, free of charge, and in any other way in my power to advance your interests hereafter. I find that I cannot write at all unless I write for public approbation and get credit for what I write. As we may probably have

a good deal of business with each other in our lives, it is best to proceed on a sure basis of confidence and good understanding, therefore I hope you will appreciate an author's feelings in the case and deal with me with your usual fairness. Please answer immediately.[25]

> Very respectfully yours,
> Stephen C. Foster

This letter reveals several things about Foster and about the state of minstrelsy at midcentury. Foster had been ashamed to be associated with the minstrel genre, because the early minstrel songs were crude and musically uninspired, and as the composer himself said, "trashy." He had intended to write songs "of another style" that would appeal to the better classes, but the overwhelming success of "Old Folks at Home" among "refined people" convinced him that he could finally associate his name with Ethiopian songs without shame. By "making the words more suitable to their taste," Foster had indeed upgraded the genre, but Christy was also a popularizer of refined minstrelsy, and he may have felt that his interpretations of the songs and his presentations had as much to do with their success as the composer. Christy filled his programs with emotion-laden songs by Foster and others, since sentimentality accorded with the performer's notion of his particular brand of minstrelsy. Consequently, when Foster asked to be released from the agreement, Christy refused. On the back of the letter, he scribbled that Stephen "was mean and contemptible, and a vacillating skunk and plagiarist!"[26]

Stephen was so anxious to reverse the terms of the "Old Folks at Home" arrangement that he offered to return the money Christy had paid for the privilege of being known as the song's composer. Morrison claimed his brother received an impressive five hundred dollars, but a New York friend revealed that Stephen told him he sold out for a mere fifteen dollars.[27] But no matter how much money was involved, from the minstrel's perspective, Stephen was "a vacillating skunk." Two years earlier, Foster had told Christy, "I wish to unite with you in every effort to encourage a taste for this style of music so cried down by opera mongers."[28] One year later, when "Old Folks" was being published, he asked Christy to put his name on the cover as composer. And in 1852 Stephen flip-flopped once again and said he wanted to reverse the terms of the agreement.

By the time Stephen made his futile request, "Old Folks at Home" was being published all over the English-speaking world without the Foster name. In his handwritten manuscript book, to the side of the page on which he had written "Way down upon de old plantation," Foster scribbled lengthwise "Cramer, Beale, & Company Music publishers 201 Regent Street & 67 Conduit Street London." The large British company published "Old Folks" in 1851 as "Old Folks at Home, American Song, Arranged by D. Godfrey." No mention was made of Stephen Foster. A half dozen other London publishers came out with the song in the same year without mentioning Foster's name, although the Christy name was mentioned frequently and one British edition was published as "Composed and adapted by Herbert Linley," a name few heard of in America. If Stephen mailed "Old Folks at Home" to Cramer, Beale & Company with the idea that the London publisher would recognize him as the song's rightful composer and publish his name on the title page, he was setting himself up for disappointment.[29]

In spite of the damage Christy caused Stephen's ego, for several years Foster and the minstrel did have a special, if ill-fated, business relationship. They each had something that the other wanted. Edwin Christy staked his reputation on chaste, refined, emotional performances, and Stephen Foster was known for writing refined, sentimental minstrel songs that could bring the audience to tears. Stephen wrote the minstrel songs that appealed to a "refined" (read "well-heeled and paying") audience, and Christy knew how to perform them, culling the sentimentality in the song until it elicited the emotional experience that the public loved. Edwin Christy, the minstrel best known for performing refined, emotion-packed songs, and Stephen Foster, the composer best known for writing sentimental plantation songs, had a few productive years together. In the middle of the nineteenth century, the middle classes were coming into their own and were on their way to establishing their culture as the one to be emulated in America. Refinement, sentimentality, and avoidance of crude mannerisms were very important to these rising men and women, and Foster's songs as sung by Christy had those defining characteristics.

Even with burnt cork makeup, the Christy Minstrels made sure their image was refined.[30] Edwin Christy did not wear the heavy, black, masklike makeup worn by the performer Al Jolson, who left the area around his mouth unpainted and made his eyes appear bulging when he sang "Swanee River" in the 1920s. Promotional pictures of Christy and other performers of Foster's sentimental minstrelsy from the early 1850s show the actors looking like any other working-class men, except their complexions are darker. In the pictures, their entire faces are covered with the ash of burnt cork, but the makeup is not used to exaggerate and distort facial features the way minstrels did at the end of the nineteenth and in the early twentieth centuries. The minstrel Charles White, who sang Foster's "Nelly Was a Lady," went all out to portray onstage an image of a refined-looking black man that would measure up to the protagonist in the song. In every promotional picture, he wears only a light dusting of burnt cork, not grease paint, and looks like a decent man with whom white men and women could empathize. In one image, White is dressed up like an African American artist, holding a palette while painting a portrait. He was not crude or inhuman looking, like the Jim Crow character of earlier days or the grotesquely masked minstrels of the next century that inspired disgust and ridicule. When Christy and White sang sad sentimental minstrel songs, their stage personae had to reflect the sympathetic characters that their songs portrayed musically, so they adopted a sartorial style and made up their faces to look like refined, dark-skinned men who commanded sympathy, and to a limited degree, respect.[31]

In line with his refined physical appearance, Christy's advertisements promised "chaste performances" and comedy that was less crude than that of their competitors, which was sure to attract the "elite and fashionable in all the principal cities of the Union":

> Far famed and original band of Ethiopian Minstrels . . . whose unique and chaste performances have been patronized by the elite and fashionable in all the principal cities of the Union . . . respectfully announce that they will give a series of their popular and inimitable concerts, introducing a variety of entirely new songs, choruses, and burlesques. Admissions, 25 c.[32]

Edwin Christy was smart enough to know that he could draw women and the better-paying classes into his theater by adding refined, sentimental music in the parlor tradition to the "robust comedy, song, and dance" of the minstrel stage.[33] Of course, Christy himself helped bring in the women. He was good looking, with fine features and fair hair and eyes, and his persona, like Foster's, represented respectability. Soon, other minstrel troupes followed his example by refining and upgrading their shows. The Ethiopian Serenaders, for example, drew in a better class of audience by offering more sentimental songs and calling their minstrel shows "blackfaced concerts."[34]

Christy's personal attributes attracted the middle-class customers that made him more successful, but the inclusion of Foster's plantation songs gentrified his shows, because whatever Stephen wrote came across as sentimental and emotionally moving. *Lady's Godey's Book*, the preeminent nineteenth-century women's magazine and the revered guide to refined lifestyles, designated Foster's minstrel songs the benchmark to which all other minstrel songs should be compared, because of their gentility. This endorsement meant that his plantation songs were refined enough for feminine parlors, and it was acceptable for ladies to perform them at home.[35]

How minstrel music became an entertainment acceptable to the genteel classes was a development engineered to a large extent by the desire for greater profits. When Stephen wrote Christy that by his own "efforts" he had "done a great deal to build up a taste for the Ethiopian songs among refined people," he was only partially correct. Sentimental songs like Foster's had become commodities for which the new middle class would fork over hard-earned dollars as proof of their genteel status, and they purchased Foster's songs for the same reasons they purchased pianos and fine carpeting and furniture. Refined plantation songs like "Old Folks at Home" came about in part because the music publishers wanted to expand the audience for minstrel songs to include women of the cultured classes, who were the primary purchasers of sheet music. The pianos in their homes and the ability to play them, as well as the songs they chose to sing, were the credentials of superior social standing. When Foster wrote "Old Folks," although he was in the vanguard of the transformation, he might not have realized that minstrelsy was moving into the parlor and being refined in the process. Had he realized that fact, he might not have relinquished his name on the cover, but it is fairly certain that he understood what was happening when he asked Christy to restore his name as composer.

To successfully move minstrel songs into the parlor, the publishers and composers had to adapt their subject matter, words, sentiment, music, and covers to make them more attractive to the ladies. Foster's plantation songs reflected on appropriately sentimental subjects, like love, death, and loss and longing for the past—concepts that appealed to the women, but the slave dialect in the words had to be minimized and eventually removed to make them more acceptable to the middle class. The word "darky" replaced the more offensive term in the sheet music, and any words the parlor girls felt awkward singing or pronouncing were left out or replaced with words they were comfortable singing. Even the names of the songs were designed to appeal to the ladies, as when Foster gave his minstrel love songs two-part, female names like "Nelly Bly," "Dolly Day," and "Melinda May."[36]

Foster's plantation songs were readily welcome in the parlor. The song sheets were arranged for the piano, the instrument of choice for the ladies, with a vocal part and piano accompaniment, and the melody line was comfortable to sing, with just enough embellishments and octave interval leaps to be challenging and interesting to the educated singer, but not too difficult. The publishers also put out "Old Folks at Home Variations" for piano only (with no vocal line or words), which was suitable for dancing, as the variations were listed for "polka," "quadrille," and "hornpipe."[37] The more accomplished players enjoyed fast-paced minstrel tunes, but the sentimental, slower-tempo songs that drew out emotional responses were easy to sell to female buyers and formed the basis of the new plantation repertoire.

The choruses in the plantation songs were also changed to make them more considerate of the ladies. Foster's minstrel and plantation songs had three- or four-part choruses at the end of each verse, but they were originally written with male minstrels in mind. When "Lou'siana Belle" was published in 1847, the four-part chorus was listed top to bottom, "1st tenore, 2nd tenore, alto, Bass." "Dolly Day," published in 1850 and performed by Christy, read the same. But note the change in 1853 with "My Old Kentucky Home," a plantation song that easily found its way into the parlor. The four-part chorus top to bottom read, "tenor, 1st soprano (air), 2nd soprano, Bass," indicating the song could be sung by two men and two women.[38]

The sheet music covers for plantation songs also had to be redesigned to be accepted in the parlor, and that could mean featuring a respectable-looking, clean faced white minstrel star on the cover or veering away from representational art altogether. When Edwin Christy's portrait appeared on the title page of a minstrel song (not by Foster) in the 1840s, he was portrayed without makeup, hovering over five

or six elegantly attired, blackface minstrels seated in a classic pose holding their musical instruments. Foster's minstrel and plantation song
covers from the 1850s, however, often feature nothing but large, fancy
lettering that informs the purchaser of the song's title, the composer's
and publisher's names, and when pertinent, the name of the minstrel
performer.[39] In an effort to make the music covers more acceptable to
the ladies, title pages with decorative script only, or sketches of imaginary plantation scenes, replaced the five or six minstrels who were
featured on the sheet music covers in the previous decade. The change
seems to indicate that while the crude imagery of early minstrelsy was
unacceptable in the parlor, placing elegantly attired, dark-hued minstrels on the title page was going too far, suggesting that white women
were welcoming them into their homes.[40]

The care taken with the music covers of minstrel songs and the
amount of minstrel music published clearly indicate that the genre had
worked its way inside the home by the 1850s. But sentimental parlor
minstrelsy in turn influenced public performances. The theater impresarios took the same route as the music publishers, and although it is
difficult to say who came first, the results were the same. When the
impresarios realized that they could make more money putting on
shows that conformed to the tastes of the moneyed classes, they began
to put on more refined shows. In the early days of minstrelsy, theaters
catered to proletarian tastes and offered crude, one-man minstrel
shows. Dan Emmett of the Virginia Minstrels described the crude activities the men engaged in when watching a show at the Bowery Theater in the Jacksonian era of the early 1830s:

> When their mouths were not filled with tobacco and peanuts, they
> were shouting to each other at the top of their voices . . . . Their chief
> pastime between the acts, when not fighting, was to catch up a
> stranger or countryman, and toss him from hand to hand over their
> heads until forced from fatigue to resist.[41]

By the middle of the 1840s, the large minstrel show had taken over and
later in the decade, thanks in large part to Christy and Foster, featured
more refined acts and sentimental songs. The impresarios went along
with the change, even encouraging more refinement, because they noticed that crudeness was costing them their better customers. When the
middle classes were no longer willing to be seated in the same audience

with mechanics and laborers who were loud mouthed and displayed uncouth habits while watching the shows, they walked out and built their own theaters that offered more exclusive entertainments. Then the minstrel impresarios decided the best way to keep their patrons was to refine their programs and upgrade their buildings to appeal, not only to a better class of men, but also to their wives and children.

This was a novel idea. Before midcentury, the only women frequenting the theaters were prostitutes and actresses, who were often considered the same thing. But all that changed when entrepreneurs began to "redefine the theater as a place safe for mothers and children," and refinement and sentimentality became the new direction in minstrelsy.[42] By 1856, the playbill for one minstrel show announced a "new and magnificent TEMPLE OF AMUSEMENT IS NOW OPEN" at 444 Broadway. Actually the building was remodeled, not new, but the minstrel impresario promised "a place of Public Amusement Regardless of Labor or Expense, at once Elegant, Attractive, Spacious and Well Ventilated . . . . The Most Magnificent Place of Ethiopian Entertainment in the World."[43] The following year the *Spirit of the Times* reported that this same Christy and Wood's theater had "a marble facade and floors, pianos and brocade sofas in the foyer, magnificent chandeliers, and other luxuries comparable to those in the best theaters." The *Spirit* assured its readers that "the ladies will be enraptured with the new house, and indeed they appeared so last night." The major minstrel theaters in the city quickly followed by example, as did P. T. Barnum, who made an effort to upgrade his museum and circus. All underwent makeovers and refined their jokes, their music, their décor, and their performances, with profitable results.[44]

Although all classes of white men and women seemed to be rushing off to the minstrel shows, the same could not be said of African Americans, who attended the shows much less frequently. Rarely was a colored gallery mentioned in the minstrel playbills as was the case for other types of entertainment, and few contemporaries remembered seeing blacks in the audience.[45] Still, some of the minstrel shows were patronized by a racially mixed audience of urban workers who sat side by side and laughed at the same jokes.[46] The upper-class blacks did not like the shows, however. The black physician Martin Delany took up his pen "reproving in a very severe style (too severely we think)," according to the *Pennsylvania Freeman*, "not only the minstrels, but also the newspapers that praised their performances."[47] Frederick Douglass did not like minstrel performances either, but he did approve of Foster's plantation songs, recalling that free blacks and slaves sang them often. He thought they expressed sympathy for his race, which actually helped the cause, but he did not like to see the songs performed in blackface.[48]

As Edwin Christy was the foremost performer of refined sentimental minstrelsy, Stephen Foster was the preeminent composer in the same genre. Christy used refined language and sometimes sang without adopting the slave dialect, which minimized the barrier between the black stage persona and the white audience, and Foster's songs employed the tropes of the sentimental—longing, weeping, death, long ago—which created sympathy and evoked tearful emotional displays in the listeners. When Christy performed Foster's songs, they had to show sympathy for the slave's suffering, if they alluded to the slave at all.

Proslavery Southerners agreed. Some years later, when Christy's Minstrels ventured to Charleston, South Carolina, at the very inopportune moment just as Charleston seceded from the Union, the minstrels were greeted with such hostility that they were forced to run into hiding, barely escaping with their lives. Southerners regarded Christy's shows with Foster's songs as much too sympathetic to the slaves for their tastes. In Alabama, in July 1861, a few months after the Civil War broke out, the *Mobile Register and Advertiser* wrote glowingly of a new development, their own homegrown Confederate Minstrels who dressed up as slaves on the stage and spoke only words of regret about the threat to their peculiar institution.[49] According to the southern newspaper, the Confederate Minstrels showed "an entire absence of that abolition sort of songs which have been too long tolerated on the Southern Stage, where we hope never to hear [Foster's] 'Swanee River' or [B. R. Hanby's] 'Nelly Gray' again."[50]

10

SHIRAS AND THE ANTISLAVERY IMPULSE

When the sentimental minstrel songs Foster wrote and Christy sang worked the audience up to an emotional state that brought tears to the eyes, those watching and listening might be feeling sympathy for the black protagonists on the stage. The sight of suffering, even if only in a theatrical performance, was important to a society wrestling with the morality of slavery, ever since the philosopher Jeremy Bentham argued that the ability to suffer was the determining factor in deciding if "the greater part of the species under the denomination of slaves" ought to be enslaved.[1] When performed correctly, sentimental minstrel songs brought out the strongest emotions in the audience. Even William Makepeace Thackeray commented on a "minstrel with wool on his head, and an ultra-Ethiopian complexion, who performed a negro ballad that I confess moistened these spectacles in a most unexpected manner. . . . [A] vagabond with a corked face and a banjo sings a little song, strikes a wild note which sets the heart thrilling with happy pity."[2]

Stephen Foster was probably first introduced to the antislavery cause in Cincinnati, where everyone was talking and reading about slavery. After he returned to Allegheny, he heard about it even more when he renewed his friendship with his neighbor Charles Shiras, a man of a very similar mindset to the Cincinnati editor William Gallagher. A boyhood friend of Stephen and Morrison and a member of the Knights' club, Shiras had enjoyed musical evenings in Allegheny before he became a reformer and antislavery advocate. As an adult, he was infected with the optimism of the age, and became convinced that while there was "no panacea for social evils . . . the world will surely progress to a greatness which we cannot conceive."[3]

After Stephen moved back to Allegheny, he and Shiras rekindled their friendship. They had much in common, since both men were married with daughters and still lived at home with their mothers. When Stephen began to spend time at Shiras's mother's house, his friend worked to indoctrinate him with the antislavery message. Shiras was a reformer who had shown no talent for business. He lost most of his money on bad real estate investments and then turned to writing and publishing weekly newspapers.[4] *The Evening Day Book* was more literary in nature and may have served as a venue for Shiras's own poetry, but the *Albatross* was an abolitionist newspaper Shiras started in 1847, the same year he met William Lloyd Garrison and walked with him in the hills above Allegheny City, where secret conversations with the publisher of the *Liberator* inspired him to start his own newspaper.[5] The paper was short-lived, but it was later picked up and reinvented as *The Saturday Visiter* [sic] under the editorship of Jane Gray Swisshelm, Pittsburgh's own, resident, female abolitionist.[6]

Shiras's poetry championed the oppressed, whether white men whose spirits and bodies were broken in factories or black slaves who suffered the lash of the master. His best-known poems were the anti-slavery "Bloodhound's Song" and the labor manifesto "The Popular Credo" or, as it was more popularly known, "Dimes and Dollars." The Pittsburgh publisher W. H. Whitney included both in a collection of poems titled *The Redemption of Labor* published in 1852, the same year *Uncle Tom's Cabin* went to press, but the "Bloodhound's Song" also appeared in the antislavery *Bugle* in Ohio.[7] Shiras wrote the latter in October 1850, when he and "others were asking for the repeal (not nullification) of the notorious Fugitive Slave Law,"[8] and outraged citizens of Allegheny assembled in public rallies to denounce it.[9] In the "Bloodhound's Song," the poet exhorts his "brothers" to take note that the new Fugitive Slave Law has moved slave catching out of the South and onto the "the highways of the North."

> O brothers, awake! For the time has come
> To brighten the bloodhound's fame,
> They've opened a nobler field for us
> To follow our human game!
> We'll hunt no more in the Dismal Swamp,

> Where the snake and the wild beast hide;
> But we'll course on the highways of the North,
> Where the fields are fair and wide. [10]

For oppressed whites of the working classes, Shiras composed the pro-labor "Dimes and Dollars," a marvelous poem that appeals to those with "empty pockets" in any century. Stephen's wife Jane claimed that her husband set the poem to music, but the song was never published. [11]

> Dimes and Dollars! Dollars and Dimes!
> An empty pocket's the worst of crimes!
> If a man is down, give him a thrust
> Trample the beggar into the dust!
> Presumptuous poverty's quite appalling,
> Knock him over! Kick him for falling!
> If a man is up, Oh! Lift him higher
> Your soul's for sale, and here's a buyer! [12]

Music publishers may have turned down "Dimes and Dollars" because it was too radical and threatened to cause disturbances between capital and labor. Mid-century America, which witnessed the slavery issue bubble to the surface, also experienced embryonic labor struggles, especially in cities like Allegheny and Pittsburgh, where industry was growing and attracting workers who labored under less-than-fair conditions. [13]

Stephen Foster maintained a close relationship with Shiras from 1850 through 1853, the years he wrote his greatest plantation songs. These were also the years Shiras was involved with the abolition movement. Though underrepresented in the history books, the city at the three rivers made a less visible, but still vital, contribution to the antislavery cause. The local antislavery centers in Allegheny and Pittsburgh were easily accessible to Shiras by foot or carriage. He might have been introduced to the African American John Vashon, whose barber shop on Third Street in downtown Pittsburgh was a meeting ground for abolitionists. He also could have known Dr. McDowell's protégé Martin Delany, who published the antislavery *Mystery* on Third Avenue and Market Street, before he left for medical school. The most impressive abolitionist, and one Shiras was sure to know, was his wealthy neighbor Charles Avery, a former cotton merchant turned lay preacher who reportedly lectured at the Methodist Protestant Church next door to the Foster house. [14] The official story is that while Avery was on a cotton-buying expedition to the South, he was moved by the suffering of the slaves, experienced a religious awakening, and decided to devote his time and immense wealth to fight the slaveholders.[15]

In 1849, the year before Stephen moved back home from Cincinnati, Avery opened the Allegheny Institute and Mission Church on the corner of Nash and Avery Streets to advance the education of blacks. The three-story, brick building that housed the Institute featured a library and classrooms on the first floor for men and women to study everything from liberal arts to useful vocational trades. Runaway slaves were hidden in the basement of the building, which was rumored to be a stop on the Underground Railroad, where an old canal line served as a passageway to the Allegheny River that carried the refugees north on their journey to freedom. The top floor of the Mission Church was reserved for religious services, where not only sermons but also the rich voices of the students singing African American spirituals could be heard in the summer from the open windows.[16]

When considering the powerful emotion in Foster's plantation songs, it is natural to imagine that Stephen and George Shiras, who lived only a few blocks away, hung about outside the Mission Church or stepped inside just to listen to the music. Frederick Douglass described the slave songs as "the most pathetic sentiment in the most rapturous tone." He believed "the mere hearing of those songs would do more to express some minds with the horrible character of slavery, than the reading of whole volumes of philosophy on the subject could do."[17]

> They told a tale of woe that was then altogether beyond my feeble comprehension; they were tones loud, long, and deep; they breathed the prayer and complaint of souls boiling over with the bitterest anguish, every tone was a testimony against slavery, and a prayer to God for deliverance from chains. The hearing of those wild notes always depressed my spirit and filled me with spirit and felled me with ineffable sadness. I have frequently found myself in tears while hearing them . . . . To those songs I trace my first glimmering conception of the dehumanizing character of slavery . . . . The songs of the slave represent the sorrows of his heart, and he is relieved by its tears. At least such is my experience.[18]

Stephen allegedly spent "all his time" at Shiras's house when he was composing "Old Folks at Home," "Oh! Boys, Carry Me 'Long," and "My Old Kentucky Home," and Shiras's mother and daughter believed

Charles Shiras was very influential in the creation of these songs. His daughter Rebecca was only two at the time of her father's death, but she was told, probably by her mother, and believed that her father provided the words to several of Foster's compositions. When a reporter from the *Leader* interviewed her in 1879, she told him:

> I know that it ["Old Folks at Home"] was composed in this very house, between the years 1850 and 1852. My father and Foster were fast friends, the latter spending nearly all his time at our house. Foster would compose the music and my father the words, but in all cases Foster was forbidden in any way to attach my father's name to the songs, as father, or in fact, no one else at that time, considered them worth anything, and he would not allow his name to appear in connection with any such trash.[19]

Shiras's mother reaffirmed the idea: "I know my son wrote many of the songs and helped to write many more of the songs. Right in that front room yonder he and Stephen would sit night after night."[20]

Exactly how much Charles Shiras contributed to Stephen's plantation songs may never be known, but the conclusion drawn by the poet's nephew George Shiras III is reasonable: "The *Leader* interview as a whole gives the impression that Stephen Foster came often to the Shiras house over a period of years and that a good deal of work went on there. Thus it is at least possible to suppose that Stephen consulted or worked with Charles on the words for a number of the songs." Surely, Stephen's line from "My Old Kentucky Home," "They hunt no more for the possum and the coon, On the meadow, the hill and the shore" is reminiscent of Shiras's line from the "Bloodhound's Song," written three years earlier, "We'll hunt no more in the Dismal Swamp, Where the snake and the wild beast hide." More importantly, even if Shiras did not pen a single word in Foster's songs, it is possible to credit the poet with influencing the composer to look more sympathetically upon the antislavery cause, and as a result, to imbue his greatest plantation songs with a subtle antislavery trajectory. It is unlikely that the two "nice young men" could have spent very much time together without an exchange of ideas, and the sympathetic feeling in the songs suggests that Shiras gained the upper hand, at least for a while, in countering the influence of Foster's conservative Democratic family. Rebecca Shiras's assertion that "no one else at the time considered them [plantation

songs] worth anything" rings true considering that in 1851 Foster did
not want his own name to be associated with "Old Folks at Home."[21]

Morrison Foster, of course, denied that Shiras wrote the words to his
brother's songs. On February 14, 1886, he responded to a newspaper
article published in Chicago:

> The author of the article evidently knows nothing personally about
> what he writes. My brother Stephen C. Foster and myself, being
> nearly of the same age were intimately associated together from in-
> fancy until the time of his decease.
>
> I had personal cognizance of every song he ever wrote, at home. I
> mean in Allegheny County. His regular practice was to compose the
> music first, and then write the words afterwards, to suit the music. In
> writing the words his practice was to write a verse or two at a time,
> submitting them to me verse by verse for my opinion or to his moth-
> er, who possessed a fine poetic fancy. At rare intervals he wrote
> music to the words of others, but he always preferred to write his
> own words in order to harmonize them with the previously written
> music. Charles P. Shiras was an intimate friend of ours . . . . He and
> his mother lived on Hemlock Street Allegheny City in a two story
> brick house.[22]

Morrison believed that "Shiras' style of poetry was too heavy and som-
ber for Stephen's music." He said Stephen collaborated with Shiras on
only one published song, "Annie My Own Love," in which case Shiras's
name was printed as author of the words on the title page and Stephen
made sure that Shiras received half the royalty payments. Morrison also
contradicted the claim that Shiras had a piano in his mother's house
that his brother used, saying that "Stephen had his own piano at home
which he bought from H. Kleber & Bro. and on it practiced and composed." Finally, Morrison said of the songs the newspaper article attributed to Shiras, including "Old Folks at Home" and "My Old Kentucky
Home," "I personally and distinctly remember the writing of the words
of all of them by Stephen." Thus Morrison Foster, in the last years of his
life, closed off any suspicion regarding outside authorship or influence
on the words to Foster's famous planation songs.[23]

But Morrison could not deny that Charles Shiras influenced his
brother to become interested in the antislavery cause and to infuse his
plantation songs with antislavery messages. "Oh! Boys, Carry Me

'Long," published in 1851, bears a strong resemblance to a West Indian poem associated with the antislavery cause. Foster's song about a dying slave who is still cognizant enough to direct his own burial shows sympathy for the elderly slave who has lived beyond his years of usefulness. He tells his companions to "Carry me long, Carry me till I die, Carry me down to the burying ground, Massa, don't you cry." In his younger years, the protagonist in the song had "hoed the fields," planted the cotton and tobacco, and "minded the corn." Now he bids farewell to all, master and "boys," because there is "No use for me now."[24]

Foster's song is very similar to the Jamaican antislavery song or poem, "Carry Him Along," that was included in Matthew Gregory Lewis's *Journal of a West India Proprietor* and published in London in 1834, the year after Great Britain abolished slavery in Jamaica. Not only the titles, but the plots are also very similar. The Jamaican poem describes a pitiful situation in which strong, healthy slaves are directed to carry "Along" an old, worn-out slave to a "Gulley" where he will be left, still alive, to die. Then the master orders the board he is carried on and the frock he is wearing to be returned to be used again. In the West Indian poem the slave is objectified, as the title of the song is "Carry Him Along," whereas Foster's title, "Carry Me 'Long," gives more agency to the black protagonist. There are two voices in the West Indian song poem, for one voice commands, "Take him to the Gulley! But bringee back the frock and board." A second voice pleads, "Oh! Massa, massa! Me no deadee yet!" In Foster's song, the black protagonist is in charge and he is directing his own burial. But there is something eerie about the song, for the protagonist directs the "boys" to "Carry me til I die." That is, he implores them not to abandon him at the burying ground while he is still alive, which is what happened to the slave in the Jamaican poem.[25]

The similarity of "Oh! Boys, Carry Me 'Long" to the West Indian song-poem only confirms the legend that there was a connection between that song and the mixed-race, "bound," servant girl Olivia Pise who worked for the Fosters when Stephen was a child. Morrison Foster said "Oh! Boys" was influenced by strains of music Stephen heard at a "church of shouting colored people" when he was a child attending services with Olivia. Exactly which black church Foster would have attended with "the mulatto daughter of a French dancing master from the West Indies" is not known. An African Methodist Episcopal Church that burned down in Pittsburgh's Great Fire of 1845 was located on Front Street in the city's downtown. Olivia could have brought him to that church when the Fosters were boarding in the city. It is also possible that he accompanied her to a black church in Allegheny Town, since Olivia continued to work for the Fosters "from time to time" after they moved to Allegheny.[26] Olivia may have known these West Indian songs and sung them to Stephen when he was a child, but it seems more likely that he was inspired to write "Oh Boys! Carry Me 'Long" after he read the poem in Matthew Gregory Lewis's *Journal of a West India Proprietor*. Charles Shiras may have had a copy of the book and shown it to Foster, or the poem might have been reprinted in one of the abolitionist newspapers like the *National Era* or the *Liberator*, which Shiras certainly read.

Like the Jamaican poem, "Oh! Boys, Carry Me 'Long" dealt openly and directly with the burial of a slave, whereas Foster's other songs, even those that honored the dead, usually avoided the subject of burial altogether. Foster in 1851 did not envision a happy earthly future for the bondsmen. In "Oh! Boys," the dying slave sings out, "Dere's no more trouble for me; I's gwine to roam in a happy home, where all de niggas am free." Foster's family indicated that he was "decidedly fatalistic about the institution of slavery," regarding it "as an intolerable burden under which the black race stumbled helplessly and hopelessly."[27] He seemed to believe at the time he wrote the song that freedom for the slave would come only with death, an idea that was also expressed in many African American spirituals.

The antislavery message carried in "Oh! Boys, Carry me 'Long" is subtly expressed through its sentimentality and the sympathy it creates in the audience, but that was not always the case. For a brief time, in 1850 and 1851, Foster wrote minstrel songs that expressed a subversive message rather openly in the last verses of the songs. In each example, a slave disobeys his master and has to run away or is sold away. In some of the cases, the slave fights back. The timing for the songs was appropriate. The 1850 Fugitive Slave Act had just passed or was being discussed, permitting slave owners or catchers to come to the North, and with no proof, claim that any black man on a Northern street was his runaway slave, and force him back South. The slave catcher could even demand the assistance of any Northerner standing by.[28]

In "Oh! Lemuel," Foster's protagonist encouraged insubordination by urging the slaves to take the day off and stop working: "Go down to de cotton fields, and bring de boys away, go down and call de Nigga boys all, we'll work no more today." Lemuel himself has abandoned his work, "gone today to take de morning air," so that he can "make de fiddle hum, [and] . . . make de banjo tum." In "Angelina Baker," the protagonist "is left to weep a tear," because his beloved Angelina has spoken to the master about freedom, and was sent away as a consequence. In the next verse, we learn that "Angelina likes de boys" and "used to run old Massa round, to ax for him to free dem." In the fourth verse, the protagonist says "I ax for Angelina, And dey say she's gone away, I don't know wha to find her." Angelina was sold away because she harassed the master. Both "Oh! Lemuel" and "Angelina Baker" were published by F. D. Benteen of Baltimore, which is surprising because Baltimore was a very Southern city at the time.[29]

"Way Down in CA-I-RO," published by Firth, Pond and Company in 1850, has a similar message. Cairo is the southernmost city in Illinois and the juncture where the Ohio River meets the Mississippi. Anything south of Cairo is slavery; north of it is freedom. In this song the protagonist bemoans his fate, "Way down in Ca-i-ro dis Nigga's gwine to die." But he had accepted life philosophically until he crossed his master: "Sometimes de nigga's life is sad, sometimes his life is gay, when de work don't come too hard he's singing all de day." Because he wanted to impress "all de ladies in de land and all de genmen, too" when he played in the "darky band," he took his master's "'bran new coat to wear it to de ball." The result was predictable: he leaves his "true-lub" to weep while he is sold down river to Cairo.[30]

The last song, the one with the most subversive message, is "Ring de Banjo," published by Firth, Pond and Company in 1851 as a "New Ethiopian Melody." The song is filled with purposeful subterfuge and suggests violence. In the first verse, the protagonist says, "the darky never groans" and times are "nebber dreary" as long as he can play the banjo, piano, and the bones. In the third verse, the protagonist says his master set him free and he went to Kentucky, but he came back willingly and will never leave again. But in the fourth verse he tells another story, the meaning of which appears to be purposely confusing. The protagonist sings, "ob a lubly summer day, the master send me warning, he'd like to hear me play on de banjo lapping; I come wid dulcem strain, Massa fall a napping, he'll never wake again." In the fifth verse, the protagonist is on the go again. He tells his true love he has to leave "while de ribber's running high." What can we make of this? Did the slave kill his master? Or did the master simply die, and the slave took to the river because he no longer had a kindly master to care for him? Most interpretations favor the first scenario, that the protagonist in "Ring de Banjo" killed his master.[31]

"Ring de Banjo" had a lively catchy tune, but the song did not sell well. Perhaps the message was too confusing or dangerous for the times. The devoted "darky" comes back after being set free, but he returned only to murder his master.[32] Foster followed "Ring de Banjo" with "Oh Boys! Carry Me 'Long," which was just as antislavery, but Stephen had learned to use sentimentality to translate the messages that were hidden behind the burnt cork. Foster came into his own when he began writing sympathetic minstrel songs that offered cryptic messages of compassion. Foster never had to say anything himself, because his songs did and they had far greater reach than his personal voice. He had learned to keep his opinions to himself and let his inner voice be expressed through his music.

Foster's plantation songs built up an emotional response in the audience, but the composer never openly acknowledged a commitment to the antislavery cause.[33] He seemed to express himself best by creating emotion in the songs, and letting the emotion do the work. This was the original idea of the abolitionists, too. Harriet Beecher Stowe prayed that if her reader's eyes welled up with tears of sympathy, that would be enough to end slavery. William Lloyd Garrison was of the same opinion. He published *The Liberator* every day for over thirty years believing that slavery would end if he could just reach the hearts of the slaveholders. Perhaps Foster felt the same. Either because of his timidity in the face of his family or because he wanted to keep his political views private, he did not make an open commitment to antislavery, then or later.

Foster was not the only composer to write songs with an antislavery message that was supposed to work by making the audience feel sympathy. Benjamin R. Hanby, whose father was active in the Underground Railroad, wrote the tragic "Darling Nellie Gray" about a female slave sold away from her loved ones and her home. "The white man bound her with his chain," sang the broken-hearted, black lover. "They have taken her to Georgia for to wear her life away, As she toils in the cotton and the cane."[34] Similarly, "Mary Blane," "Cynthia Sue," and "Miss Lucy Neal" were songs about couples whose masters sold away a beloved spouse. In the last song, Lucy's lover stands up to protect her, crying out:

> Oh! Dars de white man coming, to tear you from my side
> Stan back! You white slave dealer, She is my betrothed bride.
> De poor nigger's fate is hard, De white man's heart is stone,
> Dey part poor nigga from his wife, And brake up dare happy home.[35]

Minstrel songs went through a series of developmental stages from 1843 through 1852 whereby they changed gradually from insulting songs to a more sentimental mode that was comparatively sympathetic to the plight of the slave.[36] Robert B. Winans characterized the development of minstrel songs during the years Foster contributed to the genre as a gradual shift toward a sentimental medium that offered compassion rather than ridicule. During the first stage, from 1843 through 1847, the comic song dominated and "at best, poked gentle fun at blacks, but more often heavy ridicule was involved." Foster's "Oh! Susanna!" on first glance fits into this category of comic minstrel music because of its nonsense lyrics and the description of "De buckwheat cake . . . in her mouf." "Uncle Ned" exhibits elements of both the comic and the sentimental, with his description of Ned as blind, toothless, and bald. Interestingly, the subtle disparagement in the song is not based on race, but on old age.[37] During the second stage from 1848 through 1852, when Stephen wrote his greatest plantation songs, more sad, sentimental, even tragic, love songs were introduced into the minstrel shows, which influenced minstrelsy to become, for a few years at least, more compassionate in its portrayal of blacks. The most repeated story in the sad songs being introduced followed the outline of "Nelly Was a Lady," that of "a black man grieving at the death of his mate, with the black characters, especially the women, given sympathetic treatment."[38]

Foster wrote songs about slaves, but he had rarely, if ever, seen any. In Pennsylvania and Cincinnati he saw free blacks, but a trip South in 1852 gave him the opportunity to see enslaved men at their labors and inspired him to write a song that in its original incarnation was open and obvious about its antislavery sentiment. After Dunning Foster left the commission agency in Cincinnati, he bought his own steamboat called the *James Millingar* and started a business that kept him on the water all the time, transporting passengers and cargo between Cincinnati and New Orleans. In February 1852, he offered to take Stephen, his family, and some old friends down the Ohio and Mississippi rivers to New Orleans and then back to Pittsburgh. Stephen and Jane, already experiencing strains in their marriage of less than two years, may have viewed the trip as a good chance to rekindle the sparks in the relationship. Susan Pentland Robinson and the Lightner girls—Julia the soprano and Jessie the contralto—were also on board the steamer, and the sisters charmed the passengers singing duets of "Wilt Thou Be Gone, Love?" and "Old Folks at Home." Strangely enough, Richard Cowan, Morrison's friend and Stephen's competitor in the suit for Jane's hand, was aboard, too. We have to wonder what, if anything, this man's presence meant to the sensitive Stephen, whether it caused him to feel insecure or jealous. Something upset him on the trip. Stephen was an "inveterate smoker," according to Susan Pentland Robinson, and one evening on the boat he "suffered a coughing spell that almost choked him to death." He may have had an asthmatic condition that was aggravated by the smoke, but emotional stress could have triggered it, too. According to family lore, he was saved by the Irish nurse who brought out the stereotypical pot of steaming potato water, which cleared his lungs and allowed him to breathe.[39]

With Stephen recovered, the *James Millingar* moved slowly south along the majestic Mississippi, stopping along the way at different Southern ports. When they reached New Orleans, Dunning turned the boat around and brought his passengers back to Cincinnati, where he transferred them to the *Allegheny*, a new boat that carried them all back to Pittsburgh on March 21, 1852. Everyone had a great time, but more importantly, the cruise might have influenced Stephen's musical development. It was the only time as an adult that he traveled south, and the views that he saw aboard the steamboat, or that greeted him if and when he got off the boat, supposedly became distilled in the Southern imagery in his famous plantation songs. Richard Cowan suggested that the Southern flavor in Foster's songs came from observing the South at a distance from the deck of the *James Millingar*. "When we reach'd the warm latitudes," he said, "we used to sit on deck to enjoy the moonlight and the sight of the negroes burning brush and cotton stalks at the plantations."[40]

When Foster returned from the trip, he wrote his next great plantation song, "My Old Kentucky Home." Because of this, some scholars
concluded that on this trip he stopped off at Federal Hill in Bardstown,
Kentucky, the house that became identified with the name of a song,
but that would have involved getting off the boat and taking a carriage
ride some miles inland. If the visit did take place, it inspired him to
write the Kentucky song from a different perspective and with a different purpose. After spending the two previous years in the company of
his abolitionist friend Charles Shiras, the scenes Stephen saw of slavery
on this river trip, or at Federal Hill, may have convinced him to turn an
interested eye toward Harriet Beecher Stowe's just published novel and
to feel compassion for all the worn-out slaves he saw laboring under the
setting sun.

"My Old Kentucky Home" was a song with documented antislavery
antecedents. Even if this is not apparent in the published version, Foster's handwritten manuscript book, in which he wrote out the words to
most of his songs from 1851 until he moved to New York in 1860, shows
that "My Old Kentucky Home, Good Night" was modeled after the
characters in *Uncle Tom's Cabin*. In the manuscript, Stephen ended the
original version of the chorus with the line "Poor Uncle Tom, Good
Night," rather than the well-known "My Old Kentucky Home, Good
Night." Harriet Beecher Stowe's novel reached the public in book form
in March 1852, the same year but months before the song was published. (The book was serialized in the abolitionist *National Era* the year
before that.) Considering the date it was written and the evidence in
Foster's own handwriting, there is no denying that "My Old Kentucky
Home" was inspired by the famous antislavery novel.[41]

Exactly why Foster changed the words is not known. He may have
felt pressured by his brother Morrison to avoid openly associating his
music with the abolitionist crusade, or as an artist, he may have wanted
to stay on neutral ground. The book was an enormous success, and
Uncle Tom songs, poems, and plays were flying off the presses everywhere. The songs were sold as sheet music, used in minstrel skits, and
interpolated in theatrical adaptations of the novel. So prolific were they
that they became almost a genre and included instrumental pieces as
well as songs. But Uncle Tom songs did not last as long as the novel, nor
did they live on the way "My Old Kentucky Home" did. At any rate,

Stephen demonstrated sound artistic judgment when he changed the words and title to something that would have more universal appeal. [42]

The theme of "My Old Kentucky Home" is separation of loved ones, and as in *Uncle Tom's Cabin,* the separation was caused by the slave system. Whites could identify with suffering caused by family breakups, because it was an experience many had undergone, whereas enslavement appeared to upset very few. When the song's protagonist cries out, "The time has come when the darkies have to part," Foster predicted a hopeless future: "No matter 'twill never be light." Death, not freedom, would bring an end to Uncle Tom's troubles in the song, just as it did in the novel. [43]

In Stowe's book, Uncle Tom was sold to the wicked Simon Legree, because even good plantation masters fell into financial difficulties or died. After the kindly Augustine St. Clare was killed in a knife fight, his heartless widow sold Tom away from his family and his home in Kentucky. Stowe realized her crusade would be more successful if she damned the slave system rather than the slave masters and Foster appeared to follow same line of thinking: "Tis summer, the darkies are gay" tells us that the slaves could be contented when the family was left intact and food was plentiful, when "the corn top's ripe" and "the young folk roll on the little cabin floor." As it was with the Fosters in their early home the White Cottage, "All [was] merry, all happy and bright" until "Hard Times comes a knocking at the Door." Foster would deal with hard times for the white, working classes a few years later in a song inspired by Charles Dickens's novel with a similar sounding title. "My Old Kentucky Home" and "Hard Times, Come Again No More" have similarities, though. Each has at its root an economic system that is responsible for the suffering of the oppressed—slavery for blacks and laissez faire capitalism for whites.

The most troubling part of "My Old Kentucky Home" is the chorus, which somehow seems out of sync with the rest of the song:

> Weep no more, my lady,
> Oh! Weep no more today!
> We will sing one song for the Old Kentucky Home,
> for the Old Kentucky Home, far away.

Before the song's association with Stowe's *Uncle Tom's Cabin* was readily acknowledged, the Rowan family claimed that the Federal Hill house that Charlotte Foster visited shortly before she died was the inspiration for the song. No documents exist to support the legend that Stephen ever stopped at Federal Hill, although Morrison Foster said that his brother was a "frequent visitor" at the plantation. Still, it is possible that Charlotte's visit to the house did inspire Stephen to write the song, but in a far more ghastly way than imagined.

On August 25, 1852, George W. Barclay of Kentucky notified his Foster cousins that they would have to make arrangements to have their eldest daughter's remains "removed and deposited in some suitable resting place." Charlotte lay buried in the Bullitt Cemetery in Louisville for twenty-three years, but now the city was taking over the burial site and using it to build houses. On September 5, Morrison was in Kentucky to retrieve his sister's body and on September 11, Charlotte was reinterred in the new Allegheny Cemetery near the old White Cottage in Lawrenceville. The removal and reburial of her beloved daughter would have brought torrential tears to Eliza, who was given a clipped lock of Charlotte's red-golden hair to preserve as a memento. Stephen was at the dock with his brother Henry on September 10 to meet Morrison and Dunning when their sister's body arrived in Pittsburgh, and he must have conflated the loss of Charlotte long ago with the sorrow expressed in the "Old Kentucky Home" song. Even the proximity of the dates of Charlotte's reinterment and the song's composition reinforces this notion. On January 15, 1853, Firth, Pond and Company advertised "My Old Kentucky Home" as "just published," but the song is believed to have been composed the previous fall. Stephen may have inserted the lines in the chorus, "Weep no more, my Lady" to help his mother finally say "good night" to her long lost daughter and Kentucky. [44]

Stephen may have been saying good night to minstrel songs in general when he published "My Old Kentucky Home," because that was to be the last minstrel-type song he published for seven years. In the summer of 1853, Stephen left Allegheny for New York to work for Firth and Pond arranging an anthology of parlor music. Somehow in between office duties, he found time to write the very popular "Old Dog Tray" and two other parlor songs, "Old Memories" and "Little Ella," which were not so successful, but he still would not write a note in the minstrel tradition. Instead, in the fall of 1853, he returned to Pittsburgh to work on a different type of music altogether. Stephen and Charles Shiras collaborated on what was called a "grand musical spectacle," *The*

Invisible Prince, or the War of the Amazons, a play with music and costumes, suggestive of the musicals that would became prominent in the next century. Stephen wrote the music for an original libretto by Charles Shiras based on the well-known fairytale *Le Prince Lutin* by the seventeenth-century writer Marie-Catherine D'Aulnoy.

The really curious question is how Stephen and his friend became interested in putting on a fairy spectacle in Pittsburgh. *The Invisible Prince, or the Island of Tranquil Delights*, based on the same fairytale with a libretto by James Robinson Planché, the author of twenty-three fairy spectacles, had debuted in England in 1846, and played briefly at the Park Theater in New York the following year. Stephen may have heard about Planché's fairy spectacle when he stopped by the office of the *Musical World and New York Musical Times* in January 1853 and the editor encouraged him to "turn his attention to the production of a higher kind of music."[45] But it is more likely that the manager of the playhouse who presented the show in Pittsburgh came up with the idea.[46] Joseph C. Foster, who was unrelated to the composer with the same surname, managed the stock company that presented Stephen and Shiras's musical at the Foster Theater in their hometown. Joseph would have known about the *Invisible Prince* that opened in England, but he probably decided he wanted to produce his own version with an original libretto by a local poet and music by a local composer. Hence, the theatrical manager probably made the proposition to Shiras and Foster that they collaborate on a fairy spectacle and present it in Pittsburgh. Stephen collaborated well with his friend Charles, however much his brother Morrison denied the fact, and it is easy to imagine the two enjoying themselves while they worked with a flamboyant group of theatrical people on a musical play. We usually think of Stephen confined to a little downtown office space or sitting alone in his piano room on the top floor of his Allegheny house, writing the words and adjusting the melody line to fit. But here we can imagine him not only as a composer, but actively involved in staging, costuming, and directing the glitzy, multifaceted, musical production. Stephen loved theater, and his daughter Marion said that as a child he took her with him to the theater whenever he could.[47]

The Invisible Prince played seven times from November 5 through November 11, 1853, at Foster's Theater. The manager must have had faith in the reputation of the librettist and the composer, however, because he put money into staging and advertising, and the local news-papers reported favorably on the show. On November 9, the *Pittsburgh Post* said the play would be produced "in a style of splendor for which manager Foster is so noted. No expense has been spared in the scenery, decorations, etc. necessary to the proper production of the play. The well-known talent of Mr. Shiras and the admitted power of Mr. Foster as a composer form a sure guarantee that the play will be worth seeing." Joseph Foster used "all the actors and actresses connected with the theater" and brought in extras to play "soldiers, citizens, courtiers, Ama-zons, and Fairies," although the main fairy was played by Mrs. Foster, the manager's wife.[48]

Neither the words nor the music to the *Invisible Prince* was pre-served or published, as the trend in the early days of musical theater was for the music directors to work from manuscripts only. The No-vember 5, 1853, *Pittsburgh Post* said, "S. C. Foster, Esq., we under-stand, contributes the musical portion of the piece," and the *Evening Chronicle* of November 7 said the show had "music by another gifted son of old Pittsburgh, Stephen C. Foster," but none of the newspapers made a definite comment on the compositions. Jane Foster believed her husband set "Dollars and Dimes" to music at this time and used it on the night of November 11, when the performance was given as a benefit concert for Shiras and all proceeds were allocated to the sickly poet. Shiras was suffering from "consumption" and needed money for the support of his daughter and soon-to-be-widowed young wife. The Knights of the Square Table, truly a brotherhood, worked diligently to sell as many tickets as they could at fifty cents apiece since the money was to benefit one of their own. The show "turned out admirable," according to the newspaper accounts, especially considering that the composer and the lyricist were novices in this type of production.[49]

Almost immediately after Foster's musical spectacle closed, *Uncle Tom's Cabin* opened on November 17, 1853, also at the Foster Theatre. Hoping to avoid any negative comparisons to the National Theater's New York production, Joseph Foster brought over additional actors from his Cleveland theater and incorporated Stephen's sympathetic plantation songs, "Old Folks at Home," "My Old Kentucky Home," "Massa in the Cold Ground," and "Lilly Dale" into the show. Stephen was kept busy during rehearsals ensuring that his songs were performed with the right amount of pathos, knowing full well that they would now be associated with the antislavery cause. Whether or not the newspaper notice was propaganda, the Pittsburgh *Dispatch* on November 22, 1853, urged the public to visit the performance "before Judge Grier issues his injunction against its further performance." Apparently the play, augmented by Stephen's sorrowful plantation songs, was thought powerful enough "to stir up sympathy for the negro slaves, give offense to the people of the South, and bring into disrepute the institution of slavery."[50]

Uncle Tom's Cabin had a very successful two weeks' run in Pittsburgh when it closed on December 2, 1853, to much acclaim. The play continued to travel throughout the North, reaching tens of thousands of people and spreading its antislavery message, but the story was more effective as an antislavery tool when Foster's songs were included. As Dale Cockrell wrote, "If, as Lincoln suggested, *Uncle Tom's Cabin* was the cause of the Civil War, it was Stephen Foster who got everyone singing, in chorus, a strongly voiced refrain of support for that cause."[51] Ironically, the dramatized version was said to look like a minstrel show, albeit a sympathetic one. "Plantation scenes were as ubiquitous in *Uncle Tom's Cabin* as they were in minstrel shows," one musicologist noted, and the slave auction scene where the slaves were supposed to demonstrate their abilities by dancing and singing and playing the banjo, "looked like the olio section of the minstrel show."[52]

Uncle Tom's Cabin must have influenced Foster, because he abandoned minstrelsy after he worked on Stowe's musical play at the end of 1853, and did not return to the genre for seven years. There were many reasons for his decision, including what he learned from the abolitionist theatrical production, but world events came into play as well. According to more than one authority, the year he published his last minstrel or plantation song, was the last year that minstrel shows presented a sympathetic portrayal of blacks. "The gentle, lyric plantation song was to endure for scarcely more than a decade," wrote the music historian Charles Hamm. "In the years immediately preceding the Civil War, the minstrel song became strident" and abandoned its more sympathetic treatment of blacks that was a defining characteristic of Foster's sentimental minstrelsy.[53] If minstrel shows had been "sensitive to charges that slavery was brutal, oppressive and undemocratic," all that changed as the theater managers attempted to cater to the whims of their audience, who were looking for scapegoats on which to pin the problems of the rapidly disintegrating nation.[54] Rather than blame the chaos on slavery, the minstrels allowed the audience to vent their anger on the faux slaves on the minstrel stage, where they "eliminated all but the most servile and disparaging images of blacks from their shows." When slavery appeared to threaten the union, the minstrels ceased making objections to the institution and presented instead caricatures of contented Southern slaves and unhappy, black, urban dandies. The historian Mel Watkins wrote:[55]

> From about 1853 to the Civil War, then, nearly all vestiges of black humanity were excised from minstrel performances. During this period the portrait of the plantation was made even more idyllic, and the stereotype of black males as childlike, shiftless, irresponsible dolts was heightened. Freed blacks, in particular, came under pointed attack. They were invariably pictured as inept, hopelessly inadequate souls, who longed for the guidance of white men and the security of the "ole plantation," or, perhaps worse, as arrogant, near-bestial reprobates who, with disastrous consequences, foolishly took on "white" airs and lusted after white women. The comic, degrading image of blacks had almost reached its peak. America's most popular entertainment form had become a forum in which white performers posing as blacks actively lobbied for the continuation of slavery by presenting degrading, consciously distorted comic stereotypes intended to "prove" that slavery and black subordination were justified, or even more insidiously, to demonstrate that blacks actually preferred serfdom.[56]

A disease seemed to sweep across Europe and America in 1853, infecting the minds of even the most educated of men. In that year, one of the scientific racists, a Frenchman named Arthur Gobineau, published his *Essay on the Inequality of the Human Races*, an astounding treatise in French, which postulated that all men were not created equal, overturning everything Jefferson and the founding fathers had stood for. Gobineau's ideas only reinforced Alabamian Josiah Nott's theory of polygenesis, which said blacks were created as a separate species from whites, an idea many Southern slaveholders had been advancing for years.[57] The next year, the Kansas-Nebraska Act said men have a right to choose to enslave other men, and a mini–civil war erupted in what came to be called "bleeding Kansas." This was also the year that Nott's bestselling book *Types of Mankind* came off the press arguing that race is everything and that the "negro achieves his greatest perfection . . . in a state of slavery."[58]

Other reasons to stand clear of minstrelsy were that Edwin Christy, Stephen's one-time collaborator and nemesis, retired from the stage in 1854 at the age of thirty-nine, some said partially mad.[59] Even if the minstrel made him seethe with anger over "Old Folks," at least he projected the message of compassion Stephen wanted in his songs. He was replaced by George Christy, a younger man who adopted the Christy name and continued the Christy Minstrels, but presented a far less sympathetic portrayal of blacks than had his predecessor. When George Christy put on a skit based on *Uncle Tom's Cabin, or Life among the Lowly*, he burlesqued it as *Life among the Happy* and made the tragic Tom figure "more worthy of laughter than humanistic concern."[60] Stephen wrote no new songs for George Christy, although the minstrel continued to sing "Old Folks at Home" without crediting the composer on either the playbill or the songsters that he sold in the theater lobby.[61] Of course, George may have felt that he had proprietary rights to the song since Edwin Christy's name still appeared as composer on the title page, and minstrels did not pay royalties for performance rights anyway.

Foster did not write new minstrel songs during these years of increased racial denigration, but his old songs were not deleted from the minstrel repertoire and the manner and performance style of the minstrel actors may have altered the original sentiment in the songs. When "Old Folks," or any of his other sentimental plantation songs, was performed on the stage after 1853, they may not have been sung with the same amount of pathos Stephen had intended, and the tragic sentiment may have been perverted into satire and sarcasm. With no way of knowing if the style or even the lyrics were changed and used to denigrate rather than empathize, Stephen chose to take a definite break from the genre in the explosive years leading up to the Civil War.[62]

Foster also had personal reasons to avoid minstrelsy. Even if plantation songs with a sympathetic agenda had not fallen out of fashion, Foster no longer had anyone to inspire him to write the songs that carried messages of compassion. If he still wanted to compose songs with an antislavery trajectory, he had to write them on his own because his friend and mentor Charles Shiras was dead. The kind-hearted abolitionist poet, just thirty years of age, succumbed to tuberculosis on July 26, 1854, the same year the minstrel stage became more denigrating to blacks. Foster put minstrelsy aside and turned his attentions to parlor songs. He would not produce another minstrel song until 1860, and then he would write only a few. [63]

11

PIANO GIRLS AND PARLOR SONGS

After Stephen stopped writing minstrel songs, he turned his talents to the production of refined songs that had nothing to do with minstrels, the South, or "darky" dialect. These so-called parlor songs would be performed by amateur musicians in their homes and included such musical gems as "Come with Thy Sweet Voice Again," "Maggie by My Side," "Ah! May the Red Rose Live Alway!," "Molly, Do You Love Me?," and "Sweetly She Sleeps My Alice Fair." The songs included solos and duets, and they discoursed on sensitive topics that struck a meaningful chord in the years a few historians have called "the sentimental age." Some were musical expressions of lighthearted love set to poetry that emphasized nature's elements, like flowers, song birds, moon light, and beauty both earthly and celestial. Others were darker, poignant testaments to regret, loss, and death. From 1853 through 1859, Foster devoted himself exclusively to the production of these genteel songs for the parlor, avoiding any connection to minstrel or plantation songs whatsoever.

Morrison Foster said his brother Stephen's "poetic fancy ran rather to sentimental songs," but the decision to put minstrelsy on the shelf had specific ramifications that Morrison did not discuss. Exclusive devotion to parlor songs removed him from the realm of the masculine to the sphere of the feminine, from the raucous to the genteel, and from a pseudo-black public stage to the private stage of the white middle class. In other words, Foster moved back to the familiar musical space of the home parlor, where he had heard sentimental songs performed throughout his life. If he were too young to remember Charlotte's plaintive tones, he heard many of the same songs when his sisters Ann Eliza and Henrietta played them on the piano or guitar, and of course, the girls at his youthful musical club in Allegheny and his neighbor Susan Pentland were experts at sentimental songs.

Foster's decision to write parlor songs exclusively was probably cemented by the attitude of the New York music critics and editors, who openly denigrated his plantation songs, no matter how much the public loved them. In spite of the phenomenal success of "My Old Kentucky Home," when the singer Anna Zerr included it on her concert program in 1853, one critic compared the soprano's music selection to "picking up an apple core on the street." Of these formidable critics, the one with the most influence on Stephen was probably the editor of the *Musical World and New York Musical Times*—most likely Richard Storrs Willis. A composer himself, Willis had studied in Germany, claimed Mendelssohn as a friend, and had recently written the melody for the Christmas favorite "It Came upon a Midnight Clear."[1] On January 29, 1853, just two weeks after "My Old Kentucky Home" came off the press, the music editor publicly deplored Foster's propensity for writing Ethiopian melodies and expressed the opinion in his paper that the song writer should devote his talents to a higher class of music. When Foster met the editor in person at his office in New York, he assured him that henceforth he intended to write "White men's music."[2]

> Mr. Foster possesses more than ordinary abilities as a composer; we hope he will soon realize enough from his Ethiopian melodies to enable him to afford to drop them and turn his attention to the production of a higher kind of music. Much of his music is now excellent, but being wedded to negro idioms it is, of course, discarded, by many who would otherwise gladly welcome it to their pianos. We were glad to learn from Mr. F. that he intends to devote himself principally hereafter to the production of "White men's music."[3]

Between the lines, the writer even suggested that "Mr. F." would make more money with parlor songs, because they would be welcomed "to their pianos" by a better class of people. In his decision to abandon the "negro idioms," Foster had to consider economics. Even if sentimental

songs that focused on love and dying maidens were not always his
biggest sellers, perhaps they would be more profitable in the long run
when sold directly to the public, thereby bypassing the minstrels. In
addition, parlor songs sold as sheet music were protected by copyright
and provided royalties, and they had a growing market among the people with money. But it was a risky business. No composer before Foster
had earned his living solely on sheet music sales. Songwriters were
either publishers or entertainers, or they depended on another line of
work. Even Henry Russell, whose compositions sold phenomenally well
in America, made his living performing the songs he wrote.[4]

Foster's parlor songs would be purchased mainly by the so-called
"piano girls" who spent hours every day developing just enough skill at
the keyboard to dazzle friends and family. The famous music critic
James Huneker coined the term for these proficient home performers
at the end of the century,[5] and so popular was their image in the nineteenth century that they became icons in ladies' fiction, appearing in
the novels of Jane Austen, William Makepeace Thackeray, and Louisa
May Alcott. Literature was filled with piano girls, some sympathetic
creatures like Beth March from *Little Women*, but also more conniving
characters like Becky Sharp from *Vanity Fair* and Jane Fairfax from
Emma who tried to use their musical skills to marry well and improve
their social status. Most of the young ladies belonged at least to the
middle classes, because only they could afford the pricey square pianos,
music lessons two or three times a week, and costly sheet music with
elaborate lithographs on the cover. Foster's song sheets ranged in price
from 25 to 38 cents, too high for the average working-man's daughter.
Because of their expense, the individual song sheets were bound in
leather volumes, with the owner's name engraved in gold tool on the
cover. In this way, the girls ensured that their music would endure years
of practice and performance, and even be handed down to their own
daughters.[6]

The piano girls were crucial to Stephen Foster's success as a popular
song composer, and were some of the most important disseminators of
his music around the country and even abroad. Before the invention of
the radio or recordings, a woman's parlor performances from sheet
music comprised an important means of bringing music and culture
into the home. The young lady was often in her teens, as once she
married and had children of her own, she did not have the time to

devote to music practice. Nonetheless, she was expected to entertain the family and pass on the tradition, seeing to it that her own daughters mastered a certain proficiency in the musical arts. These ladies were prized for their hard-earned accomplishments, which included painting and drawing, embroidery, and language arts, in addition to music. Demonstrations of their talents turned them into decorative proof of the family's social status, and they were responsible for popularizing many of Foster's songs. John Mahon, Stephen's New York friend in later years, claimed he heard "Oh! Susanna" and "Uncle Ned" in 1852 "in Patras, Greece . . . brought there by the family of an English sea captain." We can presume it was the daughters of the sea captain who performed them for Mr. Mahon, which shows that Foster's minstrel songs were being sung by the ladies even in far-off parlors.[7]

One of the primary reasons musical skills were encouraged in young women—in addition to their status enhancing ability—was the belief many mothers held that skill at the piano or the vocal arts would make their daughters more successful in the marriage game—that is, in securing a wealthy and pedigreed husband. Few women questioned the point of forcing girls into the drudgery of daily tedious music practice: "Would not you, as a good mother, consent to have your daughter turned into an automaton for eight hours in every day for fifteen years?" The good mother answered without hesitation: "I would give anything to have my daughter play better than anyone in England. What a distinction! She might get into the first circles in London! She would want neither beauty nor fortune to recommend her! She would be a match for any man who had a taste for music."[8]

An entire business developed as a result of this "frenzy for accomplishments." Families scrimped on necessities to put money away for "fine-toned" pianos, music lessons, and sheet music. Before they were manufactured in the West, pianos were hauled over the mountains to Pittsburgh with great difficulty and expense. By the 1830s, steam-driven presses turned out sheet music in large enough quantities to satisfy the growing demand for the product, and lithography graced the covers of the songs with appropriately sentimental pictures. Young women also required lessons in the instrument of their choice, usually the piano and harp that Charlotte Foster played, or the guitar, favored by her sister Henrietta. Vocal training was also mandatory. Families with money could send their daughters to exclusive female seminaries to acquire these accomplishments, where at the end of the year, the young ladies made a demonstration of their newly acquired skills on musical instruments bedecked with flowers. Those with restricted funds could send their daughters to the informal music schools that operated in the back room of the teacher's house, where two lessons per week for a term of three months was a standard schedule.[9]

That "accomplishments" made a woman marriageable in the nineteenth century is open to debate, but the belief was firmly entrenched in the middle classes and in Eliza Foster's world view. She probably would have concurred with the woman who said, "A young lady is nobody, and nothing without accomplishments; they are as necessary to her as a fortune . . . . Next to beauty, they are the best tickets of admission into society."[10] Eliza relayed a story in her journal about one Mary O'Hara of Pittsburgh who impressed an exceptional suitor through her musical skills, but the story does not prove that accomplishments equaled wealth in the marriage game. A schoolmate of Charlotte Foster's, Mary is known today as the mother of Mary Croghan Schenley, the woman who donated the three hundred acres that were turned into Schenley Park a few miles east of downtown Pittsburgh. Eliza described the competitive courtship that brought Mary O'Hara together with the wealthy Kentuckian William Croghan, the man who called on Charlotte but did not call again. Mary was visiting relatives in Philadelphia when she was introduced to Mr. Croghan, who had come north on business. The scene around the piano involved two suitors:

> Miss O'Hara was in the midst of another song, when the bell rang and Mr. Croghan made his appearance . . . . He remained perfectly quiet until she had completed her song when after saluting her, he observed "Will you have the goodness to learn this little song for me?" The last line of each verse read, "thou shalt be mine and I will be thine." . . . She looked over the song and the already deep blush upon her cheek was greatly heightened . . . . "I have already learned this song, Mr. Croghan. It was once a favorite of my sister's. I will run it over for you." [Another suitor, the less favored Mr. Tillotson, was also in the parlor when Mary O'Hara's relative said:] "Mr. Tillotson begs that you will favor him with a song accompanied by the guitar, before he takes his leave." . . . Mr. Tillotson rose and presented the instrument [guitar] to her, which she [Mary] played with the same ease and brilliance of execution that she did the harp or piano.

[After Mary finished her song, Mr. Tillotson, feeling somewhat defeated in his efforts, left, giving William Croghan the opportunity he
was waiting for.] "My dear Miss O'Hara," said Mr. Croghan, "as this
is the first opportunity I have found, permit me to make known to
you the sentiments of my heart. I have deeply loved you since the
first moment I saw you."[11]

In Eliza's telling, music leads the heart, and Mary O'Hara married
William Croghan and moved to his plantation in Kentucky. What many
of the anxious mothers who heard the story refused to recognize was
that the beautiful Mary O'Hara had more to offer than "accomplishments." As the daughter of Pittsburgh's wealthiest businessman, she
was also very rich.[12]

Stephen grew up in the culture of piano girls and amateur singers,
literally surrounded by them—as sisters, friends, relatives, and neighbors—and their music. Susan Pentland, the girl next door in Allegheny,
played his newest songs on her piano and sang them so he would know
how they sounded in a soprano voice. Frances Welles, Stephen's friend
at the Athens Academy, was an accomplished pianist for whom he
wrote his first composition, "The Tioga Waltz." She continued to play
Foster's songs well into her seventies, and her grandson "grew up hearing Stephen's airs played daily." Other piano girls included the enchanting musical sisters Rachel, Mary, and Margaret Keller, whose home on
Penn Street was "a favorite gathering place for the glee club." Even in
Cincinnati, Stephen spent many an evening at the homes of talented
piano girls, including Sophie Marshall and the raven-haired Eliza Russell, who played the piano whenever Stephen stopped by.[13]

All the Foster boys enjoyed the company of piano girls. Henry married Mary Burgess who played the piano. Julia Murray, a Pittsburgh
beauty who broke Morrison's heart in 1851, had "a sweet voice" and
participated in the neighborhood musical gatherings. Morrison's next
sweetheart and wife was the singer Jessie Lightner, the girl with the
delightful contralto voice. Ironically, the only Foster not to marry a
piano girl was Stephen. Even Brother William's sickly wife Mary practiced the piano daily until death stilled her hands forever. Although
there is no mention that Stephen's mother was a piano girl, she encouraged participation in musical soirees, inviting the neighbors over to her
house in Allegheny, where piano music, singing, and laughter made for
a joyous occasion.[14]

Certain characteristics made the parlor songs popular with the piano girls for amateur performances. For one thing, they were simple, offering a clean melody line and simple piano accompaniments. Most of Foster's moderate-paced ballads had chords that were easy to play because they repeated often and did not demand rapid or frequent finger changes. Similarly, parlor songs avoided unnecessary ornamentation in the melody line, making them easier to sing. In Foster's songs, the vocal line went no higher than F or G on the staff, and there were no high Cs or demanding trills that only an operatically trained singer would be comfortable performing. The simplicity in the songs was not because the composer lacked the musical skills to write more complicated works, but because the genre demanded it.[15] Parlor songs were supposed to transport the listener to a higher emotional consciousness and many people believed that only a simple melody line could elicit the true sentiment of the text and bring out real emotions in the listeners. In fact, vocal music was preferred to instrumental music because the words in the song were believed to have a superior ability to convey emotions.[16]

Stephen's parlor songs were patterned after different national song models, which he drew on to weave together a unique and splendid musical tapestry. His songs combined characteristics from Irish, Scottish, and English folk and popular songs; Italian opera; and several other ethnic ingredients. His early songs like "Ah! May the Red Rose Live Alway" were composed along the English song model after Henry Bishop, the composer of the ever-popular "Home Sweet Home," which nearly everyone in Foster's generation knew. The Scottish influence is seen in his use of the Scottish snap in his signature octave leap that accented and elongated the second syllable of key words in his songs. Elements from Italian opera can be seen in the flowing melody lines and arpeggio-like accompaniments to his most lyrical parlor songs, like "Wilt Thou Be Gone, Love?," "Come with Thy Sweet Voice Again," and "Come Where My Love Lies Dreaming," his best examples modeled after opera. Finally, the German style to which Henry Kleber introduced him is evident in "Sadly to Mine Heart Appealing," which opens with a melodic and rhythmic pattern reminiscent of Schubert.[17]

For the most part, Foster's parlor songs were dependent on Irish roots, and musicologist Charles Hamm has pointed to Thomas Moore's sentimental *Irish Melodies* as the most influential model in print for

Foster's parlor songs.[18] Moore created the popular song collection by adapting traditional Irish airs to his own nostalgic poetry, and hiring professionals to arrange and write the music. An exact contemporary of Stephen Foster's parents, he wrote songs that found their way into just about every middle-class, American parlor in the first quarter of the nineteenth century, when they were heralded for their ability to bring on a visible emotional state. *The Irish Melodies* included many of Charlotte Foster's favorites—"The Harp that Once through Tara's Halls," "Come, Rest in This Bosom," and "Oft in the Stilly Night."

Similarities between Foster's and Moore's music abound, not surprisingly, since not only Charlotte, but also her younger sisters played Moore's songs when Stephen was a child. An example of an Irish-influenced melody is Foster's lullaby "Sweetly She Sleeps, My Alice Fair" with words by Charles G. Eastman. The opening phrase is pentatonic, and the tune is fairly reminiscent of several of Moore's songs. Other popular Foster songs that capture the Irish flavor are "Maggie by My Side," "Willie, We Have Missed You," "Jeanie with the Light Brown Hair," and "Gentle Annie." Ultimately, Foster combined all the different strains of music into something that was uniquely his own, and uniquely American.[19]

Foster's parlor songs discoursed on various topics in appropriately sentimental and florid language. For the first few years after his marriage, he wrote more happy, lighthearted songs about love. The duet "The Hour for Thee and Me," published in 1851, is an intimate love song, as if he were saying to Jane, now is our time to love, "When day breaks forth on the dewy lawn, And all seems mirth and glee, when birds their sweetest songs awake."[20] These songs were appropriately sentimental. In "Willie My Brave," when a young man is lost at sea, we hear the maiden calling, "Come o'er the billow, Ride on the wave, come while the wind bloweth."[21] In "Maggie by My Side," published in 1852, a storm rages outside, but the protagonist is not worried because his true love is nearby.[22]

More often, Foster's parlor songs were "sad, emotional, and poignant" creations about loss and regret that can be divided into two categories. Songs about physical loss dealt with family separations and death. Songs about nonphysical loss longed for the past, bygone days, and youth, and often emphasized regret. Both categories of songs were exceptionally sad. The sorrow emanated not only from the plaintive melodies, but also from the poems and their subject matter, and Foster gave added emphasis to the emotional content by writing from a first person perspective, and describing the emotions the protagonist was feeling from within.[23] Many of the songs were ambiguous about the exact nature of the loss being mourned. In most cases, the songs simply combined several types of loss, as when "Old Dog Tray" mourned the passing of youth and dead loved ones, and "Willie My Brave" mourned separation and, eventually, death. Home in all its connotations was commemorated along with a dead mother in "A Dream of Mother and My Home." Whether Foster's protagonists sang about a dead loved one or lost hopes, however, his songs of loss were meant to console.

Songs that pined for that which "can never come again" elicited strong emotions. A subtle concept, longing for the past was fully embraced by the generation in question, which seemed obsessed with holding on to such evanescent objects as youth and yesterdays. Foster's songs of regret were replete with such negative phrases as "Gone are the days when my heart was young and gay," "Oh! Those happy days are o'er!" and "Never will come those happy, happy hours." One reason Foster's generation seemed obsessed with the past and regret was that they had not yet come to terms with the changes around them. Steam-driven boats plied their rivers, railroads smashed through their quiet corn fields, and impersonal factories transformed their work world. And while the new order was exciting, to be sure, it left many feeling lost and uncomfortable.[24]

The changes also filled Foster's generation with a strange sort of sadness because people undergoing major transformations in their lives often feel sad about what they have left behind. "All changes," according to the writer Anatole France, "have their melancholy; for what we leave behind us is a part of ourselves."[25] Foster's songs helped them navigate their losses and heal, because when people suffer a serious loss, they need to mourn before they can move on. Pining over the past, which Foster did often in his songs, is a special kind of mourning similar to the mourning that accompanies death, but it helped people come to terms with the changes and accept their new lives. Consequently, songs of "hopes and dreams that never come true" or youthful days flitting by were very sad, but they served a purpose in the society.[26]

The most painful loss—one that plagued the antebellum society—was the death of a loved one in the prime of life. Since Foster's generation had become accustomed to expressing their feelings, the loss of their young elicited stronger demonstrations of grief than that expressed by their ancestors. In response, a special category of song—those I have called "mourning songs"—was created to console the bereaved. Some of these sad songs made incidental reference to death, through the mention of a tomb or a departed form. Others, like Foster's beautiful "Ah, May the Red Rose Live Alway," honored the dead subtly through a poignant question, "Why should the beautiful die?" In the context of the song, the phrase suggested the fragile rose, but it also signified the fragility of life, especially of the young and the beautiful. Other songs, such as "Gentle Annie" and "Where Is Thy Spirit, Mary?" were written specifically with a recently departed young lady in mind. No one could misinterpret their meaning. Foster composed and dedicated these last two songs to the memory of the dead girls, and then personally carried the sheet music to the families of the departed as bereavement gifts.

Mourning songs created especially to deal with grief have been misunderstood by the generations that followed Foster's. These songs comprised a sizeable portion of nineteenth-century parlor music, when the death of children and loved ones in the prime of life was a common occurrence. Because they were misunderstood outside of the context of the era in which they were written, and because their function has never been fully explained, mourning songs have been denounced for their saccharine, morose, or overly sentimental qualities. Yet mourning songs were very important to Foster's generation because the death of children and young adults was prevalent in the society and the bereaved needed consolation. The purpose of the songs was to console the many grief-stricken mothers, fathers, sisters, brothers, husbands, wives, and lovers who watched helplessly as their loved ones, often children or teens, succumbed to nameless diseases with unknown and unknowable causes. It was not without reason that Foster's song asked, "Why should the beautiful die?"[27]

That men and women frequently confronted with the death of their young found value in songs that guided them through the grieving process should come as no surprise. Victorians created an entire genre of literature, including novels, biographies, mourner's manuals, prayer manuals, mourning poetry, and hymns, which functioned primarily to console the bereaved. Historian Ann Douglas named the genre "consolation literature," whose purpose was "to reach and comfort those suffering bereavement or loss."[28]

"Mourning songs," a subset of parlor songs to which Foster and other composers of his generation contributed, employed sentimentality and euphemisms to transform the image of death as disintegration into an image of death as restoration and redemption. Sheet music covers featured angels hovering above the dying who wore a smile of beatitude and resignation as they were escorted to heaven. Euphemisms in the song lyrics taught that the loved ones were not dead, but "peacefully sleeping" and at "home." Through the discourse of sentimentality, the dead children in the songs were transformed into angels to make their deaths easier to bear. Stephen Foster participated in this euphemistic discourse with the now incredible sounding titles "Little Ella's an Angel" and "Tell Me of the Angels, Mother."[29]

Mourning songs also comforted through community. When young women sang their sad songs of death in a parlor filled with family and friends, they encouraged individual and communal healing. Mourners came together to sing, play, or listen to mourning songs and were consoled. Perhaps tear-inducing, sentimental songs facilitated the mourning process by providing "the means for navigating our bruised souls through our loss, for discarding that which is no longer feasible."[30] In "Gentle Annie," Foster offered communal resolution when, in the chorus, he switched to the plural, "Shall we never more behold thee, never hear thy winning voice again?" Singing about death in a communal setting functioned as a consolation technique by encouraging the bereaved to reenact the pain of their loss, which helped them to let go.

Another consolation technique favored by the antebellum generation during bereavement was the creation of an enduring memory of the loved one, the "equivalent" something that becomes the recipient of the feelings that the dead person once elicited. According to a famous psychoanalyst, when the bereaved replace the dead person with a memory of the loved one, the memory converts grief, which is painful, into mourning, which is characterized by acceptance and healing.[31] Singing mourning songs thus helped the bereaved because they were reminded of the dead person when they sang, and remembering helped "to close the gap." When people gather together at funerals and reveal their own fond memories of the dead, it is to help the living heal, and Foster's mourning songs mentioned memory often.

Foster's songs relied on the concept of replacement as a mourning technique, working very subtly through the creation of a remembrance to restore that which has been lost. Rather than talking about a heavenly afterlife, Foster employed at least four insignia to serve as restorers of the past in his mourning songs: dreams, memories, melodies, and nature. His 1850 song "Lilly Ray" never mentioned the word death or dead, although it referred to Lilly Ray as "a gentle form passeth away." Lilly was the "lonely, departed one," but Foster was able to bring her back by restoring her in "dreams" or "visions." In dreams, Lilly lived again; she was re-created. The dream became the replacement that was needed for healing:

> When slumber's dreamy light, O'er me is thrown
> Calling in visions bright, Days that are gone,
> While round my drooping heart, Joy seems to play
> Fondly I dream of thee, Sweet Lilly Ray[32]

Another song in which dreams were the purveyors of the past is "Old Dog Tray." Although the dog's fidelity to his master is emphasized, the real point of the song is that "The lov'd ones, the dear ones have all passed away." Yet Foster tells us that they can be replaced:

> It brings me a dream of a once happy day,
>   Of merry forms I've seen, upon the Village Green.[33]

The composer imbued dreams with the power to re-create lost objects. In "Come with Thy Sweet Voice Again," loss was signified by "Bright visions long vanished," but these "bright visions" can be summoned by dreaming: "Let me dream in the lap of thy sighs." In the song "Ellen Bayne," dead loved ones—"forms long departed"—reappeared in dreams. In "Thou Art Queen of My Song," the protagonist laments that "cold forms surround us," but dreams restore the joy that is past: "But still while I'm dreaming the smiles are o'er me beaming." To Victorians, dreams offered the chance to restore happy days gone by and "more of inner truth than we can find in waking hours." In "Beautiful Dreamer," dreams carry the sleeper away from "the sounds of the rude world" to a sublime state where "all sorrows depart."

In some cases, the dream state needed a catalyst to be brought into action. In "Lilly Ray," melody seemed to usher in the dream state and the reinstatement of the lost loved one, "When Liquid melody falls on my ear, Then I impulsively dream thou art near." In other songs, like

"Old Memories," memory alone served to replace that which had been lost. Foster tells us that even when departed smiles do not return, memories "never depart" and instead preserve early joys "now gone." In this way, "memories" can be permanent in a world where everything else is transitory.[34]

> Fondly old memories recall round my heart,
> Scenes of my early joys, that never depart.[35]

What is lost can also be captured in melody and then transferred for permanent safekeeping to nature. Mary Keller sang Foster's newest melodies when he tried them out on his young friends in Allegheny City. After she died unexpectedly, Foster published "Where Is Thy Spirit, Mary?" Mary's friends thought that the girl's spirit "lingered in the air," but Foster found it in the melody of "an old time ballad, Low and plaintive was the strain." In a subsequent line, Foster asked where Mary's spirit dwelled and then located it in the song of "spring birds now returning, with their music fill the air, And we know by that sweet warning, That thy spirit lingers there."[36] Foster, like a true antebellum artist, located and re-created Mary's spirit in natural elements and in melody. Nature was all-powerful when the Hudson River artists showed man as small and insignificant in comparison, but Foster never made the spirit of a human being insignificant. Mary's spirit mingled with the song of the birds, all in a loving and equitable collectivity.

12

HOBOKEN AND DEATHS IN THE FAMILY

When Stephen showed up in New York alone in the summer of 1853 to work at the Franklin Square office of Firth, Pond and Company, nobody seemed surprised. Problems had been brewing between him and Jane for at least six months. The previous Christmas, Henrietta, now remarried, arrived at the Allegheny house with her second husband Jesse Thornton and her three children, and as soon as Stephen and Jane opened the door, she sensed trouble. Later, she confided the details to her brother Morrison: "How sorry I feel for dear Stephy, though when I read your letter I was not at all surprised at the news it contained . . . . I last winter felt convinced she [Jane] would either have to change her course of conduct or a separation was inevitable."[1] As for an explanation of the offensive "course of conduct," we are left in mystery, although Jane's "tempestuous outbursts" were singled out as the culprit. If any excuse were offered for the outrageous behavior, it was that Jane was "exceedingly pretty and had been spoiled and petted at home," the implication being she was not going to be pampered in the Foster household and she might just as well get used to it.[2]

None of the Fosters suggested that Stephen's impetuous and erratic behavior made him a difficult man to live with, nor did they discuss his increasing tendency to find solace in drink or the resentment he may have felt toward his wife. But Stephen Foster may have unwittingly revealed clues to what was bothering him about Jane and his marriage in a letter he wrote on February 14, 1853, to the same editor of the *Musical World and New York Musical Times* who had pushed him to write "White men's music." Stephen's so-called "Valentine's Day letter" was published a few weeks later in the *Musical Times*, accompanied by a critical retort that left the composer feeling embarrassed and unwilling to put his opinions before the public again.

Stephen penned the damning letter in response to something he read in the January 8 edition, an article probably written by Richard Storrs Willis for his series "Musical Studies for the Million."[3] The article dealt with basic music theory and harmony and stated, "The leading note, or 7th of the scale, may not be doubled, and must resolve upward to the 8th."[4] Regrettably, the editor published Foster's response in the February 26 edition and used it to demonstrate that the composer was "acquainted with the rudimentary rules of harmony and not much more."[5] Others discredited the Valentine's Day letter as an embarrassing attempt at self-promotion and a misguided plan to market his celebrity.[6] More damage accrued after Stephen's death when, perhaps from such negative critiques as this, the idea circulated that Foster was "an untutored genius . . . with scanty musical training," a myth that musicologists have now overturned.[7]

Whatever reason the editor had for pointing out Foster's alleged musical deficiency, the letter is interesting for what it reveals about his attitude toward his wife and the opposite sex. If the editor had read between the lines, he might have noticed that Foster's mind on that Valentine's Day appeared more occupied with matrimony than harmony. He began by querying, "Might we not have a musical gender?" and then went on to advocate dividing chords into genders, "a distinction suggestive of matrimony." To the masculine gender belonged "the sturdy prime and the valorous *fifth*,—which, when sounded together, to the exclusion of others, suggests trumpets, and 'the big wars that make ambition virtue.'" To represent the "feminine notes of the harmonic family," Foster suggested "the conciliating *third*, and the complaining, though gentle (minor) seventh, as they seem to lean for support on the sterner notes." The feminine seventh, he noted in the excerpt below, was useful "in creating discord":

> The males, though noisy and boisterous, may be doubled or reinforced with propriety, while the females (bless their dear hearts) can speak for themselves . . . . In support of this idea, is the fact that the seventh has a natural penchant for the third, or sister tone of the succeeding chord, where it usually resolves itself in order to unfold

its sorrowful story; a proverbial weakness of the sex, confiding their
secrets to each other . . . . the aforesaid *seventh* can sometimes be
used to great advantage in creating *discord*, but it would be ungallant
to dwell on this branch of the argument.[8]

If the letter is suggestive of what was going on in Foster's life at the
time, *discord* was a gentle explanation. If we try to read between the
lines, it appears that Jane was complaining to one or more of her sisters,
"confiding their secrets to each other," probably about his drinking, and
the result was chaos. Something happened in May of 1853—we don't
know what—but Jane was angry enough to pack and walk out with baby
Marion. The details of the breakup are hidden because it would have
been "ungallant" for the husband to "dwell on this branch of the argument." Perhaps the underlying source of the dispute had something to
do with the fact that on May 5, 1853, Stephen signed an exclusive
contract with Firth, Pond and Company that guaranteed a 10 percent
royalty on the retail price of all new Foster songs the firm sold. Although the new agreement was better than his previous 8 percent
contract, Jane may not have wanted her husband to sign the agreement
at all. She may have wanted him to try another line of work, something
steadier that would not demand he travel and live in New York. This is
only conjecture, but it looks like a good possibility. After Jane stormed
out with the baby, she probably moved in with her mother and sisters in
the McDowell house, conveniently located across the river in Lawrenceville.[9]

Stephen responded to Jane's departure with a similarly strong emotional outburst. He sold his furniture in the Allegheny house to his
father for seventy-five dollars and left for New York on June 13, 1853, a
month after Jane walked out. Of course, it is almost certain that the new
contract with Firth and Pond demanded that Foster move to New York
to work closely with his publishers on their forthcoming anthology, *The
Social Orchestra*, a fact that might have infuriated Jane. She may not
have wanted to move, since she had a small daughter to consider and
New York's reputation as a "dangerous city" was only growing. And she
may have been unwilling to leave her community of friends and family
behind.

Jane could not have complained about the discomforts of traveling to
New York, though, because the trip to the big city was easy by this time.
The previous year, the train made its first complete journey all the way

through to Pittsburgh from the East in one day instead of four. Brother William, as one of the men responsible for the feat, was the honored guest of the Pennsylvania Railroad when he and his family arrived on December 11, 1852, at the Pittsburgh station and all the Fosters came out to greet them. Stephen took the train to New York in January 1853, when he met with the musical editor, and he took the train again in June when he sold off his furniture and rushed to his publishers in New York to begin compiling a new musical book for amateur instrumental performances.

When Firth, Pond and Company commissioned Foster to work on the *Social Orchestra,* he became totally immersed in the parlor tradition. His job was to arrange miscellaneous songs and melodies "from among the most popular operatic and other music of the day" for performances on the flute and violin. When completed, the *Social Orchestra* had eighty-three pages of music, including some Foster songs, arranged "in an easy and correct manner, as Solos, Duets, Trios, and Quartets, suitable for serenades, evenings at home etc."[10] Foster was selected for the job because his publishers wanted someone who could transition classical European models to amateur performances and the composer already had a reputation for writing people-friendly music. In the introduction to the book, the publishers said they had "confided the task of selecting and arranging the melodies to a gentleman of acknowledged musical taste, and composer of some of the most popular airs ever written in this or any other country, as will be seen by reference to the name on the title page."[11] Stephen must have been honored by the publisher's choice, even if the work entailed leaving his wife and daughter behind.

After he moved to New York, even with sound reasons for doing so, the chronology of Foster's life becomes lost in a maze of unsubstantiated facts, accusations, and hearsay. The family was embarrassed about the couple's separation and did not want the public to know the details leading up to or immediately following his move in June 1853. Although he had steady employment, he seemed perennially short on cash, and less than a month after settling into Manhattan, Stephen asked his brother Morrison to advance him some money. A note issued by Firth, Pond and Company for $125 passed back and forth between the two brothers, because Stephen had already signed it over to Morrison in payment of an earlier debt. When he realized how desperately he needed the cash, he asked Morrison to return the note to him, reassuring him that the music publisher would soon be advancing him $500. But Morrison Foster was already experiencing financial difficulties of his own. The cotton business had been failing in Allegheny for some time, and Morrison's position became precarious. The following year, his boss would become very ill and transfer one of the factories of the Hope Cotton concern over to an Isaac Pennock, who found less and less work for Morrison.

Stephen, in the meantime, had plenty of work in New York but seemed to have been drinking regularly. "Taylor's new saloon great," he wrote Morrison on July 8, 1853, of the bar on the first floor of Taylor's International Hotel, where he probably lodged. The hotel with its magnificent tiled lobby at the corner of Broadway and Franklin Street was a few steps from his publishers who were still at No. 1 Franklin Square. No doubt he was spending his afterhours at the saloon, where the alcohol was certainly flowing, but he did make time for the attractions of the great metropolis in spite of his busy schedule. He spent the Fourth of July on Staten Island with friends of the family, and visited New York's Hippodrome, the great circus, and the opera where he heard the German soprano Henrietta Sontag. The newly constructed Crystal Palace on 42nd Street was also on his itinerary.[12] The immense, steel-girded glass structure, an icon of industry, put on display the marvelous inventions of the new era and made a man proud.

The Social Orchestra was scheduled to be printed by November 1853, but production was delayed for one reason or another. Still, Stephen finished his part of the job and returned to Pittsburgh that month to stage the *Invisible Prince* with Charles Shiras and to incorporate his plantation songs into the stage production of *Uncle Tom's Cabin*. On this trip home, Stephen reconciled with his wife, and the couple moved with little Marion back into the Foster house, where they remained through Christmas. Most likely, Jane had stayed at her mother's house while Stephen was in New York. Around January 26, 1854, when the *Social Orchestra* came off the press, Stephen returned to New York with his wife and daughter and rented a large new house in Hoboken, New Jersey, the town on the opposite side of the Hudson River, just a ferry ride from New York.

Apparently, Foster believed his luck had turned around and he was optimistic that more profitable offers would be coming his way.[13] The corner, four-story, brick row house that he rented at what is today 601 Bloomfield Street cost more than Stephen could afford, but it was Jane's first real home without her in-laws since her marriage. As if to take note of this achievement, she proudly signed her Episcopal prayer book "Jane D. Foster, Hoboken." The building was only two years old when Stephen and his family moved in, and Hoboken was a delightful neighborhood of newer townhouses that must have reminded him of Allegheny and the Commons he had just left. A few decades earlier a Colonel Stephens had turned the undeveloped grassland into a resort for upper-class men and women who wanted to escape the noise and din of Manhattan across the river. He even constructed America's first yacht club in the town in 1844, and a six-mile path along the waterfront known as River Walk that led to the Elysian Fields, expansive gardens and meadows where the nation's first organized baseball game was played. During these years, Hoboken was inhabited by the famous and the well-to-do, including Horace Greeley and Henry Ward Beecher, and even John Jacob Astor built a vacation house on Washington and Second Street.[14]

That Stephen chose to live in such an up-and-coming neighborhood says something about his striving for middle-class respectability after he completed the *Social Orchestra*. The decision appears rash and foolish, in hindsight, for Firth and Pond paid him a flat fee of $150 and no royalties for his contribution. In his optimistic carefree frame of mind, he spent everything he had trying to impress his wife and himself that he was indeed the successful man whose songs were being sung and hummed and performed the world over. But when new contracts were not forthcoming, it became apparent that he could not handle the mounting expenses of maintaining the family in such a large house. He wanted his wife to be proud of him, surely, and he probably thought his publishers would offer him more steady work, but they did not. *The Social Orchestra* was successful over the long term, bringing in a steady stream of moderate returns for the publisher for decades, but Foster had no claim to royalties and it was not the smash hit that "Old Folks at Home" had been.

The reviews of the *Social Orchestra* were generally favorable. The *Musical World* described the work as aiming to "improve the taste of the community for social music," and the editor said "no work is better adapted for such a purpose than one that gives opportunities of combining instruments." He also approved of Foster's "writing for such instruments as are more commonly the object of practice among amateurs— the violin, the flute and the violoncello." But the review was not without criticism. Foster was familiar with the flute and violin, for which the *Social Orchestra* was specifically designed, but the editor regretted "that Mr. Foster has omitted to arrange some pieces for the tenor [viola]." He also complained, "We do not entirely approve of the management of the second violin, written as it is from beginning to end in doubled chords, which renders the part tedious." In the end, the editor said the *Social Orchestra* "well deserves the favor of the public" and he was confident that "this is not the only work of the kind which he [Foster] will find the public calling for at his hands." Unfortunately, neither the public nor Firth, Pond and Company requested a sequel to the book. [15]

The next published works by Foster were individual parlor songs in sheet music form. In February 1854, "Ellen Bayne" came off the press, followed in March by "Willie, We Have Missed You," a happy sentimental song that tells the story of a young wife who waits up late into the night to greet her husband with a loving embrace. The lithographed cover of the Firth, Pond song sheet represents an idyllic scene of home and family that was popular at midcentury, and the sentimentality in the song is especially powerful at the moment of the reunion of the couple. Stephen devoted pages 76 through 81 of his manuscript book to the song that, contrary to what the lyrics say, may have been inspired by the love of a faithful mother. [16] Although published in the first quarter of 1854, the reunion that suggested the emotional scene in "Willie" was Foster's own homecoming at the end of the previous year. Eliza, not Jane, waited up for Stephen when he returned to Allegheny around the beginning of November 1853 to work with Charles Shiras on *The Invisible Prince* and Morrison Foster believed that was the inspiration for the song. Stephen had just returned from New York when he broke down in tears at the sight of his mother standing in the doorframe of the Union Avenue house, and he took a few minutes to regain his composure. Eliza, according to Morrison, recognized the sound of her youngest son's footsteps on the porch and rushed out to greet him with open arms. [17]

There is some concern that Stephen Foster's close attachment to his mother was a strong deterrent to a close relationship with his wife. [18]

The argument would only hold up if Stephen found a mother figure in Jane with which to replace Eliza, but Jane was not one to take on the nurturing role. She quarreled with her husband at the start of the marriage as they both struggled to determine just what their respective roles would be. Morrison Foster wrote that Stephen's "love for his mother amounted to adoration. She was to him an angelic creature."[19] Jane, in contrast, does not come across anywhere as "angelic" or consoling, which may have been one of the problems with the marriage. Jane had been a pampered daughter, and she did not want to be the one to pamper Stephen, the way his mother did. Eliza had a close emotional bond with Stephen, to be sure, but it is not likely that his affection for his mother, or hers for him, competed with the devotion due his wife.[20]

The next song Stephen wrote was inspired by his wife, or rather, her hair. In June 1854, Foster published "Jeanie with the Light Brown Hair," a love song that is most associated with Jane Foster. The lithograph on the title page of the Firth, Pond and Company sheet music shows a middle-class young lady with long, dark hair, parted in the middle with loose curls running down to her chest.[21] Most illustrations at the time featured young women with their hair tightly pulled back and up off their necks. Although the song was not officially dedicated to Jane on its title page, in family lore there was never a doubt that Stephen wrote the song with his wife in mind. Family sources assert that Jane Foster "was often addressed by the affectionate diminutive, Jennie," which was the name Stephen used when addressing her in private.[22] "Jennie" was also how the name appeared in the manuscript version, and the original title to the song on page 82 was simply "Jennie." By page 84, where he wrote out all the stanzas on one page, he lengthened the title to "Jennie with the Light Brown Hair," but it was still not "Jeanie."[23] His publishers probably changed the name because Jeanie is easier to sing and it rhymes better with dream. The song in the Irish style of Thomas Moore is beautiful and has lived on after Stephen's more popular plantation songs fell out of favor, as its AABA melodic structure with slight variations became increasingly common in subsequent decades.[24] Particularly noteworthy are the song's "references to vocal sounds" where his wife's "melodies," or the composer, are "sighing like the night wind and sobbing like the rain."[25]

"Jeanie with the Light Brown Hair" was crafted to allow the singer the experience of using the notes to emphasize the meaning of the words. When the vocalist sings "Bourne like a vapor," the first syllable of "vapor" is a sixth above the preceding note, with no rest in between, and the singer must jump up to the note and land on it ever so lightly, so as not to destroy the fragile vapor as well as the musicality of the song. When Foster wrote "I dream of Jeanie," "I see her tripping," and "I long for Jeanie," he used dotted quarter notes for the words "dream," "see," and "long" because dreaming, seeing, and longing can be expressed as fairly enduring states. In a similar fashion, when Foster wrote "tripping where the bright streams play," the words dance on eighth notes because the word "tripping" represents light, rapid movement. The meaning of the words and the duration of the notes are again coordinated when Jeanie is "floating like a vapor" and the protagonist is "Never more to find her." Here Foster placed a fermata over the first syllable of the word "vapor" and over "find," letting the singer get carried away holding the note. The fermata expressed the futility in trying to hold on to a vapor or in looking for the "never more."[26]

In the song, Foster likens his wife to a "vapor," which was used as a synonym for spirit at a time when many men and women were convinced they could communicate with the dead in séances. The analogy suggests that Jane was not a concrete physical presence, but something ephemeral that came and went as she wished, and disappeared like a vapor into thin air, which was the case many times in their marriage. The words "I long for Jeanie" even suggest he might have been separated from Jane when he wrote the song, but there is no way of knowing if the couple was living together or apart when he penned the delightful song, or for how many years they lived together as man and wife. Family lore has it that "in the first few years of Stephen's and Jane's married life, there are several home comings and several leavings, and Jane went oftener to New York while Stephen was there than the record shows."[27] It is nice to believe they lived together in the Bloomfield Street house for ten months, but quite possibly Jane enjoyed her own home for only a few months before she took Marion and moved back to her mother's house in Pittsburgh. Even if they did not separate during their residency in Hoboken, the months they shared the house were not always peaceful, as indicated by the following poetic inscription written by Stephen in his manuscript book, next to the completed version of "Jeanie with the Light Brown Hair":

HOBOKEN
Where wranglers bid you to their scenes of strife
In wrong conception of your plan of life.[28]

Whenever Stephen was away from Pittsburgh, especially when he was alone, his siblings worried about him and commented in their correspondences about their brother's strange way of life. Apparently, he did not write often and when he did, he must have revealed that he was under financial pressure and unhappy. When Henrietta first learned that Stephen had moved to New York without Jane in June 1853, she extended an invitation for him to stay with her in Ohio, not understanding that her brother's career opportunities were in New York in close proximity to his music publishers. Dunning Foster also expressed concern over Stephen's chosen path in life: "Have you heard anything from Stephen lately?" he queried Morrison in March 1854. "It is a subject of much anxiety to me, notwithstanding his foolish and unaccountable course—I hope he will continue to make a comfortable living for himself."[29] Maybe Dunning thought going into the music business instead of taking over his commission merchant agency in Cincinnati was the "foolish and unaccountable course."

All the Foster boys, in fact, were working hard to become established in various business ventures, but they could not help but worry about their youngest sibling who struggled to make a living as a composer. In addition to his poor financial prospects, they worried about his increasing dependence on alcohol, noting that he was sinking into a kind of hopeless despair, which he frequently soothed with drink. Interestingly, when Stephen worked on a song called "When the Bowl Goes Round," he penned in two choices in the blank space after "No heart so bright, but finds its____." His choices for the conclusion to the sentence were "might" and "blight," suggesting he knew that alcohol offered the illusion of strength but would ultimately destroy him.[30]

Eventually, Stephen left New York, with the same impulsivity he demonstrated when he walked out of Jefferson College within a week of starting classes. The story in the family is that one day in October 1854, with little or no discussion, he simply sold off his furniture and put his wife and daughter and himself on a train to Pittsburgh. Jane must have struggled with her husband's sudden decision to pull up roots and move. She had purchased the furniture less than a year earlier, fixed up the house, probably sewed curtains, and suddenly she was on her way back. And to what? To the house in Allegheny crowded with too many Fosters that her rich brother-in-law William owned. Morrison was always cordial and gave Jane money when she needed it, but his biography of his brother barely mentions his sister-in-law, and there seems to have been no love lost between them. Perhaps their politics were too different and, in Morrison's eyes, she was too outspoken and independent minded for a woman. As for Jane's feelings about the Fosters, there are no extant letters that might hint at them, and no one ever mentioned that Jane felt gratitude or affection for the brother-in-law who supplied the house she lived in.

After they returned to Allegheny, Stephen, Jane, and Marion moved back into Brother William's house since Stephen could not afford to rent a house of his own, and living with the Fosters was better than boarding. The couple knew from firsthand experience what it was like to dine at a communal table in a boardinghouse, where strangers watched every bite that went into their mouths and the landlord did not provide enough food to go around. Consequently, Stephen and his family moved into the crowded household on Union Avenue, where he was expected to write songs in a feverish manner to help put food on the table, but Jane did not stay long. On October 26, Ann Eliza's son James Buchanan, who was staying in the Allegheny house while he studied law in Pittsburgh, wrote his father that Stephen intended remaining in Pittsburgh that winter, but that Jane "will not be here however. I believe he wants to get her out to Youngstown with Aunt Henrietta."[31]

Stephen and his wife might not have been getting along, but Henrietta needed help caring for her sick daughter Mary who had "suffered for the last two months with fever and ague."[32] A month later, however, Jane and Henrietta showed up together at the Allegheny house with Mary who "was brought here to be recuperated." Apparently, Jane had antagonized the Fosters before she was banished to Youngstown, but over what is not known. James said about his aunt Jane, "to tell the truth I never have found out what the nature of her sin was." In any case, by November, Stephen's wife was "fairly fixed and at her ease in Allegheny" where the Fosters acted "perfectly oblivious to all that is past."[33]

Stephen went back to his composing, but he was unable to produce enough songs in 1854 to make his publishing contracts profitable. The year after he renounced the minstrel genre, he wrote five parlor songs: "Willie, We Have Missed You," "Jeanie with the Light Brown Hair,"

"Ellen Bayne," "Come with Thy Sweet Voice Again," and "Hard Times Come Again No More," entered for copyright on December 16. As beautiful as "Jeanie" and "Willie" were, they did not make the money that "Old Folks" and "My Old Kentucky Home" commanded, yet Stephen did not return to minstrelsy. After the publication of "Jeanie," he made several starts on emotion-filled verses that were never turned into complete songs. One began "Old partner of our youthful mirth, Thy fruits are scattered o'er the earth." Perhaps he intended the words to be a song commemorating Charles Shiras's recent passing. Perhaps "thy sweet voice" that he beaconed to "come again" in his last song for 1854 belonged to the deceased poet, whose friendship had inspired him to write his greatest songs.

On December 21, 1854, Stephen signed his third contract with Firth, Pond and Company, which should have inspired him to be more productive. The new contract, in the composer's own handwriting, was more advantageous than his previous contracts, indicating that he had matured into an astute businessman, or what is more likely, that one of his brothers dictated the content. Foster's second contract from May 1853 had given exclusivity to Firth and Pond, but the new contract did not. The last article in the third contract protected Stephen by stipulating that any manuscript must be relinquished by the publisher if he "shall delay during more than a reasonable length of time to publish it." That way they could not hold on to a song just to prevent another publisher from getting it. Another interesting addition was that the publishers were obligated to "issue at all times a sufficient number of copies of said music to supply the demand." One wonders what prompted Stephen to put in the addendum. Perhaps he believed his publisher's November 11, 1854, advertisement that claimed they sold more than 130,000 copies of "Old Folks at Home," 90,000 copies of "My Old Kentucky Home," and 74,000 copies of "Massa's in de Cold Ground." As fate would have it, even with a history of hundreds of thousands of sales and a new and improved contract, Stephen would not produce more songs the following year.

On Christmas Day 1854, Stephen, Jane, and three-year-old Marion were together in the Allegheny house with nearly the entire Foster clan to celebrate the holidays. Although Brother William and Ann Eliza and their families could not join them, Dunning Foster and Henrietta and her family did. Mary must have recovered because Dunning commented that Henrietta's "girls are just at such an age as to require considerable expenses in keeping up appearances in a city."[34] The occasion was a joy for the whole family, but there was much—perhaps too much—pressure placed on Eliza. In October she had taken a train straight through to Philadelphia, where she visited son William and daughter Ann Eliza, both of whom now resided in the fair Pennsylvania city.[35] Her grandson James Buchanan accompanied her and visited his own parents at the same time. Eliza was very tired when she returned at the end of the month to a house that was overly crowded with too many people to look after and too many chores.[36] Most of her labor went to caring for her very sick husband, and Dunning worried "that our dear Mother is likely to have her health injured by her attentions to Pa."[37]

Dunning's concerns were merited because the 1854 Christmas turned out to be the last the family would spend together. On January 18, 1855, Eliza Foster took a carriage from Allegheny over the bridge to Pittsburgh for a leisurely day of shopping, and suffered a fatal heart attack after purchasing some trinkets, including "a length of blue satin ribbon."[38] She felt the attack come on in front of a neighbor's house, collapsed at their front door, and was carried inside where she died. When Ann Eliza received the news in Philadelphia, she fell into a fit of crying. Long anticipating her sickly father's death, she was shocked to learn that her mother had left the earth first. In fact, Stephen's father never knew his wife had died, since he was mentally as well as physically incapacitated at the time of Eliza's death. Six months later, on July 27, 1855, William Barclay Foster also passed away. He was laid to rest next to Eliza in the new Allegheny Cemetery in Lawrenceville, where Charlotte's remains had been reinterred only a few years earlier near the old White Cottage.

How Stephen felt about his father's death can only be conjecture. No one discussed his feelings toward his father. During the last months of his life, when the senior William was confined to his bed more dead than alive, more ineffectual than he ever had been, did his son pity him? Despise him? Relief that he was finally gone surely colored some of his emotions. In addition to being relieved from the caretaking chores the invalid required, Stephen no longer had to stare at him day in and day out wondering, "Will I be like this?" Or worse still, "Am I like this already?" Surely he wondered if his fate would be determined by the character of his father. William was the father who could not support his family, impractical and idealistic, chasing after a world that no longer existed. In describing William Barclay Foster, Stephen must have worried that he was describing himself. Stephen wrote no songs in praise of his father. The one song, "Oh Boys, Carry Me 'Long," which was rumored to have been inspired by the senior William, was published years before his passing and was about the burial of an old sick slave.

However he felt about his father, Morrison Foster claimed that Stephen never got over the loss of their mother, whom he idolized and who apparently idolized him. Young James Buchanan said of Eliza Foster shortly before she died, "Grandmother loves her son Stephen with a wildness of which you can hardly form a conception."[39] Still, he functioned rather well on the domestic scene after his mother's death. He remained in the Allegheny house with Jane and Marion, caring for his sick father "with regularity and system" until the latter passed on. Far from being lonesome, Stephen seemed rather comfortable with the house less crowded. He had the help of two Irish servant girls—"Biddy is my main stay . . . and Margaret is also an excellent girl"—and after some guests or boarders left in March 1855, he wrote his sister Henrietta, "I get along much better without having any strangers in the house except as servants."[40]

After Eliza's death, Morrison moved out and went to live in a boardinghouse, probably because he felt intrusive after Jane became mistress of the house on the death of her mother-in law. Later that year he moved to Philadelphia where, through some Democratic connection, he was appointed army quartermaster and put in charge of funneling military supplies to "bleeding" Kansas. Fighting had broken out in the contested territory the year before over whether slavery would be allowed and Morrison most likely supported the proslavery faction.

Stephen was content to handle the chores and maintenance of the house, but after his father died, he fell behind in the thirty-one dollars quarterly rent he owed his brother William. Apparently, Stephen's musical creativity suffered after his parents' deaths and he could not write enough songs to pay his bills. Although "Hard Times Come Again No More" came off the press in January 1855, just after his mother's death, Stephen had written it the year before when Charles Dickens published *Hard Times*. The famous novel highlighted the hardships of the British poor, but the current economic despair in Stephen's hometown may have drawn him to the book. In 1855, Pittsburgh suffered after the closing of many of the area's cotton mills, and the song became more meaningful than it would have been without hinging on a real-life situation.

At the end of June, Firth, Pond and Company came out with two additional Foster songs, both with more lighthearted titles. Henrietta's daughters Lidie and Mary Wick were visiting when their uncle wrote "Come Where My Love Lies Dreaming," and the girls sang the soprano and alto parts while Stephen accompanied them on the piano. The song's structure, a composed-through song, differed from his usual model of stanza followed by chorus. Some critics suggested that his German composer friend Henry Kleber assisted him or at least encouraged him to try the more ambitious form, but it is possible that he wrote the song on his own because he was tired of doing the same old thing.

Foster's next title was "Some Folks," copyrighted on the same day as "Come Where My Love Lies Dreaming." The upbeat song worked in many ways like a self-help pep talk, repeating the idea "Some folks like to sigh, some folks do, but that's not me or you."[41] In contrast, "The Village Maiden" that Stephen published in September less than two months after the death of his father, was just the opposite, a sorrowful song about a young woman who marries and subsequently dies.[42]

There was much sadness for the Fosters that fateful year. In October 1855, Henrietta's thirteen-year-old son Thomas from her first marriage climbed a tree and fell to his death. The last title Foster published late in the year was "Comrades, Fill No Glass for Me," a song that easily fell into the temperance genre, but was an interesting case of haunting self-expression, with highly confessional words. It is interesting to note that Firth, Pond and Company did not want the song or Foster did not offer it to them. "Comrades" was published on November 23, 1855, by Miller & Beacham of Baltimore, successors of F. D. Benteen, his old publishers. If the song can be taken as a guide to Stephen's inner feelings, in light of the recent deaths of his parents, he appears to have concluded that he had failed to live up to the expectations his "parents centered in their child." The house was no longer crowded, but at the end of 1855 Foster was depressed and guilt stricken:

> When I was young I felt the tide,
> Of aspirations undefiled,
> But manhood's years have wronged the pride

My parents centered in their child.[43]

More deaths in the family occurred the next year, and Foster became even less productive. In March 1856, Dunning Foster wrote Morrison from Cincinnati that he was "quite weak," although he did not "feel ill enough for any of you to come here."[44] The damage inflicted by the disease contracted in the Mexican-American War had proven irreversible and he regretted that he "made a fatal mistake in remaining here this winter." Henry, Morrison, and Stephen rushed to Cincinnati and were with Dunning when he died on March 31, 1856, shortly after he wrote the letter. Her brother's death, which was her first loss of an adult sibling since Charlotte, "that dear creature," had died in 1829, was particularly difficult for Ann Eliza to accept. Religion finally brought her comfort and, as she told herself and her remaining brothers, "the will of the Lord be done: it is always the best." Her words echoed those of her mother who had come to terms with Charlotte's death, only after "a perfect reconciliation to the Will of the Omniscient" brought her "tranquility."[45] Now Ann Eliza wrote, "Nothing remains to us but submission to his loss."[46] Later in the year tragedy struck again when the younger William became a widower for the second time. William had anticipated the death of his wife Elizabeth for some time but he still found the prospect of losing her agonizing. Ann Eliza said her brother had "made up his mind to part with her," but "his grief at the prospect he says is beyond expression."[47]

The sorrows of so many deaths in the family in such a brief time weighed heavily on Stephen, who managed to produce just one song for his publishers in 1856, "Gentle Annie." Even that was a mourning song, composed, according to some sources, to commemorate the death of a neighbor's child who had been run over by a horse.[48] Stephen was dressed and preparing to leave for a formal evening function, when he learned that the neighbor's daughter had been killed. He immediately went to the child's home and sat through the night with Annie's grieving parents. The sentiment in the song is so powerful that an anecdote has been passed along involving Abraham Lincoln. Supposedly, the mother of a Confederate soldier went to see Lincoln in the White House to beg to have her son released from a Union jail. The woman brought her little daughter along who stood quietly by, while the mother pleaded her case with the President. Lincoln then went to a window and stood there, silently looking out. The little daughter, in the meantime, walked over to the piano in the room, and started to play "Gentle Annie" while the President remained standing, lost in thought. On hearing the song, his eyes welled up with tears, and when the little girl had finished playing, Lincoln granted the distraught mother her wish. [49]

Although the Foster daughters like Ann Eliza were religious in the traditional sense and church going, the Foster men were different. "Gentle Annie" may provide a window into Stephen's spiritual side, revealing some clues to his ideas about religion and his belief in God and the supernatural. In the song, Annie's body lies buried in the earth, but the composer re-creates the girl's spirit in the "wild flowers scattered o'er the plain." Death is never mentioned, only alluded to in the mention of the "tomb" in the last stanza. Annie "wilt come no more," but her form does not reappear in dreams or memories, as happens in many other Foster songs. There is a suggestion that Annie's spirit has been reborn in the scent of the wild flowers, "While they mingle their perfume o'er thy tomb." Annie's spirit has found pantheistic reincarnation, in the perfume of the flowers over Annie's grave. Foster's beliefs are perhaps akin to that of the Transcendentalist Ralph Waldo Emerson, who wrote, "Nature is so pervaded with human life, that there is something of humanity in all . . . that behind nature, throughout nature, spirit is present." [50] This may be the closest we can get to an understanding of the composer's religion.

Since Stephen did not find comfort in organized religion, although he attended church services on occasion, he still needed to find relief from the sorrows of the many losses in the family. Sad, but true, he appears to have turned to spending nights out with friends and drink to assuage the pain that tore at his heart for several years after the deaths of his parents. Although Stephen may have belonged to the Philharmonic Society in Allegheny, more stories attest to evenings spent in "jolly, boisterous gatherings" and drunken "serenading expeditions" with questionable friends in Pittsburgh and Allegheny, than to staid concert going.

One story that came to light decades after the composer's death was offered by an "anonymous" companion. The author of the *Pittsburgh Press* article lived at Pittsburgh's Iron City Hotel, from where, he said, Stephen and about a dozen young men would set out nightly to serenade beneath the windows of the upper-class residents of the city. Stephen was a married man at the time of this particular venture, because the anonymous writer said one of the favorite songs Stephen sang was "Old Dog Tray," which was published in 1853. When they serenaded at the house of Judge Irwin on Stockton Avenue in Allegheny, someone sent down a jar of homemade pickles lowered on a string from an upstairs window. If Stephen brought his oak cased melodeon along and set it under the judge's window, the combined sounds of the instrument and the voices would have echoed into the night.[51] That no one opened the door and handed the men the jar seems to indicate that the Irwin family found the serenading party too rowdy to deal with. The writer, of course, claimed that the pickles, prepared by the judge himself, were the best in town and were a compliment to the singers. But however one interprets the offering, Jane Foster would not have been pleased with a gift received in such a manner.[52]

Another story about Stephen's nightly adventures came from Jane and was reported by the composer's granddaughter Jessie Welsh Rose. Stephen and his "lifelong friend next door on Union Avenue" belonged to a small company of musicians who played the banjo and guitar. One summer evening, after staying out all night practicing and partying, the two men were "assisting one another home in the wee, small hours of the morning [when] they passed the old Allegheny Market" and bought a live goose as "a peace offering" for their "unconciliating wives." When they arrived at Stephen's house, Jane opened the door to find her husband clutching a screeching "terrified goose" to his breast, while he exclaimed "Oh, Jenny, see the nice goose I have for you, honey." Jane's response "ran something to the effect that it would be a matter of fine distinction to know t'other from which."[53]

Stephen was obviously still inebriated and Jane had to come to terms with the fact that she was married to an alcoholic who had a difficult time growing up. Perhaps in Allegheny it was all too easy to fall back into the role he had played before he married, that of a talented youth who wrote songs and performed them for his neighborhood Knights. But Stephen was a grown man now who, like many of his friends, had the responsibility of a wife and child. Stephen next turned his talents to writing campaign songs, something that sounded grown up and manly, but as the musical director of a glee club that was to sing James Buchanan into the presidency, he spent just as much time drinking and serenading in the wee hours of the night.

1. Stephen's parents, Eliza Clayland and William Barclay Foster.

2. White Cottage, the Foster family home in Lawrenceville, Pennsylvania.

3. The Federal Hill mansion in Bardstown, Kentucky.

4. Sheet music cover featuring Thomas Dartmouth Rice.

5. Brother William, Stephen's successful older sibling.

6. Stephen's sister Ann Eliza and her husband, Reverend Edward Y. Buchanan.

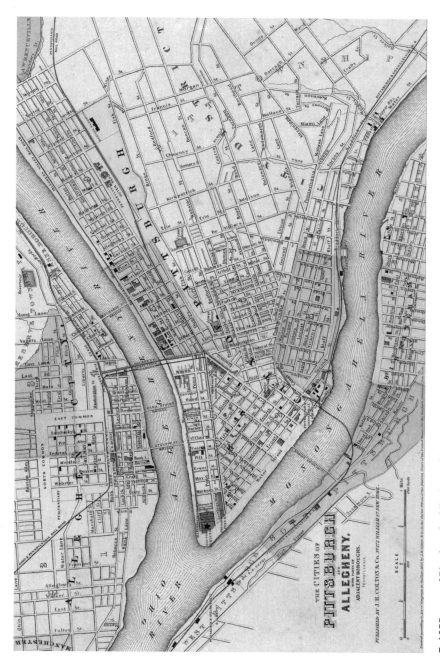

7. 1855 map of Pittsburgh, Allegheny City, and surrounding rivers.

8. Lithograph of the African American musician Francis Johnson.

9. Henry Kleber, who taught Stephen music theory and encouraged him to write songs.

10. Framed daguerreotype of Stephen Foster portrait showing his scar.

11. Dunning Foster, who employed his brother Stephen as a bookkeeper.

12. F... town ... Bu ... Ja ... ... R... ... c1848 C... ... ... in ... ... fronts ... on St ... L... ... ...

13. Marion Foster, Stephen's and Jane's only child.

14. Martin Delany, who studied medicine under Stephen's father-in-law.

15. Stephen's brother Henry Foster, who tried to get the composer into West Point.

16. Minstrel Edwin P. Christy, who sang Foster's plantation songs.

17. Stephen's "Old Folks at Home" sheet music, with Christy as composer.

18. Minstrel Charles White, an African American artist.

19. Hoboken row house where Stephen wrote "I Dream of Jeanie with the Light Brown Hair."

FIRST PRESIDENTIAL RESIDENCE —OCCUPIED BY GEORGE WASHINGTON, FRANKLIN SQUARE, N. Y., JUST DEMOLISHED. (SEE PAGE 414.)

20. Firth, Pond & Company at Franklin Square.

21. James Buchanan, a politically valuable in-law.

22. Stephen Foster in 1859.

23. Stephen's brother Morrison Foster, who was closest to the composer.

24. Clement Vallandigham, leader of the Copperheads.

25. "Political Cock Fighters" cartoon from 1844, portraying presidential candidates Clay and Polk.

THE COPPERHEAD PARTY.—IN FAVOR OF *A VIGOROUS PROSECUTION OF PEACE!*

26. Copperhead cartoon portraying Peace Democrats as snakes.

27. Stephen's sister Henrietta Foster and her second husband, Major Jesse Thornton.

28. Stephen Foster in New York.

29. Stephen Foster with soldier-lyricist George Cooper (on the right).

30. George Cooper, featured on the cover of sheet music.

CITY of NEW YORK.

31. Map of the City of New York, 1860, showing Lower Manhattan, where Stephen
lived his final years.

32. Famous comic singer Tony Pastor.

33. Andrew Carnegie in 1861.

34. Drawing of a New York concert saloon where the newest variety songs debuted.

35. Theater manager Laura Keene, who staged musical extravaganzas on Broadway.

36. Actor Charles W. Couldock on stage with his daughter Eliza.

37. The surviving Foster siblings after Stephen's funeral (clockwise): Henry, Morrison, Henrietta, and Ann Eliza.

38. Leather pocketbook and a scrap of paper with Foster when he died.

13

THE BUCHANAN GLEE CLUB

When Ann Eliza's brother-in-law James Buchanan ran for president of the United States on the Democratic ticket, Stephen wrote two lively campaign songs for the man, and in the process, helped bring "the worst president in the history of the country" into the White House.[1] There was no question about the Fosters doing anything they could to help Buchanan into the "White House Chair," the name of one of Stephen's campaign songs. He had done much for the family, and perhaps could do more if he won the presidency. Just as the Fosters depended on Brother William, they lately turned to James Buchanan, if not for money, then for recommendations that would bring rewarding jobs and government posts. Buchanan's party machine connections in Pennsylvania, and even his signature, brought good fortune. Henry had lost his clerkship in the Treasury after the Whig Zachary Taylor came to office, but when the Democrats returned to power with Franklin Pierce in the White House, James Buchanan saw to it that Henry was reinstated. A flattering letter of recommendation addressed to "His Excellency Franklin Pierce," assured the President that his "kin through marriage [Henry Foster] was a reliable & active Democrat, a gentleman of great respectability & highly esteemed in the city of his residence."[2]

The Fosters were long-time Democrats, even before they could claim a connection to James Buchanan. Stephen's father William supported Andrew Jackson from the time he risked and lost his fortune sending supplies to help win the Battle of New Orleans, and he continued to support Jackson and his Democratic Party through thick and thin from then on. In 1825, William won a seat in the Pennsylvania legislature in Harrisburg and was reelected to the position in 1828.[3] In 1842, he became Allegheny City's third mayor and remained in office two years. Many of his reasons for sticking with the party of Jackson were personal. "Old Hickory," for example, had closed down the infamous Bank of the United States that foreclosed on the White Cottage, and the Democratic Party's patronage system for years led to jobs, financial rewards, and government appointments for William's sons. His party connections provided Henry with the clerkship in Washington worth about $1000 a year, and his behind-the-scenes finagling helped son William secure the appointments that were key to his professional advancement.

James Buchanan was much older than Stephen Foster, by almost thirty years, making him about the same age as the younger man's father. He was born in 1791 in a log cabin at the foothills of the Allegheny Mountains in southern Pennsylvania, and like the senior William, his kinsmen were Scots-Irishmen who crossed the ocean to Philadelphia before settling in Mercersburg, Pennsylvania. Buchanan's father became a prosperous merchant and sent his son to Dickinson College in Carlisle, Pennsylvania, where he became a lawyer and served in the Pennsylvania Assembly. The young Buchanan was six feet tall, blond haired, and genetically beardless. At the age of twenty-eight, he became engaged to a wealthy socialite who broke off the commitment after her fiancé appeared more interested in her money and politics than he was in her. When the young woman died for no apparent reason soon after ending the engagement, people suspected suicide and a whiff of scandal followed the future president for many years afterward.[4]

Buchanan never married, and as America's only bachelor president, there have long been suspicions about his sexual preferences. Although he flirted with women at Washington levees, he was never known to be seriously involved with any. As a Congressman in Washington, he boarded with the handsome Senator William King from Alabama and the two remained intimate until the latter's death in the early 1850s. Many people in Washington commented on Buchanan's effeminate qualities, including Andrew Jackson who called him an "Aunt Nancy." At Buchanan's death, his niece destroyed the correspondence received over the years from King, and King's niece destroyed the letters Buchanan sent to her uncle. There is evidence that the Fosters did not always have flattering things to say about James Buchanan either, but many of their comments have also been consigned to the flame by protective and self-conscious relatives.

One consequence of Buchanan's permanent bachelor state was his generosity with his many impecunious relations. He lavished gifts, money, and political appointments on his younger brother Edward and his wife Ann Eliza, and when they settled down in Paradise, Pennsylvania—before ending up in Philadelphia—James Buchanan bought them a large house, which enabled them to move out of the boardinghouse they were renting. He even purchased the All Saints Episcopal Church, the historic parsonage in Paradise where Edward served as the pastor.[5] In later years, Ann Eliza's daughter spent a great deal of time with her president uncle, although she was not the daughter of his sister Jane, the favored niece Harriet Lane, who lived at the White House and took over the duties of first lady. James Buchanan did all he could to further the career of Ann Eliza's son, the president's namesake, James Buchanan Jr. Young James served as his uncle's secretary in the White House, and when the elderly former president died, he left quite a large fortune to his brother Edward, Ann Eliza, and their children.[6] Even if the Fosters were not in complete agreement with him politically, it would have been financial suicide for them not to have campaigned for James Buchanan.

Buchanan had excellent credentials and was very experienced when he ran for the presidency. He had served several terms in the House and the Senate, was appointed minister to Russia, and became Secretary of State under President Polk. But that was not why the Democrats wanted him as their candidate. He was chosen because of his absence from political involvement during passage of the Kansas-Nebraska Act that inaugurated a disastrous reign of violence and bloodshed in the territories. Buchanan was, in fact, out of the country during those contentious years, serving as minister to the Court of St. James, where he did a good job of keeping Britain out of Central American affairs. Unfortunately, his name was also irretrievably linked with the Ostend Manifesto, which would have added Cuba to the United States as another slave state.

His most peculiar attribute, and ultimately his downfall, was his devious devotion to Southerners, which earned him the name "doughface" for his malleable politics. Some critics thought the excess fat around his face in middle age would have branded him with the name anyway. When everyone was talking about what should be done with the new lands acquired from the Mexican-American War, he opposed the Wilmot Proviso, which would have kept slavery out of the new territories. When the Compromise of 1850 was finally worked out, he supported the new Fugitive Slave Law that gave federal marshals more money if they returned an escaped slave than if they freed him. When a slave catcher and his son were killed trying to retake a runaway slave in Christina, Pennsylvania, fifteen miles from Buchanan's country estate in Lancaster, Buchanan was appalled by the outcome and blamed the abolitionists for endangering the Union. He was too blinded by his partiality to the South to realize that slavery was becoming an anachronism in the age of industry and free labor.

Buchanan faced two competitors in the presidential race—one many years his junior—but he was not worried. John C. Frémont, the handsome young Republican known as "the pathfinder" for making daring forays into the unchartered West, was considered a dangerous radical, whose victory would lead to the nation's destruction. The other contender, the middle-aged former president Millard Fillmore of the American Party, ran on a platform of hatred of foreigners and Catholics, and had no chance of winning. Buchanan, at sixty-five, was indeed elderly when only 3 percent of white men lived to that ripe old age, but he appeared venerable. A shock of white hair dignified his cool, unruffled appearance, and he stood very erect except when he cocked his head to one side to accommodate his bad eye, while assuming the posture of an intent listener. Somehow he convinced himself and others that he was the only mortal capable of saving the Union.

When Stephen volunteered to write campaign songs for James Buchanan, it was not the first time he became musically involved in a political campaign. In the fall of 1851, when William Bigler ran for governor of Pennsylvania on the Democratic ticket and his brother John ran for governor of California, Stephen penned the verses for the campaign song "Hurrah for the Bigler Boys," but he did not write an original melody for it. He set the words to the tune of his already published "Camptown Races," a song everyone knew and could sing along with. The words were benign compared to the scathing words he would use against the Republicans to achieve Buchanan's election. "Going to run again? Johnston, your insane. I'll bet my money on the Bigler Boys, for the Whigs have had their reign." Stephen called the "Union . . . our cherished dream," but he seemed naive when he wrote "If South Carolina makes a fuss . . . Oh, why should we be in the muss?" His objective was simply to turn out the Whig opponent, which he did. Bigler won the election and became the Democratic governor, and Stephen had his first experience singing in a political victory.[7]

To help Buchanan win the White House five years later in 1856, Stephen joined with Morrison to form the all-male Buchanan Glee Club. Morrison was the treasurer of the club, and Stephen became its musical director. Thus Stephen's sole business with the Buchanan campaign involved writing songs and conducting a "political marching and singing band" that would hurrah Buchanan and his vice-presidential running mate, Kentuckian John C. Breckinridge, into the highest offices in the land. Music and midnight torchlight parades were highly regarded by both parties for bringing in the votes, and often carried more weight than political ideology. Foster's singing band may have filled the night air with the clang of brass instruments and the irritating sound of off-key, inebriated singers, but the Republicans who hurrahed for Frémont conducted midnight parades that were just as loud and boisterous as those put on by the opposition:

> The [Republican] campaign went on, in a blare of Fremont torchlight parades . . . giving the famous new staccato cheer, distributing handbills, shouting for "Bleeding Kansas" and for "Free Labor, Free speech, Free Men, Free Kansas and Fremont," drowning out the Buck and Breck[inridge] of the Democratic Buchaneers with the promise to "take the Buck by the horns." . . . And the Democrats laughed at the Republicans' "shrieks for freedom," and made a point of decorum and quiet dignity.[8]

Not that the activities of the Buchanan Glee Club were any more decorous. Billy Hamilton, who met Stephen in 1855, described the club's serenading experience when the singers, all Democrats, got into a fight with men from the volunteer fire company, who were campaigning for one of the opposing political parties. Even if the club's purpose were ostensibly political, the shenanigans appeared no different from any of Foster's nightly escapades. Hardly a week passed when they did not have some concert, musical, or serenade, and Hamilton described the summer and fall of 1856 during the campaign as exciting times. "I was a

Democrat then and so was Foster, and we organized a Glee Club for the purpose of booming the campaign in Allegheny." They had a "body guard" of fifty to one hundred men who formed the chorus when Stephen, Morrison, Hamilton, and Tim Smith sang the solo parts. "We would march through the streets singing campaign songs, and had many interesting conflicts with the Whigs and other political clubs."[9]

When the different political clubs bumped into one another in the street, the meeting was not amiable. One evening the Glee Club with its huge chorus stopped to serenade in Lawrenceville, and some stranger joined the crowd and insisted on singing the solo parts. When the appointed soloists asked him to stop and he refused, the chorus "body guard" gave him "a blow on the left ear" and knocked him down repeatedly. The Pittsburgh firemen, across the street, jumped into the fray and a vicious fight ensued. Hamilton described how he and the handful of "vocalists" escaped unscathed:

> In a twinkling, our peaceful body of serenaders was transformed into a howling mob. Foster, his brother [Morrison], myself and other vocalists hastened out of the crowd. We were all too small for our ages and had no business around where any fighting was going on. We always left that to our body guard and they protected us most effectually in that case. None of us was hurt, and few of the members of the guard suffered but the firemen were completely routed and driven back into their headquarters. They had attacked the wrong crowd that time.[10]

The firemen probably campaigned for the new Republican Party, or perhaps some favored Millard Fillmore's American or Know-Nothing Party, but disgruntled Whigs, the troublemakers Hamilton mentioned, could be found in either of these parties.[11]

If the "serenaders" that night in Lawrenceville sang anything like Foster's "Great Baby Show or the Abolition Show," they would have easily antagonized the firemen. Stephen set the "The Great Baby Show" to the popular "Villikins and His Dinah," a stage song based on an English folk ballad that everyone knew well enough to sing along with loud and clear. The new words were very offensive, yet there can be no doubt that Stephen wrote them because he devoted pages 128 through 137 in his manuscript book to Buchanan campaign songs. (Stephen, in fact, wrote the first eight verses of the song, and Morrison penned the less poetic-sounding last two.) The "Great Baby Show" attacked Republicans, calling them abolitionists, unknowing youths, border ruffians, and even New Englanders, and the song insulted further by suggesting that many of the followers of the Republican party were mere youths, who knew not what they were doing: "They had young men on horseback, so nice and so gay, Aged Seventeen years on this Seventeenth Day." Foster lumped together "gemmen ob color" with "jokers and clowns" and identified Republicans with "grim border ruffians" after the fanatics who attacked proslavery families in Kansas. People of New England stock were singled out as objects of ridicule, not only because Midwesterners had a common prejudice against them, but also because Buchanan hated New Englanders whom he associated with lunatic "isms" like abolitionism.[12] In the song's final published form, one verse appears as follows:

> They had Ohio Yankees of Western Reserve,
> Who live upon cheese, ginger cakes and preserves.
> Abolition's their doctrine, their rod and their staff.
> And they'll fight for a six pence an hour and a half.[13]

When Foster first experimented with "The Great Baby Show" on page 131 of his manuscript book, however, he became distracted from politics long enough to castigate the "Ohio Yankees" for mistreating their wives. After the line about "cheese, ginger cakes and preserves," he had written, "Their wives are their slaves and cold water their staff." Then he crossed out "slaves" and penned in "servants" above it, until he finally ran a heavy line through the whole sentence. What was he thinking?[14]

The "Great Baby Show" was written as a spoof or a satire of the massive Republican political rally staged in Pittsburgh and Allegheny City on September 17, 1856. The words to Stephen's song, without the music, were later published in the *Pittsburgh Post*, the Democratic paper, on September 26, 1856. What really bothered Stephen and Morrison was that the Frémont procession, named for the Republican presidential candidate, was phenomenally "successful even beyond the most sanguine anticipation of the warmest friends of the cause of Freedom." In comparison, the Democrats' convention held "only a week ago" was an abject failure. According to the Republican *Pittsburgh Gazette*, "the Buchanan men, after the labor of weeks, held a convention, and their procession contained only some fifteen hundred persons, with a few banners and no exhibition of the trades, or manifestation that the masses were interested in their cause."[15]

The Republican procession attracted 100,000 spectators and participants and was counted "the greatest political convention of the people ever held in Western Pennsylvania, and probably in this State." On that fateful Wednesday, the "seventeenth day" of the month, "every avenue leading to the city was crowded with every description of conveyance," as trainloads of people from the outlying areas augmented the size of the local Fremont crowds. "The windows of every house on the line of the procession were crowded with ladies, waving banners and handkerchiefs," and the streets were decorated with brightly colored flags and decorative "mottoes." The newspaper reported that the motley crowd of humanity that made up the procession was estimated to have extended from seven to nine miles in length, moving cumbersomely down the streets of Pittsburgh at the rate of three miles per hour. Included in the actual procession were at least 10,000 people, 1,700 horses, and 400 wagons and vehicles of every kind. The Frémont crowd annoyed the Fosters even more by setting up on the North Common, in Allegheny, right in their own neighborhood. Four stands were assembled, with speakers busy at every one, and neighborhood stores, shops, and manufactories were closed for the occasion.

Most upsetting, perhaps, was that the Republicans attracted the working class, men previously claimed by the Democrats and the determining factor in Pittsburgh's vote. While the Fremont procession represented "nearly every profession, art, trade and employment," tradesmen took the starring roles. Like actors in a play, "The stalwart blacksmith was hammering out his iron, the carpenter was pushing his plane, the moulder was preparing his moulds, the engine builder was turning his lathe." Indeed, the *Pittsburgh Gazette* found the key to Frémont's success in the city's workingmen: "Our convention was a great success. It has cheered the hearts of the friends of Freedom and carried dismay into the ranks of the Pro-slavery party. The procession gave unmistakable evidence that the workingmen, the mechanics, the farmers, and the laborers are with us."[16]

Foster's second campaign song, "The White House Chair," for which he wrote his own music, was published in the *Pittsburgh Post* twelve days later on September 29, 1856. The words reflected the concern that was paramount in the minds of Northern Democrats, the threat of disunion, and was far less offensive than Foster's earlier song:

Let all our hearts for Union be,
For the North and South are one;
They've worked together manfully,
And together they will still work on.
Then come ye men from ev'ry state,
Our creed is broad and fair;
Buchanan is our candidate
And we'll put him in the White House Chair. [17]

Yet both "The Great Baby Show" and "The White House Chair" spelled out themes and fears that appeared over and over again in 1856 in the *Pittsburgh Post.* The city's Democrats feared that abolition would allow thousands of freed slaves to move into Pittsburgh and take jobs away from whites. One newspaper article warned about the slaves, "They are mechanics!" while another suggested that abolition would lead to a reduction in wages for the white workers who would have to work for freedmen's wages. The Democrats put themselves on record as favoring freedom, saying, "Could slavery be abolished and the negroes removed to a separate home and country we would rejoice at it." But in the end economics ruled. Abolition "would be to subject the white laboring classes to an irresistible and most ruinous competition with cheap negro labor." The white working class also feared social equality and racial amalgamation. They opposed the idea that black "children shall go to the same schools with the white children. That their men shall labor together in the same occupations . . . [and] mingle in the same churches . . . That they shall go to the ballot boxes together." [18]

Stephen's attack on the abolitionists through his campaign songs appealed to the Democrats of Pittsburgh. Many viewed abolitionists as bloodthirsty fanatics and madmen who would stop at nothing to have their way—neither murder, mayhem, nor fratricidal warfare. They blamed the warfare in Kansas on the abolitionists, who, they said, had no respect for the new doctrine of Popular Sovereignty that allowed men to vote for or against slavery in a territory and was acceptable to many Democrats. Fearing civil war, disunity, and the end of their beloved republic, the Democrats warned Pittsburghers not to vote the Republican ticket, which they identified with the abolitionists: "Nothing but grim visaged war will suit abolition and pro-slavery agitators for without their pabulum . . . they will sink to the level of peaceful citizens and be heard of no more!"[19]

In spite of the economic ruin and bloodshed that the Democrats predicted a Republican victory would bring, John C. Frémont won in Pittsburgh by convincing the tradesmen and mechanics that Democrats were pro-Southern in sentiment, and had no respect for free labor, since Southerners thought labor was reserved for slaves. The *Gazette* quoted a South Carolinian gentleman who said that "Slavery is the natural and normal condition of laboring man, whether white or black." He even said working men were not "fit for self-government." When the *Gazette* quoted a Southern Democrat saying Northerners were "Greasy Mechanics, filthy operatives . . . struggling to be genteel," that was more than Pittsburghers would take. The following day, Pittsburgh's Allegheny County gave a majority of votes to Frémont and the Republicans. "We can hurrah over our own county, if over nothing else." James Buchanan won the presidency and Pennsylvania, but not Pittsburgh. Identified as a "national man equally acceptable to both North and South," he appeared to be the best candidate to those Americans who were still geared toward compromise.[20]

If "The Great Baby Show" affronts our sensibilities with its direct attack on abolitionists, the feeling is only intensified when we recall that the minstrel Edwin P. Christy identified Stephen as a "vacillating skunk." For only a few years back Stephen had flirted with the antislavery cause and written sympathetic plantation songs when he was involved in a personal and professional relationship with his abolitionist friend Charles Shiras. By 1856, Shiras was dead and the composer reversed his stand and attacked the Republicans so scathingly as to suggest something other than politics was goading him on. Of course, campaign songs in the nineteenth century were expected to be insulting, and "The Great Baby Show" is not nastier than most. But some other force appeared to be at work. Foster would have been pressured into believing that he was somehow betraying the family if he had not supported Buchanan, whose success impacted the family's financial well-being, and whose watchword throughout the campaign was antiabolitionism. Buchanan always maintained the abolitionists were the seed of the nation's problems, and in his last State of the Union Address, given when he was leaving office in December 1860, he pointedly blamed them for tearing the country apart. The culprit, said the depart-

ing president, was twenty-five years of "agitation against slavery" promoted in the press, when "all that was necessary" to "settle the slavery
question forever" was to leave the slave states alone to manage their
"domestic institutions" in their own way.

Buchanan may have convinced the thirty-year-old Stephen, as he
had so many others, that a Republican victory would mean the end of
the Union. He identified the Republicans as abolitionists, which they
were not, and over and over again assured the public that the South
would secede if the Republicans won, which it did four years later. The
abolitionists were easy to attack in 1856, now that their methods were
associated with violence. Five years earlier when Stephen worked on
sympathetic minstrel songs in Shiras's front parlor, the weapon of
choice for antislavery men and women was talk, moral suasion, and
sympathy. Now both abolitionists and anti-abolitionists took up bloodier
weapons. In May 1856, when Charles Sumner, the senator from Massachusetts denounced a South Carolina congressman on the slavery issue,
the latter responded by beating him nearly to death with his walking
cane. In Kansas, the fanatical abolitionist John Brown dragged unarmed
proslavery men out of their houses at night and hacked them to pieces.
Abolitionists were being characterized as fanatical madmen who would
stop at nothing to make liberty for the slave a reality. That Stephen was
antislavery in his heart, there is no doubt, but as with many men in
1856, the threat of fraternal bloodshed and national dissolution was
perhaps too high a price to pay for the slave's freedom.

The Buchanan campaign certainly kept Stephen busy and probably
turned his thoughts away from the family's recent losses, but it did not
make him productive in a way that would solve his financial problems.
He was the head of the house on the East Common and had a wife and
a daughter to support, but he was unable to pay his bills. Even with
royalties coming in from songs he had written in previous years, he had
to write at least a dozen new songs each year to make his current Firth,
Pond and Company contract profitable, yet he wrote only one commercial song in 1856, "Gentle Annie." His mother or father may have provided a small inheritance that enabled him to squander his time for a
while, but it is more likely that he was too disturbed to write. With a
heavy heart, fretting over finances and personal losses, Stephen vented
his frustration in song, attacking the new Republican Party and the
abolitionists. All in all, it appears that Stephen Foster's involvement

with President Buchanan's campaign and the Buchanan Glee Club was very little motivated by politics. Rather, it was a familial obligation, offering at the same time the chance to drown out his sorrow in mind-numbing activities that involved music, drink, and boisterous merriment.[21]

There was an irony in store for Stephen as soon as Buchanan moved into the White House. Foster's great plantation songs had portrayed blacks as sympathetic human beings, but the Dred Scott ruling made sure that African Americans would not be considered men at all. In February 1857, one month before Buchanan took office, Supreme Court Justice Catron of Tennessee told the new president that the justices were split on their decision about the Missouri slave who sued for his freedom and asked him to do something about it. Buchanan immediately sent secret messages to his friend Justice Robert Grier, "urging a comprehensive judgment that moved beyond the particulars of Dred Scott's individual status into that of all black Americans—slave and free, North and South." He wanted the court to reach a decision that could be used to end the slavery issue once and for all. Grier talked things over and, two days after Buchanan's inauguration, Supreme Court Justice Roger Taney ruled that slaves were private property without any rights white men were "bound" to respect. The Missouri Compromise was nullified, slavery could not be prohibited in the territories, and in fact could grow up almost anywhere. After the Dred Scott decision, a black man was not a man at all.[22]

During the campaign, Stephen seemed to have adopted Buchanan's politics, all for the sake of security and financial gain for the family. Buchanan won the election and moved into the White House, but he did not leave office gracefully. The man who built a twenty-two room house in Lancaster, Pennsylvania, surrounded himself with dozens of his nieces and nephews, and then showered them with monetary gifts, government positions, clerkships, and promotions. Ann Eliza's son James Buchanan moved to the White House and served as his uncle's personal secretary. But President Buchanan paid the price for his generosity and nepotism. In his last year in office he was investigated on charges of corruption and almost impeached. The lesser charges made against him were for his generosity in doling out offices and patronage jobs to his relatives. One citation was for "a nephew through marriage" who was given a post and never showed up on workdays, only on paydays. As one historian explained, "He ran a family employment agency dunning his political friends for patronage positions for some of his nephews as government clerks." Considering that Henry Foster was a clerk in the Treasury Department for many years, and that Ann Eliza's son James enjoyed educational gifts courtesy of his strange uncle, the Fosters were lucky they were never implicated.[23]

On a blustery March 4, 1857, James Buchanan, victorious over his younger opponents, stood before a large crowd in Washington to "take the solemn oath" to "faithfully execute the office of President of the United States." Edward Buchanan and several of his eight living children, including the president's namesake James, were present to witness their uncle's inauguration and to enjoy the festivities of the occasion. Ann Eliza was sick and had to stay home in Philadelphia. Stephen, who had adjusted his moral compass to make a musical contribution to Buchanan's crowning achievement, was not present at the victory celebration either. He missed hearing the new president boast how he had settled the question of slavery in the territories forever and how he would preserve the nation intact and free from corruption. When he left office four years later, Buchanan had broken every promise he had ever made.[24]

14

ROYALTIES SELLOUT

Three weeks after James Buchanan gave his inaugural address and promised an enduring union and abundant prosperity for the nation, Stephen found himself homeless. On April 13, 1857, William Foster Jr. sold the brick house on the East Common, along with two other frame houses he owned in Allegheny, to a Dr. John S. Kuhn. Exactly when Stephen learned his brother planned on selling the house he called home for the past twelve years has not been determined. William could have mentioned it when he brought his wife Elizabeth's body back to be buried in the Allegheny Cemetery in February 1857. Or Stephen may have known earlier because he began working on his finances the month before. On January 27, 1857, he must have known something was amiss because on that day he made up a list in his manuscript book estimating the value of his songs in terms of future royalties. His income was almost entirely dependent on royalties, and excluding the Buchanan campaign songs, he had written only one song in 1856.

The sad fact was that Stephen's songs were well known throughout the nation and in far off places around the globe, yet he could not earn enough money to maintain himself and his family. Only five days before, on January 22, 1857, John B. Russell, a friend from his Cincinnati days, published an article in the *Cincinnati Daily Gazette* praising the worldwide popularity of Foster's music:

> If popularity is any test of merit . . . probably no man's ideas have been more often repeated, when we consider singing, playing, whistling, etc. His tunes are a perpetual solace to the miner of California,

the slave in the cotton fields of the South, and they gladden the tedious watches of the sailor in every sea reached by American or English enterprise. It is hardly too much to assert there is not a family in this country where any musical taste exists, that has not been cheered with the melody of his songs. In fact, they are sung all over the civilized world, the seacoast cities of China not excepted. We lately read of an American traveler (Bayard Taylor, we think) teaching "Uncle Ned" to the Arabs in Africa, and explaining to them, at their request, the meaning of the words, in their own dialect. A Paris correspondent of a Boston paper says, on hearing "Oh, Susannah," whistled through the streets, he enthusiastically cried out, "America forever!" Dickens speaks of its popularity in the prisons of England; and a friend who has spent some time in Central America, says he has heard the natives amuse themselves by the hour, in singing snatches of Foster's early songs, which they had caught from the roving Californians.[1]

On January 28, 1857, the day after he compiled the fateful list, Stephen thanked Russell for the "complimentary notice of me and my music" in the *Gazette*, which he said he would forward to his New York publishers "for insertion in any paper." Realizing the irony that a man whose music was world renowned could not earn enough to keep the respect of his wife, Foster wrote, "How a man likes to show these little flattering testimonials to his wife! If it were not for that, the benefit to me of your kind and friendly action would be half lost."[2]

For several months, Foster held on to his list of future royalty values, probably waiting to see what would happen while he debated whether or not to approach his publishers with a sellout proposition. Money, or rather its lack, was a source of constant worry, but he did not let on about it to his friends. To Billy Hamilton, to whom he wrote in the middle of January, he revealed nothing. Instead, he joked about the dog Billy had given him that earned the name "Rat-Trap" for its omnivorous appetite for "shoes, stockings, spools, the Cat and everything else that he could find lying around loose."[3] Even to his brother William, he said nothing about the anxiety that overwhelmed him on a daily basis. On March 11, 1857, he sent him the manuscript for Buchanan's campaign song, "The Great Baby Show or the Abolition Show," which he had written the previous year, and attached to it a cordial note: "Herewith I send you the words of the show song in full, with one verse of the music. We are all quite well." Stephen kept his own counsel and made no decisions about his royalties until after he learned the house had been sold in the middle of April. It was a serious blow to all the occupants, including Morrison and his nephew James Buchanan who still lived in the house, but the blow was particularly devastating to the composer and his wife and daughter.[4]

Firth, Pond and Company had paid Stephen $9,436.96 in royalties from November 14, 1849 to January 27, 1857. In his calculations of their future value, he originally estimated that his copyright interests were worth at least $2,786.77, but Firth and Pond only agreed to give him $1,872.28. That amount was reduced further because he had already drawn out $640.00 and on March 19 he took another $300.00 advance. He had also been paid the January 1 royalty amount of $267.72. In the end, his publishers only owed $1,200.00 as the onetime fee for future royalties, which they paid on May 30, 1857, six weeks after William sold the house. Foster was in such a hurry that "on May 27, three days before the notes were dated, he discounted the three four-hundred dollar notes at the Pittsburgh Trust Company" and put the money into the bank, drawing on it "until December 29 of the same year (1857)."[5] He also made a similar arrangement with his Baltimore publisher, accepting $200.00 for all future royalties on the sixteen songs that F. D. Benteen had published for him over the previous decade.

Stephen thought he could survive with his small family for a year on the $1,200.00, but he went through the money in six months. He was surprised because he had lived on $1,100.00 in 1856, considerably less than the $500.00 a quarter he claimed he earned in the past. From the time he signed his first contract with Firth, Pond and Company seven years before, his actual earnings averaged $1,425.84 a year, an amount that would have kept his family in a modest style of comfort, had he been able to keep up production and not been forced to ask for advances.[6] But the muse had not visited him lately, his income was shrinking as a consequence, and he did not expect things to get any better. Now he grabbed at the money and he and his family devoured it.

A major factor in Foster's decision to sell off his copyrights must have been the knowledge of the impending sale of the Union Avenue house, but what compelled William to sell in the first place is open to speculation. There may be more than one answer, but William's health was a crucial consideration. After his wife Elizabeth died late in October 1856, he himself began to show signs of a serious illness and confided to Morrison that he had "a weak (left) breast," possibly a symptom of tuberculosis. "This, of course," he told his brother circumspectly, "is all for your own information, as I don't want the impression to get out that my health requires any such precaution" like a trip to a "warmer climate." His bosses noticed something was amiss, however, and ordered him to take a month's vacation.[7]

Another factor in William's decision to sell the house was the economy. In the summer of 1857, several months after President Buchanan thanked a higher being for America's abundant prosperity, a bust cycle attacked the western sections of the country. Pointing to the inflation in land prices from buying and selling on easy credit, one newspaper headline predicted, "Things cannot last!" But Stephen's savvy older brother, who was then vice president of the Pennsylvania Railroad, would have expected as much. He had insider information and probably already knew that the booming economy depended on the over-expansion of the railroad lines, a factor later cited as a cause of the depression. When the Panic of 1857 hit the nation full strength in September, banking institutions suspended payment and closed their doors, stocks plummeted, farm and land sales stopped, and more than 5,000 businesses failed. Western cities like Pittsburgh seemed to suffer the most and even the mighty railroads fell into the hands of receivers, along with small farms that had been foolishly mortgaged to purchase railroad stock. William's knowledge of the railroad's finances would have been enough to convince him to put his houses on the market in the spring, and he could have told Stephen at the beginning of the year to prepare for the worst. Foster's early biographers scorned his decision to sell off his royalty rights, but he may have made the only decision he could in view of the disastrous financial depression and his anguished mental state.[8]

William's decision to sell the Allegheny houses and to pull all support from Stephen when he did still seems heartless and leaves questions unanswered. Even with his health deteriorating and the economy faltering, could he not have left one of the houses for his hapless younger brother? It is a difficult judgment call, especially after learning that William did not have as much money in 1857 as would be expected of a man in his position. When he informed his brother Morrison of his weak lung, he wrote, "having no estate, my life is all to my children."[9]

He probably felt he needed to liquidate all his assets as quickly as possible to protect his children should he die. Other factors that come to mind are resentment for the many years the Fosters pressured him for financial support. Maybe William began to sense that he was an enabler, making it too easy for Stephen to shirk the manly duty of providing a home for his family. With growing health problems and flagging finances, he may have simply felt too tired and worn-out to worry about the Fosters anymore. He had long since repaid his debt to his adoptive parents Eliza and William, which ended with their deaths two years earlier. Morrison, who had been living in the house since January, was still a bachelor and could live comfortably in a boarding-house, and young James Buchanan could always find a home closer to his president uncle—or even move into the White House. That left only Stephen, Jane, and Marion. Of course, if he had kept the one house on the East Common after selling off the others, and turned it over to Stephen, such generosity would have been an act of benevolence, but for some reason he chose not to.

The loss of his home for the second time in his life marked the beginning of the composer's final emotional and financial decline. Stephen never really knew the White Cottage, which was subsequently so altered by the new owner's renovations that he could only imagine what it must have looked like when his parents lived there. The brick house at 605 Union Avenue in Allegheny was the only permanent home known to him and Morrison, and its sale was unsettling to all involved. As if repeating the life story of Stephen's parents, the ousted Fosters became boarders and moved into a succession of rented rooms and houses in Pittsburgh and elsewhere. Around the middle of April 1857, Stephen, Jane, and Marion settled into the Eagle Hotel at 274 Liberty Street in Pittsburgh where they paid the proprietor John Mish twelve dollars per week, always paying late, according to Stephen's account books. [10] Morrison, who found "his belongings scattered," moved into a Mrs. Leech's establishment on Penn Street, until February 1858, when he turned down a job offer from the Pittsburgh Canal and moved to Philadelphia to live with his brother William. Henry Foster, although gainfully employed at the Pittsburgh and Steubenville Railroad Company, was living with his wife and daughter in a large house in Lawrenceville near the Allegheny River, but it was not his house. It belonged to his mother-in-law, so he was not at liberty to invite in the homeless Fosters.[11]

The boardinghouse lifestyle, which became the couple's predominate mode of existence after the sale of the Allegheny house, did not agree with Jane and probably contributed to increasing resentment against her husband. Stephen was used to boardinghouses, since he spent portions of his childhood in a variety of them, but they would have been highly disagreeable to Jane, and an unpleasant reminder that her status in society was sinking since her marriage to America's favorite composer. She had grown up in a single family house where all five daughters found plenty of room for privacy, with a parlor for entertaining and receiving guests. Jane must have wondered how little Marion would achieve respectability when her mother and father had no parlor of their own, and worse still, how she would attract suitors when she was of courting age. Single men, and even women, lived in boardinghouses, but married couples, especially if they came from the better classes and had children, did not want to share living space with strangers.[12]

Stephen was more accustomed to boarding-house life than his wife, but the move to Pittsburgh still depressed him and squelched his creative energies. He missed Allegheny, and the neighbors missed the familiar sight of the composer and his little daughter strolling side by side through the parkland in the summer, when the flowers were in full bloom and the Commons a bright green. Marion often walked with the little, black Scotch terrier Stephen had exchanged for Billy Hamilton's troublesome dog, gripping the leash with one small hand while clutching her father's hand in the other. No longer would they stand together watching the barges and passenger boats glide by on Allegheny's waterways, or stop to talk with the toll house collector who admired Stephen's music without knowing he was chatting with the famous composer himself.

Stephen seemed to enjoy being a father, once Marion was old enough to be a little person. After Jane bought her dancing slippers, her father brought her to her lessons on Liberty Avenue in Pittsburgh every Saturday afternoon and returned after the class to pick her up. He was fun loving in the presence of his daughter, except when he was under pressure to compose. Then, it was said, his personality switched from "warmhearted and affectionate" to "amazing irritability." Since he could not tolerate "interruptions when he wanted to work," Marion had to be "kept out of his study until the song was completed," after which Stephen "turned again into the merry, romping comrade, and her laughter was music in his ears."[13]

In 1857, Stephen published only one new song, "I See Her Still in My Dreams," about a lost loved one, and he arranged "Gentle Annie," the song he composed the previous year, for the guitar. Firth, Pond and Company still paid royalties on new compositions, but Foster's output was too small to earn enough money to defray his family's expenses. He needed cash to pay his landlord at the Eagle Hotel for past due rent and to cover the down payment on the house or apartment he rented in April 1858, from William and James Murdock. It is not clear how long the Fosters stayed with the Murdocks. His account book mentioned "5 quarters" at a cost of forty dollars, but a few months later in August the Fosters were living with a "Mrs. Johnston," possibly at the Johnston Hotel at East Liberty Station, where he paid nine dollars per week for the family.[14] Stephen was also spending on alcohol, because with his increased anxiety since the loss of the house, he turned more and more to drink.

On February 9, 1858, Foster took the train to New York to draw up a new contract with Firth, Pond and Company, one he hoped would bring in more money. Although he would earn nothing from his old songs, the new agreement promised 10 percent royalties on all new songs and one cent on instrumental arrangements, but his publishers had once again grown impatient with his requests for advances. The previous month, on January 1, 1858, having earned just $31.25 in royalties on new songs, he had asked for and received an advance of $100.00. Now they asked not only for exclusivity, but that his accounts be settled quarterly, with full settlement on demand, and Foster accepted. He was desperate and upon signing the new contract, he renounced all royalties from "I See Her Still in My Dreams" in return for an additional $25.00 advance. On February 25, his publishers gave him a "loan" of $50.00, and he took another $43.75 for his traveling expenses to New York. In 1858, Stephen was only able to produce five parlor songs for Firth, Pond and Company, most about loss, death, and separation. In addition to the melodic "Linger in Blissful Repose," he wrote "Lula is Gone," followed by the repetitive sounding "Where Has Lula Gone?" Other titles were "My Loved One and My Own or Eva," and "Sadly to Mine

Heart Appealing," copyright on December 28. Although five songs in 1858 were more than he had produced in the past two years, the numbers were not satisfying to either the composer or his publisher.[15]

After vacating the Allegheny house, Stephen spent less time composing and more time socializing with friends, which served to distract him from his problems. Stephen was said to prefer highbrow entertainment, or else Jane thought that morally uplifting theater would keep him from his drinking companions. Whatever the case may be, he and Jane spent intimate "Musical evenings" in the company of Morrison and Jessie Lightner, Henry and his wife Mary, Andy and Susan Robinson, the Blairs, and Dick Cowan. The couple attended a performance of *Anthony and Cleopatra* because Stephen was very fond of Shakespeare, and they dressed in evening attire for the musical concerts "presented by Henry Kleber, Professor Rohbock, and William Evens' choral societies." Stephen could be a severe critic, however, and was known to "stamp indignantly out of the theater at some especially offensive discord by the singer or orchestra." He could also be derisive and mock the classical musicians since, as noted before, he was a wonderful mimic. When they lived in the Allegheny house, Stephen was known to return home from a classical recital in "a stuffy music hall" and "go to the piano, dash back his hair from his forehead, flip out the tails of his long-tail blue, and proceed to give a 'fantasie brilliante' on 'Jim Crow' or 'Camptown Races' in the frenzied manner of the artist of the evening."[16]

Even if Stephen had a preference for classical music concerts and Shakespeare, he obviously still enjoyed the humor and vitality of the lowbrow entertainments. Morrison had introduced Stephen to minstrel shows when they were children, but he also introduced him to the circus, and to his good friend, Daniel McLaren, who became a world-famous clown. The fourteen-year-old McLaren was employed at Massingham's stable at Front and Ferry Street in Pittsburgh, caring for the horses, when he met Morrison, who was working a few blocks away at Cadwallader Evans' Mill at Ferry and Water Streets. Morrison, Dan, and Stephen hung around together, and whenever a circus or minstrel show came to the city, they obtained the best seats they could afford and, mesmerized by the spectacle, squeezed together three in a row.

Dan McLaren became the most famous and highest-paid clown in the country after he changed his name to Dan Rice, benefiting from sharing a surname with the famous minstrel Thomas Dartmouth Rice. Minstrelsy and clowning had much in common. One performer wore black paint and a wooly wig, and was more adept at song and dance. The opposition wore white paint and an unnatural, colored hairpiece, and was more talented with acrobatics and horses. But clowns sometimes put on blackface and took the parts of minstrels. When Dan Rice started his stage career, he appeared in blackface as an Ethiopian Serenader and later with Dan Emmett and the Virginia Minstrels. Clowns, like minstrels, often spoofed their social betters in skits that were crude and bawdy but without the darky accent, and the whole thing—the musty animal smells, the brightly colored costumes, the loud noises, and the death-defying acts—appealed to the lowbrow tastes of immigrants and workers. [17]

Dan Rice must have reminded Stephen of the minstrel performers. If the minstrels bantered back and forth with the master of ceremony, Rice the clown bantered with his ring master and proved the clown was no fool. If Stephen felt frustrated with the minstrel shows and what they had become, if he became sick with remorse just thinking about Edwin Christy and the great song he had surrendered, he could still find joy in the spectacle of the circus, and for years, whenever Dan Rice came to town, Morrison and Stephen had free passes to front row seats. [18]

Being a spectator at an entertainment, whether a staid music concert or a flamboyant circus act, was one thing, but Stephen knew that, with the limited number of songs he was writing, he needed to cut back on his evenings out and do something that would make him more productive. The house on Union Avenue had a piano in a third floor room to which he could retreat for privacy, but with the boarding-house lifestyle, he had no place to compose. [19] Starting in July 1858, Stephen leased a studio for about a year (until August 1859), probably at the same location at 112-114 Smithfield Street where he had maintained an office after Marion was born. He also rented a piano for twelve dollars a quarter from Charlotte Blume, wife of the local piano dealer Frederick Blume. [20] The office was in the vibrant, artsy section of downtown Pittsburgh, where the local musicians, writers, and artisans congregated. Henry Kleber, the classically trained musician who was once Stephen's music teacher, opened a new music store at 53 Fifth Street, about two blocks from Stephen's office, and Mellor's music store was also nearby, as was Gillespie's, a favorite hangout for the famous Pittsburgh genre painter David Gilmour Blythe.

When Foster stepped outside his office, he could easily be distracted. His boyhood friends from the Knights of the Square Table club were grown up now and some had offices nearby. If they stopped to chat with Stephen, these young men with rising careers might have been painful reminders of his own failure. Even if he did enjoy their company, their success staring him in the face could have driven him to seek solace in drink. And the logistics were easy and inviting. Foster's studio on an upstairs floor of an office building was right above Robert Wray's grocery, at a time when liquor was freely served in the backrooms of groceries or could be purchased with some small items of food in the front section of the store. It is easy to imagine Stephen sitting at the piano in his office, becoming frustrated, and slipping downstairs for a drink or two to ease the writer's block or the nagging sense that his muse was out flirting with some other artist.[21]

Stephen, more and more, was spending nights out with his rowdy friends, serenading, carousing, and mostly drinking. Although Jane had tried to discourage the habit by asking him to restrict his evening activities to classical concerts and dramatic plays, the plan did not work. She must have worried that Marion was old enough to notice when her father did not come home at night, and she did not want her to witness Stephen's alcoholic revelries. Therefore, in the fall of 1858, she encouraged her husband to accept an invitation for a river excursion to Cincinnati aboard the steamboat *Ida May*, even though she did not approve of the boat's captain. Billy Hamilton was the Buchanan Glee Club singer who had been involved in the heated confrontation with the volunteer firemen two years before. Still, Jane was ready for a getaway. They were boarding uncomfortably at Mrs. Johnston's and the cruise would serve as both a distraction for Stephen and a much-needed vacation for all the stressed-out Fosters.[22] At the same time, she hoped her husband might be inspired to write a song or two as the boat drifted along the placid Ohio.

When Hamilton first extended the invitation, Stephen was reluctant to accept. His old friend Bill Blakely, like his deceased brother Dunning, had contracted some disease while serving in the Mexican-American War. Stephen brought him medicine, but he had shown no improvement after taking it, and was in fact dying. "Bill looks worse than when I last saw him," he informed Morrison after visiting him on October 22, 1858.[23] A week later, Stephen was still unwilling to leave his sick friend and looked around for a replacement. "Neither Henry nor I feel inclined to go to Cincinnati," he told Morrison, "but our old friend Tom Smith says he will go willingly." They also knew a "hard working Glass blower" with family in Cincinnati who would gladly trade places with them.[24] But on the morning of November 11, Bill Blakely died and Stephen made a quick decision to take the cruise after all.

It was Jane's and Stephen's first visit in ten years to the city where they had started their courtship, but the boat was too crowded for romantic intimacies. This time their daughter traveled with them, as did Stephen's niece Mary Wick, Henrietta's daughter from her first marriage. Marion was seven years old, just the same age Stephen was when his mother took him downriver to Cincinnati and Kentucky. She had grown to be a beautiful child with dark hair and intense dark eyes, and she looked very much like her father. Stephen wanted her to experience the pleasures of the riverboat he had known as a child, and he welcomed the excursion in spite of the weather, which, on the day before departure, had turned "cloudy, dull cold . . . with scarcely a gleam of sunshine." In a letter to Morrison dated November 11, 1858, Stephen wrote, "Mary Wick, Jane, Marion and I start tomorrow for Cincinnati on Billy Hamilton's boat, the *Ida May*. . . . [T]he trip will be a recreation and variety for me. Siss [Susan Pentland Robinson] gets along very well since her mother's death. We had a nice duck supper with her the other evening. She had plenty of jokes about [her husband] Andy, as usual."[25]

While onboard, he completed the song "Parthenia to Ingomar" for which he wrote only the music. Stephen's young actor friend, William Henry McCarthy, contributed the words. Since the death of Charles Shiras, McCarthy was probably the first poet Stephen worked with in a collaborative relationship, and he seemed to like it. The two men used to meet for "lively musical evenings" at the home of Harry and Rachel Keller Woods in the Hazelwood section of Pittsburgh, where they worked out the intricacies of fitting notes and words together. As a team, they would publish two additional songs in 1859, "For Thee Love, For Thee" and "Linda Has Departed," proving to Foster that collaborative songwriting could be efficient, creative, and enjoyable. Perhaps, since leaving the Allegheny house, he felt more inspired working with another person rather than in the solitary confinement of the studio.

Unfortunately, the trip did not turn out exactly as Jane planned. Once the *Ida May* docked in Cincinnati, Stephen and Billy Hamilton took off to have the kind of fun for which Billy was known. An early-season storm covered the roof tops with an inch of compacted snow but neither the storm nor the pleadings of Jane could keep Stephen from serenading the night away with Billy and his equally rough companions.[26] Billy was not the man Jane wanted her husband to hang around with after hours, but she could do little to confine or control Stephen, especially in another city in another state. The following is a description of their adventure:

> On their way down Broadway, they [Stephen and Billy] heard music and discovered a party of serenaders in a yard . . . . "Why," said Stephen, "they're singing my song, 'Come where My Love Lies Dreaming'." "Yes," responded Billy, "and making an awful bungle of it, too. Let's go over and help them out." Accordingly, Stephen and Billy crossed over and joined in with the singers. After the song was finished, the Cincinnati boys turned on the newcomers and demanded to know why they had intruded. Billy Hamilton introduced himself and stated that his companion was Stephen Foster, the composer of their serenade. The singers scoffed at the idea and began to grow so belligerent that Billy asked them if they knew Cons Miller down at the *Gazette* office. They replied that they did, and Billy asked them if they would take Cons' word for it . . . . Cons Miller identified them both beyond question and assured the skeptical Cincinnatians that the brown-eyed stranger was indeed Stephen C. Foster, the composer. Nothing was too good for the visitors after that, and instead of returning to the steamboat, Stephen and Billy spent the evening in the company of their new friends, serenading the entire neighborhood, and otherwise making merry.[27]

We have to sympathize with Jane's predicament. She was married to a man who at the age of thirty-two still serenaded the night away in the company of rowdies like the "Cincinnati boys." Without a doubt, drink figured strongly in the evening's activities. Presumably Jane waited on the *Ida May* for her husband to return, but the couple's verbal exchange would not have been pleasant when Stephen showed up at the boat just before dawn the next morning. She could not have been happy watching her husband throw off his grown-up skin and revert to the antics of an adolescent. He revealed two different sides to his personality, a change certainly exaggerated by the alcohol. Foster could project the image of an intensely sensitive man, almost effeminate in his emotional displays, whose eyes filled with tears when he sang a sentimental song, or he could reveal a spirited side few spoke about or witnessed. As his brother Morrison explained, "This sensitive man had the nerve and courage of a lion physically."[28]

Morrison Foster told a story about Stephen that sounds barely believable considering his size and demeanor. If true, he might have been in an alcohol-induced state. Morrison said his brother was walking over the bridge from Pittsburgh one night, on his way home to Allegheny, when he came across "two brutes abusing and beating a drunken man." Stephen "of course interfered and fought them both . . . . He managed to pick up a piece of a board . . . with which he beat one almost senseless and chased the other ingloriously from the field." For his efforts, Stephen earned a scar on his cheek, "which went with him to the grave."[29] The scar is clearly visible in an 1859 daguerreotype, but the story about how he earned it is less credible. With his slight build and five-foot-seven-inch frame, he hardly seemed capable of taking on two fighters, "rough and tumble all over the street," unless in self-defense. Perhaps he was the man attacked by the "two brutes" when he stumbled home in the wee hours of the morning after a night of alcoholic serenading, or perhaps one of the firemen confronting the Buchanan Glee Club carved the knife wound on his face.[30]

In the spring of 1859, Stephen, Jane, and Marion were boarding with a Mrs. Miller, but Jane took whatever opportunity she could to bring herself and her nine-year-old daughter somewhere else. They alternated between visits to Jane's sisters in eastern Pennsylvania or her husband's sister in Warren, Ohio, a small town eighty miles northwest of Pittsburgh where Henrietta settled after she married Jesse Thornton. Stephen missed his daughter when Jane took her away, but he understood why she did so. Seeing Marion grow up in a boardinghouse must have reminded him of his own childhood and been painful to watch. So when Jane took her little excursions with Marion, he missed her but became resigned. At least Henrietta welcomed her sister-in-law into her home now and appeared to be less critical than she had been in past years. The reason for the friendlier relationship between the women was probably that Henrietta could see that while Jane had matured and accepted the responsibilities of adulthood, her younger brother would not.

At the close of the year, Stephen grew increasingly anxious knowing his money would run out in 1860. The exclusive contract with Firth and Pond from February 9, 1858 was due to expire the following August and he began to look around for new publishing opportunities. A small Pittsburgh paper known as *Clark's School Visitor* that was geared to teachers and students began reprinting some of Stephen's songs in 1859, publishing them either with the composer's original poetry or with special words that would appeal to children. To the tune of "Uncle Ned," for instance, they set the following words:

> There's a great deal of pleasure in the school I attend,
> And I do love to go, love to go!
> With pleasure our lessons are all made to blend,
> And we learn what we all ought to know.

Since the words were not Foster's, perhaps the composer believed the exclusivity clause with Firth, Pond and Company did not apply. Although *Clark's* republished "Mass'a in the Cold Ground" in their December 1859 issue, they did so with the permission of his New York publishers. The following year *Clark's School Visitor* was bought out by Daughaday and Hammond, a Philadelphia firm, and Foster began to consider making a permanent move to New York. There he might renew his contract with Firth and Pond, establish a closer relationship with *Clark's* new owners, or reach out to new publishers in Manhattan. In any event, Pittsburgh no longer felt like home to Stephen. Instead, it had become a painful reminder of "the voices that were gone." Mother, father, and Dunning were all dead. Although Henry Foster stayed on in Lawrenceville, he had a wife and children who demanded all his attentions. And Morrison, the brother to whom Stephen was closest, suddenly decided to move far away to another state.[31]

After the cotton business went under in Pittsburgh, Morrison found himself unemployed with no viable prospects in his home town. His boss McCormick, who had been parceling off the Hope Cotton business for the last several years, asked him to find a buyer for the one remaining factory so that he could devote his money to "iron and steel." Morrison managed to sell the machinery for $45,000, but nobody had cash for the property. Eventually, the factory ended up in the hands of a

James H. Childs who kept the mill going making "seamless" cotton bags.[32] McCormick went into the iron business and Morrison, after twenty years in cotton manufacture, looked about for new opportunities. Finding nothing in Pittsburgh, he moved to Philadelphia because his brother William, who was very ill and dying, asked him to. William needed Morrison for emotional support, and offered him some temporary work while the unemployed brother figured out his next step in life.

At the beginning of 1860, Morrison returned to Pittsburgh, still without permanent employment, and decided it was time to marry. Nearly a decade had passed since the beautiful but fickle Julia Murray broke Morrison's heart to marry a scion of the abolitionist LeMoyne family and inspired Stephen to write the duet "Wilt thou Be Gone, Love?"[33] On February 23, 1860, having remained a bachelor longer than his contemporaries, Morrison took his vows at the advanced age of thirty-seven, and the bride he chose was Jessie Lightner, the contralto who a decade earlier sang Stephen's parlor songs to perfection.[34] Little more than a week after the ceremony, William Foster Jr. who was too sick to attend the wedding, died in Philadelphia, his head inclined across the shoulder of his loving stepson. An infected "carbuncle on his neck" that closed over and spread into his bloodstream was identified as the cause of death, but other factors were involved. William had been ill for more than three years, even before he told Morrison in 1856 that he suffered from "a weak (left) breast."[35] Brother William was fifty-two when he died on March 4, 1860.[36]

The day after the wedding, Morrison and his wife Jessie packed up and left for Cleveland, Ohio. Jessie's relatives in Georgia and Missouri were known "secessionists," and during these volatile days with the country on the brink of civil war, his marriage to a lady with Southern connections may have had something to do with his leaving town, for Pittsburgh had turned into a Republican city. Morrison supposedly became involved in an iron business in Cleveland, but in reality he spent most of his time with the curious pro-Southern politics of his newly adopted city. Pittsburgh had indeed become a lonely place for Stephen.

The War between the States was fast approaching, and even if people could not fathom it, disturbing incidents appeared in the papers daily to remind them that the two sections of the country were becoming two nations. The previous fall, the abolitionist John Brown made his

famous raid on Harper's Ferry, an act that some Northerners interpreted as heroic but that Southerners considered a threat to life, limb,
and civilization as they knew it. The Democratic Party split over the
issue of slavery in the territories, leaving a big gap for the Republicans
to achieve a resounding victory in the upcoming presidential election.
In the midst of these confusing and unsettling events, with the Foster
family and the nation facing dissolution, Stephen decided it was time to
get out of Pittsburgh, to take his wife and little girl, and move once and
for all to New York.

Just before leaving, he wrote his first minstrel song in almost seven
years. As he said good-by to Pittsburgh for what turned out to be the
last time, Stephen returned briefly to the now-contentious medium of
minstrelsy with the publication of the jaunty and somewhat autobio-
graphical "Glendy Burke." The song was ostensibly about a steamboat—there was a real boat with that name in the harbor—but in reality
Foster was composing a going-away song for himself. Just as he was
packing to leave Pittsburgh, he wrote almost bitterly, with only a hint of
slave dialect: "I'll take my pack and put it on my back, When de Glendy
Burke comes down. I'm going to leave this town." The chorus shouts
Foster's determination to get out of town, but with a senseless direction. Although he was in fact moving North, to New York, his song
persona calls out, "Ho! For Lou'siana!" and then croons sheepishly, "I
can't stay here, for dey work too hard." But why Louisiana, if the song's
protagonist was looking for an easier life? One explanation is that the
captain of the real *Glendy Burke* was from New Orleans, but in the real
world, blacks worked much, much harder in the Deep South and Foster
could not stay in Pittsburgh because he had not worked hard enough. [37]

On their way east, Stephen, Jane, and Marion stopped in to see
Henrietta and her family in Warren, Ohio, which was due west of New
York and not out of the way. The Fosters moved in with the Thorntons
for the summer, but when his sister's house began to feel too
crowded—Henrietta had four more children with her second husband—they moved to the fairly new Gaskill House that opened its
doors to the public in 1853 with a grand ball celebration. The hotel
must have been a nice place when Stephen and his family stayed there,
since "a huge assembly hall and ball room, reached by a circular stair-
way, occupied the greater part of the fourth floor." In fact, "Sally Todd,
daughter of the Governor, swept down the grand staircase attired in the

height of the fashion of that period" while Marion Foster stood by with the proprietor's daughter "watching with awe."[38]

The Schoenbergers, the owners of the Gaskill House, had two daughters who as elderly women reported their memories of the Fosters' visit seventy-four years earlier: "Mrs. Foster," one of the proprietor's daughters recalled, "never left her room and Marion always took her meals up to her." There seems to have been some animosity between Jane and the landlady. "Now and then my mother would talk to her [Jane] but mother was a very busy woman and the hotel kept her busy all the time. She did not have much time for idle conversation."[39] The implication here is that Jane was haughty and demanding, but it could have been simply that Stephen and Jane were behind in the rent. Stephen had written to Morrison on May 31, 1860: "I desire to pay Mr. Schoenberger (the landlord) at the end of the month as I engaged to do, and have told him that I would pay him when I would hear from Cleveland."[40] Hearing from Cleveland meant getting money from Morrison. Obviously, Stephen could not afford the lavish Gaskill House, but Henrietta for one reason or another could or would no longer accommodate her brother and his family.

In April and May of 1860, Stephen wrote two letters to Morrison pleading for money. "Please send me by return mail $12—I have received from F. P. & Co. a letter stating that they cannot advance me any more money till I send them the songs now due them . . . as our present agreement is about expiring. They show a disposition to renew the agreement, but, very properly require payment in music before any new arrangement."[41] In another letter written a month later, Stephen sent Morrison a draft on Firth, Pond and Company for fifty dollars, which he wanted his brother to "hold for ten days, and if you can conveniently, please send me the amount by return mail."[42] Even with the late rent payments, Stephen and Marion were popular with the Schoenberger daughters:

> Mr. Foster would sit in the big public parlor on the second floor in the evening and play and sing. I recall that a Frank Leroy, a photographer of Warren of that time, used to be in the company . . . . I remember Marion Foster, the daughter of Mr. Stephen Foster. We used to go up to the big ballroom and play "dolls" and have a grand time together. She was a beautiful dancer and her father would stand in the doorway and applaud when Marion danced and kept time with

castanets. . . . He always wore a high silk hat and was gentle and kind to us. I thought he was a very handsome man. [43]

The proprietor's second daughter remembered the sad day Stephen, Jane, and Marion bid farewell to the Gaskill House and set out for New York. She recalled that "when the stagecoach pulled up and Mrs. Foster swept into it, followed by her husband and daughter," Stephen "lifted his hand high and waved goodbye." Later she confided, "I know we all felt very badly." [44]

15

NEW YORK "POTBOILERS"

When the summer flowers blossomed for the last time in 1860, Stephen Foster knew it was time to move on. At the end of April he had informed his brother Morrison, "I expect to be in Cleveland very soon on my way to New York," but whether or not he ever visited him in the city on the shore of Lake Erie is not known.[1] Stephen arrived in New York in late summer or early fall of 1860 with his wife and daughter, and the three Fosters moved into a comfortable boardinghouse owned by a Louisa Stewart on Greene Street, just a few blocks west of Broadway and Stephen's music publishers. Stewart had a piano on which Stephen tried out many of his new compositions and, like the owner of the Gaskill House, had two daughters who "grew very fond of Jane and Marion, and the latter's funny little ways."[2] Although not lavish or spacious like their large row house in Hoboken, Mrs. Greene's establishment was reputable and acceptable for the family of a young composer. It was also conveniently located within walking distance of dozens of theaters, in a neighborhood where Stephen could learn what was happening on the music scene, and possibly introduce himself to a few publishers.

In spite of his reduced income, Foster's songs gave the couple a sort of celebrity status during their first year in New York, when they were frequently invited out and "at once drawn into musical circles." The Fosters received invitations to musical events and to the homes of theatrical professionals, and at parties that attracted the top billed "musical lights" of the stage. The actors were as interested in meeting the composer of "Old Folks at Home" as he was in meeting them. Ste-phen's granddaughter Jessie Welsh Rose told a reporter of the *Pitts-burgh Post*, "People entertained musically to a large extent in those days. There were balls, singing clubs, minstrels, concerts, etc., with invitations often to the Fosters."[3]

Relatives (including nieces and nephews) and old friends and neigh-bors also on occasion stopped in New York, where Stephen and Jane escorted them around to catch the latest musical plays and extravagan-zas. But the gala evenings and social diversions did not last long, since the composer was always pressed for cash and soon found himself scrambling about in search of any means to make money. Family lore has it that when the couple was invited to a costume party, Stephen was so desperate he spent the evening in the orchestra playing "first violin," wearing a disguise of a false beard with cotton "plumpers" in his cheeks. The story is hard to believe since Stephen played the flute and piano, but he probably picked up a degree of proficiency on the violin from his father, who played the fiddle. What is true about this fantastic account, however, is that he needed money, badly.[4]

Not long after settling in New York, Foster realized that he needed to expand his professional publishing contacts if he were to make his living as a songwriter. His old publishers, Firth and Pond, had not sought to renew the exclusivity article of the February 9, 1858 contract, and although they opted to continue publishing his songs after the old contract expired on August 9, 1860, they made no guarantees and re-jected some of his new compositions. This compelled him to pound the sidewalks looking for publishers who were ready and willing to buy. He became aggressive at this stage, with a wife and child to support, and in his first year alone entered into contracts with at least four new publish-ers. He was desperate and accepted whatever deal they offered, agree-ing to write whatever type of song they desired. These new publishing assignments put very little money in Stephen's pockets, since they were not based on royalty rights, but they forced him to produce more pro-digiously than ever.[5]

Foster ran into difficulties after he arrived in New York, for many reasons. Since his parents' deaths, his musical creativity had come more in spurts than floodwaters, and over the past few years he disappointed Firth and Pond with his limited production. Once in New York, he was spurred on to write more, but the mood of the nation was in flux and neither Foster nor the publishers knew exactly what was wanted. Theaters closed down as soon as war threatened, and there was no telling when they would reopen. Tastes in music were changing, too, and the songs Foster wrote when he first moved to New York were not the right songs for the times, which were becoming increasingly volatile. Foster was still writing sentimental ballads in the antebellum style, but with the nation about to erupt in civil war, the songs he was comfortable writing and his publishers were used to publishing neither interested nor comforted the people. With the economy off-kilter and no one sure which direction to take, it was a bad time to be in the songwriting business.

Foster's annual output of published music had shrunk considerably even before he arrived in New York. His contract with Firth and Pond called for twelve new songs a year, but from 1857 through 1859 he produced about a dozen in total. After he vacated the Union Avenue house, he composed very little, even after renting an office space and turning on occasion to outside poets to supply the lyrics. His reduced productivity reflected the discomfort and anxiety he was experiencing after he sold off his royalties, when he constantly worried about where the next paycheck would come from. It was a dangerous cycle, because the more he worried, the less he wrote, which in turn drove him to drink and made him worry more. Stephen once bragged to a friend that his songwriting brought him an income of nearly $1,500 per year, approximately $75,000 to $100,000 in today's money, but that was true only in his best days, when he still could rely on his royalties. Although Firth and Pond continued to pay royalties on any new songs he wrote and, to show good faith, Foster proved himself more productive in 1860, the relationship was irredeemable by the time the contract came up for renewal in August 1860.[6]

Stephen had contracted with *Clark's School Visitor* when he and the magazine were still in Pittsburgh. On May 2, 1860, he agreed to write six songs for Daughaday and Hammond, *Clark's* new publisher in Philadelphia, over the course of a year. He also granted them the "privilege of renewing at the end of that time for, say—one year more." Foster was obligated to the terms of his exclusive contract with Firth and Pond until August, but he must no longer have felt bound by them because he made Daughaday and Hammond "the independent proprietors of such songs as I may send you for publication," and he promised to send "a song for each alternate issue of the School Visitor." *Clark's* later claimed that "for the six beautiful songs written for us by Mr. Foster, our publishers paid the sum of $400.00 or $66-2/3 apiece for the manuscripts."[7]

Stephen and Jane were still in Warren, Ohio in July 1860, when "Jenny's Coming O'er the Green" came off the press in Philadelphia and *Clark's School Visitor* proudly announced across the top of the cover page, "Stephen C. Foster, the Celebrated Song Writer, special contributor to the Musical Department." Realizing the tumultuous political situation infecting the nation, the editor assured his readers that "nothing sectional or sectarian shall ever appear in our columns." There was nothing of the sort in Foster's song, although a legend developed that the song nearly caused a state of war in his marriage. When he first wrote the song, "Jenny" was described as aged "seventeen." Jane, who thought she had a proprietary claim on the name Jenny, was past thirty and reportedly became angry and demanded that "seventeen" be removed from the lyrics. Whether or not the story is true, seventeen was probably too old for the readers of *Clark's School Visitor*, and Foster took out the reference to age altogether.[8]

Clark's publishers probably believed their payment to the desperate composer was generous, but $400 was not enough for Stephen and his small family to survive, even if it helped make up the gap between what Firth, Pond and Company paid him for new songs and what he needed to live. But Foster, who had not been able to meet the terms of his contract with his original publishers, could not satisfy the less demanding terms of *Clark's* contract. Although he did eventually write six songs for them, it took him more than two years to do so, not one, as he originally promised. *Clark's* followed "Jenny's Coming O'er the Green" with the "Beautiful Child of Song" and "The Little Ballad Girl."

The Fosters were living in New York City when "The Little Ballad Girl" came off the press in December 1860. Consequently, Stephen would have had the chance to see the pitiful sight of hundreds of nearly frozen huckster girls standing on street corners peddling artificial flowers, colorful boxes, cooked foods, clothing, or anything that would put a few pennies into their pockets. It must have been the sight of these desperate children and the fear that his own daughter would end up in similar circumstances that inspired him to write this unusual song, which tells the story of a young girl who hawks printed song ballads on the streets of New York. The song could be sung by two voices and involved a conversation between a potential customer and a child, in which the former asked: "Ho! Little girl, so dressed with care! With fairy slippers and golden hair! What did I hear you calling so loud, Down in that heartless motley crowd?" And the second voice answered: "'Tis my father's song, And he can't live long; Everyone knows that he wrote it; For I've been down at the hotel door, And all the gentlemen bought it." Foster must have imagined little Marion hawking "Old Folks at Home," the song some people (but not everyone) knew he had written, since Christy's name continued to be printed on the cover as composer. The image of the pathetic huckster girls must have stricken Stephen with a morbid sense of anxiety, urging him to write more prolifically than ever.[9]

Foster delayed fulfilling his contract with *Clark's*, but out of simple desperation, he managed to surprise Firth and Pond with an additional four new songs before the end of 1860. Like "The Glendy Burke," they were written in the plantation style, which must have been what his publisher requested, but they were in fact different. "Old Black Joe" is listed as "Foster's Melodies No. 49" on the title page, and it is written in standard English, not in dialect. It is, in fact, a song lamenting lost youth. Joe asks, "Where are the hearts once so happy and so free?" Except that the protagonist is called "Black Joe" and his friends are "gone from the cotton fields," he could be any old man. What friends of the slave were happy and free even in childhood? Joe is not longing to return to the old plantation, but to the happier days of his youth. But the song is dominated by elements of the sentimental: death will reunite him with the "friends" who "come not again" and "the forms now departed long ago."

Foster's next creation published in 1860 and stemming from the minstrel tradition is "Down Among the Cane-Brakes," which would not appear to be a minstrel song at all except for the words "canebrakes on the Mississippi shore." Again, the protagonist sings in standard English, not dialect, and he is, like Black Joe, longing for "life's early day," when he "could laugh and play . . . free from care." Foster must have written "Down Among the Cane-Brakes" to accommodate his publisher and he turned it in with a vengeance. Like other songs in the antebellum style, it laments that "Happy Days are o'er" and "will come back no more," but the protagonist does not want to return to Mississippi; he wants to return to his youth that he happened to spend in Mississippi. Firth, Pond and Company did not even identify "Down Among the Cane-Brakes" as a "Plantation Song" as they did with "The Glendy Burke." Rather, it is identified simply as "Foster's Melodies No. 50." "Virginia Belle," Foster's last 1860 song in the Southern tradition, is not a plantation song in the traditional sense either and is the most interesting. Copyrighted soon after Lincoln's election, when the Southern states were threatening to secede, the song appears to be a plea for Virginia not to leave the Union—but in disguise, for the words could be interpreted to suggest a girl who has died. "She bereft us when she left us," the protagonist wails, "She was taken without warning, Sweet Virginia Belle!"[10]

"The Glendy Burke," "Old Black Joe," "Down Among the Cane-Brakes," and "Virginia Belle" were copyrighted in November 1860, making a total of nine delivered to Firth, Pond and Company by the end of that year. Although still short of the dozen called for in Foster's earlier contracts, his output looked promising. In March 1861, "Don't Bet Your Money on De Shanghai," another minstrel song, came off the press although it may have been written, like the others, late in the previous year. These five songs were the first in the minstrel and plantation tradition that Stephen had written in seven years. Pressure from his publisher, as well as empty pockets, must have been the deciding factors because Foster's venture into the minstrel medium was clearly an anomaly.

Stephen and Jane moved to New York at a momentous time in history. On November 6, 1860, Americans voted in the country's most consequential and unusual presidential election. Abraham Lincoln, the candidate for the new Republican Party, faced two Democratic contenders after the party split, Stephen A. Douglas of Illinois and John C. Breckinridge of Kentucky. Northern Democrats favored Douglas but tensions ran high as states from the South threatened to secede, and many people feared a Republican victory, with Lincoln at the helm, was sure to bring civil war. Foster needed only to look down the street to see that Manhattan was a Democratic stronghold, when 30,000 rowdy demonstrators in bright red shirts marched along Broadway and the Bowery, ominously swinging lanterns in the night and clamoring for Stephen Douglas. The politics of the city, with its Democratic mayor and multiethnic residents, would have been familiar to Stephen, but the scene on the street still appeared threatening.

When New York toughs paraded about clamoring for Douglas in the fall of 1860, Foster may have written "Don't Bet Your Money on De Shanghai." He had already written campaign songs for James Buchanan, and here was another chance to bring in a solid Democratic victory. The song is ostensibly about a cockfight, a bloody sport that was popular among the working-class men who voted the Democratic ticket and attended minstrel shows. Firth, Pond and Company put an engraving of a large rooster on the sheet music cover, a subtle reference to a popular figure of the San Francisco underworld, whose escapades interested the Bowery inhabitants. Nicknamed the "Shanghai Chicken," Johnny "Shanghai" Devine had been a young New York tough when he was shanghaied to the San Francisco waterfront, where he turned gang leader and terrorized other young men into becoming unwilling crew members. Stories about his clawing victims to death with his hooked hand appeared frequently in the newspaper the year of the presidential election.[11]

The first two verses of the song do not generate questions, but a careful reading of the third verse suggests a political allegory, in which the Northern Democrat Douglas stands "in de middle ob de ring" between the extremes of the Southern Democrat Breckinridge and the Republican Lincoln. "Don't Bet Your Money on de Shanghai" involved a moneyed bet on a cockfight, but a political message could have been cleverly relayed through the words: "De Shanghai's tall but his appetite is small, He'll only swallow eb'ry thing that he can overhaul." Abraham Lincoln was tall and many feared he would "overhaul" the Constitution and the institutions of the South, were he to win. Foster's song advised, "Take de little chicken in de middle ob de ring, But don't bet your money on de Shang-hai." In a presidential election that had more than two contenders, the five-foot-four-inch Douglas was easily identified as "de little chicken in de middle ob de ring" compared with the six-foot-four-inch "Shang-hai" Lincoln.

Betting on the outcome of political elections was not new to the Foster boys, who as young men placed bets "on every possible occasion" on election results. Similarly, the idea of portraying presidential hopefuls as clawing and scratching roosters was not a novel idea either. An 1844 cartoon entitled "Political Cock Fighters" showed two roosters engaged in combat with outstretched wings and flying feathers, but in place of the roosters' heads, the cartoonist drew in the faces of the competing presidential candidates Henry Clay and James K. Polk. Standing around the ring were other famous political figures, including Daniel Webster, whose cartoon blurb read, "I'll bet one of my best Chowders on the Kentucky Rooster."[12]

What does an allegorical reading of "Don't Bet Your Money on de Shanghai" demonstrate? Among other things, it shows that Foster was conservative and, like many Americans, did not want to risk seeing the country broken apart by a Republican victory. His thinking was like that of many New Yorkers who, before the firing on Fort Sumter, wanted to take it easy on the South, work toward compromise, and avoid war. Before the war erupted, he probably believed a vote for Douglas would save the Union. But an allegorical explanation also suggests that Stephen was more comfortable expressing his political opinions through charade and symbolism than through direct and open communication. This should come as no surprise, as blackface minstrelsy is about "ambiguity" and was long used to express the sublimated antagonism of the working classes against their social betters.[13]

Had the "Shanghai" song been published before the election, it would presumably have been picked up by a minstrel to sing on a New York stage to the rowdy men who frequented the theater and voted the Democratic ticket. They would have understood that the rooster and the chicken represented the main contenders in the presidential race, and they would have cheered for Douglas, the little chicken. But either Foster pulled back and decided not to publish the song then, or his publishers did not want to put out a song that was even subtly political and had a limited lifespan. In any case, by the time it came off the press, the message in the song would have been diluted. Abe Lincoln, the "Shanghai Chicken," was already president of a ruptured nation and Stephen Douglas at forty-eight had only one month left to live.

Writing under allegorical cover may have been the best way for Stephen to express his politics without directly confronting his brother Morrison, who voted for John C. Breckinridge. The Kentuckian had been James Buchanan's vice-president, and Buchanan was still Ann Eliza's brother-in-law, which may have been reason enough in Morrison's mind to vote for Breckinridge. But it was clearly a vote for the South and a demonstration of where his politics were taking him.[14]

Morrison's vote was an anomaly in his hometown of Pittsburgh, too, where the city voted overwhelmingly for Lincoln, and the diehard Democrats cast their vote for Stephen Douglas.[15] But Morrison had already left Pittsburgh and was living in Cleveland, where he quickly allied himself with the conservative wing of the Democratic Party and began denouncing President Lincoln.

In an attempt to please his publishers, Stephen had produced four new minstrel titles in 1860 and 1861, but his relationship with Firth, Pond and Company continued to deteriorate. While struggling to get Stephen to produce more, they would have been peeved to learn that *Clark's School Visitor* reissued Foster's songs as sheet music through the Philadelphia firm of Lee and Walker. This company had come into existence a dozen years earlier when Julius Lee and William Walker, employees of George Willig of Philadelphia, broke away and started their own firm.[16] Because of Foster's prior association with Willig, Lee and Walker employed Stephen in the production of the sheet music they issued for his songs, although he did not relocate to Philadelphia. In any event, Foster did not receive royalties from Lee and Walker or *Clark's*, while Firth, Pond and Company continued to pay royalties on everything new he wrote. Even if *Clark's* had the legal right to issue sheet music through another publishing house, it could hardly have seemed ethical to Foster's original publishers. Of course, Stephen would have had no say in what *Clark's* did with his songs, but it must have appeared like a breach of faith. Firth and Pond continued to publish Foster's songs for the rest of his life, and posthumously, but they were never again his exclusive publishers and they put out fewer and fewer of his songs, in comparison to the publishing houses that paid him a flat rate per song—and very little at that.[17]

Constant requests for advances, an inability to produce regularly to fulfill the terms of his contract, and the sale of his songs to new publishers led to the fatal rift, but additional factors figured in the deterioration of the relationship. John Firth and Sylvanus Pond appeared unwilling to take a risk on songs that suggested anything new. Unable to gauge what people were feeling when war loomed in the shadows, they continued to publish the same, old-style Foster songs. With the exception of "Don't Bet Your Money on de Shanghai," the Foster titles they published in 1861 were in the sentimental genre about love or dead or dying children. "Molly, Dear Good Night," a lovely parlor song, was copyrighted in April, 1861, about one week before the firing on Fort Sumter and the start of the Civil War. It was formally dedicated on its title page to "Mrs. J. Edgar Thompson," wife of the Pennsylvania Railroad president and sister to Brother William's wife Elizabeth. She was also the appointed guardian of William's children. The next month, Firth, Pond and Company published "Our Willie Dear Is Dying," a "ballad" that would have had more impact if Willie were a soldier, but Willie was a mere child, whose "mother's heart is watchful" and sorrowful. "Farewell, Sweet Mother," copyrighted in October of the same year, focused on the death of a young person without mentioning whether a girl, boy, or soldier were dying. The publisher, however, would have had little difficulty selling these last two songs because their titles were suggestive of battlefield deaths.[18]

Stephen's relationship with Firth and Pond continued to deteriorate, and by 1861 they had refused some of his songs and were no longer his main publishers. Early that year, while looking about for publishers who would show greater interest in his songs, Stephen made the acquaintance of John Mahon, a middle-aged, financially strapped newspaperman of sorts. The Irish-born writer became a close friend and, in spite of his own pecuniary difficulties, opened up his "apartments" at 311 Henry Street as a comfort zone for Stephen when he was not running himself ragged looking for publishers. Stephen spent many an evening sitting at Mahon's piano working out his songs before offering them to publishing houses, and Mahon's wife and daughters became a surrogate family, especially after Jane left him alone in New York. Foster taught the Mahon girls to sing, and when the eldest daughter married in 1863, Stephen attended the wedding and played and sang several of his own compositions.[19]

Mahon knew Stephen needed to boost his earnings and was able to introduce him to some minor music publishing houses with which he had connections. While less esteemed than the prestigious firm of Firth, Pond and Company, they would not refuse Foster's songs.[20] John J. Daly, whose office was located in a storefront at 419 Grand Street, was one of the publishers Mahon introduced to Stephen. Daly was impressed with the composer's reputation and was ready to publish anything with the Foster name on it. Whatever Daly paid for the songs, the onetime payment for outright ownership was "a pittance of what he got before," yet Foster was glad to get it.

Publishers were not eager to buy songs once the war broke out. Since sheet music sales usually followed successful stage performances, the publishers wanted the theaters to fill up before they published new songs, and for a while impresarios faced empty seats. Even Firth, Pond and Company seemed reluctant to buy new songs until they knew what their war-strained customers wanted. Foster must have felt fortunate when Daly offered to publish eight of his songs from June through December 1861, all but one in the old antebellum style. Rather than an actual contract, an informal understanding may have existed that as long as Foster continued to write and the songs sold, Daly would publish them.

The first song Daly copyrighted, on June 4, 1861, was "Our Bright, Bright Summer Days Are Gone." Stephen had offered the song to his old publisher, but Pond refused it without giving a reason. John Mahon described how the composition ended up at Daly's and how the publishing relationship between Foster and Daly started. Foster was out of work, as Mahon recalled:

> I remember one evening, when we were both pretty "hard up"— indeed, neither of us had a cent, and I had a family besides—and suddenly he sat down to the piano. "John," said he, "I haven't time to write a new song, but I think I can write 'Our Bright, Bright Summer-days are Gone,' from memory." He sat down, and wrote the words and music from memory in about an hour and a half. "Take this round to Daly," said he, "and take what he will give you." Mr. John J. Daly, now of 944 Eighth Avenue, was then my publisher, and was at 419 Grand Street. I took the song to Mr. Daly. He was proud to get a song from Foster. He tried it over, and it was really beautiful. He offered a sum which, though not a tithe of what Foster got in his better days, was still considered very handsome; and this "stone which the builders (Pond & Co.) rejected" became very popular. Subsequently the late Thomas D. Sullivan composed brilliant variations for this song, and it is a favorite to this day.[21]

There was rarely anything new about the songs Foster wrote for Daly, who finished out the year and continued into the next publishing such nonconfrontational Foster titles as "Sweet Little Maid of the Mountain," "Little Belle Blair," and "Nell and I." Finally, in recognition of the ongoing war, he published Foster's first innovative title to date, "I'll Be a Soldier." Although the song acknowledged the national conflict, Foster's personal struggle with his wife was not far from his mind, as when the protagonist bids "Farewell! My Own Lov'ed Jenny Dear," an obvious adieu to Jane.[22]

The words were appropriate because sometime in the summer of 1861, Jane packed up and left New York and Stephen. She took ten-year-old Marion with her to Lewistown, Pennsylvania, a town along the Juniata River sixty miles northwest of Harrisburg, where they moved in with her sister Agnes Cummings and her doctor husband, along with their five children. Marion started school in Lewistown and was "a most excellent child in every respect."[23] In October, Jane borrowed money from Morrison to visit her husband, after telling her brother-in-law that "it is very necessary that I should be with him." She took a train to New York with her daughter, but when Marion came down with an illness, she used that as an excuse to move back to Lewistown.[24] It was a hard life for all concerned. Aside from the sporadic visits Jane made to New York, Stephen would spend his remaining years alone.

Jane's decision to leave her husband was difficult, but she was frustrated with their living conditions and eager for her daughter to grow up in a more stable environment. The couple's first few months in New York were comfortable and interesting, even if they "boarded during most of the time they lived together" in the city. Their rooming houses were clean and respectable, but the good times quickly evaporated. Foster's inability to provide a steady income led to a precarious hand-to-mouth existence, and Jane became increasingly unhappy as her husband's resources and prospects dwindled, while his drinking increased. For a woman reared in middle-class comfort, the situation would have been intolerable, and Jane certainly is deserving of sympathy during this chaotic period in her life. After she returned to Lewistown, Foster produced song titles like "Why Have My Loved Ones Gone?" that suggested he missed his family and was wallowing in self-pity over what he perceived as abandonment.[25]

At the beginning of 1862, Foster contracted with the firm of Horace Waters at 481 Broadway, which eventually published more than twenty songs for him. The first songs off the press, with names like "Little Jenny Dow" and "I Will Be True to You," indicate that Jane was still very much on his mind. Horace Waters must have entered into an official contract with the composer because the sheet music covers had numbers set out boldly to tell eager buyers that more Foster songs would be forthcoming, without mentioning specific titles. Like the publisher of *Clark's School Visitor*, Waters had some arrangement with an out-of-state firm—in this case Oliver Ditson—to publish Foster's songs in Boston, and the composer was not paid royalties by either firm.

Foster continued to write songs reminiscent of the antebellum days during the first half of the year, offering very little that was original. "The Merry, Merry Month of May," for example, published for *Clark's* in April, uses a melody "nearly identical" to Foster's old campaign song "The White House Chair," indicating that the composer was feeling burnt out and not putting in enough effort.[26] Nor did Foster offer Waters anything novel with "A Dream of My Mother and My Home," in which the protagonist reverts to the composer's old habit of recalling by-gone days. "Slumber My Darling," however, published around August, 1862, is a charming lullaby written in an appropriately swaying 6/8 time signature.

By the second half of 1862, in response to the demands of the times, Foster was making subtle stylistic changes that were evident even in his parlor songs. After he contracted with S. T. Gordon at 706 Broadway, his songs began to exhibit something new and uplifting—in the music anyway, even if the words were still reminiscent of the antebellum days. "No One to Love," published by Gordon, hints at the self-pitying sentiments found in some of Foster's older songs, but the melody, with its moving 3/4-time signature, is pretty and refreshing. Similarly, "No Home, No Home," copyrighted by John J. Daly in July 1862, recalls the antebellum model, with the lost soul wandering "in sorrow where e'er I roam."[27] But there is something different here: the music does not convey the same hopelessness expressed by the words, and instead suggests a positive resolution in the future.

Perhaps Foster was affected by the nation's exuberant fighting spirit, when men all around him rushed to enlist and expressed excitement about the future instead of listlessly pining over the past. By the end of the year, it was apparent that while Foster still wrote sentimental parlor songs, many had lyrics that sounded more positive than the words he had written earlier in the year, and in the previous year. Daly published "Happy Hours at Home," a home song that pined for school days, summer joys, and Christmas toys "that can never come again." Whereas "home" in the antebellum songs had many metaphorical connotations, "home" in this song and in others written during the war suggested concrete examples of happiness in the here and now.

"Gentle Lena Clare," copyrighted by S. T. Gordon on the last day of 1862, was similar in some ways to "Jeanie with the Light Brown Hair." The protagonist boasts of his loved one's "careless winning ways" and "wild and birdlike lays," but the song is lighthearted in melody, with a catchy tune in the chorus. Lena Clare is a real girl, with "deep blue eyes and waving hair," not a vapor or shadow figure. Written in 2/4 time, the song has plenty of eighth notes and leaps up a sixth in true Foster fashion. A soldier could have sung the song, while dreaming about his girl. There was nothing morbid about it. Similarly, "The Love I Bear to Thee," published in January 1863 by Horace Waters, is a love song that uses the tired phrases "thy form lies calm in sleep" and "childhood's hours now passed and gone." But the song is not heavy with despair, nor is "Lena Our Loved One Is Gone," even though Lena is dead and "gone from the earth." The protagonist asks where Lena's soul roams, but the song does not exhibit the deep pathos found in "Gentle Annie," which Foster wrote a decade earlier about another dead girl.

During the war, angel songs and mother songs were especially popular as a mechanism for dealing with the overwhelming losses of the nation, but they were not as tragic as Foster's antebellum "mourning songs." Horace Waters published several "angel songs" with words and music by Foster, including "Little Ella's an Angel," "Willie's Gone to Heaven," and "Tell Me of the Angels, Mother." These now insipid sounding titles sold as sheet music with piano accompaniment for twenty-five cents each, but Waters also included them in the anthologies of religious music he was fond of publishing.[28] "Mother songs" made up another very popular song category that Foster wrote and Waters published. "Oh! Tell Me of My Mother," "Farewell Mother Dear," "Farewell Sweet Mother," "Bury Me in the Morning, Mother," and "Leave Me with My Mother" are some of the titles Foster contributed to the genre that became more prevalent the longer the war continued.[29] Angel and mother songs, surprisingly, were characterized by neither regret nor great pathos. But there was a demand for them, they provided small comfort to a grieving parent, and Stephen needed the work.

Foster's early biographers condemned most of his New York songs, including the angel and mother songs, without acknowledging that he was trying something new that would satisfy the public and his publishers. His earlier songs had exhibited a pathos tied to regret, a leading trait of the antebellum songs and a painful human emotion, but Americans no longer wanted songs that focused on regret. The war had made the world so sad and the losses so great that Americans did not want to dwell on their sorrows. Even Foster would not allow himself the luxury of his usual self-pity and lament over what was past and gone. In "The Voices That Are Gone" he eschewed regret with the words, "May there be no vain regretting, Over memories I would shun." Even the music to the song, with repeating arpeggios in 3/4, waltz time, reinforces the idea, so that the song is not truly sorrowful. In his earlier songs, Foster thrilled to regret and languished in memories, but once the war began, feelings were jarred and desensitized, and people refused to find virtue in despair.

The critics did not appreciate the changes Foster was making to his songs, and ended up lumping nearly all his 1860s compositions into a category of inferior, mass-produced titles they labeled "potboilers." The "angel" and "mother songs" were easily relegated to the "potboiler" category, but the critics reserved another genre for that characterization—songs that did not deserve the insulting designation. In the second year of the war, Stephen Foster devoted his creative efforts to writing songs that supported the Union war effort. They were beautiful, functional, and, unfortunately, scorned and denigrated.

16

WAR SONGS AND COPPERHEAD RELATIVES

In the second year of the war, Stephen Foster began to write Civil War songs in earnest. In response to the changing tastes of the people and probably the demands of his publishers, when pining over the past, even in song, seemed like a foolish option, Foster began to compose some of his most purposeful creations—war songs. Nearly every war sponsored them, even if they were quickly forgotten melodies that lasted only as long as the conflict itself. Foster wrote marching songs and recruiting songs that inspired men to enlist in the Union Army. He wrote songs to comfort the sweethearts, mothers, and sisters waiting at home for their soldier boys; others conveyed battle news, praised President Lincoln, and referenced current events. These songs encouraged and aided the war effort, and they allowed the composer to become subtly involved with the political landscape without openly expressing his convictions or directly confronting his Democratic relatives. If we accept these songs as an expression of Stephen's wartime loyalties, they provide a key to understanding a politically circumspect man.

While Stephen was busy writing songs that helped recruit soldiers to the Union cause, his brother Morrison was busy recruiting converts to the Copperhead cause. Northern Democrats like Morrison Foster, who were sympathetic to the South and defied Lincoln's war policies, were contemptuously labeled Copperheads, and there were plenty of them in Cleveland, where Morrison was living after the war broke out.[1] When fewer Democrats in the Smoky City boasted of being proud to be called by the name associated with "poisonous reptiles,"[2] Morrison settled into Cleveland and became an outspoken advocate of the Copperhead cause. On February 28, 1861, he published an article in *The Plain Dealer*, a Democratic newspaper in Cleveland, titled "The Uses of the Slave States" and argued that the slave states were too valuable to be lost. Concerned mainly with the economics of the situation, he pointed out that the goods produced by slave labor amounted to hundreds of thousands of dollars and he argued for appeasement. Admitting that "the natural prejudices of our people against slavery in its general sense" had blinded them to the fact of the mutual dependence of the North and the South, he assured his readers that he was "not one of those who have adopted this error."[3]

When Morrison expressed his opinion in the Cleveland newspaper, he was still championing "king cotton" even though he no longer worked for McCormick's factory in Allegheny and the cotton industry in Pittsburgh was dead. But he acted like he did, and continued to champion cotton, which continued to be very important to the American economy, as it had been to him personally. Several reasons come to mind as to why Morrison should be so pro-Southern. One may have been personal. His first sweetheart left him, not simply for a Northerner, but for the son of an abolitionist, after which he married a woman with relatives who fought on the Southern side. Other reasons were more grounded in economics and history. Morrison had benefited from Pittsburgh's cotton industry, and he could not forget that the city had for years enjoyed fruitful economic relations with the South. When the Allegheny Mountains formed an insurmountable barrier to eastern trade, before the canals and the railroads made travel to the East rather easy, merchants who relied on the Ohio River to connect them with trading partners formed strong ties with the South and West. Morrison had business relationships with Southerners early on and he continued to believe that the nation's economic well-being depended on staying on amiable terms with the South. He put the almighty dollar first and would acquiesce to the slaveholder's every demand in the name of peace and prosperity over union and national honor.[4]

After Morrison moved to Cleveland, he became even more devoted to the Copperheads. Cleveland was the central location for the traitorous group's activities, and Morrison became involved with that city's peculiar politics as soon as he and his wife moved there. Morrison's fanaticism over the cause increased after his introduction to the Copperhead leader Clement L. Vallandigham, a man who became a regular visitor at Jessie and Morrison's Cleveland home. The Ohio congressman was several years older than Morrison and had attended Jefferson College in Canonsburg, Pennsylvania, the year before Stephen spent two uneventful weeks at the school. During the war, Vallandigham became a peace advocate and made intense verbal and written attacks on President Lincoln, publicly castigating him for continuing the carnage. The Copperhead instigator found his largest following among Midwesterners, including Richard Cowan, who many years earlier had courted Stephen's wife Jane. When Cowan took his seat in the Senate, the *Pittsburgh Post*, a partisan Democratic paper, declared itself "the especial defender of Senator Cowan" for the latter's devotion to the Copperhead cause.[5]

Vallandigham was fair-haired and good-looking, with a dangerous talent for leading and inciting an audience. His charismatic tirades managed to attract large numbers of men and women in Ohio who opposed the continuation of the war, and his popularity increased as the economic depression in the upper Mississippi Valley deepened. Cities like Cleveland, whose prosperity depended on the sale of farm surpluses to the South, suffered the most from the war, when the Ohio River trade collapsed, farm prices declined, businesses closed, and unemployment became widespread. Consequently, Midwesterners were quick to blame the Lincoln administration and eagerly absorbed the harangues of their outspoken leader, who wanted the president to negotiate immediately for peace with slavery left intact. Vallandigham saw "more of barbarism and sin in the continuance of this war than in the sin and barbarism of African slavery." In a speech before Congress, he proudly claimed that he was "one of that number who have opposed abolitionism or the political development of the antislavery sentiment of the North and West, from the beginning."[6]

Morrison was easily swept up in the tidal wave of the famous Copperhead's harangues. Clamoring for immediate peace, he called Lincoln a tyrant and, like Vallandigham, insisted that the South could never be forced into submission. Before long, Morrison and Jessie's radical politics and anti-Lincoln sentiments alienated "their Republican friends and neighbors" and they ended up restricting their socializing "to just a trusted few," like the circus clown Dan Rice and the Shakespearean actor Charles Couldock.[7] Presumably, the "trusted few" were men of similar politics. The British born Couldock, who appeared in a performance of *Our American Cousin*, though not on the night Lincoln was assassinated, probably remained sympathetic to the South through much of the Civil War. Dan Rice, in all likelihood, held the same views, although he was known to change his routine to suit the geographic interests of his audience.[8]

The Fosters, like many Americans—including the Lincolns—had friends, family, and in-laws who took opposing sides in the great national conflict, which caused hurt feelings and angry outbursts and sometimes complete estrangements among family members. Morrison's wife Jessie was a native Pittsburgher, but she had brothers and cousins who fought on the Confederate front. Henrietta's husband Jesse Thornton served the Union cause, but his wife joined the Copperheads at Morrison's house in Cleveland. Ann Eliza's sons fought on the Union side, but her preacher husband lost some of his parishioners because his president brother had a reputation for being soft on Southerners. Many believed James Buchanan was complicit in the treasonous activities of his Secretary of War John Floyd, who tried unsuccessfully to transfer arms from the Arsenal in Pittsburgh to forts in the South. Stephen himself was not immune to family squabbles, innuendos, and hurt feelings. When he wrote songs that honored Lincoln and the Union, Morrison and Jessie became furious.[9]

Morrison's extreme politics, which outraged the typical Northern Democrat, must have baffled Stephen, a conclusion best supported by an analysis of the Union war songs he began writing the year after he moved to New York. No one really knows exactly what Foster's politics were. Even if he claimed to be a Democrat, all Democrats were not alike during the Civil War. The party split and there was a marked difference between Copperheads like Morrison, or Peace Democrats as some were known, and Democrats like Stephen, who put politics aside to support the Union, the war, and the president. Surely Foster's politics changed over time, swinging in one direction and then the next. But camouflage and ambiguity as a means of self-protection came naturally to him, since for many years he was involved with the minstrel stage where opinions were hidden behind a blackface mask. Secrecy may have been the easiest way to deal with Morrison, and as an artist Stephen may have thought it best to keep his politics hidden from the public. If Stephen's Civil War songs, like his plantation songs, contained messages that accurately reflected his thoughts, they reveal that he became a staunch supporter of the Union and the president once the war began.

Before Lincoln's election, Foster, like his fellow New Yorkers, may have favored Stephen Douglas who stood in "de middle" politically, but once the Southerners fired on Fort Sumter, Stephen renounced partisan politics and stood firmly by the president. Like a good Union man, he wrote songs for the men in blue, and when Lincoln needed men to volunteer their services and in some cases, their lives, he wrote songs that encouraged them to enlist. Foster even dedicated some of his songs to President Lincoln, an act skeptics may explain as a ruse prompted by his publisher to sell songs, but the words in Foster's war songs demonstrate that he was an uncompromised patriot. In contrast to his brother Morrison who encouraged a disruption of the war effort, Stephen encouraged fighting to save the Union, and wrote songs that disparaged Southerners. If a rift developed between the brothers after Stephen moved to New York, it may have been in part politically motivated. Rather than argue, Stephen chose to keep his political opinions to himself and to express them only in his songs.

The first song in which Stephen expressed a positive sentiment about the war was "I'll Be a Soldier," published in July 1861, the same month the Union Army engaged the rebels at Bull Run in northern Virginia and was sorely defeated. In the song, Foster openly declared his devotion to the Union and encouraged enlistments by advertising soldierly pride. He modeled his soldier protagonist after the flashy dressers in New York's elite Seventh Regiment who wore grey—not blue—uniforms with white or black cross belts. At this early stage in the war, Foster, like many romantics, envisioned soldiering more as an exercise in sartorial elegance than the bloody nightmare it would become. When the Seventh answered the president's call for volunteers to serve three-month terms, these high society boys, including young merchants, bankers, and professional men, showed up accompanied by their regimental bands and personal servants. Throngs of New Yorkers rushed to greet them as they set out for Washington, when women waved handkerchiefs and threw flowers at their feet. In spite of their enthusiasm and commanding presence, they served only thirty days instead of the requested three months. Still, they were a class act and

Foster was impressed enough to write a song about them and perhaps, to fancy himself one of them. But the message Foster urged was clear: join the Army![10]

The next war song Foster wrote was "That's What's the Matter," published in April 1862. The song is remarkable because Foster not only tells us that he is going to write a new type of song, but he even explains why he is going to try a new genre: "We live in hard and stirring times, Too sad for mirth, too rough for rhymes; For songs of peace have lost their chimes, And That's what's the matter!" The song announced the composer's realization that Americans preferred stirring patriotic songs to sweet sentimental songs. These were songs men could sing, and ladies too, but they would also unite friends and families and provide camaraderie and inspire patriotism. Morrison and his secessionist wife Jessie did not appreciate "That's What's the Matter," and the line "The men we held as brothers true, Have turn'd into a rebel crew" caused Jessie to get up in arms since her young brother Isaac Lightner was fighting on the Confederate side. But Stephen's lyrics also offended Morrison because, in addition to calling Southerners a "rebel crew," this song renounced all "party feeling" and maligned those "Democrats" who were willing, in Foster's own words, to "take their [Confederate] side" and "let the Union slide."

> The rebels thought we would divide,
> And Democrats would take their side;
> They then would let the Union slide,
> And that's what's the matter!
> But, when the war had once begun,
> All party feeling soon was gone;
> We join'd as brothers, ev'ry one!
> And that's what's the matter! [11]

The song expressed Foster's and, for the moment, New York's attitude that devotion to party politics would have to take second place to loyalty to the Union. The next year, after Lincoln announced the Emancipation Proclamation and the draft, many New Yorkers changed, but for the time being they were united in support of the president and the Union. The composer probably took note of engaging headlines in the newspapers when he wrote the lyrics to "That's What's the Matter," which echoed the words of a repentant Mayor Fernando Wood who told his constituents, "We know no party now." After the firing on Fort Sumter, even the Democratic mayor publicly supported Lincoln, offering the president his "services in any military capacity consistent with my position as Mayor of New York City." Now men "bursting with pugnacity" lined up along the Bowery to enlist their services to fight to preserve the Union, irrespective of party affiliation. [12]

Foster's next war song, published by Horace Waters, was optimistically titled "Better Times Are Coming!" While Lincoln looked in vain for a general who could fight and lead the Union to victory, the song's lyrics boldly recited the names of the many Civil War generals who had tried but so far failed to free the land "from its clouds of despair." Foster followed the song about generals with a song for sisters. Published in August 1862, again by Horace Waters, the spirited, yet poignant, "Was My Brother in the Battle?" delighted Northern piano girls with its urgent words that seemed to dance along to a sprightly lilting melody. Composed almost completely in eighth notes, the melody has a graceful yet energetic movement and is well placed for the soprano voice. "Was My Bother in the Battle?" offered a soldier's sister the opportunity to sing about the war from the perspective of a sibling's loss. It was a powerful tonic for young women whose brothers were injured or died in the war, as it assuaged their losses with patriotic pride and kept up feminine morale, an important contribution to the war effort.

In the summer of 1862, President Lincoln desperately needed soldiers and he issued a call for 300,000 volunteers. In response, S. T. Gordon published the rousing "We Are Coming Father Abra'am, Three Hundred Thousand More" for which Foster supplied the music only. The words were adapted from the very popular poem "Three Hundred Thousand More," by the Quaker abolitionist James Sloane Gibbons, which first appeared in the *New York Evening Post* on July 16, 1862. More than a half dozen composers rushed to set the poem to music, including Firth and Pond who published the same Gibbons poem to music by William B. Bradbury. But Foster's version, published in September 1862, was far superior to songs with the same title by other composers, and his title page featured in large clear type the words, "Respectfully Dedicated to the President of the United States."

"Father Abra'am" was clearly a man's song, or rather a song for a chorus of men. The "We" instead of the usual "I" set the pattern from the beginning, and the image of several hundred thousand men rallying to the Union cause is suggested by the chorus of a multitude of male voices. S. T. Gordon also published "We're a Million in the Field," another song for male voices, but this time Foster wrote both the words and the music. Here he identified his Southern brethren as "foes" who "kept their blighting plans concealed," and the protagonist urged Kentuckians to stay true to the Union at the very moment Lincoln agonized over keeping them on his side. About the blue grass state, Foster wrote: "True and plucky, They know that the Union is their shield. And they'll do their duty, In all its beauty, when they find we're a million in the field." Foster or his publisher Stephen Gordon, a New Hampshire–born Yankee, made sure the title page of this song read "Dedicated to the Union Army."[13]

Surprisingly, while Stephen was busy writing militant pro-war Union songs, his sister Henrietta wrote an antiwar poem, titled "Five Hundred Thousand Dead," which she published in 1862 in a local newspaper. Stephen's songs encouraged the soldiers to volunteer and fight, but Henrietta's poem preached the opposite:

> Dear land of mine, for thee my tears are shed,
> Five hundred thousand of thy sons lie dead!
> If blood were needed this great strife to end,

> An ocean has already flowed in vain,
> Then how much more is yet required to wash
> The grievance out, and bring us peace again! [14]

Henrietta had jumped on the Copperhead bandwagon at the same time her husband Jesse Thornton was a Union captain in the Commissary Department of the Army of the Potomac. Captain Thornton's absences from home during the war left Henrietta lonesome enough to make extended visits with her children to Morrison and Jessie's house, where she quickly fell under the spell of the handsome Vallandigham, who was a frequent visitor.

Morrison's wife Jessie was already writing rebel songs and poems when Henrietta showed up in Cleveland and began voicing her own peace sentiments in verse. Later generations would call her an antiwar activist because her poems grieved "for friend and foe alike, for the unholy, the unchristian method of settling a misunderstanding between men born brothers." [15] Eventually, General Burnside ordered Vallandigham's arrest for undermining the war effort by his constant verbal assaults. Lincoln, in an almost comical gesture meant to punish the Copperhead leader gently but not severely enough to turn him into a martyr, exiled him to the South where he was not wanted and was allowed to "escape" to Canada. After Vallandigham's arrest, however, Henrietta's poetry became even more incendiary, this time directly denouncing Lincoln and his war policies. Originally Henrietta's peace poems played up the Copperhead cause without mentioning names, but after her hero went into hiding in Canada, Henrietta wrote verse after verse addressed directly, "To the Hon. C. L. Vallandigham, in Exile." Consciously or unconsciously, she was competing with her brother Stephen who dedicated Union songs directly to President Lincoln.

> Tho' thou art in exile, Vallandigham, now,
> The Laurel e're long shall encircle thy brow;
> Tho' banished, and branded as traitor, thou art
> Yet still doest thou live in the people's great heart.
> Thine eloquence comes from the Canada shore,
> We hear it above the wild cataract's roar. [16]

On January 1, 1863, Abraham Lincoln issued the Emancipation Proclamation that promised freedom to all slaves residing in those states currently in rebellion against the federal government. Lincoln's proclamation also stated that able-bodied black males would be accepted into the Union Army to bear arms and fight for their own freedom, and newspaper advertisements offered ten dollars a month and support for the families of black men who enlisted. Martin Delany of Pittsburgh, one of the first men the Army "engaged as a Recruiting Agent of Black Troops," was employed to recruit for the Massachusetts Fifty-Fourth, the famous black regiment that fought under Robert Gould Shaw at Fort Wagner. Although 180,000 black soldiers eventually served in the Union Army and many died fighting, the president's decision initially caused a great deal of controversy. For many New Yorkers, black soldiers fighting for their own freedom was not the problem, but emancipation made New Yorkers less willing to risk their own lives in a conflict they now perceived as a war for the freedom of slaves. [17]

On March 3, 1863, three months after the Emancipation Proclamation was issued, the federal government stunned New York's working classes by announcing a draft that forced them to fight for a cause they no longer believed in. With fewer volunteers, the Civil War Military Draft Act became all-inclusive in its application. It covered all white men between the ages of twenty and forty-five, whether citizens or immigrants who had filed for citizenship, but it excluded married white males thirty-five and older. What infuriated the working classes the most about the law was that it specified that a rich man could buy his way out of military service by paying another man $300 to sacrifice, what clearly appeared to be, his less valuable life. Although he was not living with his wife, Stephen Foster at thirty-six was over the age limit for a married man, and hence, exempt from the draft, which fell most heavily on poor, single young men who could not afford to pay a substitute, or to bribe the government for official exemption.

With blacks being enlisted in the Army and whites being forced to fight, African American soldier skits and "colored brigade songs" entered the minstrel repertoire. Surprisingly, minstrels approved of black soldiers, and favored the idea of arming them and having them do their own fighting. "If darkies want their freedom," one minstrel said, "they should be drafted and fight for it." [18] Of course, when minstrel performers impersonated black soldiers on the stage, they still could not offend their white audience by portraying them as equals. Minstrels never suggested that blacks in uniform would rape or plunder, or that they could not be trusted to carry arms, but the white audience still found them threatening. Consequently, minstrels dispelled their fear "by laughing at black soldiers" and portraying them "like children who imitate without understanding." Black troops given the order to "fall in," for example, jumped into a lake, reinforcing the popular image of African American soldiers as cowardly and incompetent buffoons. In one skit, a member of the "Black Brigade" promised to fight the South, but only "by word ob mouth," for "to fight for death and glory, am quite anudder story."[19] When the stage commander told the black soldiers to strike for their country and their homes, one minstrel soldier replied, "some struck for der country, but dis chile he struck for home."[20]

When black soldiers became a popular subject to lampoon on the minstrel stage, Foster wrote the music to "A Soldier in the Colored Brigade," copyrighted by Firth, Son, and Company at the end of May 1863. (Foster's original partners had separated at the beginning of the year and John Firth opened his own store at 563 Broadway, while Sylvanus Pond and his son William continued publishing down the street as William A. Pond & Co.) Foster's new song in the comic tradition fit the formula of black brigade minstrel songs and expressed the sentiment held by many working-class New Yorkers: freedom for blacks was not worth the destruction of the Union or the forced sacrifice of thousands of white soldiers. But the song still promoted the idea that African Americans should become soldiers and fight for their own freedom. Was not black blood as good as white blood on the battlefield? George Cooper, the white Union soldier from New York who penned the words to the song, reaffirmed that sentiment and even encouraged whites to accept black soldiers. In the fourth verse, he subtly reassured the audience that black soldiers were alright by mentioning that General Jackson had used them to fight the British at New Orleans—which he had.[21]

The song was Stephen Foster's last contribution to blackface minstrelsy, but he composed only the music. Cooper's attitude toward black soldiers can only be surmised from the lyrics—the poetic young man had seen enough of the horrors of the battlefield to think that nothing was worth the sacrifice—but whatever he wrote had to express the philosophy and politics of the minstrel stage and its white audience. The comic elements dominated in the song, yet the political ideology sprinkled throughout appealed to the show's audience. Just as the lampooning of blacks in earlier minstrel shows was meant to dispel the anger of the poor against their rich bosses, after the new conscription law said a rich man could buy his way out of military service, the minstrel stage served the same purpose. It allowed the men in the audience to vent their anger by laughing at African Americans instead of attacking the rich who made the law and were benefiting from it. The minstrel sings the line, "I'll be a Colonel in de Colored Brigade," and anticipates a laugh at the idea that a lowly African American can rise as high in rank as a colonel. The next line also develops the comedy through contradiction, but includes a message:

> With musket on my shoulder and wid banjo in my hand,
> For Union and de Constitution as it was I stand[22]

The "Union and de Constitution as it was" suggests conservative Democratic ideology and the continuation of slavery, but the phrase when used on the minstrel stage suggests old-style, contradictory nonsense. How could a black soldier who was fighting the war as a free man say he stood for "the Union and the Constitution as it was"? The last few sentences were even more disconcerting:

> Some say dey lub de darkey and dey want him to be free,
> I s'pec dey only fooling and dey better let him be.
> For him dey'd brake dis union, which de're forefadders hab made,
> Worth more den twenty millions ob de colored Brigade![23]

The last line in the song, "Worth more den twenty millions ob de colored Brigade," is unclear. Was preserving the Union worth more than the freedom or the lives of African Americans? "Twenty millions," of course, was hyperbolic writing on Cooper's part, but Lincoln must have thought the Union was worth the lives of 600,000 white men, because saving it and winning freedom for the slaves cost more than that number. Still this line has suggested to some scholars that Foster never emerged from the unthinking young man he was when he wrote "Oh! Susanna" fifteen years earlier, and included the line "De lectrie fluid magnified, And killed five hundred nigger."[24] George Cooper wrote the words to "A Soldier in the Colored Brigade," and whether they expressed the opinion of Cooper or Foster, both or neither, is not known. But it hardly makes sense to ignore the moral progress Foster made over the past fifteen years based on a few lines in a song he did not write. If it looks like he was momentarily in retreat, perhaps he was.

When the song was published, the nation despaired that the war and the loss of life would ever end. He may have had a lapse of judgment that allowed him to use the words just as Cooper penned them, or he may have been trying to please some minstrel performer. "A Soldier in the Colored Brigade" was the only minstrel song he wrote using Cooper's lyrics. When Stephen composed his own minstrel songs in 1860 and 1861, most of them were sentimental ballads that longed for bygone days and were written in the minstrel guise to please his publishers. Foster, in fact, had spent the two previous years in New York writing Civil War songs that encouraged men to join the fight that ultimately ended slavery.

Cooper may have written the spiteful words in the last line to appease the festering working classes, whose anger erupted in the devastating Draft Riot a little more than a month after the song was published. Apparently, venting anger on the minstrel stage was not enough. For four days beginning on July 13, 1863, white men throughout Lower Manhattan raged, rioted, burned, plundered, and murdered. Two years earlier, Foster had seen patriotic New York toughs line up to volunteer to fight to preserve the Union, but after the conscription law went into effect, he saw these same men terrorize the city rather than serve their country. The mayhem had not been sparked by the Emancipation Proclamation or even by Lincoln's recruitment of black soldiers, which had happened seven months earlier. What set them seething was the new draft law that insinuated the lives of working-class men were worth only $300 while "they pay $1,000 for negroes."[25]

The riot began on Monday morning, when thousands of workers from the southern tip of Manhattan marched northward to the site of the draft lottery on Forty-Seventh Street. Along the way, they cut telegraph poles, pulled up railroad tracks, broke store windows, and attacked police officers. The angry crowd, including men, women, and children, swelled to twelve thousand by the time they converged on the Upper East Side to attack the homes of wealthy Republican abolitionists and the offices of the *Times* and the *Tribune*. By noon the crowd turned on the free black population of the city. Their most heinous act was setting fire to the Colored Orphan Asylum on Fifth Avenue, where, miraculously all but one of the children was pulled to safety through a back door. Another group of rioters attacked African Americans in their tenements along the downtown waterfront, while a mob in Foster's neighborhood hanged black men on lampposts and burned the bodies as the crowd cheered for Jefferson Davis.[26]

The elite of New York wasted no time. Seeing in the riot contempt for the law and private property, the merchants, financiers, and businessmen banded together and pressured their new Republican Mayor George Opdyke and Secretary of War Edwin Stanton into ordering the regiments just returned from Gettysburg to march in and put down the rabble. The riot concluded with the elite Seventh Regiment, the same men Foster had eulogized in "I'll Be a Soldier," pointing howitzers at the slums of Five Points and Lower Manhattan. The experience must have been horrifying for Foster who lived close enough to smell the fires and hear the pounding footsteps of the angry men and the screams of their victims.

Sometime in 1863 Henrietta Foster wrote a poem called "Sound the Rally" that was used as a campaign song for Vallandigham, when he ran for governor of Ohio in the fall (while still hiding out in Canada). Henrietta wrote the words to fit the tune of "Better Times Are Coming," her brother's song about Union generals published in the early summer of 1862.[27] Some questions come to mind here. Did Stephen have anything to do with Henrietta's decision to set her poem to his music? Did he even know that Henrietta's poem would be sung to this particular melody and used as a campaign song for Vallandigham? Did he care?

The least damaging and most plausible explanation is that Henrietta supplied her own words to the tune of "Better Times Are Coming"—without her brother's knowledge. She would not have been the first. Both Democrats and Republicans set campaign songs to Foster's most popular tunes during the 1860 presidential election, and it was easy enough for Henrietta to get a copy of the song and set her own poem to it.[28] She might have even chosen this particular song to spite her brother for taking a political position so opposed to that of the family. "Better Times Are Coming" demonstrated confidence in Abraham Lincoln and his administration, making it highly unlikely that Stephen would have knowingly allowed his sister to use the melody to support Lincoln's enemy in the gubernatorial campaign.

Foster penned nine verses to "Better Times Are Coming," and most contained the names of Union officers who were actively engaged in fighting the war. He mentioned Generals Siegel, Halleck, Fremont, Scott, and Grant; Captains Foote and Ericson; Colonel Corcoran from the Irish brigade, and the names of other legendary fighters. Stephen still had faith in General McClellan, even though his lack of fighting spirit retarded the Union advance: "Your faith in McClellan put, for we are sure he's right." The second verse demonstrated confidence in Lincoln and his administration:

> Abra'm Lincoln has the army and the navy in his hands,
> While Seward keeps our honor bright abroad in foreign lands;
> And Stanton is a man, who is sturdy as a rock,
> With brave men to back him up and stand the battle's shock.

Most tellingly, while identifying Southerners as traitors and rebels, the song praised General Burnside, the man responsible for Vallandigham's arrest:

> And Burnside, victorious, he rides the ocean's breast,
> The traitors and the rebels will soon meet their doom;

In stark contrast, Henrietta's poem voiced the ideology of the Copperheads or the Peace Democrats, the designation she would have preferred, and viciously attacked Lincoln as a dictator and a despot, who "scoffs at the people's rights" and "strikes at liberty." It appears that Henrietta adopted the melody of "Better Times Are Coming" for Vallandigham's campaign because she wanted to make a mockery of the pro-Union sentiment her brother expressed in the song.

SOUND THE RALLY

> Democratic freemen of the Buckeye State,
> Hasten to the rescue before it is too late;
> Look out for your liberties—hesitate no more,
> Up, up, and be doing, boys, "the wolf is at the door."

Chorus:

> Hurrah! Hurrah! Hurrah!
> Sound the rally for Vallandigham and Pugh!
> Hurrah for the Union and the Constitution too!
> The Dictator Lincoln has put us under ban,
> He has exiled Vallandigham for speaking like a man;
> He scoffs at the people's rights, we are no longer free,
> Unless we stop the despot who strikes at liberty.[29]

Even with Foster's music attached to Henrietta's campaign poetry, the Copperhead leader was sorely defeated in the Ohio governor's race by the War Democrat John Brough. Morrison Foster was convinced that the Peace Democrats who would have voted for Vallandigham had been intimidated at the polls into not voting. For the rest of his life he retained a calico backed ballot as evidence, scribbling in pencil on the back: "This ticket (calico backed) is a sample of the means used to intimidate those who wished to vote for Vallandigham." In the days of open balloting, Morrison Foster recalled that any man who carried a calico backed ballot was identified as a Peace Democrat or a supporter of Vallandigham, and was promptly thrown out of the polling station by Lincoln's soldiers who stood around menacingly supervising the election.[30]

Morrison and Henrietta Foster were not alone in criticizing Lincoln and accusing him of dictatorial and unconstitutional practices. While some thought the war justified the president's strong-arm tactics, many others in the North opposed what they considered Lincoln's disregard for personal liberties. On April 27, 1861, two weeks after the war started, the president had suspended the writ of habeas corpus and arrested and jailed dozens of suspected Southern sympathizers. When Chief Justice Taney, the man behind the Dred Scott decision, declared that the president's actions went outside the law, Lincoln simply ignored him and curtailed the activities of anyone who tried to obstruct the war effort. Perhaps Henrietta Foster was fortunate that Lincoln did not arrest her for her peace poems and her campaign songs. Lincoln, however, was more interested in suppressing voices that had greater reach than Henrietta's.[31]

The newspaper publisher Benjamin Wood, whose one brother was the mayor of the city and the other the minstrel star Henry Wood, was the type of man who attracted Lincoln's attention. Benjamin Wood published the Copperhead *New York Daily News*, which in one issue labeled the president an "unscrupulous chief magistrate" who spoke "an ocean of falsehood and deceit." Believing he needed to control the antiwar demonstrations that grew up in pockets and threatened the war effort, Lincoln ordered the postmaster general to stop delivering Wood's newspaper in order to keep it from influencing the public. With an official ban on delivery, the *New York Daily News* went into bankruptcy and in short order closed down.[32]

Stephen probably knew the Wood brothers through his connection to Henry Wood who occasionally bought songs from him to sing at his minstrel theater on Broadway, but the composer was not involved with the brothers politically. During the war, after the Democrats splintered into irreconcilable factions, the War Democrats called the Peace Democrats traitors because of their reluctance or refusal to fight to restore the Union. Even the popular Fernando Wood was labeled a traitor and lost the contest for mayor to the Republican George Opdyke. Stephen did not have to worry that he would be accused of taking the wrong side in the political battle. In spite of the confusion and demoralization with which he viewed the war, his songs indicate that he stood for Lincoln and the Union.

As the battles raged on in the bleak first half of 1863, an all-pervading sorrow over the continuation of the war shaded the society in gloom. Before Gettysburg, with few military victories for the North and no end in sight to the suffering, Foster expressed his and the nation's frustration with what appeared to be a never-ending tragedy. "When This Dreadful War Is Ended," with words by George Cooper, was published by Horace Waters sometime after March 10, 1863, with a title that sounded very much like "Weeping Sad and Lonely, or When This Cruel War Is Over," with music by Henry Tucker and words by Charles Sawyer.[33] Tucker's song became a national favorite, but both songs were published the same year and expressed similar sentiments: a war-weary nation wanted a return to peacetime bliss. Foster's song, however, composed almost entirely in eighth and sixteenth notes, is lively, upbeat, and determined—not maudlin or tragic like Tucker's.

Foster's protagonist wants a return to normalcy but only after victory. He longs to see his home and his girl: "Soon I hope the day will come, Love's own star will lead my footsteps, Safely back to you and home." But this soldier wants to go home only after "the threat'ning storm is past, And the flag our foes have planted, Flies in shreds upon the blast." "When This War Is Ended" suggests that Foster believed in fighting the South into complete submission and putting everything aside to win. The one constancy in Foster's politics seemed to be his optimistic belief that the day would come when America's stars and stripes would wave once again over a united country, even if that meant leaving the South in a state of ruin and becoming a persona non grata in his brother Morrison's house.[34]

The Copperheads' time in the sun lasted but a brief moment. They were loudest at the end of 1862, after Lincoln announced his preliminary Emancipation Proclamation, and they continued as a formidable force for much of the following year. In June of 1863, when Robert E. Lee was intent on marching his army through Pennsylvania, Pittsburghers spent days building up defenses around their city in anticipation of a possible attack. But Lee never went for Pittsburgh. In the first days of July, Lee's army stopped at Gettysburg, Pennsylvania, which lay just south of Harrisburg. There the armies of the North and the South met in a great battle that appeared to decide the future of the war in favor of the Union. Lee was defeated at Gettysburg and turned his army southward, while another battle in the West at Vicksburg also ended in defeat for the Southerners. In less than a year, the Copperheads had reached a high point in their hatred, but their decline after Gettysburg was nearly as precipitous, although it was not until Sherman marched his troops into Atlanta the following September that their forces completely collapsed. In the meantime, bewildered by the trauma of the war and the disturbing, some might say, traitorous activities of his family, Stephen Foster became increasingly estranged from them. He spent most of his time collaborating with the soldier lyricist George Cooper, writing innovative songs that made major strides toward a new direction in popular music.

17

THE FOSTER-COOPER "SONG FACTORY"

If Gettysburg proved to be the turning point in the war, it may have been a turning point in Foster's musical career as well. It was after that momentous battle that a young Union soldier named George Cooper returned to New York and entered into an innovative musical collaboration with America's favorite melodist. It was not the first time Foster worked with a lyricist or adapted existing poetry to his music, but in the past he did so infrequently, and only when he felt like it. Now he was propelled by good business sense to utilize outside talent on a regular basis, and his decision to collaborate with Cooper was a conscientious and wise one. At the beginning of 1863, even before he started working with Cooper, Stephen had contracted with Horace Waters to write the music for two hymn books, and the commission involved setting words other than his own. Although collaboration was not a new experience for Stephen, writing for religious publications was. In addition, Waters gave him the opportunity to work with talented women lyricists who wrote inspirational poetry and a few who wrote abolition and temperance songs.[1]

Horace Waters was committed to both the antislavery cause and temperance, but he was also a very religious man who, in the past, had been successful publishing hymn books and believed that hymns set to Foster's melodies would sell well.[2] *The Golden Harp for Sunday School* and *The Athenaeum Collection of Hymns and Tunes for Church and Sunday School*, both completed in 1863, contained ten original compositions by the composer known for popular music, and the hymns as

Foster wrote them were pretty and pleasant to sing. Stephen either collaborated with Waters's staff writers, such as the ladies known as O. S. Matteson and M. A. Kidder, or he wrote the words himself.[3] More often, he set hymns from Waters's many anthologies of religious music or adapted a famous poem like "The Pure, the Bright, the Beautiful" by Charles Dickens. How he felt about writing religious music is not known, but at least it started him on a pattern of collaborative songwriting that would have far-reaching effects in the future.[4]

Stephen was in his middle thirties when he met the twenty-two-year-old George Cooper and the two formed an exciting, collaborative, songwriting team. The poet and the composer were introduced at the alcohol-dispensing, German-owned "Dutch grocery" just east of the Bowery at the corner of Hester and Christie Streets, most likely by another young poet named George W. Birdseye, who had himself met Stephen only a few months earlier.[5] The date of Cooper's introduction is not known, but it was sometime before February 11, 1863, the day Foster told Birdseye he would be willing to "arrange Mr. Cooper's melody when my hand gets well."[6] The offer to arrange Cooper's melody appears generous, but Stephen was destitute and probably expected to be paid for his work. Later, the men entered into a mutually beneficial business arrangement whereby Foster wrote the music and Cooper contributed the words.[7] Cooper's poetry and Foster's melodies fit perfectly together, and as soon as they met, Stephen knew he had found the right man for his partnership—a poet who could write the light-hearted lyrics that a public, overwhelmed by tragedy, wanted and needed.[8]

Their partnership probably bothered Birdseye, who wrote war poems and would have been thrilled to collaborate with the man he later described as "the most popular song-composer in the world." Unfortunately, when Stephen set Birdseye's poem "Down by the Gate" to music, the song was never published and a working relationship never materialized.[9] Birdseye, who wrote a lengthy poem eulogizing General Grant and another in praise of women, did not have the talent for writing song lyrics, and was too much like Stephen to form a complementary team.[10] Birdseye even ended his long life in strikingly similar circumstances—destitute, alone, and forsaken by a wife and child he could not support.[11] Birdseye was only eighteen years old when he met Stephen, but youth did not bother Foster who seemed to prefer the company of younger or older men when he lived in New York. Some years after Foster's death, Birdseye published an unflattering account of the composer's last days, when he said they spent time together, but his reminiscence may have been partly colored by jealousy.[12]

George Cooper was several years older than Birdseye, but far more mature and experienced. He had just returned home after an unfortunate military campaign in central Pennsylvania, where he had just missed the opportunity of a lifetime. He was a private in Company B of the Twenty-Second Regiment of New York's National Guard and, years later, claimed that he served in the Gettysburg campaign from July 1 through July 3 in 1863. Close enough, but during the famous battle, the Twenty-Second's division of 9,000 men remained in Carlisle, Pennsylvania, twenty miles to the north. General Halleck sent telegrams summoning them to move south, but the starving Twenty-Second did not meet up with the Army of the Potomac until a few days after the battle. Then they marched from town to town in Pennsylvania and Maryland, in a futile attempt to catch up with Lee, who had crossed into Virginia by the time the Twenty-Second reached New York on July 24.[13]

The returning soldier lived in the same Bowery neighborhood as Foster, but Cooper resided at 176-1/2 Bowery, probably with his parents, on one of the street's more reputable blocks that was home to some small businesses and residential housing. Cooper's father owned a general merchandise store on the Bowery near Bond Street, and Embree's Music Store was located nearby at 134 Bowery. Although they worked together for less than a year, it was time enough for the men to write more than twenty songs, and Foster called Cooper the "left wing of the song factory," a phrase that indicates he considered the relationship a solid business decision.[14]

Although collaborations between composers and lyricists were not unknown, Foster's early biographers and music critics judged his decision to work with Cooper as evidence that he had lost touch with his muse. One very damaging assessment of the Foster-Cooper relationship was written by biographer John Tasker Howard in 1934: "The collaboration with George Cooper produced little that was worthy of Stephen's talents in early years." Even the wonderful comic songs "Mr. & Mrs. Brown" and "If You've Only Got a Moustache," both collaborative efforts, were defined as "trifles."[15] Stephen's niece Evelyn Morneweck perpetuated the insult in her chronology of the family when she

called the Foster-Cooper songs "short lived productions of little consequence," "mere potboilers," and "mediocre productions" written "despite his [Foster's] growing intemperance."[16] More recently, a highly
acclaimed music historian concluded that Foster's "song 'factory' was
fueled by pecuniary pressures."[17]

The negative assessments carried over to nearly all his New York
productions, whether he wrote them on his own or with a lyricist. One
critic concluded, "Foster wrote much during his last three years because he needed the money, and because publishers . . . did not have to
pay highly for them."[18] Another stated that "some of his Civil War songs
are sad for reasons other than their author intended."[19] The general
opinion seemed to be that "Numerous as they are, if Stephen Foster
had written nothing but these songs of his later years, his name would
have been forgotten long ago. Most of them are extremely commonplace, and obviously are pot-boilers."[20]

These denigrations of Foster's last musical creations appear harsh
and based on ignorance and bias. The critics who disparaged his last
songs were enamored of the antebellum plantation style and were unable to accept the idea that music changes to meet the needs and whims
of the public. The dominant opinion that, with the exceptions of "Beautiful Dreamer" and "Old Black Joe," Foster produced almost nothing of
value in New York is dependent on the bias of the critics, who had a
preference for the older songs and judged that very few of those written
during the war were quality products. Such a harsh judgment fails to
recognize that many of the new works, while different from older models, were artistically just as good as the earlier creations. Of course, not
everything written in New York, especially those songs turned out
under duress, deserves a glowing review, but the songs he wrote with
George Cooper, and most of his Civil War songs, are marvelous artistic
creations. If they appear different from Foster's antebellum songs, they
were meant to be, because they were written in response to changing
tastes, which in turn were molded by changing national events. After
the Civil War broke, Americans needed a new music that would help a
war-torn nation endure and work through its ordeal, and for one reason
or another, Stephen produced this new music best when he collaborated.

The Foster-Cooper "song factory," as Stephen referred to the partnership, was especially adept at producing innovative songs that satis-

fied the people's desire for more upbeat positive music. The team wrote uplifting sentimental songs, stirring and poignant war songs, and splendid comic songs that anticipated the next generation of popular music—variety, vaudeville, and musical comedy. Unfortunately, these achievements have gone unrecognized because critics failed to notice that the composer's New York compositions stood in the vanguard, anticipating new trends that took over the industry in the years after the war. These same critics failed to consider the possibility that Foster's last years in New York moved him beyond the antebellum model to new and original compositions that have been misunderstood or rather not considered at all. The critics and music historians who could not disassociate Foster from the pre-war genres, which they themselves preferred, ignored the fact that Foster with Cooper took popular music in a new direction because times had changed.[21]

The second half of the year 1863, in the wake of Gettysburg, marked not only an end in sight to the hopeless continuation of the war, but for Foster also the beginning of a new songwriting style that was reflective of postwar music. Intuitively, Foster knew that on his own he could not pen the words to the new-styled songs. He was astute enough to know that, if he wanted to satisfy the needs of the people, he had to find a poet who could write the words to the energetic, fun-loving songs that people craved. Foster willingly renounced his own poetry in favor of Cooper's because he knew his own was often too sad and sentimental for the times, while George had a talent for writing lyrics in an upbeat style. Cooper's youthful optimism overrode what could almost be described as Foster's antebellum cultural pessimism. Together they complemented each other's talents and shortcomings, and formed an innovative team that ushered in late nineteenth- and early twentieth-century music.

Even Foster's sentimental melodies, when combined with Cooper's lyrics, were forward sounding, suggestive of "Silver Threads among the Gold" and the Irish-inspired songs that became popular in the 1870s. The Foster-Cooper team published eighteen songs in six months, showing that the men were prolific working together. (Additional songs by the team, like the Irish-sounding "Sweet Emerald Isle That I Love So Well," were published posthumously, after Foster's death.) When Cooper penned the words to Foster's songs, they had just the right amount of sentimentality to make them moving, but not tragic, and his comic songs were funny and uplifting. In "Katy Bell," the protagonist's love interest does not die in the song. Instead, her suitor waits "Till the sun was sinking low, and I had won her for my Bride." In "Kissing in the Dark," with words by Cooper, the physical expression of love—kissing—is glorified in the lyrics and in the title: "Not a sweeter note of music, Sings the morning lark, Than is heard when lips are meeting."[22]

Even the war songs Foster and Cooper wrote together were never morbid. "Bring My Brother Back to Me," a song title that is reminiscent of Foster's "Was My Brother in the Battle?" is urgent and joyful. When Foster penned the words, the brother was dead, whereas in Cooper's lyrics, the sister is confident that the brother will return "safe . . . to my longing arms." In "When this Dreadful War is Ended," the departing soldier tells his sweetheart how happy he will be to know she will be true. And he urges, "Be not mournful now my darling; Let me kiss away each tear. . . ." He is confident he will return after the war and mentions the "kiss" in sensitive terms. In "My Boy is Coming from the War," the first two verses are optimistic. Not until the final verse do we learn that "her boy was lying dead! And the mother sadly waits" for one "who'll never come." The protagonist "drummer boy" in "For the Dear Old Flag I Die" hears "the angel band calling from the starry shore," but the sorrow in the song is mitigated when the boy is turned into an angel.[23]

The Foster-Cooper song factory produced many excellent ballads and war songs, but they were at their best when they produced clever comic songs that seemed custom-tailored to the music hall. The best and most innovative songs that the team wrote together were four songs in the comic tradition, which took major strides toward the variety and vaudeville stage. "There Are Plenty of Fish in the Sea," in keeping with the storytelling tradition, relates in several verses the antics of a stubborn and foolish spinster, who turns down every proposal of marriage because she thinks her youth and beauty will last forever. The protagonist calls out defiantly, "There are plenty of fish in the sea," until in the last verse she faces the prospect of a lonely spinsterhood when she realizes that as youth fades, the "fish" are no longer so easy to catch. The song would have struck a sensitive chord in the females in the audience, for the Civil War death toll turned many young women into lifelong spinsters.[24]

Another great comic song, "My Wife Is a Most Knowing Woman," tells of a drinking man unhappily married to "a most knowing lady" who recognizes her husband's bad habits only two well. The song did not portray the wife in sympathetic terms, but the audience knows better. If they could not laugh at the poor henpecked husband, the marriage would have been tragic. Although the words were composed by Cooper, the details offer an all-too-intimate glimpse into Foster's own marriage. The wife is depicted as a shrew who "would have been hung up for witchcraft, If she had lived sooner . . . ." She knows all her husband's "secrets"—his nightly drinking bouts—because "her eyes are like those of a lynx." In the second and third verse, the husband confides:

> She would have been hung up for witchcraft,
> if she had lived sooner I know
> There's no hiding anything from her,
> She knows what I do, where I go
> And if I come in after midnight, and say
> "I have gone to the lodge,"
> Oh, she says while she flies in a fury,
> "Now don't think to play such a dodge!
> It's all very fine, but won't do, man,"
> Oh, my wife is a most knowing woman.
> Not often I go out to dinner,
> And come home a little "so-so,"
> I try to creep up through the hall-way,
> As still as a mouse, on tip-toe,
> She's sure to be waiting up for me,
> And then comes a nice little scene,
> "What, you tell me you're sober, you wretch you,
> Now don't think that I am so green!"[25]

Toward the end of the song, the harassed husband concludes, "One might as well be 'neath a tombstone, As live in confusion and riot," and in the last verse, he is resigned to "stay at home now like a true man." If the song is an accurate reflection of Foster's marriage, which it seems to be, it offered Stephen a chance to reveal his marital miseries to the public, behind the words to the song. The effect is comical, however, and multiple verses could have been performed in their entirety as a single variety act. "My Wife Is a Most Knowing Woman" has lasted the test of time and was recorded in 1992 with virtuosity and humor by the great baritone Thomas Hampson.[26]

"If You've Only Got a Moustache" is a delightful Foster-Cooper song in the comic tradition and arguably one of their best collaborations. The

song's four carefully balanced verses assured the listener that a moustache would make any man attractive enough to find a mate and happiness.

> Oh! All of you poor single men,
> Don't ever give up in despair,
> For there's always a chance while there's life,
> To capture the hearts of the fair.
> No matter what may be your age,
> You always may cut a fine dash
> You will suit all the girls to a hair
> If you've only got a moustache.[27]

Subsequent verses rely on the moustache to quickly dispose of all "woe"
and prove that even an "empty"-headed man could end up with "a wife
and ten heirs, all through a handsome moustache." This song, identified
on its title page as a "comic song," has been sung by concert and opera
singers, including the mezzo-soprano Marilyn Horne.[28]

The last of the comic song collaborations, "Mr. & Mrs. Brown," is a
duet for male and female voices, and it is best suited for the stage.
Identified as a "comic duet" on the first page, it would have been a
perfect piece to perform at a music hall, where it would be thoroughly
enjoyed as a single act or interpolated into a musical play. The song is a
witty, conversational battle, which has been set to music, between a
man and his wife. The couple is arguing on the stage, and the male and
the female voices sing individually and jointly. The wife complains that
the husband is away from home every night, drinking no doubt. When
she teases him that a male friend named Jones visits her regularly, the
husband gets jealous and promises to stay at home. In the end, the
couple is reconciled, as the husband sings, "Now come and kiss me do,
Jones is a bosom friend to me, but needn't be to you." The song, which
has directions on how each verse is to be performed—"furiously," "indignantly," "coaxingly," and "lovingly"—must have been written with
stage possibilities in mind.[29]

The difference between the songs Foster wrote with Cooper and
those he wrote on his own is apparent to the ear. The Foster-Cooper
songs simply sound like they were meant to be performed in a music
hall or on a variety stage. Foster's earlier ballads, designed with simple
piano accompaniments and vocal lines suitable for trained amateurs,
were meant for an intimate performance in the parlor, while his planta-

tion songs could be performed either on the minstrel stage or at home. But the songs with Cooper's lyrics had great theater potential, and toward the end of the century and into the next, they would carry popular music to the stages of vaudeville, Tin Pan Alley, and Broadway.

Even before the war had ended, the songs Foster wrote with Cooper exhibited the traits of the postbellum style. Music historian Nicholas Tawa describes some of the defining characteristics of the songs that became popular after the war from 1865 to 1900, and the Foster-Cooper songs show some of these same subtle differences in sound, mood, structure, and lyrics. These postbellum qualities were present in most of the songs Foster wrote in collaboration with Cooper in the early 1860s.

According to Tawa, "During the [mid-eighteen] sixties and seventies, compositions started to appear that were altered in some individual details." Tawa found that songs composed in the popular music tradition from 1865 to 1900 were characterized by "acceptance of reality" and an interest in the here and now, in contrast to the antebellum preference for singing about "the arcadia that might have been and the paradise to come." They also used "forward looking lyrics" that described "practical experiences" rather than the "idealized relationships" emphasized in the earlier songs. These postbellum songs did not emphasize a divine presence or such non-concrete ideals as loyalty, devotion to parents, or "right conduct." In the new songs, a cynical attitude toward human nature replaced the "nobility discoverable in ordinary people" evidenced in the older songs. In general, the postbellum songs were concerned with enjoying life, rather than longing for perfection and making selfless commitments, and they seemed to reflect a new, more secular, viewpoint. Another notable difference was that the antebellum songs acknowledged the continuation of the spirit after death, but the new songs paid tribute to the present material life, however brief it may be.[30]

Tawa also comments on the changes in the musical structure of the postbellum songs. More of these songs were written in 3/4 or 6/8 time. "Songs moved at a faster pace, fewer andante's appear," writes Tawa, concluding that as the "pulse of the new American society was quickening, so was the music." The new songs were lively, as were the Foster-Cooper songs, and like "Kissing in the Dark," they dealt with "slice of life fragments of actual experience," and "dismiss the lofty, unphysical love that was highly lauded by American songwriters of the antebellum days." The new songs "treat love as it really exists," not as an ideal, pointing to the "evanescent quality of anything connected with happiness and beauty."[31]

Foster was not really stuck in the antebellum mold, since, with Cooper, he wrote songs that reflected many of the identifying characteristics to be found in popular song after the war. His new songs, for instance, celebrated the everyday pleasantries of this world, including worldly love and women in the flesh. Most noticeably, instead of pining for days gone by, they demonstrated an optimistic regard for the future, in spite of (or because of) what the nation had just lived through. Even when singing of separations, growing old, and dying, the newer songs do not project the overwhelmingly sad emotions that were a trademark of Foster's antebellum songs. They seek happiness in *this* world, not in a glorified past or in a heavenly reunion in the next life.

With Cooper's lyrics, Foster's music takes on a whole new sound. There are the "antebellum Foster" songs and then there are the "Foster and Cooper" songs. The collaboration inaugurated a whole new dimension to Foster's songwriting. Being sensitive to the society's changing musical tastes, Foster chose to collaborate with Cooper to write a new style of music. The poetic muse had not escaped him in the last year of his life. Rather, it was that Foster the artist always tried to act like a businessman. He understood that popular music develops in response to the mood of the people and he chose to write the songs that suited the new mood. Just as he abandoned minstrel and plantation songs when the political scene was boiling over in 1854 and such songs were beginning to appear inappropriate, he now pushed aside the parlor songs that glorified the past, ethereal women, spiritual delights, and the resolution of problems through death. Instead, he wrote sentimental songs with more muted emotions and he wrote comic songs that helped people laugh as they dealt with life's problems. Foster's New York years should be commended for introducing a whole new musical direction that looked forward to the era when songwriters would be known only by their last names and as teams, such as Gilbert and Sullivan, Rodgers and Hammerstein, and Lerner and Loewe are today.

Foster and Cooper wrote songs that the people wanted. And the team knew what that was because they heard the lively new music all around them. Whether they took a stroll down the Bowery, or crossed through Canal or one of the narrower side streets to Broadway, they had the opportunity to hear the new sound loud and clear by stepping through the doors of any of the many music halls that proliferated in the neighborhood. Another way to learn about the new music was to stop the performers, impresarios, and music publishers when they were out walking on Broadway and ask them which songs brought the most applause and what song sheets sold the most copies. The interaction between these creative types was important because it made possible the collaborative effort that held the entertainment industry together. The composer and the lyricist had to know what type of song the performer wanted, and the publisher in turn needed to know what songs received the best response from the audience before committing to the expense of publishing. The area surrounding lower Broadway and the Bowery, vibrant thoroughfares for purveyors of entertainment, became an exchange arena for clues to what audiences wanted and what the new trends in popular music would be.

New York around Broadway, even in the early 1860s, was the happening place for anyone involved with theater or music. The neighborhood had about a dozen and a half theaters offering everything from legitimate theater to minstrelsy, each claiming to offer the most exciting shows to draw in the most customers. Squeezed in between the theaters on Broadway were Foster's music publishers, including the now separate establishments of Firth, Son and Company and William A. Pond and Co. Others on the same street were P. A. Wundermann, S. T. Gordon, and Horace Waters. The reason for their proximity was obvious. The entertainers in the theaters and music halls would be able to get copies of the publishers' songs right off the press, and the music publishers in turn could anticipate increased sales in their showrooms from the men and women who walked out of the theaters next door, singing and whistling the songs they just heard on the stage.[32]

For Stephen and George, walking from the Bowery to Broadway was a regular part of their business day. They could easily stop off at one of their publishers to sell a song as soon as the ink was dry, or they could try to sell the same song to one of the managers or proprietors at the new music halls or to one of the minstrel performers. In fact, it was often easier to sell songs to performers during the war than to publishers, although the venture usually went hand in hand. That is, the publishers preferred to publish songs that they knew would be performed before an audience. George Cooper explained how Stephen "wrote with great facility and without the aid of a piano. . . . [on] whatever paper he could find," after which "these first drafts were taken out and sold to a publisher or theater manager, practically without correction."[33]

Foster must have sold songs to many impresarios and theater managers on Broadway, but when interviewed years later by Foster biographer Harold Vincent Milligan, Cooper only provided an account of their interaction with Henry Wood, who bought songs directly from Foster on an "as needed" basis and paid very little for them. The minstrel would catch Foster walking down the street with a new song in hand, and call out, "What have you got there, Steve?" A deal would be struck, "for whatever they [Foster and Cooper] could get for them, which was never much." Wood gave him a onetime payment with no royalties, an unprofitable arrangement Stephen made with nearly everyone he sold his songs to in New York.[34] Milligan described the transaction:

> The song "Willie Has Gone to the War" was written one morning and after it was finished, Stephen rolled it up and, tucking it under his arm, said, "Well, where shall we put this one?" Cooper says that he remembers it was a cold, raw, winter day, with snow falling drearily and the pavements covered with slush. Stephen's shoes had holes in them and he had no overcoat, but he seemed oblivious to discomfort and misery. As the author and composer proceeded up Broadway, they passed Wood's Music Hall, and the proprietor, standing in the lobby, hailed them as they passed with the question, "What have you got there, Steve?" The song was sold then and there, Wood paying ten dollars cash, fifteen dollars more to be paid at the box office that evening. Stephen called Cooper "the left wing of the song factory," and most of their songs were written and sold in very much the same manner as "Willie Has Gone to the War." They sold all of their songs for cash, receiving no royalties on any of them.[35]

Cooper called Wood's theater a "music hall" but the building at 514 Broadway was actually known as Wood's Minstrel Hall, which the entertainer opened in 1862 from a converted synagogue.[36] Cooper also claimed Henry Wood purchased "Willie Has Gone to the War" for a onetime payment, but he may have been mistaken here, too, because that title was published by William A. Pond, who did pay royalties. There is always the possibility that Wood paid Stephen for the right to perform the song first and have the publishers print his name on the cover. The description above is reminiscent of Foster's financial arrangement with Edwin Christy and his early days in Cincinnati, when he sold his unpublished songs in manuscript form to the minstrel performers at the stage door. Wood paid Stephen a total flat rate of twenty-five dollars per song, and when he published Foster's song lyrics in his songsters, he paid him nothing for the privilege.[37]

The songs Henry Wood purchased from Foster and Cooper in the early 1860s were not the same type of songs Wood sang in the mid-1850s. At that time, Wood performed Foster's plantation songs in dialect and blacked up. A decade later, Wood changed his act to rely less on plantation ditties and more on the new style songs. He did not sing in "darky" dialect and usually did not wear blackface. Foster and Cooper wrote white men's songs for Wood to sing in the 1860s, which shows how minstrelsy was changing and adapting to the times. "Willie Has Gone to the War" was written for the minstrel to perform without blackface, as the song anticipated the happy day when a soldier returns home and the battles are over:

> And still I will hopefully wait, The day when these battles are O'er,
> And pine like a bird for its mate, Till Willie comes home from the War.

Wood also sang "Jenny June," another white man's song, with a melody that many years earlier had appeared in Foster's "While the Bowl Goes Round." Cooper liked the melody so much that he added a new title and rewrote the words into a song about happiness in the here and now: "Did you see dear Jenny June, When the meadows were in tune, with the birds among the bowers. . . . All the robins increased their song."[38] In the 1850s, Wood sang "My Old Kentucky Home" in blackface. Now, he sang a white man's love song by Foster and Cooper, and he wore no makeup.

If paying a small, flat fee for the songs while pocketing phenomenal amounts on ticket sales seems particularly callous, the minstrel Wood was not the only one taking advantage of Foster at this time in New York. Biographers never fail to mention the negative interaction the composer had with minstrel performers like Henry Wood, Edwin Christy, or Charlie White, but few have considered the possibility that

Foster wrote songs for the newer genres of the stage, such as variety acts and fairy spectacles, and the entertainers and impresarios who ran those shows may have taken advantage of him in much the same way.[39]

18

CONCERT SALOONS AND VARIETY MUSIC

When Stephen walked along Broadway carrying a song to sell to Henry Wood, the soles of his shoes were wearing down at the heels and the cloth of his jacket was so threadbare that the wind ran through to his chest. He no longer felt hunger pains, since eating irregular meals had dulled his appetite. But the chill in the air as night fell about him increased his yearning for the comforting warmth of rum slinking down his throat, just enough to deaden the emotional pain that threatened to engulf him every evening. He would sell to Henry Wood, or to any performer or impresario, at whatever price they wanted to pay, because he could exchange the few coins he earned for drinks at the new concert saloons a few doors down the street. The strangely hospitable environment of this new entertainment venue offered comfort and the chance to watch and listen to the newest songs being performed on a stage. Huddled around the bar, bodies pressed close together, the boisterous, all-male clientele raised their glasses to their lips, laughed at the comic songs, and for a few hours, forgot about their problems.

Clearly the world and its music had changed in the decade since "Swanee River" had been on everyone's tongue. With death and destruction all around, people craved songs that were uplifting and energetic, with words they could sing to help them forget—like the songs Foster and Cooper were writing in the song factory. It was an altogether new music, aptly named "variety" because it was sandwiched between diverse acts, one after the other, and performed in such a way that was spellbinding. The audience was mesmerized by the contrast that the numerous acts provided, as they seemed to rush by like whirlwinds. A delicate ballerina appeared on the stage, followed in quick succession by a vocalist who sang a comic song like Foster and Cooper's "Plenty of Fish in the Sea," which in turn was followed by a daredevil acrobatic display. The most attractive innovation in variety entertainment, one that appealed to the soldiers who loved the shows, was that real women sang and danced on the stage, rather than female impersonators, as was the case in minstrel shows.

Variety entertainment, which grew directly out of minstrelsy, circuses, and the British music halls, thrived in the environment of the concert saloons, which really took off at the start of the Civil War, when soldiers on furlough found an escape in the laughter, glitter, and fast-paced acts that provided respite from the miseries of the war. Many proprietors, of course, preferred to call their establishments by more refined names, like concert room, concert garden, or music hall, but they all came equipped with a stage for singers and a bar for alcohol, and they offered a good time at half the price of the old minstrel shows.[1] The first concert saloons were built underground in cellars along the Bowery and they relied on "conspicuous transparencies" to notify potential customers on the sidewalk above what entertainment awaited them below. Others opened above ground in storefronts, and when they had proven their success, large pretentious music halls that featured song and dance, orchestras and music directors, and tantalizing individual variety acts opened up on Broadway.[2]

The shows were usually free at the concert saloons, included in the price of the drink, because their real purpose was to encourage the boys in blue to linger and buy more drinks while waiting for the next act. The catch was that the drinks were served by pretty young waiter girls who often wore provocative clothing such as short skirts, high red boots, tights, and low-cut blouses. These not-so-innocent girls sat with the customers and flirted, encouraging them to buy round after round of their favorite alcoholic beverage. Many of the girls were aspiring performers, who walked on the stage to sing a song or two, but more than a few were known to sell themselves as prostitutes.[3]

Because many of the managers of the early variety theaters had been minstrel performers, variety shows followed a familiar format. Like minstrel shows, they were initially arranged in three acts, and the first two acts presented a series of unconnected specialty acts without a story line to tie them together, very much like the "olio" section of the minstrel show. The audience was treated to a succession of singers, dancers, jugglers, and acrobats, while musicians accompanied their performances. The third act in the larger music halls was a spectacular presentation, or "afterpiece," that was presented as a spoof on a popular or classic play, similar to the third act in the minstrel show, except that it was not a plantation scene.[4]

Concert saloons came in different degrees of opulence. The smaller, unpretentious ones on the Bowery, sometimes called "free and easies," had simple stages at one end of the saloon, a piano, amateur performers, rather uncomfortable seating, and plenty of alcohol, but with no admission charge; the soldiers pushed their way in and lingered long enough to spend their dollars. The fancier ones on Broadway, like the Melodeon, Canterbury, and the American Music Hall, distinguished themselves from the Bowery saloons by calling themselves "concert" or "music halls." They charged an admission and had a large auditorium with a professional stage, a music director and an orchestra, and professional performers. Patrons from all walks of life rubbed shoulders at the music halls, especially when snugly seated on pew-like, wooden benches fitted in the back with slats to hold the customer's drink.[5] The Canterbury Hall accommodated 1,500 people and was lined with gold-framed mirrors to triple the spectacle, while acts "of the most varied character," including Spanish and French dances, ballet, and flying trapeze, dazzled the eyes and the senses.[6] Robert Butler, manager of the nearby American Concert Hall, took advantage of his circus background and offered pantomimes, acrobats, equestrian performers, and tightrope walkers.[7]

The first concert saloons were masculine domains, with an ambiance that was coarse and boisterous. The *New York Evening Post* noted in 1862 that "especially on Saturdays nights . . . . all parts of the house are crowded by male visitors . . .who wear their hats and caps at pleasure."[8] The comedy could be robust, too, drafted to appeal to the laborers, soldiers, idlers, and "very young men" who huddled around the bar with a drink in hand, although on occasion a judge or low-level banker squeezed in for a taste of the seamy side or a chance to gape at the waiter girls.[9]

Considering the pleasure he took in music, it makes sense to imagine that Stephen enjoyed his drinks, at least some of the time, at several of these new saloons that sprouted in his neighborhood during the war. There were seventy-five concert saloons in lower Manhattan when Stephen was living there, and most provided free musical entertainment. Foster's erstwhile friend George Birdseye recalled that the composer liked to entertain the people at the bar by singing his own songs, especially after a few drinks, when he gave a moving rendition of "Hard Times Come Again No More." There would have been a piano that he or someone else could play while he sang, and his comrades at the bar could join in, since they all knew the words to at least the chorus.[10] If the fifty establishments along the Bowery were not to his liking, Stephen could have crossed over to Broadway and found twenty-five more respectable variety or music halls that offered the same drinks with better entertainment and ambiance. The music halls were convenient, too, since most of them were only steps away from Foster's publishers. In fact, the new Firth, Son, and Company at 563 Broadway was located on top of the Melodeon Music Hall, which bore the same address, only the latter was in the basement.

The Melodeon on Broadway would have appealed to Stephen, with its alcoholic drinks and "males and females who sing comic and sentimental songs," and "a German-American middle aged lady who does opera with all the shakes and trills common to prima donnas."[11] But its history might have bothered him. The music hall's first owner was Charles White, the minstrel who liked sentimental songs and tried to steal "Nelly Was a Lady" by having it copyrighted in his own name. White opened the Melodeon at 53 Bowery in 1849, originally offering minstrelsy, but he offered variety acts when he reopened on Broadway in 1857. White's talents never took to variety and his theaters failed, but he set the pattern for what variety—with lavish respectable performances and more professional performers—would become in the next decade. He was the first to charge an admission because the elaborate shows he wanted to put on could not be paid for with alcohol receipts alone. On Sundays he offered alcohol-free performances, but charged a six-cent admission and proved that people would pay just to watch the shows.[12] In 1861, White sold the Melodeon to Frank Rivers and went to work for the many variety impresarios on Broadway, sometimes blacking up for a single minstrel act sandwiched between a song and dance, and at other times donning the whiteface makeup of a clown.

Sources allude to Foster's presence at local drinking establishments and to his drink of preference—homemade rum mixed by "the barkeeper from French spirits and brown sugar"[13]—but no one knows exactly where he liked to drink. George Cooper recalled that Stephen bought some of his drinks at the "groceries," where he could make "a meal of apples and turnips from the grocery shop, peeling them with a large pocket-knife," and a grocery at Christie and Hester Street has been mentioned.[14] But there were too many exciting concert saloons in Lower Manhattan for "groceries" to have been the only place where Stephen enjoyed his alcohol. The groceries were "dark, dirty, depressing looking establishments" that supplied the neighborhood with necessities like "fuel, soap, candles, crockery, pipes, and tobacco," and stored food in large wooden barrels or "behind the counter in tin boxes." Intoxicating spirits, including the grocer's own "bottles of poisoned firewater," were available to anyone who requested them, but the quality was inferior.[15]

If George Cooper did not mention concert saloons when he was interviewed by biographer Harold Vincent Milligan years later, the oversight was understandable. because concert saloons were associated with "waiter girls" and prostitution and were considered evil. During the war, their reputation became so sordid that the government enacted a law to try to close them down. The real problem was that the established theaters suffered when concert saloons became so popular that they drew customers away from respectable venues like Wallack's and Niblo's Garden. When the owners of these posh establishments were threatened with empty seats, they attacked the concert saloons for corrupting the morals of soldiers and teenage boys who sneaked inside to peek at the waiter girls. On April 17, 1862, the theater impresarios joined forces with the moral enthusiasts to push through a state bill that would "enable the authorities to effectually shut-up the concert saloons in the city." John A. Kennedy, the superintendent of police, urged its passage. That a man named Kennedy would support a law that aggravated the Irish residents of the community seems strange, but he did, and his action was not forgotten. The next year, when the Draft Riots broke out in New York, Kennedy was beaten by the mob until unrecognizable.[16]

The Concert Saloon Bill stipulated that all places of amusement in New York had to be licensed, that no alcohol could be sold at a concert saloon, and that no females could serve the refreshments.[17] The new law made it "unlawful to conduct any kind of performance on a New York stage unless a license had been obtained from the city," but a license for a stage performance could not be issued to any establishment that offered beer, wine, or spirits on its immediate premises. Finally, the law forbade any theater owner from holding both a liquor license and a theatrical license, and threatened fines and imprisonment for those who did not comply.[18] The law was aimed at the "waiter girls," who, next to the music and show, were the main attraction that men paid to see, but full compliance would make the concert saloon as it was then known, unrecognizable. When the law went into effect on April 24, 1862, for a few months in the summer it appeared to be working. The Canterbury went out of business, along with many of the smaller halls, but by the end of the summer and into the fall, many had revived and new ones opened to take the place of those that failed. With the soldiers on furlough, there was too much demand for them, and as long as the war lasted, the nation had more serious worries than corrupting the morals of its youth. According to one authority, "Throughout 1863, the world of the concert saloons operated as it had before the Legislative action; entertainment, refreshment, and pretty waiter girls were all available for patrons."[19]

The concert saloons and music halls survived throughout the war, each in its own way. Some followed the law and managed to work around it by operating as saloons without offering entertainment. Others attempted to stay in business without obtaining a license and risked being raided by the police. Those with money complied by building a full wall separating the bar from the auditorium and stage. The alcohol was still available, but patrons would have to enter the bar from the street to buy their drinks, and they could not drink or be served by waitresses while they watched the show. A few cleverly circumvented the law by firing the singers, keeping the piano, and encouraging the audience members to participate in sing-alongs, or "glee singing." These proprietors were not breaking the law when they continued to serve alcohol, because they no longer had performers or a stage. Still others kept the stage hidden inside a closed off room, where they continued to offer entertainment and alcoholic beverages.

Stephen and George most certainly dropped in at the music halls and the concert saloons, because doing so was part of business. The most enticing thing about the concert saloons was that they offered the song factory duo the opportunity to try out their own songs on a real audience and to promote them. Even on Bowery Street, where the talent and entertainment was second rate, they could find a piano and a singer for a practice run of their newest songs. They could also sell their songs to theatrical managers or performers at the concert saloons, because Stephen and George were writing just the type of comic and sentimental songs they needed for their acts. The new sentimental songs for the variety stage were usually performed by sexy young women who sang of failed courtships or fondness for their homeland, but they did not sing of loss and death. The songs had to be lighthearted and flirtatious, not maudlin, and the situations encountered in these new songs were resolvable.[20]

The team could have brought their songs to the concert saloons to be performed before a live audience either before or after they were published, since hearing them would create a demand for the printed song sheets. Songwriters were constantly supplying the entertainers with a steady stream of new material just to get exposure, even if they were paid very little, in food or drink, or not at all.[21] Handing out new songs to performers as a means of promoting, or "plugging," them was a good means of marketing and the publishers might have encouraged the policy as a contingency for publication. At any rate, the proprietors of the music halls would have been happy to have their performers, or even the customers at saloon sing-alongs, present the Foster-Cooper songs.

A popular means of promoting new songs during the Civil War and a generation later was to encourage audience participation in sing-alongs around the bar by passing out slips of paper with the lyrics written on them. Tin Pan Alley publisher Edward B. Marks claimed, "The best songs came from the gutter in those days!" and explained that from "its initial break in the beer saloon, a song might work up to the smaller variety houses," until it reached the top theaters in the city. "If a publisher knew his business," said Marks, "he always launched a sales campaign by impressing his song on the happily befogged consciousness of the gang in the saloons and beer halls. When a number was introduced from the stage of one of the more pretentious beer halls, that was a plug!" Perhaps some of Foster's publishers encouraged him to "plug" his songs at the better variety halls on Broadway, too.[22]

The preeminent concert saloon during the Civil War was the American Music Hall at 444 Broadway, an address previously advertised as "the Most Magnificent Place of Ethiopian Entertainment in the World."[23] At the beginning of the war, when it was converted to a variety theater under the management of Robert Butler, the star performer was Tony Pastor, advertised as the "the greatest clown and Comic Singer of the age." At the time, singing was an important means of presenting comedy and the comic song became the means by which talented male performers captivated the audience and became stars. Minstrel performers had sung comic songs in blackface, but with variety music the Irish and the German immigrants became the butt of the jokes. The songs were performed in an Irish or German accent, or in standard English, but not in a Southern, slave dialect. Many ditties for the variety stage were parodies of famous or well-known songs, and while some performers sang cruel parodies of the Irish, Pastor gave sympathetic portrayals of the ethnic group that comprised a large segment of his audience.[24]

Tony Pastor's theater looked like any other on the inside, especially after the handsome bar at the entrance was walled off to accommodate the new Concert Saloon Bill, but his show at the American Music Hall was like no other. "Beautiful women danced upon the stage, amazing Negro [blackface] comedians created much laughter, and dexterous acrobats" held the audience "in breathless yet fearsome delight." Admission was twenty cents a seat, much higher than the Bowery venues at six-and-a-half cents, yet his theater filled to capacity every night. On April 17, 1861, a few days after the bombardment of Fort Sumter, Pastor stunned the audience at 444 Broadway with his incomparable rendition of "The Star Spangled Banner." One patron recalled enthusiastically, "I thought the roof of the building would fly off . . . . It was tremendous." This was the first time the "Star Spangled Banner" had been sung on a variety stage, but so successful was Pastor's rendition, that he closed the show every night with it throughout the war.[25]

Tony Pastor was born sometime in the early 1830s on New York's West Side below 14th Street.[26] Like the Foster children, he improvised his own play house, but converted the family cellar instead of a carriage house, and starred in everything from blackface minstrelsy to the burlesques of Shakespeare. He purchased a tambourine and a "negro wig," and appeared with a professional minstrel troupe at the corner of Chatham Street before going to work at P. T. Barnum's "dime" museum at the corner of Anne and Broadway. In 1847, Tony joined a circus that offered a variety of exciting acts, from tightrope to juggling, while he played both the blackface minstrel and the whiteface clown. Soon after the death of his father, his mother apprenticed him to John J. Nathans's circus and he traveled the circuit, performing in Allegheny City, Stephen Foster's hometown, before moving on to Cincinnati in 1849, where cholera forced the troupe to disband. Tony was still a teenager when he returned to New York an experienced performer and took on different roles at the theaters on the Bowery. At the start of the war, he was hired as a comic singer at the American Music Hall at 444 Broadway, where he became a sensation and his career took off.[27]

When the Concert Saloon Bill went into effect, Tony was not worried.[28] His shows were top quality and patriotic, and he maintained tight enough connections with the Tammany Hall Democrats to get around the law, but he chose instead to go along with it.[29] Pastor fired the waiter girls and set up the bar "next door with no inside communication between it and the theatre," and was more successful for doing so.[30] By forcing the concert saloons to abandon the scantily dressed girls, the alcohol, and the risqué jokes, the new law encouraged variety to transform into the respectable entertainment known as "vaudeville." Pastor was willing to clean up his act because he knew that upgraded shows attracted a better clientele and would be more profitable in the long run. Rightly suspecting that the bawdy concert saloons would lose customers after the war ended and the soldiers left town, he wanted to be ready to greet his new clientele.[31]

In his desire to promote respectability and profits, Pastor may have reminded Foster of Edwin Christy, the minstrel who a dozen years earlier had whitewashed his own reputation by performing refined blackface minstrelsy for the better classes. Foster composed songs for Christy years before, and now he had the opportunity to do the same for the man who would be regarded as the father of vaudeville. The Horace Waters Publishing company at 481 Broadway, where Stephen worked on *the Athenaeum Collection of Hymns and Tunes*, was just a few doors down from Pastor's music hall at 444 Broadway, and Foster could not have missed the sounds of boisterous laughter emanating from the fabulous new theater. It was no coincidence, then, that Stephen wrote the music for "The Song of All Songs," which Pastor performed regularly in his shows. According to an article in the *New York Clipper*, "Tony had the words set to music by Mr. Foster" who composed the song "expressly for Tony," while the entertainer was touring in Boston.[32]

Published in December 1863 by D. S. Holmes, the song with the strange title was really a publicity vehicle because it listed more than sixty songs that Pastor popularized at "444," including Foster's "Jenny's Coming O'er the Green" and "We Are Coming Father Abraham."[33] The list "that will cause you to smile" seems endless and only hints at the 1500 titles that were in Pastor's repertoire:

> There was "Abraham's Daughter," "Going out upon a spree"
> With "Old Uncle Snow," "In the Cottage by the Sea"
> "If your foot is pretty, show it," "At Lanigan's Ball,"
> And "Why did she leave him" "On the raging Canawl?"
> There was "Bonnie Annie" with "A jockey hat and feather"
> "I don't think much of you" "We were boys and girls together"
> "Do they think of me at home?" "I'll be free and easy still"
> "Give us back our old Commander" with "The sword of Bunker Hill!"[34]

It is not certain who wrote the words to "The Song of All Songs," but several possibilities come to mind. In Pastor's *Comic Songsters*, "The Song of All Songs" was promoted as an "An Original Conglomeration of Titles, Written and Sung by Tony Pastor" to the air "The Captain with His Whiskers," but in the *New York Clipper* article, Pastor told the reporter that John F. Poole, the in-house writer of skits and satires at "444," contributed the words to the sheet music version.[35] Pastor often wrote his own words to his songs, drawing on ideas from current event articles he found in the newspapers, but he tapped into many different sources for the music.

"The Song of All Songs" claimed original music by Foster, although Pastor usually set his words to well-established tunes that everyone in the audience knew. He also adapted songs from the British music halls and relied on his own musical directors, such as Ferdinand Van Olker and the classically trained David Braham from England, to supply him with melodies. But Pastor also admitted that he "borrowed" from fellow entertainers or "purchased" his songs outright, presumably from destitute composers, and paid very little. "I generally pay $15 for a good song," he told the reporter for the *Bowery Autocrat*. "Why, would you believe that I receive on an average one hundred songs a week from different persons, and out of each thousand I'll get only ten good songs?" We have to wonder how much he paid Stephen to write the melody for "The Song of All Songs." The names of most of the composers who sold him melodies or lyrics, or both, are lost to posterity, but even when a well-known composer like Foster supplied the music, we expect that Pastor paid very little.[36]

In the same year that Pastor published the "Song of All Songs," he copyrighted the "Combination Song," described on the title page as "a bunch of penny ballads as sung by him [Pastor] in New York & Boston with great applause." The "Combination Song" was published by Oliver Ditson of Boston, the firm that had published Foster's songs years before. All five verses are nearly identical to those in the "Song of All Songs," and are to be performed "Allegretto con Spirito."

> As you walk through the town, on a fine summer day,
> The subject of my song you have met on your way;
> On railings and on fences, wherever you may go,
> You will see the Penny Ballads stuck up in a row,
> The titles for to read, you may stop for a while,
> And some are so odd, they will cause you to smile;
> I've noted them down, as I read them along,
> and I've put them all together to make up my song.[37]

Since no composer's name appears on the title page of the "Combination Song," the question of authorship comes up. Did Tony Pastor's music director write it? Did he pick it up from some unknown composer or develop it himself from a familiar tune? Or did Stephen Foster compose the music for "The Combination Song" at the same time he wrote "The Song of All Songs"?

It was acceptable practice in the early 1860s for musical performances to have "interpolated" songs that were taken from elsewhere and put into the show, and unless the songs used in the show were well-known, the composer's name would rarely be mentioned.

Pastor was happy to tell the *New York Clipper* reporter that Foster wrote the music for the "Song of All Songs" because Stephen was already dead when the article appeared in March 1864. The master of the comic song would have found many of the songs from the Foster-

Cooper factory a good fit for his shows. We can even imagine, although there is no proof, that the comic song "If You've Only Got a Moustache" was written especially with Pastor in mind, for the famous vaudevillian wore a large, dark moustache that curled up facetiously at its ends. Foster and Cooper wrote just the sort of songs the audience at "444" wanted. Pastor found patriotic songs useful for "ballyhooing the Union Cause and chasing away blue devils at every opportunity," and he alternated rousing marching songs like "Freemen, Rally" and "We Are Marching to the War" with songs about famous battles like "The Monitor and Merrimac."[38] Pastor was gifted when it came to performing comic songs and particularly enjoyed songs about "the scolding wife," a topic that the Foster-Cooper team handled adeptly. But Pastor did not limit himself to performing "new and original songs on the topics of the day." Always looking for the best way to use song to make people laugh, "the world renowned comic vocalist" learned to convulse the audience with parodies of the most popular songs of the day.[39]

Pastor's numerous *Comic Songsters*, which sold in the lobby of his music hall, contained parodied lyrics to well-known songs. Written either by Pastor or one of his henchmen, the altered words rhythmically fit the original tunes and were published with the directive "to be sung to the air of," followed by the name of the original song.[40] When Pastor parodied well-known Foster songs like "Willie, We Have Miss'd You" or "I Dream of Jeanie," the new words often turned a sentimental ballad into a laughable farce. Pastor's parodies of Foster's sentimental songs lead us to wonder how the composer felt if he stopped by "444" and heard his songs spoofed on the variety stage. He might have fumed, but maybe he just laughed along with the audience, realizing that imitation is the best form of flattery and also good advertising. Of course, Tony Pastor was not the only one parodying Foster's songs. Phil Gannon had been a minstrel performer in 1850 before he became a jig dancer and comic singer in the concert saloons. His very popular "My Good Ould Irish Home" was sung to the melody of "My Old Kentucky Home," and in Gannon's version, it is the Irish immigrant who longs to return to his "poor, unhappy home far away."[41]

> Och, my heart still yearns for my good ould Irish home,
> Though grieving may all be in vain,
> Bad luck till the day that I ever thought to roam,
> For I'll never see my country again.

Methinks I can see my little cabin door
The thought makes my poor bosom swell
But sad is my fate—I will never see it more
So my good ould Irish home fare thee well.

Foster's songs were not the only ones that Pastor parodied. Any of the really popular tunes in any genre were considered fair game. The sensitive Civil War song, "Mother, Is the Battle Over?" by Benedict Roefs, was parodied as "Mother, Is the Bottle Empty?" He also parodied George F. Root's 1864 song "Just before the Battle, Mother" with new comic words by Eugene T. Johnston:

Just before the battle mother,
I was drinking mountain dew,
But when I saw the rebels marching,
Unto the rear I quickly flew;
Where all the stragglers were flying,
Thinking of their homes or wives—
It was not the "Rebs" they fear'd dear mother,
But their own dear precious lives.
Then farewell mother, you will never,
See my name among the slain;
For if I only can skedaddle,
Dear Mother, I'll come home again. [42]

Even the war's moving "Weeping Sad and Lonely, or When This Cruel War Is Over" was subjected to a dunking in Pastor's humor. As usual, the comic changed the words to the song, but he was gentler this time:

Dearest Sal, Do you remember, When I marched away
With my musket to my shoulder, Looking nice and gay?
Now those shining regimentals all in rags appear
Darns and patches all about them, awful times out here!
Weeping sad and lonely, Lord! How bad I feel!
When this cruel war is over, Praying for a good square meal. [43]

Pastor's "That's What's the Matter, No.1" was unlike his other parodied songs, whose words were often a play on the original. Here the lyrics bear no similarity to the words in Foster's song with nearly the same title, nor do they appear to satirize anything. The parodied version was patriotic and anti-Southern, and its anti-abolition sentiment aimed to please the angry, draft-conscious, working-class New Yorkers in Pastor's audience:

> We'd oughter take old Massa Mealy,
> And his abolition crew,
> And make them fight for the Union,
> Just as they'd orter to do.
> For it was these self-same fellows,
> That first kicked up the fuss—
> And I think we'd oughter to make them,
> Help settle up the muss.[44]

In the case of "We Are Coming, Father Abraham," Pastor's words are a parody of the same poem by Gibbons that Foster set to music. Undoubtedly clever and funny, Pastor's version appealed to poor New Yorkers who hated the idea that the new draft law allowed a man to buy his way out of military service if he could come up with the exorbitant sum of three hundred dollars:

> We are coming, Father Abraham,
> Three hundred dollars more;
> We're rich enough to stay at home,
> Let them go out that's poor.
> But, Uncle Abe, we're not afraid,
> To stay behind in clover;
> We'll nobly fight, defend the right,
> When this cruel war is over!
> We are coming Father Abraham,
> Three hundred dollars more;
> We have never smelt of powder,
> But that's the fate of war.
> Be not alarmed, we come well armed,
> We're rich enough and able;
> And with hearts that never yet knew fear,
> We'll slap it on the table.[45]

Still another parodied song, "Billy, I Have Missed You," does not mention Foster's name at all, only that it is a "Parody on Willie, We Have Miss'd You, Written by C. Sloman, and sung by Tony Pastor." Sloman's words fit Foster's tune exactly, and there is no mistaking this for a parody of any other song:

> Oh! Billy, on the tight, dear, Oft you come home,
> So it is nothing new, dear, But I wish you would not roam;
> You're muddling your poor pate, And you're ruining your poor voice,

Quite unsteady is your footstep, Why make such a life your choice?
I'll make music on your ear, If night after night you roam,
Oh! Billy, I have miss'd you, Then, Billy, *do* come home!
You're in the Station nightly, But one night of all,
The light was burning brightly, I heard my Billy fall;
Our little ones jump'd up, And the bed-clothes off they cast,
Each eye look'd like a wrinkle, Then they slept again quite fast;
I thought I heard your voice, Shouting out "Some love to roam,"
Oh! Billy, I have miss'd you, Now, drunken, you come home![46]

In Pastor's parody of "I Dream of Jeanie with the Light Brown Hair," the comic singer jokes about the latest immigrant group, the Germans. Times were changing and the audience was more interested in laughing at German accents than "darky" dialect. The songster specified that the parody was to be sung to the air "Jenny with the Light Brown Hair:"

I dreams bout Jimmy mit his prown plue hair,
A great old velar vas he,
He trinks dem schnapps till his eyepalls shtare,
Un he don't leave nodding for me.
I loves de lager un de swietzer kaese,
I loves dem pretzels rare,
But better does I love mine pretty liddle frow,
Mine Jimmy mit his prown plue hair.

Pastor also sang "Beautiful Jersey, A Parody," with new words to fit Foster's "Beautiful Dreamer."

Beautiful Jersey! Theme of my song,
What mem'ries of mud to thy regions belong;
What queer recollections my buzzum now fills,
Of thy monster musquitoes, with terrible bills.
Full many a time I've left ounces of blood,
With the insects that swarm in that region of mud.[47]

The transition from minstrelsy to variety is obvious, yet the change was gradual and developed in stages. Variety's similarities to minstrelsy are especially evident when one compares playbills from the minstrel shows of the 1850s with the playbills from variety shows appearing in the 1860s. Both entertainments were featured at 444 Broadway, and the playbills are surprisingly identical in design layout.[48]

One minstrel playbill from March 2, 1855, announced in large, bold type at the top of the page, "the original Geo. Christy and Wood's

Minstrels at Minstrel Hall, 444 Broadway." The qualifier "No connection to any other company" followed underneath to demonstrate perhaps that this show was not connected with Edwin Christy who had retired the previous year. Henry Wood was listed as "business manager" and George Christy was "stage manager." The show was clearly divided into three acts or "parts." In "Part First—Representing the Dandy Negroes of the North," company members sing selections from Verdi's opera *Ernani*, followed by performances of popular songs, including "My Old Kentucky Home." The performers wear blackface even when they sing the operatic arias. The second part began with a "Concert A La Julien" by "Mons. Julien Kneassano," obviously a reference to the minstrel Nelson Kneass who performed in the show. Diverse acts portending variety entertainment followed, including a dance or "Pas de Africane," a violin solo, several banjo acts, a comic trio performance, a Virginia reel, and a concertina solo. Part 3 was an operatic burletta entitled "Lend Her de Sham Money, or Much to do about Nothing." This was a complete play in parody with music performed by a five-piece orchestra. The characters in the burletta were "primo buffer, primo tenore, and Prime up Donna." The playbill advertised that "The Song Books and Music" were for sale "at the Ticket Office and at the principal music stores" nearby.

Compare Wood's and Christy's 1855 minstrel playbill to a variety playbill from 1862. At first glance they appear very similar, but there are subtle changes in content and style. Running across the top of the playbill are the words "American Music Hall," not minstrel hall, yet the address is the same, 444 Broadway. The music director was Ferdinand Van Olker and there was a ballet master listed. The headliner Tony Pastor, "the Greatest Comic Singer of the Age," joined forces with the former minstrel "Charley White," who had gone to work for Pastor after he sold the Melodeon. Both men have their names featured in large bold type, and White's name appears on the playbills as often as Pastor's, especially when the comic singer was out of town, but White rarely performed in blackface at the American Music Hall. Another innovation is that the names of women singers and dancers, previously excluded from minstrelsy, are printed prominently on the playbill. Most importantly, the clean-faced comic-singer, not the minstrel, and the comic song, not the pathetic ballad, are the star attractions. [49]

Tony Pastor's 1862 show at the American Music Hall emphasized the number and diversity of the variety acts. A dance medley was followed by the Tyrolean singers, a Pas de Deux, more song and dance acts, and a song by the coquettish Amelia Wells. The variety acts were similar to the skits in the "olio," or second part, of the minstrel show, but more acts appeared in the 1860s. The "Wandering Minstrels" was the only skit devoted to blackface and only one "Pathetic Ballad" was listed on the playbill. The act everyone waited for was Tony Pastor himself singing his surprise "Comic Song," the name of which was never mentioned on the playbill. If Foster and Cooper wrote the song, Pastor would not have mentioned it because, like Edwin Christy, he wanted to be known as the composer as well as the performer. Even if the playbills looked alike, there were plenty of differences between George Christy and Henry Wood's Minstrel Hall in the 1850s and Pastor's American Music Hall in the 1860s. In the "Circus" finale, the minstrel Charles White played the part of the clown, probably appearing in whiteface.

Stephen Foster really had no chance of developing a successful working relationship with Tony Pastor. The father of vaudeville was more powerful and conniving than Edwin Christy ever was. He rarely credited the composers for their songs, preferring to take credit for everything himself, and leaving little opportunity for the composers to make money. Performers like Pastor even placed ads in the *Clipper* for songwriters, bought the songs for a few dollars, and then added their own verses and a simplified accompaniment to suit their audience. Then they took the modified versions to a publisher who published them with the performer's name as composer, with no questions asked, because music associated with a well-known performer was easier to sell.[50] Foster and his talents once again fell victim to men more clever and less scrupulous that he ever could or would be.

Variety was not the only entertainment sweeping aside the older musical forms. Another popular genre that promised to enthrall with its extravagance and to blot out the images of the war was the fairy spectacle produced at Laura Keene's Theater at 624 Broadway. Keene's shows, which were precursors of the Broadway musical, were decidedly feminine, with ballet dancers in shear fairy costumes, lavish stage settings, fairytale storylines, and light-operatic music. Although the idea is speculative, it is entirely possible that Foster in some way collaborated with Keene on her fairy spectacles. When he published "I'd Be a Fairy" in 1863, just when the war was in its most crucial stage, he must have intended the song be used in one of her productions, because "I'd Be a Fairy" makes no sense at all for the time and the place it was written.

Laura Keene was born in England, the same year as Stephen Foster. An accomplished actress and playwright, she was also a proficient pianist and musician. After moving to New York in 1852, she worked at Wallack's Theatre, and the following year opened Keene's Varieties where she made history as the first woman theatrical manager in America. She is more famous, however, for adapting a play by Tom Taylor into the phenomenally successful *Our American Cousin* and starring in it on the night Abraham Lincoln was assassinated at the Ford Theatre. When *Our American Cousin* premiered at Laura Keene's Theatre in October 1858, the part of Abel Murcott was played by Morrison Foster's actor-friend Charles Couldock.[51] It therefore seems plausible that Morrison might have used his friendship with Couldock to maneuver an introduction between Laura Keene and Stephen at some time or other when he was in New York. Such networking was conceivable, since on several previous occasions, Morrison played the business manager for his younger brother, making contacts and carrying manuscripts back and forth.

Stephen was interested in fairy spectacles and had experience writing them, because in November 1853, he had staged his own in Pittsburgh, *The Invisible Prince, or the War of the Amazons*, which was well received in the local press. In July 1859 and again in May 1860, Keene staged a fairy spectacle based on the same fairytale by Madame D'Aulnoy, and called it *The Invisible Prince*. Keene, however, used the libretto that James Robinson Planche wrote for the London 1846 debut of *The Invisible Prince, or The Island of Tranquil Delights*. The name, the topic of the story, and many of the characters in Stephen's and Keene's shows were the same, although her libretto was undoubtedly different from the libretto by Charles Shiras that Stephen used in his production.[52]

The question of who influenced whom naturally comes up, although Keene certainly had enough connections of her own not to have stolen the idea from a show in Pittsburgh. Still, she might have used some of Foster's songs in her production. Unfortunately, the music from neither Keene's nor Foster's *Invisible Prince* has been preserved, but it is possible that her *Invisible Prince,* or her *Seven Sisters* spectacle which opened six months later, contained some songs by Foster.[53] Thomas Baker was the resident composer for both shows, a man highly regarded for making "music a noticeable feature of the evening," but he need not have written all the songs in the spectacles.

During the 1860s, according to musicologist Deane L. Root, "the practice of inserting musical numbers [by unknown composers] in the play remained unchanged." Resident composers such as Baker, who doubled as conductors, were often too busy to write all of their own songs or they lacked the talent. In fact, since "the music was performed from manuscript copies," it is "difficult to determine who composed the music for many of the plays and spectacles of the period."[54] Also, the playbills from Laura Keene's Theater state that medleys from a "popular air" were performed, without naming either the composer or the air.[55] Foster might have asked to contribute songs to Keene's spectacles. It would not have been surprising. His "Fairy-Belle," copyright August 19, 1859, a month after Keene debuted her *Invisible Prince*, was perfectly suited to be interpolated into her fairy spectacle.[56]

There are many unknowns, but there were too many connections not to conclude that Stephen met the century's leading female impresario. Foster was in New York to renew his contract with Firth and Pond in February 1858, when Charles Couldock was rehearsing the debut performance of *Our American Cousin*, and they could have met then. But it is more likely that he met Laura Keene in 1860 when he was invited out to one of her fairy spectacles. When Stephen's old friend Susan Pentland Robinson visited New York with her husband and son "just before the outbreak of the war," they invited Stephen and Jane to dinner at the St. Nicholas Hotel. Afterward, "they all went over to Laura Keene's Theatre" to watch the *Seven Sisters* that opened on November 26, 1860, "with new music by Thomas Baker."[57] Eliza Couldock, Charles Couldock's daughter who had shared the stage with her father ever since childhood, had a part in Keene's play that night. The aspiring actress was very close to Morrison's wife Jessie, with whom she spent time whenever Eliza and her father stopped in Cleveland. It seems almost certain, then, that after the show, Stephen went backstage to congratulate Eliza Couldock on her performance and was introduced to the famous Laura Keene.

The *Seven Sisters* was extraordinarily popular. The show played more than 250 performances and attracted 400,000 patrons in eight months, at the same time that the South seceded and the Civil War broke out. Apparently, the show's extravagant displays and fantastic storyline (based on a German play that Keene herself rewrote) provided the escapism New Yorkers needed. Thomas Baker conducted his orchestra with a showy, gold-tipped, ebony baton and Keene made use of the mechanical marvels of the age, raising and lowering the gas lights on the stage and in the auditorium with a newly patented device. What impressed people the most about the "grand operatic spectacular," however, were the scintillating scenes that offered "a delicate vision of fairyland" and dozens of "pretty women" with "firmly shaped legs," revealing "the hidden mysteries of alabaster bosoms."[58]

On the evening Stephen and Jane watched Keene's show, a very pretty girl named Jennie Engel danced in the production, and a decade later, after Engel became a popular variety singer, *Jennie Engel's Songs* were published and included "I Should Like to Be a Fairy," by Thomas W. Charles, a title that sounds very much like Foster's 1863 "I'd Be a Fairy."[59] Charles's song did not sound anything like Foster's, but spectacles and fairy dust were certainly on the composer's mind. One afternoon, soon after moving to New York, Stephen spent hours sewing sequins onto Jane's evening gown so that she could attend a costume party disguised as a fairy queen.

If Keene and Thomas Baker used Foster's music in their productions without identifying him, the fact only reinforces the tragedy in the composer's life. On September 12, 1866, one year after the Civil War ended, *The Black Crook* opened at Niblo's Garden and became known as the first musical. As was the case with the *Seven Sisters*, much of the show's appeal came from the ballerinas who flitted across the stage as fairies and sprites, in flesh-colored tights. The music was credited to Keene's old music director Thomas Baker, who contributed orchestral music for the dances and the play as a whole, but left no extant published music from the show. The "March of the Amazons" was published as original music for the *Black Crook* without a composer's name, with only the words "arranged for the piano by Emil Stigler" on the cover.[60] Another song written especially for the *Black Crook*, "You Naughty, Naughty Men," with music by George Bickwell and lyrics by

Theodore Kennick is delightful and reminiscent of the theatrical pieces from the Foster-Cooper collaboration.[61]

Foster was in the vanguard of musical comedy when he contributed to the *Invisible Prince, or the War of the Amazons* in 1853. The *Black Crook* is credited with being the prototype of the modern musical because its songs and dances were interspersed throughout a unifying story by American playwright Charles M. Barras. But Foster's musical extravaganza had had songs and dances interspersed within a "skillfully woven" storyline by Charles Shiras thirteen years earlier. A description of Foster's extravaganza in the *Pittsburgh Post* for November 10, 1853 describes it as nothing less than a complete and coherent play:

> The dialogue is spirited, very often witty, and never lags in interest. In a number of scenes, the love passages . . . are beautiful and would reflect credit upon a higher order of dramatic composition than a scenic play. The plot of the play is skillfully woven, and the termination of it leaves one nothing to wish.[62]

It appeared that anyone who had a good song suitable for Amazons and fairies could interpolate it into the *Black Crook*, but the composer would go unrecognized. Of course, Thomas Baker was familiar with many anonymous songwriters because he used their services when he was the music director at Laura Keene's Theater. Interestingly, Foster's publishers put out works associated with the *Black Crook* the year after the show opened. William A. Pond & Co. published the "March of the Amazons" and "Transformation Polka," S. T. Gordon & Son published the "Black Crook Waltz," and J. L. Peters & Bros. of Cincinnati put out the "Fairy Queen March."[63] It is not hard to notice the lines of continuity between Foster's *The Invisible Prince, or the War of the Amazons*, Keene's *Invisible Prince*, and Baker's *The Black Crook*. Not only minstrel players and music publishers, but variety stars, theater managers, and fellow composers also took advantage of Stephen all too readily.

19

LAST DAYS ON THE BOWERY

Stephen Foster resided in New York City for the last three-and-a-half years of his life, yet few documents, letters, or reminiscences exist to clue us into details about those tortured final years. From 1860 until his death early in 1864, he receded into the protective anonymity of New York's Bowery, where the sounds and sights of Lower "Manahatta," as Walt Whitman referred to his beloved city, proved to be a perfect diversion for a man who feared his own life was in a continuous downward spiral.[1] When a man is depressed, he eschews places and relationships that remind him of better days or suggest personal failure. He prefers to get lost in new and unfamiliar spectacles, and the more diversionary his world, the better off he feels. The Bowery was a diversion because it provided a brightly lit, carnival-like atmosphere, filled with a mélange of sights, smells, and sounds. Its multiethnic residents spoke with strange accents and sashayed down the street dressed in colorful clothing that looked like theatrical costumes. Members of the working class claimed the Bowery as their own, but it was also a stage where drunks, derelicts, losers, Civil War soldiers, and prostitutes could act out their roles without being recognized, in the same way that minstrel performers hid behind blackface to act out their parts on the stage.

Many men who lived and died along the Bowery severed old relationships and left few records of their existence, not because they had nothing to give the world, but because they were broken in spirit and wanted to be left alone. When he lived in New York, Foster, too, broke off relationships with old friends, and left no extant letters to his family.

Whatever the reason, the only extant documents detailing Foster's New York years are testimonials given by the few friends he met and spent time with in the city. Some of these men and women knew Foster on a fairly intimate basis, while others had only brief encounters with him. All the accounts were recorded when clouded by the passage of time, yet most of the reminiscences offer "dire descriptions" of his final years. One friend described Foster as "a man utterly careless of his appearance, having apparently lost the incentive power of self-respect." Another said the composer walked around with holes in his shoes and sold whatever new clothes were given him to buy alcohol.[2]

Two good friends of Foster's from his New York days left the most reliable records: the newspaper man John Mahon and the lyricist George Cooper.[3] Mahon described details of the composer's life in the article "The Last Years of Stephen C. Foster," which he published in the *New York Clipper* in March 1877.[4] In a personal interview with biographer Harold Vincent Milligan, given more than fifty years after Foster and he collaborated as a songwriting team, Cooper provided an invaluable account of how Foster spent his final days. A less reliable and less flattering account of Foster's last years was provided in 1867 by George W. Birdseye, the young poet who introduced him to Cooper. Finally, Effie Parkhurst Duer, a lady songwriter who knew Foster briefly during the final months of his life, offered her own somewhat foggy impression of the day she was introduced to the man who referred to himself as "the wreck of Stephen Foster." Perhaps her sympathetic yet negative remembrance was colored by that fact that in later years she composed temperance songs, including the very popular "Father's a Drunkard and Mother Is Dead," which suggests that, in addition to the intervening decades, Duer's memory might have been clouded by her anti-alcohol bias. Still, her portrait of the composer appears credible.[5]

After reading the various reminiscences, both caring and uncaring, many questions come to mind about Foster's last years. How truthful were these accounts of degradation given by acquaintances such as Duer and Birdseye? What was everyday life along the Bowery like during the Civil War? The composer's last known address was the New England Hotel at 15 Bowery on the northwest corner of Bayard and Bowery. The Foster family maintained that accommodations at the hotel were not bad at all, yet in 1857, just a few years before Stephen rented a room there, the intersection where the hotel was built was the site of a bloody urban riot, where the native-born residents of the neighborhood battled the Irish Dead Rabbits in gang warfare. A prim and proper minister named Lymon Abbott rented a room in the hotel just to peer out of his window and observe the violent spectacle below. Such startling facts make one question the credibility of the Fosters' benign description of their brother's last place of residence.

Another negative point about Foster's address is that a glance at any historical map of Manhattan shows that the lower part of the Bowery formed the eastern border of Five Points, America's most notorious slum. Effie Parkhurst Duer said Foster was sleeping on the floor of a cellar on Elizabeth Street in Five Points when she met him at a music store. Cellar habitation peaked on the Bowery and at Five Points during the war, as destitute immigrants crowded into basement rooms "as thickly covered with bodies as a field of battle could be with the slain." These rooms were usually windowless, "without air, without light, filled with a damp vapor from the mildewed walls, and with vermin in ratio to the dirtiness of the inhabitant." According to a writer from the *Tribune*, doctors could spot a cellar dweller immediately from the "musty smell" about the body.[6]

Descriptions such as this of life in New York's worst neighborhoods would have been passed along to middle-class families like the Fosters, who might have known little about the city except what they read in contemporary newspapers. Sensationalist literature like *New York by Gas-Light* and its sequel, *New York in Slices*, by George G. Foster, a writer unrelated to the composer, painted an even more fearsome portrait of a city cleaved in two both economically and socially. The narratives were exaggerations, no doubt, but to what extent? Modern historians still describe the clear-cut social division in nineteenth-century New York as "the sunshine and shadow tradition" and "the era's central cliché about the city."[7] In December 1860, *Harper's Weekly* published a two-page pictorial entitled "The Two Great Classes of Society," a series of sketches contrasting scenes of selfish extravagance with scenes of abject poverty. Representing the rich and the poor as "Two Nations," one sketch portrayed two painfully thin women hovering over a starving infant in a cradle, while a juxtaposed vignette detailed well-fed, elegantly dressed ladies at the opera who cared nothing for the plight of the poor.[8]

In the 1860s, many of New York's poor were immigrants from Germany and Ireland or their children, people who made up nearly half the city's population. The Irish, with their stereotypical reputation as criminals and fighters, lived in the Fourth, Sixth, and Seventh Wards, in the worst sections of the lower Bowery, and the better classes did everything to avoid them. The Germans made up an equal portion of the immigrant population on the Bowery, but they were educated and safe by comparison, and settled along the upper end of the street in different wards from the Irish.[9] When the native-born feared "the frequency of assaults on private citizens at night" in lower Manhattan, they moved north into exclusive enclaves that they closed off to the poor. So dangerous was the lower Bowery that the famous diarist George Templeton Strong said he never left his house at night without a pistol, especially if he had to travel downtown. When the better classes traveled downtown in the morning for business, they returned at the end of the day to the comfort and safety of their own posh, segregated neighborhoods.[10]

Foster did not live anywhere near the uptown elites or even in the proximity of the comfortable middle classes, who congregated above Bleecker Street. He was forced by poverty into the wretched streets at the lower end of the Bowery, the area usually reserved for the rough and unruly classes. At its worst, the neighborhood harbored prostitutes and men who lived lives of crime; at its best, it provided shelter for a few struggling artist types like Foster. The reputation of the Bowery, however, was increasingly marred by its proximity to the slum Five Points, which lay immediately to the west. As more toughs from Five Points crossed over to the Bowery, the better classes moved further west to the Broadway neighborhood, abandoning the Bowery to the "transients and down-and-outs" who found cheap lodgings for a quarter a night. Broadway continued all the way uptown, but the Bowery ended abruptly at 14th Street with Union Square acting as a barricade separating the lower classes from their social betters.[11]

By day, the Bowery earned a reputation as a bazaar-like, shopping emporium, the street for bargain hunters. The banter between the retailers and those "in desperate search for a deal" provided a sideshow ambience for those who watched the fierce haggling that went on over the desired object. The smell of cooked or sweet foods drew in "throngs of shoppers milling along the sidewalks," who stopped to fork over spare change to the vendors who called out their wares—from freshly shucked oysters and roasted peanuts, to baked pears floating in sweet syrup. African Americans held the monopoly on hot, roasted yams, and on cold winter afternoons "coffee and cake saloons" were good places to warm up over a hot drink.[12] Small pubescent girls hawked freshly cooked sweet corn, attracting attention with their metrically rhymed and sexually suggestive chant: "Here's your hot corn, smoking hot, just from the pot!" The minstrel Henry Wood was very successful with a popular temperance song called "Little Katy, or Hot Corn," a saga about a young girl who peddled corn on the streets and was beaten to death by her drunken mother when she failed to bring home enough money.[13] Other attractions, day or night, were pseudoviolent Punch and Judy shows, jugglers, street musicians, bagpipe players in kilts, and the characteristic organ grinder with his well-dressed monkey. At dusk, the Bowery changed its ambiance when suddenly lit up by red, blue, and green globe-shaped lanterns that directed masons, butchers, firemen, mechanics, and shop girls to the nearby cheap theaters, saloons, and noisy carnivals. Indeed, the street lit up at night like a real-life variety show.[14]

Walt Whitman described the Bowery as the place for the people: "Things are in their working-day clothes, more democratic, with a broader, jauntier swing, and in more direct contact with a vulgar life." For Whitman, the street represented "the most heterogeneous mélange of any street in the city," attracting the native and the foreign born, the young and the old, and those who liked the flamboyant and showed "a certain cocky pride in colorful wickedness, delight in the brash."[15] Only African Americans, who for years had lived with the Irish in some of the Bowery's worst tenements, were rarely welcomed, except as street peddlers.[16] For the previous two decades, before the street was overwhelmed with soldiers, its prototypical inhabitant had been the colorful "Bowery b'hoy"—pronounced as if two syllables, buh-hoy. Dunning Foster jokingly referred to this dubious resident of Lower Manhattan when he said he was "one of the beaux, not b'hoys of Cincinnati, which reputation I do not covet."[17]

The term was in common usage to describe a working-class fellow who "loved fun, adventure, hard drinking, and a night out with his pals."[18] The b'hoy walked "not exactly [with] a swagger, but a swing," and wore "a black silk hat . . . precisely upon the top of his head" to cover his "well-oiled" hair, "long in front, short behind." He wore a "cravat a-la sailor, with the shirt collar turned over it . . . black frock coat . . . black pants one or two years behind the fashion, heavy boots," and a half-smoked cigar hung from the left corner of "the mouth, as nearly perpendicular as it is possible to be got."[19] Stephen Foster could have seen the Bowery b'hoys on the nights they carried lanterns to demonstrate against the election of Abraham Lincoln, and he might have seen the character as a cultural icon on the New York stage. The play *A Glance at New York* by Benjamin Baker opened at the Bowery Theatre a decade earlier with Frank Chanfrau, a native Five Pointer, in the starring role as Mose the Fireman. The Bowery theatergoers thrilled to watch Mose in his tight black pants and red jacket running about the stage frantically rescuing babies throughout the 1850s.[20]

When Foster moved to New York, the flamboyant b'hoy was being overshadowed in the press and on the street by the "sporting man," a new, more dangerous Bowery resident who spent most of his time "gambling, drinking, and fighting in saloons." Unlike the Bowery b'hoy who had a specialized trade, the sporting man preferred a life of crime to regular employment. He wore less conspicuous clothing to blend in with the characters of the underworld, but he was a gangster who made the Bowery a dangerous place to live, and newspapers thrived on the sensationalist stories of his illicit activities.[21]

Of course the most conspicuous characters on the Bowery in the early 1860s might not have been the sporting men, but the Union soldiers of diverse ethnicities who formed segregated units based on their national origin. After German soldiers held a huge rally at the Steuben House on the Bowery, they feasted on sausage and beer and then marched off to war. The Irish formed their own Sixty-Ninth Regiment, which Archbishop Hughes blessed in front of St. Patrick's Cathedral before sending them off to the First Battle of Bull Run. The multinational Garibaldi Guard took second place in ostentatious clothing with their "red flannel basques and blue shirts" singing "German, Hungarian, Swiss, Italian, French, and Spanish camp songs." Most conspicuous were the New York Fire Zouaves, many of whom were b'hoys from the volunteer fire companies. They attracted the most attention with ballooning grey blue trousers, bright red shirts, and tasseled fezzes modeled along the French Algerian style. But the Union soldiers, no matter the unit or the ethnicity, impressed Foster sufficiently to write songs in their praise.[22]

At the start of the war, these spiffy-outfitted boys in blue could be seen lining up proudly at the many daguerreotype studios on the Bowery to have their pictures taken before marching off to battle. A year into the war, however, Foster would have witnessed a less heroic image of the soldier boys. The photographer Mathew Brady and his contingent of assistants, intent on capturing images of the war in action, carried their oversized camera equipment to the nation's growing number of battlefields. The camera shutter was too slow, however, and Brady brought back to his Broadway studio the gruesome sepia prints of dead, stilled soldiers, in various stages of decomposition. According to the *New York Times*, Brady's camera very nearly "brought bodies and laid them in our dooryards and along the streets." His startling daguerreotypes, especially those of the slain at Antietam, dispelled any illusions men might have retained about the glories of war. [23]

Sometime in 1863, Foster and his friend George Cooper dressed up and posed at one of these New York daguerreotype studios, probably intending a publicity photo for their "song factory." The two men in the "ambrotype" look business-like in oversized tailed coats with velvet lapels; George wears a bowtie. They are about the same height as they stand leaning in toward each other, with their heads turned slightly to face the camera. Their hair is neatly clipped, parted and swept to one side and both are clean-shaven in the years when facial hair was fashionable. Stephen does not look to be underfed, although his generous overcoat may be camouflaging a thin body frame. [24] Even with very limited funds, money for the photograph, whatever the price, would be found, because a portrait was considered a necessity and there was something magical about it. The Civil War generation revered photography for many reasons, mostly because, like songs of loss, the sepia print could revive the memory of the loved one who might be killed in the war. One man believed that when a photo was taken, "one of the spectral layers was removed from the body and transferred to the photograph." [25]

It was not necessary to study Mathew Brady's photographs to find real evidence of the suffering caused by the war. Everywhere in New York City, Foster could find signs of the chaos the war created, in the amputees hobbling on one leg, the frequent funeral processions, the battle-scarred soldiers reminiscing over sights few would see and live to tell. Throngs of men and women stood around to hear the names of the dead read aloud, along with the casualty lists of mutilations to the body—an arm lost, a leg shattered, a skull cracked. With the war showing little evidence of concluding, the Union generals seemingly incapable of victory, and the volunteer offices closed down for lack of enlistments, prospects of a return to normalcy seemed dismal indeed. A special military hospital was set up at Central Park and the sounds of the ambulances zigzagging through the streets could be heard throughout the night, competing only with the horrible cries of the wounded.[26]

In spite of the reminders of war all around him, Sunday afternoons on the Bowery could have been fun for Stephen. "Broadway is quiet, the lower part of the city still [yet] the Bowery is alive with excitement," according to one eyewitness who said that on Sunday the "Hebrews" who "have no conscience in regard to the Christian Sabbath" set up stands on the sidewalks and "solicit trade from all passers-by." They sold second-hand clothing or, as the case may be, bought up used clothing for resale. Morrison sent his younger brother new clothing, but Stephen usually sold what he did not need for ready cash. One can imagine the hesitant composer on a Sunday morning conducting an uncomfortable exchange with a Bowery garment man, too shy or eager for his money to haggle in the timeworn tradition of the Jewish peddler. After six in the evening, however, when shadows descended on the Bowery, the street would not have been a wholesome place. Matthew Hale Smith describes a dangerous Sunday night scene in his sensationalist *Sunshine and Shadow in New York.*[27]

> Leaving the City Hall about six o'clock on Sunday night, and walking through Chatham Square to the Bowery, one would not believe that New York had any claim to be a Christian city, or that the Sabbath had any friends. The shops are open, and trade is brisk. Abandoned females go in swarms, and crowd the sidewalk. Their dress, manner, and language indicate that depravity can go no lower. Young men known as Irish-Americans, who wear as a badge very long black frock-coats, crowd the corners of the streets, and insult the passer by. Women from the windows arrest attention by loud calls to the men on the sidewalk, and jibes, profanity, and bad words pass between the parties. Sunday theaters, concert-saloons, and places of amusement are in full blast. The Italians and Irish shout out their joy from the rooms they occupy. The click of the billiard ball, and the booming of the ten-pin alley, are distinctly heard. Before midnight, victims

watched for will be secured; men heated with liquor, or drugged, will be robbed; and many curious and bold explorers in this locality will curse the hour in which they resolved to spend a Sunday in the Bowery.[28]

The Bowery became even more dangerous in the wake of the horrendous Draft Riots when men were afraid to walk the streets after dark. In the fall of 1863, as stories of his brother's drinking and despondency trickled through the grapevine, Morrison tried to convince Stephen to leave the city. Although he promised he would return to Pittsburgh or join Morrison in Cleveland, no definite plans were made. Jane Foster also worried about her husband and wrote Morrison, "If you can persuade him to return to Cleveland with you, I am sure that all will soon be well with him again."[29] But Stephen would not be convinced, however abysmal his situation, to abandon New York to live as a dependent in the home of his rabidly Copperhead brother, nor could Jane invite him to live with her in her sister's house. His sister Ann Eliza also became involved in the effort to get Stephen out of the dangerous city when she sent her son Edward Buchanan to New York to bring him back to her home in Philadelphia. "Edward was instructed to take no refusal—he was to insist that his uncle return with him." But Stephen put on such a "cheerful and perfectly poised" front that his nephew did not dare reveal "the real purpose of his coming." Young Edward wrote home to his mother, "There was no way that I could broach the matter, without seeming very presumptuous."[30]

Stephen was busy writing upbeat songs with George Cooper in the second half of 1863, but his New York friends, as well as family members, noticed his "growing dependence on alcohol." To Stephen's brothers and sisters, the alcohol problem was of greater concern than his "frequent financial emergencies," although it is certain that the "financial emergencies" aggravated his drinking. This was the period in the composer's life that his granddaughter Jessie Welsh Rose described as "the dark pages in the life of S. C. Foster," the years when Jane Foster was "engaged with the aid of Morrison Foster and John D. Scully (a brother-in-law) in trying to put her husband upon his feet—a futile effort."[31]

Alcoholic consumption in antebellum America was very high, and its prevalence has been explained as a by-product of the anxieties that afflicted men who failed "to achieve" in a society that increasingly identified self-worth with monetary success. One historian who studied alcoholism explained, "People who have high aspirations set themselves difficult, perhaps impossible targets, fail to meet their own expectations, suffer disappointment from their failure, and thereby become susceptible to anxieties" that they can only quell with alcohol. In other words, high ambition accompanied by failure caused anxiety that drove men to drink.[32]

Stories abound from friends, acquaintances, and relatives that Stephen Foster had a drinking problem. Most sources assert that the addiction became more entrenched the longer he lived alone in the city. How much or how often he drank, and whether he can or should be identified as an alcoholic, have been debated. Drinking was a common pastime along the Bowery, and one female resident explained, "If you lived in this place you would ask for whiskey instead of milk."[33] With no real cure, and without the personal will power or outside support needed to reform, Foster's marriage, health, work, and ultimately his life became casualties of "demon rum." After his death, nearly all reminiscences and articles remarked on his drinking. George Birdseye spoke of Stephen's "insatiable appetite for liquor . . . in his later years,"[34] and even George Cooper said his friend "drank constantly (although he never appeared to be intoxicated)" and "was indifferent to food."[35] Another source, the Pittsburgh musician and newspaper owner Robert P. Nevin, who may have visited Stephen in New York, recorded in his 1867 memoir that Stephen "wrestled with earnestness indescribable" to free himself from the horrible affliction:

> In the same unfortunate direction was the tendency of habit grown insidiously upon him, a habit against which, as no one better than the writer knows, he wrestled with earnestness indescribable, resorting to all remedial expedients which professional skill or his own experience could suggest, but never entirely delivering himself from its damning control.[36]

Jane Foster, who remained in Pennsylvania at her sister's house in 1863, often sent money to Stephen to pay for "cures" for her husband's addiction. Exactly what treatment Stephen tried in the early 1860s is not known, although opium was frequently used to soothe the delirium tremens that is associated with excessive use of alcohol. Various "cures" were advertised in newspapers and magazines and sold by mail order to the wives of alcoholics, who were instructed in how to administer the patent medicine without the unsuspecting spouse ever knowing it. The wife could, for example, surreptitiously put fifteen to twenty drops of one concoction into her husband's alcoholic beverage, inducing a "nausea and disgust" that would convince the imbiber never to drink again. The "cures" themselves consisted of nearly 50 percent alcohol, but in addition, they often contained opium, morphine, and cocaine. One doctor said that he despaired of ever seeing a reformed alcoholic. Whenever there appeared to be one, the reality was that the drinker had switched his addictions and was now an opium addict.[37]

If a wife despaired of the "cures," she could try to convince her husband to join a voluntary association like the Washingtonians that, like the present day Alcoholics Anonymous, relied on personal confessions and promises of abstinence before groups of like "sinners."[38] Stephen's father William in the 1840s had taken the pledge to abstain before an assembled group of flamboyant Washingtonians, which may have kept him on the wagon for a while.

When "cures" and voluntary associations failed, men intent on reform could try to be swayed by one of the long-running temperance plays at the Bowery Theater, a short walk from Foster's room at the New England Hotel.[39] Since opening in the year of Stephen's birth, the theater featured melodramatic plays that carried messages of moral improvement for the masses. Foster could not have missed the tear jerker *Ten Nights in a Bar Room* that debuted at the Bowery Theater at the beginning of the Civil War and replaced *The Drunkard*, which had run throughout the 1850s. *Ten Nights* by Timothy Shay Arthur showcased the disastrous effects that alcohol had on everyone who came in contact with it. In the last scene Mary, the innocent young daughter of the town drunkard, died after someone accidently hit her with a shot glass. When the curtain came down, the audience was so distraught they were ready to close down the barrooms and pledge themselves to the temperance societies.[40]

Stephen Foster contributed to the temperance genre in song, even if he were unable to practice what he preached. In 1855 he wrote "Comrades Fill No Glass for Me," but in 1863, when alcohol was proving a serious contender for his affections, Foster, together with George Cooper, penned "When the Bowl Goes Round," a song that recognized the power of alcohol to make "darkling sorrows take their flight":

In the bosom dwells no sigh, While the goblet's brimming high,
All the world is filled with treasure, While the bowl goes round,
Darkling sorrows take their flight, in the wine's rich ruby light,
And the hours are winged with pleasures, While the bowl goes round.[41]

Loneliness resulting from his continued separation from Jane probably drove Stephen to drink even more, along with the haunting knowledge that while he had failed to become the self-supporting man, his wife had become the self-supporting woman. Sometime in 1863, Jane moved from Lewisburg to Greensburg, Pennsylvania, a town thirty miles to the east of Pittsburgh. When she realized that sufficient and reliable financial support would not be provided by her husband, she took a job as a telegraph operator at the Greensburg office of the Pennsylvania Railroad, where she worked twelve hour shifts from 7 a.m. to 7 p.m. Her granddaughter Jessie Welsh Rose described Jane's hectic schedule:

> Many times she told me how she was the first to break the snow down Bunker Hill, Greensburg, on her way to work, and later during this period, when she had taken into her office as messenger boy her sister's 12 year old son McDowell Cummings, she spent hours after dark delivering messages herself, because she was afraid to send the timid boy into the country alone.[42]

Jane challenged the nineteenth-century doctrine of separate spheres that maintained the husband was to go out into the world to work, while the wife stayed at home to tend to domestic affairs and care for the family. She was encouraged to challenge the system, not only from financial necessity, but by the war's endless demand for soldiers that opened up many jobs to women. Jane seems to have worked herself up to a managerial position at the telegraph office, but few details survive about her specific duties or about how she felt as a married woman going out in the world to support herself.

Interestingly enough, Andrew Carnegie, the famous Pittsburgh industrialist, helped Jane Foster secure her first job. Her granddaughter remarked, "She was given the telegraph office at Greensburg by Andrew Carnegie himself, who supplanted his cousin Miss Hogan in order to do this. Miss Hogan was moved to the Allegheny office."[43] Carnegie was twenty-eight years of age and unmarried in 1863 when he set up telegraph offices to assist the Union cause. He was working for Thomas

Scott, the man next in line to be president of the Pennsylvania Railroad, when the war came and he decided to serve his country in his own way. Believing he had more to offer the Union cause than his five-foot-three-inch frame on the battlefield, Carnegie bought his way out of military service in the army by paying a substitute $850, far more than the going rate of $300.[44] Immediately grasping the importance of maintaining communications between Washington and the troops on the front, he ran telegraph lines alongside the railroad tracks, and proved just how valuable telegraphic communication could be to a nation at war.[45]

Carnegie opened up telegraph operator positions to bright young women whom he personally trained to use the complex machinery, and in Jane's case, it seems, to run the office. Jane may have "studied telegraphy with a view to supporting herself and child," but she knew her work was important.[46] The telegraph was vital for dispatching news from one battlefield to the next, keeping Washington informed about the movement of troops and supplies, directing where medical help was needed, and informing the whereabouts of the enemy. Women earned about thirty to fifty dollars per month, half of what men received for the same job, but the salary was above average for women's pay scales, and welcomed by Jane who was badly strapped for money. Telegraph lines grew exponentially after the war and Jane continued to work as a telegraph operator at different offices for many years of her life.[47]

There were rumors that the young Carnegie, who did not marry until years later, after his mother died, had more than a professional interest in Jane. Stephen's biographer John Tasker Howard, who had access to written documents and personal interviews, wrote: "Gossip also has it that the bachelor Carnegie was not altogether platonic in his attitude toward Stephen's wife, yet those who advance such a suggestion are emphatic in stating that Jane was quick to discourage whatever advances the little Scotchman may have made to her."[48] These stories were hushed up in later years and Andrew Carnegie never mentioned the Fosters when he wrote his *Autobiography*. Howard did not say who the people were to "advance such a suggestion" nor on what source the gossip was based, but he felt confident enough to mention it in his biography. Howard, of course, backed away from any suggestion of impropriety by saying that the Fosters had connections of their own with the Pennsylvania Railroad, through Brother William who had been the railroad's vice president and his wife Elizabeth, whose sister was married to the railroad's president, J. Edgar Thompson. Howard assured us, "We may assume that Jane did not particularly need the young Carnegie's favor to keep whatever job she may have had." Still, William was already dead when Jane went to work as a telegrapher and the young Andrew Carnegie seems to have gone to a lot of trouble to get her situated in his office in Greensburg.[49]

Although the Fosters lived separately at times, stories suggest an on and off relationship with Jane traveling east to meet Stephen in New York, and Stephen traveling west on rare occasions to meet with Jane. One story about the composer's futile attempt to visit his estranged wife is more pathetic than comical. Reportedly, Stephen boarded a westbound train to visit Jane when she worked the night shift at the telegraph office in Greensburg. Rumor has it that Jane's assistant would run down to the station to see if Stephen were on the train. If she sighted him, she would hurry back and tell Jane, who would lock the door at the telegraph office because she did not want to be disturbed at her job. The story suggested that Stephen was inebriated when he sat on the steps outside her office and played the violin at the closed door while she was trying to get important work done. Jane's callous treatment of her husband is unverified, and it is not known that Stephen, after he settled in New York in 1860, ever ventured west again either to Pittsburgh or to Greensburg. Maybe he tried to visit Jane in Lewisburg, Pennsylvania, which was much closer to the East.[50]

There were other embarrassing stories about Stephen and Jane that emphasized the former's drinking habit. One was conveyed "verbally" by Stephen's granddaughter to his biographer John Tasker Howard. Jessie Welsh Rose heard the story, we presume, from Jane herself, but there are no written documents to support it. Jane and Stephen were living together in New York, or perhaps Hoboken, "when Stephen, in the habit of being away from home for several days at a time, finally returned to his wife and child. It was late at night, and Jane and whoever was staying with her heard someone picking at the lock of one of the front windows. The women were intensely frightened, thinking a burglar was trying to gain entrance. The intruder proved to be the unfortunate Stephen, mistaking the window for a door." The point of the story is that Stephen was too intoxicated to make the distinction, but an alternative explanation could have been that Jane bolted the door and locked him out. Hence, Stephen Foster was caught trying to crawl in through a locked window.[51]

Foster's New York songs about marriage are highly confessional, as almost every one of them repeats a similar sorry scene of an intoxicated husband sneaking home well past midnight. In "The Wife or He'll Come Home," with both words and music by Stephen, the wife is kindly and patient:

> He'll come home, he'll not forget me, for his word is always true.
> He's gone to sup the deadly cup, And while the long night through,
> He's gone to quaff, and talk and laugh, To while the drear night through.
> He'll come home with tears and pleading words and ask me to forget. . . .
> My heart may break, But for his sake I'll do all I can do.[52]

Jane was not as patient as this song's character that Stephen created. When the composer stayed out all night carousing with his friends, his wife became distinctly annoyed. Scenarios featuring a hard-drinking, repentant husband and a haranguing wife were reproduced in Foster's comic songs "My Wife Is a Most Knowing Woman" and "Mr. & Mrs. Brown." In the last mentioned, the wife is more forgiving, although she still scolds her husband for his "shameful" behavior and cries out, referring to his intoxicated state, "Oh! Harry Brown! You're anything but right!"

By the end of 1863, Foster was "anything but right," and his drinking, along with his deteriorating physical and mental state, alarmed everyone who saw him. John Mahon and George Cooper expressed concern about "his weakness and growing ill health," and both men offered Foster pecuniary assistance "when his funds were exhausted." Accepting the charity of his friends would have aggravated his already existing guilt over his financial failings and caused him to despair. Especially for a man who had high expectations from his own talents and his earlier success, the guilt had to be unbearable. Long ago he renounced generous opportunities to enter business and turned to music as his sole support. Foster's songs were popular the world over, but he had not been rewarded financially, and his lonely impoverished existence in New York only corroborated the feeling that he was abandoned by his family, his muse, and most tragically of all, hope.

20

ACCIDENTAL DEATH OR SUICIDE?

Stephen Foster's last place of residence was a large hotel that fronted four city lots at the corner of the Bowery and Bayard Street in Lower Manhattan and had some kind of grocery or drinking establishment on the first floor. In the early 1860s the building at 15 Bowery was called the New England Hotel, but in 1843 it was known as the North American Hotel when it claimed the dubious honor of being the birthplace of the standard minstrel show. Dan Emmett, the founder of the Virginia Minstrels, explained how the show was conceived when four young entertainers "were sitting in the North American Hotel in the Bowery" and "one of them proposed that with their instruments they should cross over to the Bowery Circus and give one of the proprietors a charivari as he sat by the stove in the hall entrance." The owner of the hotel watched the audition and was impressed enough to let them give a trial performance in the hotel's billiard room where their "charivari" of discordant sounds and impersonations was well received. From these modest beginnings, they moved on to the best theaters in New York and minstrelsy became the most original and controversial entertainment form in America's history.[1]

That the man who wrote some of the world's most popular minstrel tunes should make his last home in the same place that the standard minstrel show started is only one more example in the telltale coincidences in the composer's life. Others are his birth on the Fourth of July in the nation's Jubilee year and the fact that the hotel was constructed the same year he was born. But the story of Foster's final days in the hotel on Bowery Street is even more interesting.

The composer was residing in the New England Hotel when he died in a hospital on January 13, 1864, from injuries allegedly sustained from an accidental fall in his room. The official story, relayed by Morrison Foster in his biography *My Brother Stephen*, is that on the morning of January 10, 1864, Stephen "fainted" in his hotel room and "fell across the wash basin," cutting and injuring "his neck and face." He was taken to Bellevue Hospital where he died a few days later. Versions of this same story were repeated by Stephen's brother Henry Foster and, many years later, by the composer's niece, Evelyn Morneweck. A somewhat different story, however, was reported by his lyricist George Cooper, who said he found Foster lying on the floor "with blood oozing from a cut in his throat," and never mentioned a broken washbasin at all. It is difficult not to ask: was Foster's death a tragic accident or a suicide?

Henry Foster wrote two letters—one, dated January 23, 1864, to his friend Susan G. Beach, and another, on February 4, 1864, addressed to his sister Anne Eliza—describing very similar accounts of the sequence of events leading to Stephen Foster's death.

To Mrs. Beach, Henry Foster wrote:

> He had been going about feeling quite unwell for several days, when on Saturday evening he retired early and requested the Landlord of the Hotel, not to have him disturbed in the morning, about ten o'clock the next morning he opened his door and spoke to the chamber maid to bring him a glass of water, and turned to go back, when he fell as if he had been shot, and cut his head badly, a surgeon was sent for immediately, who dressed his wounds, on Monday and Tuesday he improved and spoke of being out again in a few days, on Wednesday he was propped up in his bed and was having his wounds dressed when he fainted away and never revived again. I have no doubt that owing to the state of his system, and the loss of blood, there was not strength sufficient left him to rally after fainting away.[2]

To Ann Eliza, Henry Foster wrote:

> [Stephen] had retired early to bed on Saturday evening, the following morning opened his door and spoke to the chambermaid and turned to go back to his bed when he fell as if he had been shot

striking his head on the chamber, a surgeon was procured immediately and his wounds dressed, he then sent for his friend Mr. George Cooper (as fine a little gentleman as I ever met) who telegraphed to Morrison and I, and persuaded Stevey to go with him in a carriage to the Hospital where he would be better attended to. On Tuesday he was much better, and Mr. Cooper was with him. On Wednesday, he was propped up and after having taken some soup was quite cheerful. When they commenced dressing his wounds and just as the person was washing out the rag, without Stevey saying a word he fainted away and never came to again.[3]

In both letters, Stephen was said to have sustained an accidental injury to his head. Mrs. Beach was told that Stephen "fell as if he had been shot and cut his head badly." Ann Eliza was told the injury occurred "when he fell as if he had been shot striking his head on the chamber," thereby confiding the less decorous detail that her brother fell onto a chamber pot. Both letters reported that a surgeon was called in to dress his wounds, but neither mentioned that the surgeon was called in to sew up a cut in Stephen's throat. Another curious item in both letters is that Henry has Stephen speaking with the door open, just before the accident, with a chambermaid. He told Ann Eliza that Stephen "opened his door and spoke to the chambermaid," just before he "turned to go back to his bed" and he told Mrs. Beach that his brother "opened his door and spoke to the chamber maid to bring him a glass of water."

More than thirty years later, Morrison Foster retold the story of the accident in *My Brother Stephen*, which he published in 1896. Morrison altered some of the facts and added the gory details about "a gash in his neck and face."

In January 1864, while at the American Hotel, he was taken with an ague and fever. After two or three days he arose, and while washing himself fainted and fell across the wash basin, which broke and cut a gash in his neck and face. He lay there insensible and bleeding until discovered by the chambermaid who was bringing the towels he had asked for to the room. She called for assistance and he was placed in bed again. On recovering his senses he asked that he be sent to a hospital. Accordingly he was taken to Bellevue Hospital. He was so much weakened by fever and loss of blood that he did not rally. On the 13th of January he died peacefully and quietly.[4]

Morrison referred to his brother's last place of residence as the American Hotel, and he had no chambermaid standing at the door talking to his brother. In his telling of the story, the chambermaid "discovered" Foster "insensible and bleeding" when she came to his room to bring the towels he had requested at some undetermined earlier time. Morrison does, however, have a broken washbasin, which is responsible for "a gash in his neck and face." And Morrison said his brother had been "taken with an ague"—an illness marked by chills and shivering—and "fever," which caused him to faint and fall "across the wash basin" in the first place.

The most important and probably only reliable account of Stephen Foster's "accident" was given personally by George Cooper to biographer Harold Vincent Milligan. Even though many years had elapsed since the events transpired—Cooper was about seventy-five years old at the time of the interview—he was the only eyewitness to the events that occurred after the accident and hence the only one qualified to report on the circumstances. Accounts given by his brothers were based on hearsay. Morrison and Henry Foster could only have learned the facts as they were relayed to them by George Cooper, Mr. Husted (the proprietor of the hotel), or the unnamed chambermaid. In 1920, Milligan published Cooper's account in *Stephen Collins Foster: Biography of America's Folk-Song Composer*.

> Early one winter morning I received a message saying that my friend had met with an accident; I dressed hurriedly and went to 15 Bowery, the lodging-house where Stephen lived, and found him lying on the floor in the hall, blood oozing from a cut in his throat and with a bad bruise on his forehead. Steve never wore any night-clothes and he lay there on the floor, naked, and suffering horribly. He had wonderful big brown eyes and they looked up at me with an appeal I can never forget. He whispered, "I'm done for," and begged for a drink, but before I could get it for him, the doctor who had been sent for arrived and forbade it. He started to sew up the gash in Steve's throat, and I was horrified to observe that he was using black thread. "Haven't you any white thread," I asked, and he said no, he had picked up the first thing he could find. I decided the doctor was not much good and I went down stairs and got Steve a big drink of rum, which I gave him and which seemed to help him a lot. We put his clothes on him and took him to the hospital. In addition to the cut on

his throat and the bruise on his forehead, he was suffering from a bad burn on his thigh, caused by the overturning of a spirit lamp used to boil water. This had happened several days before, and he had said nothing about it, nor done anything for it. All the time we were caring for him, he seemed terribly weak and his eyelids kept fluttering. I shall never forget it.

I went back again to the hospital to see him, and he said nothing had been done for him, and he couldn't eat the food they brought him. When I went back again the next day they said "Your friend is dead." His body had been sent down into the morgue, among the nameless dead. I went down to look for it. There was an old man sitting there, smoking a pipe. I told him what I wanted and he said "Go look for him." I went around peering into the coffins, until I found Steve's body. It was taken care of by Winterbottom, the undertaker, in Broome Street, and removed from Bellevue. The next day his brother Morrison, and Steve's widow, arrived. They stayed at the St. Nicholas Hotel. When Mrs. Foster entered the room where Steve's body was lying, she fell on her knees before it, and remained for a long time.[5]

It is noteworthy that Cooper has mentioned neither a chambermaid, a washbasin, nor pottery of any kind. Neither did he mention that Stephen had been ill from a fever. Instead, he noticed "a bad burn on his thigh" and "a bad bruise on his forehead." Most tellingly, Cooper said that Stephen had a "cut in his throat," which the doctor sewed up with black thread. Morrison had described his brother's injury as "a gash in his neck and face," while Cooper never used the word "neck." Cooper said very plainly that Stephen had a "cut in his throat." It is interesting how the choice of words suggests a different situation—that is, the difference in connotation between the words "neck" and "throat," and between "cut" and "gash." A "gash in his neck," the words used by Morrison, could be the result of an accident. But "a cut in his throat," the words used by George Cooper, as reported by Milligan, strongly suggests suicide. Besides, Cooper, in describing his friend's eating and drinking habits earlier, inadvertently informed us that Foster, who made a meal of "apples and turnips" at the grocery store, had ready access to "a large pocket-knife" for peeling them.[6]

Cooper's account of Foster's "accident" offered interesting details that showed how well he knew Stephen. Cooper mentioned that while he was suffering miserably from the pain, Foster begged for a drink, and that he, Cooper, went downstairs and brought up a "big drink of rum . . . which seemed to help him a lot." Another interesting fact was that Cooper said he found Stephen lying "naked" on the floor, which contradicts the story told by Henry Foster. If Foster were naked when he suffered the accident, it cannot be expected that he "opened his door and spoke to the chambermaid" a moment earlier. So Cooper's story contradicts Henry's story about there being a maid standing at the door when the accident occurred. Morrison's 1896 account of his brother's death shows that he knew that his brother died with some type of injury to his neck or throat. It is most likely that he discussed the cause of the wound with George Cooper, although Morrison failed to mention that Cooper was even present during Stephen's ordeal. Whatever details Cooper whispered to Morrison about that tragic day have been lost to history, but throughout his long life, Cooper would never forget the facts, or the expression in his friend's "wonderful big brown eyes."

In 1934, Foster biographer John Tasker Howard appeared so overwhelmed by the conflicting stories that he decided to let Henry Foster, Morrison Foster, and George Cooper relay the facts in their own words, rather than try to make one standard story from the whole mess.[7] In 1944, Evelyn Morneweck added to the confusion with her own account of her famous uncle's weird accident:

> On the morning of January 10 [1864], Stephen rose to get a drink of water, and, fainting from weakness, he fell against the washbowl, which broke and cut a terrible gash in his face and neck. The chambermaid found him lying in a pool of blood. Mr. Husted [owner of the hotel] sent for George Cooper, who came immediately. George said that when he lifted Stephen up the latter gasped, "I'm done for." He saw that Stephen was in a serious condition and called for a carriage to take him to Bellevue Hospital. Besides the wound in his neck, George reported that Stephen also had a bad burn on his thigh caused by the overturning of a spirit lamp used to boil water.[8]

Morneweck adhered to the story given by her father Morrison. Stephen fainted "from weakness" and then "fell against the washbowl, which broke and cut a terrible gash in his face and neck." The chambermaid in Morneweck's account found Stephen already terribly injured, "lying in a pool of blood." She had not been talking to him with the door opened, as Henry Foster attested. Morneweck tells us that the hotel proprietor sent for George Cooper, who came immediately to Stephen's assistance. Cooper's presence at the scene had been published by Milligan about twenty years earlier, so Morneweck had to mention it.

More recently Foster biographer Ken Emerson has retold the tale in his 1997 *Doo-dah! Stephen Foster and the Rise of American Popular Culture*. Emerson, like Henry Foster, had Stephen speaking with the chambermaid, yet he changed the story slightly. Emerson wrote that Stephen Foster spoke to the maid "at his door," which was different from what Henry had written—that Foster "opened his door and spoke to the chamber maid." Emerson wrote:

> On Sunday morning, Foster spoke to a chambermaid at his door and then, as he turned back into his room, fell "as if he had been shot," striking a wash basin or chamber pot that cut a deep gash in his neck. . . . George Cooper and a doctor were sent for. When Cooper, who lived only four blocks away, arrived on the scene, he found Foster lying naked (Steve never wore any night-clothes) with a cut throat, a bruised forehead and "a bad burn on his thigh." The tin boiler used for making hot drinks in the liquor grocery had overturned a few days earlier and scalded Foster "terribly," but he had neglected to tend his wound.[9]

Emerson's refashioning of the story, with Foster speaking to the chambermaid at the door without necessarily opening it, makes more sense given that Cooper tells us Foster was naked when he found him lying on the floor. But that scenario only works if the maid spoke to him at all before the accident. He might have called for help after he fell to the floor, or he may have crawled out to the hall for help, where Cooper said he found him lying "with blood oozing from a cut in his throat." Maybe he did ask for towels to clean himself up after the maid found him cut and bleeding, but Henry's story, that the chambermaid was in a face-to-face conversation with Foster just moments before the accident occurred, is highly suspect.

One other curious item is the claim that Stephen made a special request not to be disturbed on the morning of his "accident." In his letters, Henry Foster said that Stephen "retired early to bed Saturday evening" and "requested the Landlord of the Hotel not to have him disturbed in the morning." The hotel proprietor may have given this information to Henry, but why had Foster not wanted to be disturbed?

Morrison said his brother had been taken with "an ague and fever" which kept him confined to his room for two or three days, but Morrison was the only one to mention a definite illness. Cooper, and later Morneweck, said he suffered from a burn on his thigh.[10] But was that reason enough for telling the proprietor that he did not want to be disturbed? In other words, did Foster, in his depressed state, have a sinister plan in mind, which he did not want disturbed?

When the fateful telegram sent by George Cooper reached Morrison and Henry Foster informing them that Stephen was dead at Bellevue Hospital, Henry hurried from Pittsburgh and Morrison from Cleveland to New York City. Stephen's wife Jane showed up, too, and they all secured rooms at the fashionable St. Nicholas Hotel, an upper-class establishment on Broadway. (Andrew Carnegie stayed there when he visited New York.) Although none of the Fosters booked rooms in a hotel in their brother's neighborhood, they refused to discredit the New England Hotel. Henry Foster reported that "they found the hotel a very respectable place, and the landlord told them that Stephen did not owe him a cent, or anyone else that they could find."[11]

Not surprisingly, the stories told by the Fosters are slightly different and contradictory. Of course, people do remember events differently. But there seems to be an underlying agenda at work here that determined what the Fosters remembered and what they chose not to record. Morrison and his daughter Morneweck never used the phrase "cut in his throat" in describing Foster's injury; they said he had a "gash in his neck." Henry Foster never even acknowledged that Stephen had sustained an injury in the area of his neck or throat. He wrote that "a surgeon" had been called in to dress the "wounds" that resulted when Stephen had "cut his head badly," when it was actually his "neck" that was badly cut. In the end, the official opinion given by the family was the one told by Morrison Foster in *My Brother Stephen*, the first biography written about the composer—that his brother's death was caused by an accident sustained when he fell on "the wash basin, which broke and cut a gash in his neck and face."[12]

Perhaps because a doctor had been called in to sew up the wound, Morrison felt he could not leave out the detail of the "gash." He would have gone along with Henry's story of head injuries sustained by the fall on the chamber, but since a doctor or surgeon had sewed up Stephen's "neck," and the fact was probably recorded, Morrison had to talk about the broken pottery. But even if the chamber pot or the more decorous-sounding wash basin had been knocked to the floor and broken, the pottery need not have caused the wound. If Foster passed out and fell from the shock of a self-inflicted wound, he could have knocked the pottery to the floor, where it would have broken without having actually caused the fatal wound. Only the bruise to his head would have been caused by the fall.

In considering whether Foster's death resulted from an accident or an intentionally inflicted wound, certain questions come to mind. George Cooper said that he found Foster naked and bleeding. Do people commit suicide when naked? If so, why? Dr. Robert I. Simon, in his article "Naked Suicide," published in *The Journal of the American Academy of Psychiatry and the Law*, says that they do, and that "knowing that one's body will be found naked and taking the trouble to remove clothing has psychological import." Although the exact percentage of suicides carried out in the nude is unknown, Simon's "review of suicide cases in litigation revealed that an estimated five to eight percent had completed suicide while naked." Citing his own professional encounters with suicides and cases taken from history, he describes the "naked suicide" as one who "symbolically expresses regressive rebirth fantasies." While no definite reasons for naked suicide were given, he does suggest that "the shedding of clothes may symbolize a new beginning, a rebirth and cleansing, or a sloughing off of the world." Anger and vengeance were also cited as motivating factors with the intention of traumatizing the survivor. "The shock of discovering a naked suicide inflicts an indelible traumatic memory that can haunt a survivor for a life time."[13]

More in keeping with Foster's gentle personality than vengeance, however, is Simon's explanation that "in severely depressed individuals, a naked suicide may be an expression of vulnerability, utter despair, desolation or worthlessness." In line with Foster's habits, in cases where men have jumped to their deaths while naked, "substance abuse or intoxication should be suspected." Some people, "before completing suicide by firearm or deep cutting, arrange the suicide so that it does not create a 'mess' for their survivors. Individuals may also disrobe to avoid leaving bloody clothes." Finally, impulsivity, a trait with which Stephen Foster could certainly be identified, is another factor in naked suicides. "Most individuals spend at least some part of each day naked.

An impulse to commit suicide may strike while the individual is naked."
Simon found that "25 percent of individuals studied made attempts
within 5 minutes of having suicidal ideations." George Cooper said that
Foster slept in the nude. According to Simon's theory, then, if the
thought possessed him in the morning before dressing, the impulsive
personality would have carried out the deed without waiting to dress.[14]

The argument for suicide is supported by a description of Stephen
Foster's state of mind given by the composer Effie Parkhurst Duer,
who met him sometime at the end of 1863. Duer, who published under
the name Mrs. E. A. Parkhurst, was employed from 1864 to 1866 at
Horace Waters to write Civil War and temperance songs—after Stephen worked there compiling hymn books.[15] When she was introduced
to him at a "large music publishing house on Broadway," which may
have been Waters, she indicated that he was so isolated and crushed in
spirit that he could not commit his own melodies to paper, and he
accepted her offer to "do the work for him at his dictation." If we
discount the inaccurate details of dates or places, we can concur with
the biographer who said "her story gives a reasonably faithful picture of
Foster during his last days."[16] Duer's article from a 1916 edition of
Etude is worth quoting at length, as several items of importance are
brought to light: Foster was looking ill toward the end, he felt rejected
by the public, he could not even afford paper on which to write down
his songs, and whenever his money ran out, he slept in a cellar in Five
Points where he paid no rent.

> All that this writer knows of Stephen Foster's early days was heard
> from his own lips, when his troubled existence was drawing to its
> close. He told of the wrongs he had suffered, of the temptations
> thrown around him during his years of prosperity and popularity,
> until all he possessed was gone. With a broken heart, crushed spirit,
> health destroyed, nerves shattered, he broke away from old associa-
> tions, and secluded himself, hoping to regain his health, and position
> in the world. Nobly he struggled to conquer his foe, the "wine cup,"
> by which means, evil companions had sought his ruin.
>
> I shall never forget the day I met him. I was engaged in a large
> music publishing house on Broadway, New York City, leading a very
> busy life, although but twenty-one years of age. Every day I met
> teachers and composers, and wondered if ever Stephen Foster would
> appear. . . . One day I was speaking with the clerks, when the door

opened, and a poorly dressed, very dejected man came in, and leaned against the counter near the door, I noticed he looked ill and weak. No one spoke to him. A clerk laughed and said:

"Steve looks down and out."

Then they all laughed, and the poor man saw them laughing at him. I said to myself, "who can Steve be?" It seemed to me, my heart stood still. I asked, "who is that man?"

"Stephen Foster," the clerk replied. "He is only a vagabond, don't go near him."

"Yes, I will go near him, that man needs a friend," was my reply.

I was terribly shocked. Forcing back the tears, I waited for that lump in the throat which prevents speech, to clear away. I walked over to him, put out my hand, and asked, "Is this Mr. Foster?"

He took my hand and replied: "Yes, the wreck of Stephen Collins Foster."

"Oh, no," I answered, "not a wreck, but whatever you call your-self, I feel it an honor to take by the hand, the author of Old Folks at Home, I am glad to know you." As I spoke the tears came to his eyes, and he said:

"Pardon my tears, young lady, you have spoken the first kind words I have heard in a long time. God bless you." I gave him both hands, saying: "They will not be the last." . . . I judged him to be about forty-five years of age, but the lines of care upon his face, and the stamp of disease, gave him that appearance . . . . Stephen Foster was a man of culture and refinement . . . .

When this first visit was ended, Mr. Foster thanked me for my interest in him, and said it had done him a world of good to have someone to talk with. . . . I said if he would bring me the manuscript songs that he had not been able to write out, I would do the work for him at his dictation. He was very grateful, and from that time until he died I was permitted to be his helper. . . . When he brought me his rude sketches, written on wrapping paper, picked up in a grocery store, and he told me he wrote them while sitting upon a box or barrel, I knew he had no home. I asked him if he had a room; he said: "No— I do not write much, as I have no material or conveniences." He then told me that he slept in the cellar room of a little house, owned by an old couple, down in Elizabeth Street in the Five Points, who knew who he was, and charged him nothing. He said he was comfortable, so I suppose he had a bed . . . . [A] kind manager of a nearby restaurant had arranged to provide him with a hearty dinner every day, and he need not pay for anything until he was able to do business, and a friend had sent him some medicine which he must take. He looked at me for a moment and that fervent "God bless you" paid for all my planning . . . . We who were near him had no hope of his recovery, but the few comforts provided lessened the suffering of a dying man. This messenger of song, God had given to the world, was not appreciated, and when overtaken by misfortune, was treated as other great souls in the past, left to die, forsaken by a nation he has blessed by his living.[17]

Another negative take on Foster's last years was given by George W. Birdseye, the young poet who tried to work with Stephen before he entered into a musical collaboration with George Cooper. "A Reminiscence of the Late Stephen C. Foster," published in January 1867, is more sensationalist and less sympathetic than the account given by Duer, but "there are undeniably elements of truth in it."[18] Birdseye wrote:

It was my pleasure, a somewhat sad one it must be confessed, to be personally acquainted with Stephen C. Foster during the last year of his brief existence. It was in the latter part of the year 1862 that I saw him for the first time; and his appearance was so very different from what I had anticipated, that I was, to say the least, disappointed . . . . On the northwest corner of Christie and Hester streets stands an old tumble down Dutch grocery, and into this we entered. I followed my friend into the dingy bar-room at the back of the store, and a moment afterward was introduced to Stephen C. Foster. Let me briefly describe him as he then appeared to me. A figure slight, and a little below the medium stature, appareled in clothing so well worn as to betoken the seedy gentleman who had seen better days, his face long and closely shaven; the mouth of Silenus; soft brown eyes, somewhat dimmed by dissipation . . . a rather high forehead, disfigured by the peak of an old glazed cap that hung closely to his head, scarcely allowing his short-cut brown hair to be seen. His appearance was at once so youthful and so aged . . . . An anxious startled expression hovered over his face that was painful to witness. It was hard for me to force myself to believe that that poor, wretched looking object was at that moment the most popular song composer in the world; but it was Foster indeed! He seemed as embarrassed as a child in the presence of a stranger, and this diffidence never entirely wore off . . . . [H]e would walk, talk, eat and drink with you, and yet always seem distant, maintaining an awkward dignity . . . His conversation, made up mostly of musical reminiscences, was profitable as well as interesting; and at his kind and pressing invitation, I took many an opportunity to visit him. He slept in an old lodging-house in the Bowery as a general thing; but that dark grocery bar-room was for a long time his sole head-quarters, and many an exquisite melody has had its birth in that uncongenial place . . . . I have seen him take a sheet of brown wrapping-paper from the counter, and seating himself at a little drinking-table, or more probably a bean-box, rapidly dot down a few bars of some sweet air that has been haunting him perhaps for many days, meantime whistling over and over again, modifying it until he felt satisfied. Then would follow simple, liquid words, appropriate in sentiment—then a few more bars of melody— then more words, and thus music and words would develop themselves together, and form literally "one harmonious whole." He was not one to haggle about the price when selling his songs; and it was not seldom, in consequence, that a publisher would take advantage of his miserable condition, paying him a paltry sum for what other composers would demand and receive fair compensation.[19]

The testimonies given by Duer and Birdseye describe a desperate, nearly homeless man who has lost the ability to connect with others—a man who would be only too willing to take his own life. Of course, Birdseye's impressions might have been colored by a grudge against Stephen for choosing George Cooper as his lyricist, but his story is not much different from Duer's.

The desperation in both reminiscences is corroborated in a *New York Clipper* article by John Mahon, who said that Stephen needed money at the time of his death to pay his rent. After Mahon wrote the words and melody to a song titled "Our Darling Kate," Stephen offered to arrange the piano accompaniment in exchange for a small fee. Mahon described the situation:

The circumstances under which he requested me to let him arrange the accompaniment were very painful indeed. He was suffering from sheer want at the time, and although I offered him money for what he wanted (a bed at the New England Hotel, where he was seized with the illness which proved unexpectedly fatal), he refused it unless I would let him arrange the song, which I gladly did. Madam

Demorest, the celebrated modiste, paid me a handsome sum for it, and published it in her *Magazine* for March, 1865.[20]

But there was more, a strange coincidence that no one seems to bring up, the fact that John Mahon's wife died on January 10, 1864, the same day that Stephen Foster had his fatal accident. The cause of her death is unknown, but it is possible that Mrs. Mahon had a lingering illness, and that Stephen, as a close friend of the family, knew that she was going to die. Foster may have idealized her as an older sister or a surrogate mother, and may have become overly despondent over her impending death. John Mahon was in Bellevue Hospital on the day of his wife's death, being treated for an ulcer. Foster may have felt abandoned.

Suicides were not terribly unusual during the Civil War and in the years leading up to it. Feelings of despair and hopelessness only increased as the nation edged toward political collapse, which created widespread alienation and disenchantment, and a "genuine sense of crisis" beginning in the 1850s.[21] In 1857, Walt Whitman published an article in the *Daily Times* titled "Suicides on the Increase," which noted "something radically wrong in modern society: while wealth and luxury are on the increase, happiness and contentment are on the decrease."[22] The closer the nation came to national dissolution, the more it seemed people were interested in personal dissolution. An article published in the *New York Times* on August 3, 1859, recorded twenty-six suicides in New York City and stated that "the alarming frequency of late has excited much attention and surprise." Various causes were mentioned in the article—from insanity to overindulgence in rum. But statistics showed that men whose wives had abandoned or divorced them, and who lived in relative communal isolation outside of their own culture— such as native born, middle-class men living among working-class immigrants and far from their families, were more likely to be numbered among the suicides.[23]

In 1863 alone the *New York Times* printed notices and articles for at least seventy-five reported cases of suicide. The name of the suicide, his address, the coroner's name, and even the suicide notes were published. With the exception of a few who were wealthy, most of the suicides were poor, desperate people, but they were driven to commit the deed for a variety of reasons. Some were soldiers who had returned from the war too injured to care for themselves and did not want to become burdens to their loved ones. Other reasons given were the inability to pay their bills and the fact that they felt no more joy in the world. Their methods were confined to five techniques: poisoning, drowning, hanging, shooting, and throat cutting. Men committed suicide more often than women and they picked more violent methods. The Rhodes study of suicide completed some years after the Civil War noted that women were more likely to end their lives through hanging, drowning, or poison, but men preferred "throat-cutting, hanging, and shooting."[24]

In the last few months of 1863, the last months of Stephen Foster's life, at least a half dozen suicide articles appeared in the *New York Times* that might have intrigued him. Most of the victims were young men, who lived alone within, or in close proximity, to his neighborhood. He could have picked up the newspaper on October 2, 1863, and read the headline, "A Melancholy Suicide," followed by a dramatic account of the self-inflicted death of Frank L. Squire, who kept a lottery shop at No. 476-1/2 Broadway. Foster would have walked by the shop on many occasions, even if he did not personally know him. The twenty-six year old ended his life by "cutting his throat with a razor" in his home on Elm Street, where he lived with his mother. He was found on a sofa, "his throat cut from ear to ear." The motive was "not satisfactorily explained," said the article, although "pecuniary embarrassment" was implicated. The suicide note he left for his mother was reported in the newspaper: "My dear Mother," the letter began, "Forgive your poor erring son . . . . [A]lthough in life he did not think what he was doing, now he feels the bitter pang of remorse. Pray for him, that God may have mercy upon him. . . . I cannot live and feel the way I do now. Sell the furniture and put the money in the bank. God grant that we may meet hereafter. Oh! Mother, once more I ask your forgiveness and blessing."[25]

Less than a month later, the headline for October 29, 1863, read "Melancholy Suicide: A Book-Keeper Hangs Himself in His Room." Perhaps Stephen would have noticed this article because he had worked as a bookkeeper in Cincinnati at his brother Dunning's transit business. A John L. Manning, aged 30, who resided in a boardinghouse at No. 176 Bleecker Street in Manhattan, was found by his landlady "suspended by the neck from the footboard of his bed by a handkerchief, his lower limbs resting on the floor." His complaint was that he believed he had been drafted and did not want to serve his country.[26]

A few days later, Foster would have found another account of a throat cutting. The headline for November 4, 1863, read simply, "Suicide." The forty-five-year-old victim was a German shoemaker who was found "lying on the sofa dead, his throat cut from ear to ear" with a razor. In this case, the reason given was "insanity." He had a wife and several children, but they were in Germany and he was alone. Charlie Herring, another native of Germany about forty-five years of age, ended his life "by cutting his throat with a razor . . . in his sleeping room at No. 146 Essex Street." This man was also alone in New York, since both his wife and son had died earlier in the year. The newspaper concluded that the tragic losses induced him to take his life.[27]

The suicide articles appeared to be never ending. One woman took strychnine, another killed herself by swallowing an undetermined "poison," a deserter from the army took arsenic, and a French woman tried unsuccessfully to throw herself in the river.[28] A "respectable and intelligent appearing man" shot himself in the head at his lodgings at No. 9 Bayard Street, near Foster's hotel, and no one knew his name.[29] A Lieutenant Starkie who had served in a cavalry unit cut his throat in July 1863.[30] Adolf Davids, another soldier recently returned from the war, shot himself in the head in September at a hardware store, where he pretended to be interested in buying a gun.[31]

The editors of the newspapers tried to find an explanation for the increasing number of suicides in their city, without realizing that their editorials may have encouraged the awful trend. The New York papers discussed the details of suicides along with suicide notes on a daily basis in tabloid-like fashion, and the editor of the *Journal of Insanity* believed that such publicity encouraged people to kill themselves. "A single paragraph may suggest suicide to twenty persons," wrote the alarmed editor. "Those who inherit a propensity to suicide are vulnerable to imitation if a friend or relation commits suicide . . . . [T]he list of victims of this crime is greatly increased by the publicity which is given by the newspaper press throughout the country."[32]

If, as the editor of the *Journal of Insanity* believed, inheriting "a propensity to suicide" makes a man more vulnerable to imitating "a friend or relation" who commits suicide, it should be noted that the Fosters already had one suicide in the family. Joseph Tomlinson, Eliza

Foster's half-brother in Kentucky (whom she had visited with the seven-year-old Stephen), killed himself some years before Stephen's death, after learning that his favorite son had died from cholera. Tomlinson had just been selected president of Ohio University at Athens when he declined the appointment and fell into a state of severe depression. Interestingly, Stephen's niece Evelyn Morneweck said that the family would have covered up the story of his death "by his own hand," had they been able to do so. [33]

A suicide that would have been of special interest to Stephen was that of Edwin P. Christy, the minstrel who wanted to be known as the composer of "Old Folks at Home." On May 20, 1862, less than two years before Stephen's fatal "accident," Christy jumped out of a third story window at his house at 78 East Eighteen Street, "while laboring under temporary insanity," and died a day later. On his deathbed, Christy, in the moments he was able to speak coherently, willed his immense fortune to his mistress Mary Miller (or Maple), leaving nothing to his legitimate wife and son. Naturally his wife Harriet Harrington contested the will, as well as Christy's hasty marriage to Mary, with whom he was living at the time of his death. The story became more engaging and garish the next year. On October 16, 1863, Stephen would have read in the newspapers that Christy's body was exhumed and his cracked skull examined to determine if he could have been of sound mind when he made the will. In the end, the marriage to Mary was declared null and void by virtue of his previous marriage, but the legitimacy of the will bequeathing $100,000 to $150,000 was left "to be made in another proceeding." At the very least, Christy's suicide notice, wherein he was "reported to be very wealthy," and his subsequent exhuming would have made for intriguing, if unsettling, reading material. [34]

We may never learn the truth about the circumstances of Stephen Foster's death. The facts, however, suggested suicide to one writer who was not constrained by the need for hard evidence. When Peter Quinn included a characterization of Stephen Foster in his novel *Banished Children of Eve*, he made Foster's death a suicide.

> Winterbottom [the undertaker] rubbed his hands. "Mr. [Morrison] Foster," he said, "this is a most delicate matter."
> "You have handled it well," [Morrison] Foster said.

"The man who brought your brother to the hospital said he might go to the police. He said that, well, the gash in your brother's throat wasn't the accidental result of falling upon a piece of crockery. He said that it was deliberately self-inflicted; that your brother told him so; and that it was a civic duty to report such an act to the authorities."

"Where is the fellow now?"

"He has taken a trip to Rochester. His expenses were all paid, and he was given something additional. I saw to it."

"I'm deeply grateful." Morrison's words turned to puffs of steam. He shivered.[35]

Quinn's fictional story followed reality to a great degree. Stephen's body was taken to a New York undertaker named Winterbottom, and was probably already lying in an iron coffin when Morrison, Henry, and Jane arrived in the city.

Besides his brothers, there was another man involved in making the final arrangements for Stephen after his death, a businessman who would have had an interest, not only in absolving his own conscience, but also in keeping nasty rumors out of the news. According to Morrison Foster, "Under request of his family his [Stephen Foster's] body was immediately taken to an undertaker's, by direction of Col. William A. Pond, and placed in an iron coffin. On arrival of his brother, Henry Baldwin Foster and myself, his remains were taken by us to Pittsburgh, accompanied by his wife."[36] William A. Pond, the partner in the firm that years earlier had contracted with Foster to publish his songs, and who now ran his own publishing house, still had a large financial interest in the composer in terms of future sales of the songs to which his company still owned the rights. Death made Foster's songs more valuable and easier to sell and Pond took charge of the situation "immediately," seeing to it that Stephen's body was conveyed to the undertaker's and prepared for a proper burial. It is interesting that Pond, who published Foster's songs infrequently during the last two or three years of the composer's life, got involved at the very end to ensure that he had a respectable reputation in death.[37]

One of Foster's last songs was a melancholy poem of remorse, "Kiss Me Dear Mother Ere I Die." Published posthumously in 1869 by William A. Pond & Co., the poignant title was not unusual for a Civil War song expressing the last emotional contact between a mother and her dying son. But there is something unusual about this one. If the song were about a dying soldier boy, he would be proud even in death. But the protagonist of this song is guilty, and the song is confessional: "I have been wayward unto thee, Now I can feel it painfully, Patient and kind were thou to me, Kiss me mother ere I die."[38]

This is the voice of the pseudonymous Clinton Sanford, the name Eliza Foster used in her journal for George Sample, the eldest son of a prosperous lawyer from Pittsburgh, who disappointed his parents by loving alcohol too much. Eliza described the fate of the alcohol-addicted young man in her memoir, and Stephen would have read or heard the story. After the death of his parents, George turned to drink, but felt guilty about his useless life: "I should be at school or business and not loafing about the country from house to house," the despondent boy moaned. He complained that his father's estate supplied him with "as many clothes as I choose" but "deuce the bit of money will they give me." George even looked like Stephen, according to Eliza's description of Clinton Sanford: "His complexion was a youth about seventeen years old with a fine set of features and a splendid black eye. His jetty hair curled closely beneath his fine black beaver [hat] rounded in the crown." But even in his fine clothing, people from the better families would not "keep company" with him and "threw him off":

> Poor unfortunate Clinton Sanford, a father and mother in their graves, that made an idol of thee in thy infancy. A boy wert thou so beautiful and so wise that thy childhood's hours were counted ominous of high destiny, that thy star would conduct thee to the pinnacle of fame. Thus said the old nurse that watched thy growing charms and saw unfolding all the beauties of thy tender mind. But many a lovely boy as promising as thou wert, has been sacrificed like thee for want of resolution to withstand the tempter alcohol. Alas, a pauper's death and an unknown grave were the fate of Clinton Sanford.[39]

When Eliza wrote this, she may have been thinking about her son. Like the ill-fated George Sample, Foster drank too much and was plagued by guilt. Like many men of his generation, he believed he should become successful or "self-made," ever since Henry Clay used the term in 1832 to describe a man who could rightly claim responsibility for his own prosperity. In fact, democracy's freedom to reinvent oneself and become rich brought with it a strange new psychological affliction, the sense of being a "loser." When a man failed to achieve what he was taught by the new culture was the birthright of every American, he blamed himself, and society blamed him, too. But when he turned to drink, as Foster most assuredly did to console himself for his shortcomings, he became even more culpable.[40]

For some guilt-ridden individuals, the idea of suicide provided the possibility of forgiveness and a chance at rebirth, since what lives on, memories of the dead, are guiltless. Victims of suicide sometimes imagine their own death as a way of living on in other peoples' memories as a lost object, in the same way that Foster utilized memory to recreate dead loved ones in his mourning songs. In other words, the suicide attempts to convert himself into a lost object, which will live on in the memories of others. It has also been pointed out that an extreme tragedy, particularly in youth, or even a more recent loss such as a permanent separation, can encourage suicide if the person fantasizes that after death his memory will be transformed into a revered object. Even if the suicide has disappointed his loved ones during life, in death his memory can be born anew and cherished.[41]

Antebellum Americans paid court to the culture of achievement, but some men just gave up trying. One newspaper article urged: "Push along. Push hard. Push earnestly . . . you can't do without it . . . you must push. That is, if you would be something and somebody." But some sensitive men like Foster did not want to "push along" or to be "somebody." They wanted the world and all its ceaseless demands to leave them alone, and to disappear. They wanted an exit. Alcohol provided a temporary exit, until the next day arrived and brought with it the same problems and pain. Obviously, at least one man who lived at 15 Bowery Street wanted and found a permanent exit, a way to be left alone, and permission to reinvent himself in the guiltless image of spiritual remembrance.[42]

EPILOGUE

What Came Afterward

On March 11, 1865, a little over a year after Stephen Foster's death, the *New York Clipper* ran an announcement stating that "a new variety troupe is at present organizing in this city, under the direction of Tony Pastor and a well-known minstrel manager." Pastor and Sam Sharply, the minstrel manager, had taken over the building at 201 Bowery, formerly the Bowery Minstrel Hall and later Volk's Beer Garden, and facetiously renamed it Pastor's Opera House.[1] That first night, the curtain went up to reveal a banjo-playing comic, a songstress, a duo performing Irish songs and clog dances, and "a dapper and urbane" blackface entertainer.[2] In 1881, about fifteen years later, Pastor opened his famous Fourteenth Street Theater and presented shows that offered clean variety and operettas, and he became known as the "father of vaudeville." His latest protégé, Lillian Russell, sang with an operatically trained, soprano voice and transfixed the audience with her robust Gibson-girl figure, which had long since replaced the antebellum ideal of fragile womanhood. Pastor would forever be associated with vaudeville, although he said he preferred the term "variety" to the fancy, French-sounding name.

Minstrel houses converted to variety and vaudeville at a rapid pace in the decade following the war's end. In 1866, Wood's Minstrel Hall changed its name to Wood's Theater, "in quest of dignity," but five years later the minstrels were ousted altogether when the hall was renamed Theatre Comique and, according to one eyewitness, "the bill of fare was as varied and robust as that of most of the restaurants of the time." Statistics tell the story best. In 1865, New York City had twenty-one theaters, four of which featured variety and three of which were devoted to minstrel shows. By 1896, the metropolis boasted thirty-seven theaters, twelve of which were vaudeville houses. Three featured variety acts, and only one was a minstrel theater.[3]

Even with the writing on the wall, some old-time minstrel performers refused to accept the inevitable. They struggled to keep their shows going, enlarging their concerts to include extravagant acts and dozens of minstrels, if they could afford to do so. Strangely enough, the variety theaters kept minstrel acts in their shows, but now they parodied the actions and language of the newest immigrant groups. Some of the minstrels continued wearing blackface and African wigs while they sang on stage with German or Irish accents, which made for odd bedfellows.[4] One newspaper columnist described the show on Pastor's traveling circuit: "Mr. Pastor presents all the variety that can be desired—characters using the Irish, German, Yankee, and Negro dialect singing of various kinds and qualities and short drama acts that serve as the vehicle for character studies and imitation."[5] Ethnic comedy based on stereotypes of new immigrants reigned supreme on the variety and vaudeville stages from the 1870s to the end of the century, when nobody thought there was anything wrong with finding humor in other people's differences.[6]

No matter what changes they made to their acts, the old-time minstrels were losing out, not only to variety entertainers, but also to African Americans who, following emancipation, blackened their own faces and took to the stage as authentic minstrels. By the 1870s, white minstrels considered plantation skits the province of blacks, who were welcomed on the stage as long as they played the parts and sang the songs that whites expected of them. One example was the Haverly Colored Minstrels, a very large troupe that specialized in such skits as "The Darky as He Is at Home, Darky Life in the Cornfield, Canebrake, Barnyard, and on the Levee and Flatboat."[7] While white composers experimented with the new variety music, black composers like James Bland wrote songs in the old plantation style, including "Carry Me Back to Old Virginia," which was adopted as the state song of Virginia. The song's "theme of yearning and loss" was so much modeled on the antebellum tradition that many people were convinced Foster was the composer. Blacks did well as minstrels singing old-style plantation songs, but they also started and starred in their own musical comedy shows. Will Marion Cook, Bert Williams, George Walker, and Bob Cole are just a few of the talented African Americans who took to the musical stage.[8]

The lavish fairy extravaganza produced by Laura Keene and Thomas Baker reached its apogee the year after the Civil War ended, when Baker wrote and staged what became known as America's first musical. *The Black Crook* assembled in one phenomenal production all the dazzling entertainments that were competing for prominence after the decline of minstrelsy: comic songs, burlesque, ballet, acrobatics, surreal stage effects, and lovely-looking females. Laura Keene was no longer involved with the musical form she had done so much to popularize. On April 14, 1865, the actress played the starring role in *Our American Cousin* on the night an assassin's bullet brought down the curtain at Ford's Theater and ended the life of the nation's beloved president. As Lincoln lay dying on the floor of the theater, his head rested in Keene's lap in the folds of her dress. After the leading lady was questioned by authorities and released, she immediately embarked on a theatrical tour that took her from city to city across the North and the South. But audiences no longer listened to her voice or commented on the quality of her acting. Keene was forever associated with the assassination of the president and became an object of curiosity rather than an actress recognized for her talent and versatility. She kept the bloodstained dress she wore at Ford's Theater, displayed it on occasion to friends, and willed it to her daughter as part of her estate.

That Morrison Foster never mentioned Stephen might have met Laura Keene is not surprising. After the war, he moved to a town outside of Pittsburgh and never wanted to be reminded of his former association with Copperheads, or of anyone who had any connection to the martyred president. His friend Clement Vallandigham was out of his life, anyway. Six years after the war ended, the former congressman was defending a man in a murder case by trying to prove that the victim had accidently shot himself. In the process, he picked up a gun to demonstrate how the tragedy might have occurred and, forgetting that the gun was loaded, pulled the trigger on himself. Vallandigham proved his case by dying several days later.

Burlesque, a more risqué outgrowth of Keene's fairy spectacles, was probably the most exciting new entertainment to emerge full-blown after the Civil War. In 1868 Lydia Thompson's imported "British Blondes" opened in *Ixion* with women playing both male and female roles at Wood's new Thirteenth Street Theatre. Surprisingly, middle-class men and women attended the burlesque shows, since the girls' costumes were no more revealing than those worn by ballet dancers. Seating was in great demand, however, and *Ixion* was compelled to move to the larger Niblo's Garden, where *The Black Crook* had triumphed two years earlier. Eventually the press turned against burlesques, calling the shows indecent, yet the genre had clearly broken the gender barrier and opened the stage to a new type of female performer.[9]

George Cooper, the "left wing of the song factory," continued to write lyrics for different composers long after Foster's death. He lived well into the twentieth century and proved to be an interesting and prolific lyricist, experimenting throughout his life with new musical genres. Although he worked with some of the best-known, popular composers, he never managed to achieve the recognition he wanted for his songs, with the exception of "Sweet Genevieve," which ranked among the most popular and long-lasting of the postbellum "refined numbers." Cooper, who wrote the lyrics to the song when he was a grieving, young widower, sold the words outright to the composer Henry Tucker for five dollars, proving that he had learned little from the poor business choices of his old friend and mentor Stephen Foster. Cooper also collaborated with Hart Pease Danks, but their operetta never achieved the popularity of "Silver Threads among the Gold," which Danks composed with lyrics by another underpaid poet. Cooper maintained his connections with Foster's early publishers, including Ditson and Company, J. L. Peters, and S. T. Gordon & Son, who published many of the songs Cooper wrote in collaboration with other composers.[10] Cooper supplied the lyrics for musical extravaganzas, burlesques, parlor operas, operettas, and church hymns, but mostly he wrote dozens of comic songs for the vaudeville stage. One of his most renowned songs was the spoof on the former president of the Confederacy, "Jeff Davis in Petticoats," which was presented in a short play at Tony Pastor's Opera House and became very popular.[11]

Little more than a decade after Foster produced his hymn anthologies, the art of infusing religious music with elements from popular song—a job Horace Waters paid Foster to do—was developed more profitably and comprehensively when Ira Sankey published his anthology of *Gospel Hymns and Sacred Songs* in 1875. The collection contained beautiful songs that followed the format associated with popular music, including piano introductions, verses, and a chorus. Although Foster's contribution to religious music was minimal and has not been highly commended, his work as an example of hymns with trendy tunes that people loved to sing was on the cutting edge. One musicologist wrote that "Foster, ever aware of the public's taste, observed the growing evangelical movement taking place in the United States, and had just begun to provide its musical needs when he died."[12]

One of the most noticeable changes in popular music in the years following the Civil War was the transition to a decidedly Irish or British period. On August 29, 1881, the Irish duo of Edward Harrigan and Tony Hart left Pastor's and opened at the Theatre Comique, where their comedic musical shows sympathetically highlighted the foibles of the stereotypical Irishman in a succession of variety skits.[13] David Braham, the British composer-conductor at Tony Pastor's Opera House, joined the Harrigan and Hart team to help write the songs their mostly Irish audience enjoyed. Like the comic songs Foster and Cooper had written ten years earlier, Harrigan's music featured many lively eighth and sixteenth notes. In 1879, Gilbert and Sullivan's *HMS Pinafore*, a comic opera with many fast-paced, upbeat songs, opened to much acclaim at a theater in New York, demonstrating that the British music invasion began decades before anyone heard of the Beatles.[14]

Jane Foster's life continued to be very difficult after Stephen's death. For six years, she remained at her sister Agnes's home in Greensburg, Pennsylvania, where she worked long hours at the telegraph office because her responsibilities were not limited to the care of herself and her daughter. Soon after Stephen's death, Jane's mother was swindled out of her money by her lawyers and she moved in with her two daughters in Greensburg.[15] When Agnes's doctor husband was killed at a train crossing, the dependable Jane helped with the care and support of her sister and her five nieces and nephews, in addition to Marion and her mother. Stephen may have transformed his wife into a frail vapor woman in his songs, but his vision was far from the reality. Around

1870, Jane Foster moved back to Pittsburgh, where she met and married a nice, steady man named Matthew D. Wiley. She continued to work at the telegraph office, this time in the Allegheny depot, even after she remarried.[16]

When Jane retired she supplemented her income with "more than four thousand dollars" from the royalties on the songs Stephen had sold out in 1857. Over the years, the copyrights had changed hands as publishing companies died out and transferred ownership of their music. "Old Folks at Home," copyright in 1851, came up for renewal in 1879 and Oliver Ditson, successors of Firth, Son, and Company, offered Jane a royalty of three cents per copy for the fourteen-year renewal period. Morrison Foster handled all the arrangements with the publishers and thus did right by his brother's widow.[17] The song continued to be popular for decades and had unexpected consequences when it made a narrow river in Florida famous and helped launch the tourist industry in the state.

Jane needed the windfall from Stephen's songs because her responsibilities did not end when her daughter Marion grew up and married Walter Welsh. Marion gave birth to a daughter named Jessie, who became the Jessie Welsh Rose who reported her "Grandmother's Memories" to a newspaper reporter. For some unknown reason, Marion left little Jessie to be raised by her mother Jane when she moved to St. Louis with her husband. Just why Marion, who taught music, left her daughter behind is not known, but she must have followed more closely after her father than her mother when it came to family obligations. Marion lived to the ripe age of eighty-four and died in the house on Penn Avenue that had been the "White Cottage," but she never came back for her daughter. "My grandmother [Jane] raised me you know, after she had married again Mr. Matthew Wiley," Jessie explained. "I always remained with them, was married in their home, and they lived with me until they died." At Wiley's death, he left everything "which a man of small means could bestow" to Jessie. In spite of some early characterizations of Jane Foster as spoiled and temperamental, Jessie wrote lovingly of her grandmother and Matthew Wiley: "No girl ever had more loving parents than Grandma and Grandpa Wiley were to me."[18]

Jane's own death was tragic and horrific. In January 1903, when she was seventy-three years of age, her long skirt caught fire over the coal grate in Jessie's house, where she was living, and she died within a few hours from the burns. Thus ended the life of the real "Jeanie with the light brown hair, borne like a vapor on the summer's air."[19]

Thirty-nine years earlier, in the cold January of 1864, Stephen Foster's body was carried from New York to Pittsburgh courtesy of the Pennsylvania Railroad. Somehow his remains arrived intact, even though the train suffered a serious wreck. The Fosters had missed that train and taken another, so they arrived at the funeral unshaken by the ordeal. Stephen's old teacher Henry Kleber sang a burial hymn with much feeling at the grave and a band played "Old Folks at Home" and "Come Where My Love Lies Dreaming" after the casket was lowered into the ground. Stephen Foster was laid to rest between his beloved mother Eliza and his father William at the Allegheny Cemetery in Lawrenceville. Newspapers around the country carried notices of his death and published details about the funeral picked up from the Pittsburgh papers, which only emphasized the fact that the man whose music was beloved the world over had been abandoned in the last years of his life. He became more popular than ever after he died, however, when publishers turned out about twenty songs and falsely advertised each one as the "last song composed by Stephen C. Foster."[20]

A year after his death, friends and acquaintances began Foster's canonization by collecting letters and memorabilia and writing articles based on reminiscences of their "last days" with the immortal composer. As the years passed, the truth about the man became harder and harder to decipher, in part because the family wanted it that way. After hundreds of family letters were consigned to the flame, Morrison Foster was left with nearly a blank slate on which to reconstruct Stephen's life story in the image he wanted in *My Brother Stephen*.[21] Morrison's biography reached the public in 1896, the same year the Supreme Court decision *Plessy v. Ferguson* and the song "All Coons Look Alike to Me" reinforced the degradation of black citizenship in America.[22] After the war, Northerners and Southerners put aside the bloody shirt and reunited on race, hoping to quell the class conflict that was breaking out in industrial cities. In Pittsburgh, only four years earlier, Henry Clay Frick suppressed a strike at Andrew Carnegie's Homestead Mill, leaving mangled and dead bodies that recalled a Civil War battlefield. With blackface entertainers no longer using the minstrel stage to work out social tension, antagonisms between the classes were being played out in the streets.

At the end of the century, while the New South struggled to be born, the Old South quietly took on a life of its own in myth and legend. The antebellum world and the "Lost Cause" were immortalized in novels and poetry, and statues of fallen Confederate heroes were erected in town centers throughout the South. Foster's plantation songs were then resurrected and reinterpreted to equate pining for "days gone by" with a desire to return to a reincarnated antebellum South. Myths that associated Foster with the South gradually spun out of control, like the threads of a spider's web encircling and encroaching on the truth beneath. Americans almost forgot that Foster was a Northerner (or a Midwesterner) whose fleeting image of the South was captured aboard a moving riverboat. They also forgot, or never knew, that minstrelsy was an entertainment created to bring joy to the lives of Northern working-class men struggling with the inequities of an industrializing world, or that Foster was a Union man who wrote and dedicated songs to Abraham Lincoln.

Ideas about Foster's Southern connections became even more entrenched when the movie industry reinforced the myth in the first half of the twentieth century by incorporating Foster's music into films about the Old South. This misrepresentation reached its apogee when his plantation songs were used in *Gone with the Wind* to authenticate Southern belles, obsequious "darkies," and spectacular columned plantations. Even the hilarious 1947 *Secret Life of Walter Mitty* with Danny Kaye interjected Foster's plantation songs when the comedian daydreamed he was a gentleman of the Old South.

Minstrelsy took a long time to die out completely, mainly because minstrel shows acted as sentinels to watch and keep guard over the image of African Americans in a dominant white society. By ensuring that they looked like buffoons or worse, sometimes not-quite-human creatures dressed in rags, minstrelsy demonstrated to the public that blacks belonged at the bottom of the heap. The myth was perpetuated to ensure control of a minority population, although the image on the minstrel stage fluctuated over time as to the degree of degradation. The minstrel mask changed, too, as the society felt more threatened and became increasingly racist. The mask became darker, heavier with grease paint, and more degrading until in the 1920s and 1930s the minstrel emerged as a grotesque clown in blackface. He wore fat white gloves and, in the 1950s, the popular cartoon character Mickey Mouse danced on television sets as a minstrel reborn.

By the time the civil rights movement progressed in the 1960s, many Americans felt ashamed or indignant when confronted with Foster's plantation songs. After their initial embarrassment over blackface, scholars threw themselves into intense research trying to make sense of the peculiar entertainment of their ancestors. Minstrelsy emerged as a highly complex entertainment, but scholars managed to explain the embarrassing genre in such a way that, without denying its negative aspects, they were able to find positive developments that emerged from the scab on the nation's musical past. Most of the historians were able to agree that minstrelsy, however we view it today, provided the groundwork for the popular music forms that mixed white and black elements and dominated America's music scene in the twentieth and twenty-first centuries—forms like jazz, rap, rock, and hip hop—which was a good thing.

Still, songs that used slave dialect and racist language were problems that had to be addressed. "My Old Kentucky Home," Kentucky's state song since 1928, continues to be sung at state functions, the Kentucky Derby, and at football and basketball games at state colleges, but the offensive lyrics were altered in 1986, with "darkies" changed to "people." The problem was not so easily rectified in Florida, where "Old Folks at Home" has been the state song since 1935. When Governor Charlie Crist would not let it be sung at his 2007 inauguration, a contest for a new state song resulted in a winning entry by schoolteacher Jan Hinton, "Florida, Where the Saw Grass Meets the Sky." Floridians would not let go of "Swanee River," however, and the state ended up with two songs in 2008. Hinton's "Florida" became the state anthem and "Old Folks" remained the state song with its words officially altered: "longing for the old plantation" became "longing for my childhood station" and "Oh! darkeys" became "O dear ones."

Foster's songs served different functions and became many things to many people. Whatever men and women were looking to find—home, security, happiness, consolation, patriotic fervor, love, or laughter—his songs echoed and filled those yearnings, giving them what they needed to bravely face the trials of their changing world. In doing so, he established the modus operandi for popular songwriters everywhere and became America's first professional songwriter, even though his motivations were sometimes misunderstood. In the early part of the twentieth century, for example, when Americans desired a national folk music, he was designated "America's Folk-Song Composer" and his popular songs were conflated with folk music.[23] Foster, however, wrote for pay, when he could get it, and as such was a commercial composer in the traditional sense of the word—a man who dared to earn his living writing America's songs. Commenting some years after Foster's death, an admirer contributed the following thoughts: "May the time be far in the future ere lips will fail to move to its music, or hearts to respond to its influence, and may we who owe him so much, preserve gratefully the memory of the master, Stephen Collins Foster." May the time be far in the future, indeed![24]

NOTES

INTRODUCTION

1. George W. Birdseye, "Reminiscence of the Last Days of Stephen C. Foster," *Western Musical World*, January 1867, quoted in John Tasker Howard, *Stephen Foster: America's Troubadour* (1934; repr., New York: Tudor Publishing, 1943), p. 314.

2. Frederick Douglass, "The Anti-Slavery Movement, lecture delivered before the Rochester Ladies' Anti-Slavery Society, March 19, 1855," In *Frederick Douglass: Selected Speeches and Writings*, ed. Philip S. Foner, adapted, by Yuval Taylor (Chicago: Lawrence Hill Books, 1999), pp. 329.

3. Frederick Douglass, "The Anti-Slavery Movement, p. 329.

4. Deane L. Root, "The 'Mythtory' of Stephen C. Foster or Why His True Story Remains Untold," *The American Music Research Center Journal*, Vol. 1, 1991, pp. 20–36.

1. PIONEER ELITES

1. Morrison Foster, *My Brother Stephen* (Indianapolis: privately printed, 1932); "America's Greatest Song Writer," *East End Bulletin*, May 7, 1887.

2. Morrison Foster, *My Brother Stephen*.

3. Pittsburghers were very serious about their rights to make and sell whiskey. When a heavy excise tax was placed on their potable produce, five thousand angry men, ready to overrun the town in defense of their right to make and sell intoxicating spirits, assembled a few miles outside of Pittsburgh. In the

aptly named Whiskey Rebellion, they backed down only when they learned that George Washington himself would be leading troops against them.

4. The two political geniuses, Jefferson and Adams, were friends when they devoted their young lives to the creation of a new government conceived in liberty. In their middle years, political differences tore them apart, but in old age they reignited their friendship by focusing on their love child, America.

5. Morrison Foster, *My Brother Stephen*, p. 22.

6. Foster Family Letters, Susan Clayland to Charlotte Foster, August 16, 1826, C423.

7. Eliza Clayland Foster, "Sketches and Incidents of Pittsburgh," Manuscript transcribed by Joanne O'Connell, p. 2, Center for American Music, University of Pittsburgh, Pittsburgh, PA.

8. The neighboring plantation was owned by Colonel Edward Lloyd who "kept from three to four hundred slaves on his home plantation, and owned a large number more on the neighboring farms belonging to him." Frederick Douglass, *Narrative of the Life of Frederick Douglass, an American Slave* (Boston: Anti-Slavery Office, 1845), chapter 2. For information on the Foster family, see Evelyn Foster Morneweck, *The Chronicles of Stephen Foster's Family*, Vol. 1 (Pittsburgh: University of Pittsburgh Press, 1944), p. 4.

9. Morrison Foster, *My Brother Stephen*, pp. 10–12; Eugene A. Ferguson and Oliver Evans, *Inventive Genius of the American Industrial Revolution* (Greenville, DE: Hagley Museum, 1980), pp. 10, 35–41.

10. Evelyn Foster Morneweck, *Chronicles*, p. 5.

11. Morrison Foster, *My Brother Stephen*, pp. 10–12.

12. For information about the pugnacity of the Scots-Irish, see James Webb, *Born Fighting* (New York: Broadway Books, 2005).

13. Billy Kennedy, *The Scots-Irish in Pennsylvania & Kentucky* (Belfast, Northern Ireland: Ambassador Publications, 1998); George T. Fleming, *History of Pittsburgh and Environs* (New York: The American Historical Society, Inc., 1922), p. 471.

14. Morrison Foster, *My Brother Stephen*, pp. 10–12.

15. Morrison Foster, *My Brother Stephen*, p. 10.

16. Morrison Foster, *My Brother Stephen*, pp. 9–11.

17. Susannah Rowson, *The History of Charlotte Temple: A Tale of Youth*. The book was originally printed in 1794 in Philadelphia, but was reprinted in 1801, 1803, 1805, 1808, and 1811 by publishers in Hudson, New York, and New Haven and Hartford, Connecticut, giving Eliza Foster ample opportunity to have secured a copy.

18. Morrison Foster, *My Brother Stephen*, p. 14.

19. Charles W. Dahlinger, *Pittsburgh: A Sketch of Its Early Social Life* (New York: G. P. Putnam's Sons, 1916), p. 31.

20. Foster biographer Ken Emerson speculated in *Doo-Dah!* that young William was actually the illegitimate son of William Barclay Foster. Ken Emerson, *Doo-Dah! Stephen Foster and the Rise of American Popular Culture* (New York: Simon & Schuster, 1997), p. 21.

21. Locks of hair of the Foster children are preserved in tissue at the Stephen Foster Memorial. Brother William's hair was the same strawberry blonde coloring as Charlotte's, but William's hair showed specks of grey.

22. Biographical notes on Captain Lawrence.

23. George T. Fleming, *History of Pittsburgh and Environs*, p. 526.

24. Letter from Ann Eliza Foster Buchanan to Morrison Foster, March 5, 1872. Decades later, during the Civil War, the arsenal supplied the United States with a good portion of the cannons, guns, and munitions used by the Union Army.

25. John E. Semmes, *John H. B. Latrobe and His Times, 1803–1891* (Baltimore: Norman, Remington, 1917), p. 25.

26. Morrison Foster, *My Brother Stephen*, p. 19.

27. Foster Family Letters, Charlotte Foster in Emmitsburg, MD, to Eliza Foster, November 21, 1821.

28. Eliza Clayland Foster, "Sketches and Incidents of Pittsburgh," pp. 21, 25.

29. Morgan Neville, the son of Presley Neville and Nancy Morgan, wrote what is today considered a folktale of the Midwest, *Mike Fink, Last of the Boatmen*, published in 1829.

30. Eliza Clayland Foster, "Sketches and Incidents of Pittsburgh," p. 30.

31. Annie Clark Miller, *Chronicles of Families, Houses, and Estates of Pittsburgh and Its Environs* (Pittsburgh: n.p., 1927), p. 30.

32. Eliza Clayland Foster, "Sketches and Incidents of Pittsburgh." This idea comes from conversations recorded in Eliza's journal. She noted especially a difference between the hardworking women of her own generation and that of her daughter's more leisurely generation.

33. Scott C. Martin, *Killing Time: Leisure and Culture in Southwestern Pennsylvania, 1800–1850* (Pittsburgh: University of Pittsburgh Press, 1995), pp. 103–108.

34. Scott C. Martin, *Killing Time*, pp. 103–108, quoting from *Pittsburgh in the Year 1826* by Samuel Jones.

35. Evelyn Foster Morneweck, *Chronicles*, p. 3.

36. Eliza Clayland Foster, "Sketches and Incidents of Pittsburgh."

37. Eliza Clayland Foster, "Sketches and Incidents of Pittsburgh," pp. 33–35. Mary Ann Fulton (1789–1852) married Neville B. Craig of Pittsburgh and had ten children.

38. Eliza Clayland Foster, "Sketches and Incidents of Pittsburgh," pp. 33–35.

39. *Pittsburgh Gazette,* July 5, 1818.

40. Eliza Foster, "Sketches and Incidents of Pittsburgh," pp. 46–50.

41. Eliza Foster, "Sketches and Incidents of Pittsburgh," pp. 55–65.

42. Eliza Foster, "Sketches and Incidents of Pittsburgh," pp. 53–54.

43. Evelyn Morneweck, *Chronicles,* p. 29.

44. Edward G. Baynham, *A History of Pittsburgh Music 1758–1958,* pp. 14–17.

45. Leonard Feeney, *Mother Seton: Saint Elizabeth of New York (1774–1821)* (Cambridge, MA: Ravengate Press, 1975).

46. Foster Family Letters, Charlotte Foster from Emmetsburg, MD, to Eliza Foster, November 11, 1821. Maryland had been established as a colony where Catholics could practice their religion and have all the civil and political rights of non-Catholics, so it is not surprising that Elizabeth Seton's Catholic school for girls was successful.

47. Norma R. Fryatt, *Sarah Josepha Hale: The Life and Times of a Nineteenth Century Career Woman* (New York: Hawthorne Books, 1973), p. 24.

48. Article from *Gale's National Intelligencer,* 1830. William Foster Sr., "Scrapbook," Center for American Music, University of Pittsburgh.

49. Evelyn Morneweck, *Chronicles,* p. 42.

50. Eliza Clayland Foster, "Sketches and Incidents of Pittsburgh," p. 56.

51. Foster Family Letters, William B. Foster to Charlotte Foster in Meadville, PA, August 3, 1825.

52. Evelyn Morneweck, *Chronicles,* p. 103.

53. Letter from Ann Eliza Foster to Charlotte Foster in Meadville, PA, July 25, 1825. For information about Tom Hunter living with the Fosters, see John Tasker Howard's *Stephen Foster: America's Troubadour,* p. 53.

2. FORECLOSURE AND THE DEATH OF CHARLOTTE

1. The dates I have used were supplied by Evelyn Morneweck, Stephen Foster's niece. John Tasker Howard speculated that Stephen Foster lived in the house "for six years after his birth, for it is said that William Foster disposed of the house and some of the land in 1832." But that could mean someone purchased the property that year. Morneweck believed the Fosters had moved out by the time Stephen was three in 1829. John Tasker Howard, *Stephen Foster: America's Troubadour,* p. 70; Evelyn Morneweck, *Chronicles,* pp. 37–38.

2. Evelyn Morneweck, *Chronicles,* p. 6.

3. The amount of money William put up is not known exactly, but one source in 1897 estimated it to be about $90,000, a number that seems too high. *Pennsylvania Railroad Men's News,* August 1897, Vol. 9, No. 8, p. 259.

4. Morrison Foster, *My Brother Stephen,* p. 17.

5. Morrison Foster, *My Brother Stephen,* pp. 17, 18.

6. Morrison Foster, *My Brother Stephen,* p. 18.

7. Edith S. McCall, *Conquering the Rivers: Henry Miller Shreve and the Navigation of America's Inland Waterways* (Baton Rouge: Louisiana State University Press, 1984), pp. 87–97. Captain Shreve not only captained the *Enterprise,* he also designed and built it, using a high-pressured steam engine that was manufactured in Pittsburgh by George Evans, the son of Eliza Foster's famous uncle. The *Enterprise* was the first steamboat to travel downriver from Pittsburgh to New Orleans and, on steam power, to successfully make the upstream trip all the way back to Pittsburgh.

8. Florence L. Dorsey, *Master of the Mississippi: Henry Shreve and the Conquest of the Mississippi* (Boston: Houghton Mifflin, 1941), pp. 87–91.

9. Evelyn Morneweck, *Chronicles,* pp. 8, 121.

10. John Steele Gordon, *An Empire of Wealth* (New York: Harpers Collins, 2004), pp. 132–139.

11. Richard C. Wade, *The Urban Frontier: The Rise of Western Cities, 1790–1930* (Urbana: The University of Illinois Press, 1996), pp. 165– 166.

12. Richard C. Wade, *Urban Frontier,* pp. 66–168.

13. Richard C. Wade, *Urban Frontier,* pp. 175–187.

14. Foster Family Letters, Eliza Foster to brother William, May 14, 1832.

15. Eliza Clayland Foster, "Sketches and Incidents of Pittsburgh," pp. 118–119.

16. Foster Family Letters, Charlotte Foster to Eliza Foster, May 19, 1828, C415.

17. Foster Family Letters, Charlotte Foster to Eliza Foster, May 21, 1828, C414.

18. Foster Family Letters, Charlotte Foster to Eliza Foster, May 29, 1828, C412.

19. Foster Family Letters, Charlotte Foster to Eliza Foster May 29, 1828, C412.

20. Foster Family Letters, Charlotte Foster to Eliza Foster, June 21, 1828, C407.

21. Foster Family Letters, Charlotte Foster to William Foster Sr., June 26, 1828, C406.

22. Foster Family Letters, Charlotte Foster to William Foster Sr., July 3, 1828, C405.

23. Foster Family Letters, Charlotte Foster to William Foster Sr., July 3, 1828, C405.

24. Foster Family Letters, Charlotte Foster to Eliza Foster, August 12, 1828, C402.

25. Foster Family Letters, Charlotte Foster to Eliza Foster, August 12, 1828, C402.

26. Foster Family Letters, Charlotte Foster to brother William Foster, August 13, 1828, C401.

27. Foster Family Letters, Charlotte Foster to brother William Foster, August 13, 1828, C401.

28. Foster Family Letters, Charlotte Foster to brother William Foster, August 13, 1828, C401.

29. Foster Family Letters, William Foster Sr. to Charlotte Foster, September 7, 1828, C400.

30. Matthew Parker, *Panama Fever* (New York: Doubleday, 2007).

31. Foster Family Letters, Charlotte Foster to William Foster Sr., September 26, 1828, C399.

32. Randall Capps, *The Rowan Story: From Federal Hill to My Old Kentucky Home* (Bowling Green, KY: Homestead Press), 1976.

33. Foster Family Letters, Charlotte Foster to William Foster Sr., September 26, 1828, C399.

34. Foster Family Letters, Eliza Foster Charlotte Foster, October 4, 1828, C395.

35. Foster Family Letters, Charlotte Foster to Eliza Foster, October 18, 1828, C396.

36. Foster Family Letters Charlotte Foster to William Foster Sr., June 22, 1829, C442. According the information given by Randall Capps in his biography of the Rowans, the young John Rowan was no prize husband. He married a petite Southern belle seven years after Charlotte died, and fathered ten children. But he had difficulty sticking to any line of work, dueled, and drank. He died when he accidentally fell from the second story window of Federal Hill, apparently not sober enough to realize he was sitting on the window ledge. Capps, *The Rowan Story*, p. 19.

37. Foster Family Letters, Charlotte Foster to Eliza Foster, October 27, 1828, C395.

38. Foster Family Letters, Charlotte Foster to Eliza Foster, August 12, 1828, C402.

39. Foster Family Letters, Charlotte Foster to Eliza Foster, October 27, 1828, C395.

40. Foster Family Letters, Charlotte Foster to Eliza Foster, June 1, 1829.

41. Foster Family Letters, Charlotte Foster to Eliza Foster, June 1, 1829.

42. Foster Family Letters, Charlotte Foster to William Foster, June 1, 1829.

43. Foster Family Letters, William Foster Sr. to Charlotte and Ann Eliza Foster, June 2, 1829.

44. Foster Family Letters, William Foster Sr. to Charlotte Foster, June 11, 1829.

45. Foster Family Letters, William Foster Sr. to Charlotte Foster, June 11, 1829.

46. The child Stephen's quote, "Sister Charlotte down the ribber 'tuck in the mud!" appears in a letter written by Charlotte Foster to Ann Eliza Foster in the summer of 1829. Note attached in Foster Family Letters from Charlotte Foster to William Foster Sr., June 22, 1829, says the above letter is "in the collection of Maskell Ewing Jr. of Philadelphia, grandson of Ann Eliza," C442.

47. Georgiana survived and grew up to be a piano girl like Charlotte. Many years later brother William heard the teenaged Georgiana play the piano.

48. Foster Family Letters, Charlotte Foster to Eliza Foster, August 12, 1829, C440.

49. Foster Family Letters, brother William Foster to Charlotte Foster, August 23, 1829, C445.

50. Foster Family Letters, brother William Foster to Charlotte Foster, August 23, 1829, C445.

51. Foster Family Letters, William Foster Sr. to Charlotte Foster, September 2, 1829, C446.

52. Foster Family Letters, Charlotte Foster to brother William Foster, September 4, 1829, C447.

53. Foster Family Letters, Charlotte Foster to brother William Foster, September 4, 1829, C447.

54. Foster Family Letters, G. W. Barclay to William Foster Sr., October 13, 1829.

55. Foster Family Letters, William Foster Sr. to William Foster Jr., October 22, 1829, C450.

56. The idea of the "piano girl" comes from James Huneker, the nineteenth-century music critic who discusses them in his book *Overtones* (New York: Charles Scribner's Sons, 1904).

57. Foster Family Letters, Atkinson Hill Rowan to Ann Eliza Foster, November 11, 1829, C451.

58. Philippe Ariès, *The Hour of Our Death* (New York: Oxford University Press, 1991), pp. 430–470.

59. Lewis O. Saum, "Death in the Popular Mind of Pre–Civil War America," in *Death in America*, ed. David E. Stannard (Philadelphia: University of Pennsylvania Press, 1975), pp. 42–45.

60. Foster Family Letters, Atkinson Hill Rowan to Ann Eliza Foster, November 19, 1829. Atkinson Hill's ill-starred suit of Charlotte had all the elements of a tragic opera. In April 1830, about six months after Charlotte's death, Senator Rowan sent his heartbroken son to Spain to serve as an emissary for President Jackson and most likely to get over his grief for Charlotte. Shortly after he returned home to Federal Hill, a cholera epidemic swept through Bardstown, taking the lives of eight of the Rowans on July 27, 1833. Atkinson Hill was among the dead who were carried out of the front parlor to be buried on the grounds of the Federal Hill plantation. The Rowan son who wrote the tearstained letter to Ann Eliza describing the last hours in the life of the lovely Charlotte was only thirty when he died and had never married.

61. Foster Family Letters, Eliza Foster to brother William Foster, May 14, 1832.

3. ALL UP AND DOWN THE WHOLE CREATION

1. Foster Family Letters, William Foster Sr. to William Foster Jr., August 7, 1832, C610.

2. For the history of Harmony, Pennsylvania, see Pennsylvania Room, Carnegie Library, Oakland, PA. Family references are from Evelyn Morneweck, *Chronicles of Stephen Foster's Family*, pp. 77–79.

3. Foster Family Letters, Ann Eliza Foster to William Foster Sr., June 16, 1832.

4. Foster Family Letters, William Foster Sr. to William Foster Jr., April 10, 1833.

5. Foster Family Letters, William Foster Sr. to William Foster Jr., June 14, 1832, C593.

6. Foster Family Letters, Charlotte Foster to brother William Foster, August 13, 1828, C401.

7. William James McKnight, *A Pioneer Outline History of Northwestern Pennsylvania*, pp. 659–660, http://books.google.com/books.

8. Evelyn Morneweck, *Chronicles*, pp. 86–87.

9. Exactly how the Buchanans knew the Fosters is not known, but they were acquainted when Ann Eliza went to stay with Jane Buchanan in Meadville. The Buchanans lived in Allegheny before the Fosters moved there and they also knew the family of Jane McDowell, wife of Stephen Foster.

10. Evelyn Morneweck, *Chronicles*, pp. 50, 78.

11. Foster Family Letters, William Foster Sr. to William Foster Jr. Pittsburgh, April 10, 1833, C639.

12. Foster Family Letters, William Foster Sr. to William Foster Jr., June 1, 1833, C619.

13. Raymond Walters, *Stephen Foster, Youth's Golden Gleam: A Sketch of His Life and Background in Cincinnati, 1846–1850* (Princeton, NJ: Princeton University Press, 1936), pp. 5–7.

14. Foster Family Letters, Ann Eliza Buchanan to Morrison Foster, October 17, 1883, C455.

15. That cholera was in Pittsburgh in 1833 was stated in William Tasker Howard's biography, *Stephen Foster: America's Troubadour* and in George T. Fleming's *History of Pittsburgh and Its Environs*.

16. William Rouse Jullian, *In Memory of Stephen Collins Foster, 1826–1864* (Frankfort, KY: Kentucky State Historical Society, State Journal Co., 1949). Jullian supports the idea that Stephen Foster visited Federal Hill with his mother in 1833.

17. Morrison Foster, *My Brother Stephen*, p. 31.

18. Foster Family Letters, William Foster Sr. to William Foster Jr., May 18, 1834, C626.

19. Foster Family Letters, William Foster Sr. to William Foster Jr., August 3, 1834.

20. Foster Family Letters, William Foster Sr. to William Foster Jr., June 12, 1834, C627.

21. Foster Family Letters, William Foster Sr. to William Foster Jr. August 3, 1834, C629.

22. Foster Family Letters, William Foster Sr. to William Foster Jr., Dec. 7, 1834, C631.

23. Foster Family Letters, William Foster Sr. to William Foster Jr. December 3, 1834.

24. Evelyn Morneweck, *Chronicles of Stephen Foster's Family*, pp. 103, 112.

25. Edward Le Roy Rice, *Monarchs of Minstrelsy, from Daddy Rice to Date* (New York: Kenny Publishing, 1911), pp. 1–100; Richard D. Wetzel, *"Oh! Sing No More That Gentle Song": The Musical Life and Times of William Cuming Peters (1805–66)* (Warren, MI: Harmonie Park Press, 2000), p. 82.

26. Morrison Foster, *My Brother Stephen*, p. 25.

27. Robert C. Toll, *Blacking Up: The Minstrel Show in Nineteenth-Century America* (New York: Oxford University Press, 1974), pp. 30–31.

28. Thomas Dartmouth Rice, "Jump Jim Crow," quoted in Edward Le Roy Rice, *Monarchs of Minstrelsy*, p. 27.

29. Edward Le Roy Rice, *Monarchs of Minstrelsy*.

30. Edward Le Roy Rice, *Monarchs of Minstrelsy*.

31. Edward Le Roy Rice, *Monarchs of Minstrelsy*, pp. 1–100.

32. Robert C. Toll, *Blacking Up*, pp. 30–31.

33. Carl Wittke, *Tambo and Bones* (New York: Greenwood Press, 1968), p. 20.

34. Minstrel performers George Washington Dixon and Bob Farrell sang the famous "Zip Coon" song to the folk tune of "Turkey in the Straw."

35. Newspaper accounts from the early 1830s show that Thomas Dartmouth Rice took "Jim Crow" to many small towns along the rivers before he brought him to the big name cities.

36. Charles Hamm, *Music in America*, pp. 183–184; Maud Karpeles, in the introduction to Cecil Sharp's *English Folk Songs from the Southern Appalachians*, Vol. 1, p. xviii, in Charles Hamm, *Music in America*, p. 75; Robert C. Toll, "From Folktype to Stereotype: Images of Slaves in Antebellum Minstrelsy," *Journal of the Folklore Institute*, Vol. 8, No. 1, June 1971, pp. 38–47, http://www.jstor.org/stable/3814062); Frances Trollope, *Domestic Manners of the Americans* (New York: Dodd, Mead, 1927), p. 126–127.

37. Charles Hamm, *Music in America*.

38. Letter from Stephen Collins Foster in Youngstown, Ohio, to his father William B. Foster, dated January 14, 1837, in Calvin Elliker, *Stephen Collins Foster: A Guide to Research* (New York: Garland Publishing, 1988), correspondence #189.

4. SCHOOLDAYS IN BROTHER WILLIAM'S SUNSHINE

1. Foster Family Letters, William Foster Sr. to Eliza Foster, March 2, 1836, C638.

2. Foster Family Letters, Henrietta Foster and Mary Wick to William Foster Jr., June 9, 1836, C636.

3. Foster Family Letters, Lemuel Wick to William Foster Jr., January 9, 1838, C656.

4. Foster Family Letters, William B. Foster to William Foster Jr., June 8, 1837.

5. Foster Family Letters, Eliza C. Foster to William B. Foster Jr., June 16, 1837.

6. Foster Family Letters, Henry Foster to William Foster Jr., April 21, 1838.

7. Foster Family Letters, William B. Foster to William Foster Jr., March 16, 1835, C633. Evelyn Morneweck said one of the churches was St. John's Pequea Episcopal in Compass, Pennsylvania, which dated back to the 1700s. *Chronicles*, p. 113.

8. The birth dates and birth orders for Ann Eliza's children Charlotte and James Buchanan are from Edward Young Buchanan-Geneaology.com; The Kenneth Fabrizio Family Home Page: Information about Edward Young Buchanan, Familytreemaker.genealogy.com, http://www.genealogy.com/ftm/f/a/b/Ken-Fabrizio-Ventural/WEBsite-0001/UHP-1209.html.

9. George T. Fleming, *History of Pittsburgh and Environs*, Vol. 2, p. 526.

10. Foster Family Letters, Eliza Foster to William Foster Jr., May 28, 1836, C608.

11. Foster Family Letters, Henrietta Foster Wick to William Foster Jr., September 7, 1837.

12. Evelyn Morneweck, *Chronicles*, pp. 160–161.

13. Foster Family Letters, Eliza C. Foster to William Foster Jr., June 16, 1837, C646.

14. William Bender Wilson, *Pennsylvania Railroad Men's News*, August 1897, published by the Pennsylvania Railroad.

15. Foster Family Letters, William B. Foster Jr. to Eliza Foster, April 21, 1838, C659.

16. Foster Family Letters, William B. Foster Jr. to Eliza Foster, May 14, 1837, C642.

17. Morrison Foster, *My Brother Stephen*, p. 27; and William Bender Wilson, *Pennsylvania Railroad Men's News*, p. 260.

18. Foster Family Letters, William B. Foster to William B. Foster Jr., April 10, 1833, C639.

19. Foster Family Letters, William B. Foster to William B. Foster Jr., December 15, 1833, C623.

20. Foster Family Letters, William B. Foster to William B. Foster Jr., December 7, 1834, C631 and January 5, 1835, C632.

21. Foster Family Letters, June 20, 1838, C663.

22. Foster Family Letters, January 12, 1840, C665.

23. Foster Family Letters, August 18, 1838, C667. Brother William had already loaned his brother-in-law Thomas Wick $1,000 to stock his general store and the moneys were yet to be repaid when he died a few years later.

24. Foster Family Letters, William B. Foster to William B. Foster Jr., June 8, 1837, C646.

25. Foster Family Letters, William B. Foster to William B. Foster Jr., June 8, 1837, C646.

26. Evelyn Morneweck, *Chronicles*, p. 168. So desperate was William to see his son Morrison established in business that he originally offered his services on the terms of a bound indenture, but Evans refused, reasoning, "If he does not wish to stay and be useful without an indenture, he is not worth having." (p. 168).

27. Foster Family Letter, July 26, 1839, C682.

28. Letter from William Foster Sr. to William Foster Jr., October 23, 1839.

29. Foster Family Letter, October 23, 1841, C600.

30. Foster Family Letters, Henry Foster to Eliza Foster, March 10, 1836; letter from William Foster Sr. and Henry Foster to William Foster Jr., May 13, 1838.

31. Foster Family Letters, William Foster Sr. to William Foster Jr., December 1, 1840.

32. Foster Family Letters, Henrietta Foster to William Foster Jr., April 30, 1836.

33. Evelyn Morneweck, *Chronicles*, p. 110.

34. Morrison Foster, *My Brother Stephen*, p. 51.

35. Morrison Foster, *My Brother Stephen*, pp. 26–27.

36. Morrison Foster, *My Brother Stephen*, p. 24.

37. Charles Dickens, *Hard Times* (London: Bradbury and Evans, 1854), 41, 150.

38. Foster Family Letters, William B. Foster to Morrison Foster, January 12, 1840, C685.

39. Elsie Murray, "Stephen C. Foster at Athens: His First Composition," *Tioga Point Museum*, No. 222, 1941, pp. 2–15.

40. Harold Vincent Milligan, *Stephen Collins Foster: A Biography of America's Folk-Song Composer* (New York: G. Schirmer, 1920), p. 22.

41. "Towanda Historic District," National Register of Historic Places, http://www.nationalregisterofhistoricplaces.com/pa/bradford/districts.html.

42. William Wallace Kingsbury, quoted in Harold Vincent Milligan, *Stephen Collins Foster*, p. 24; and also in A. H. Kingsbury, "The Old Towanda Academy," *Annual: Bradford County Historical Society*, No. 4, 1910, p 21.

43. Regarding Stephen's inability to stick to school, no one spoke about such things as learning disabilities, nor were special school programs devised to compensate for what William and Eliza's generation considered inertia.

44. Foster Family Letters, Eliza C. Foster to William B. Foster Jr., August 7, 1840, C692.

45. Elsie Murray, "Stephen C. Foster at Athens," pp. 2–15.

46. Letter from Stephen Foster in Athens to William Foster Jr., dated November 9, 1840, in Calvin Elliker, *Stephen Collins Foster*, Correspondence #190.

47. Morrison Foster believed the composition was originally for four flutes, with Stephen taking the leading part, but other sources mention the possibility of three flutes. Morrison Foster, *My Brother Stephen*, p. 32.

48. Elsie Murray, "Stephen C. Foster at Athens," pp. 2–15.

49. Elsie Murray, "Stephen C. Foster at Athens," 2–15.

50. Elsie Murray, "Stephen C. Foster at Athens," pp. 2–15.

51. Letter from Stephen Foster in Towanda to William Foster Jr., dated around 1841, in Calvin Elliker, *Stephen Collins Foster,* Correspondence #191.

52. R. M. Welles, "The Old Athens Academy," Bradford County Historical Society, Annual No. 5, Towanda, Penn. 1911.

53. Letter from Stephen Foster in Towanda to William Foster Jr., dated around 1841, in Calvin Elliker, *Stephen Collins Foster,* Correspondence #191.

54. Letter from Stephen Collins Foster in Canonsburg to William Foster Jr., dated July 24, 1841, in Calvin Elliker, *Stephen Collins Foster,* Correspondence #192.

55. Letter from Stephen Collins Foster to William Foster Jr., dated August 28, 1841, in Calvin Elliker, *Stephen Collins Foster*, Correspondence #193.

56. Letter from Stephen Collins Foster in Canonsburg to William Foster Jr., dated July 24, 1841, in Calvin Elliker, *Stephen Collins Foster*, Correspondence #192.

57. William Foster Sr., March 30, 1842, quoted in Harold Vincent Milligan, *Stephen Collins Foster,* p. 34.

58. Foster Family Letters, William B. Foster to William B. Foster Jr., March 14, 1842, C515.

59. Foster Family Letters, William B. Foster to William B. Foster Jr., March 14, 1842, C515.

5. AT HOME IN ALLEGHENY

1. Foster Family Letters, William Foster Sr. to William Foster Jr., December 1, 1840.

2. Foster Family Letters, Eliza C. Foster to William Foster Jr., August 7, 1840, C692. Allegheny Town was incorporated as a city in 1840, hence the name Allegheny City.

3. Foster Family Letters, Eliza C. Foster to William Foster Jr., August 14, 1841, C708.

4. Foster Family Letters, Eliza C. Foster to William Foster Jr., August 14, 1841, C708.

5. Foster Family Letters, Eliza C. Foster to William Foster Jr., September 16, 1841, C596.

6. Foster Family Letters, Eliza C. Foster to William Foster Jr., October 18, 1841, C599.

7. Foster Family Letters, William B. Foster to William Foster Jr., September 3, 1841.

8. Charles Hamm, *Yesterdays, Popular Song in America* (New York: W. W. Norton, 1979), pp. 203–204.

9. Morrison Foster, *My Brother Stephen*, p. 32.

10. Evelyn Morneweck, *Chronicles* p. 382.

11. Foster Family Letters, Eliza C. Foster to William Foster Jr., October 18, 1841, C599.

12. Foster Family Letters, Eliza C. Foster to William Foster Jr., November 10, 1841, C601.

13. Foster Family Letters, Eliza C. Foster to William Foster Jr., September 16, 1841, C596.

14. Foster Family Letters, Eliza C. Foster to William Foster Jr., November 10, 1841, C601.

15. Foster Family Letters, William B. Foster to William Foster Jr., October 1, 1841, C597.

16. Foster Family Letters, William B. Foster to William Foster Jr., March 20, 1841, C703.

17. Foster Family Letters, William B. Foster to William Foster Jr., March 30, 1841, C703.

18. Morton Horwitz, *The Transformation of American Law, 1780–1860* (New York: Oxford University Press, 1992), pp. 228–229.

19. Peter J. Coleman, *Debtors and Creditors in America: Insolvency, Imprisonment for Debt, and Bankruptcy, 1607–1900* (Madison: State Historical Society of Wisconsin,1974), pp. 283–285.

20. Charles Warren, *Bankruptcy in United States History* (New York: Da Capo Press, 1935), pp. 25–45.

21. Lawrence M. Friedman, *A History of American Law* (New York: Simon & Schuster, 1985), pp.269–271.

22. Foster Family Letters, Eliza Foster to Morrison Foster, February 16, 1842, C522.

23. Foster Family Letters, William B. Foster to William Foster Jr., March 30, 1842.

24. Rick Sebak, "What the Dickens?" *Pittsburgh Magazine*, November 21, 2012. See also Evelyn Morneweck, *Chronicles*, p. 232.

25. Foster Family Letters, from Eliza Clayland Foster in Baltimore, March 11, 1842, C517

26. Foster Family Letters, Eliza Foster in Baltimore to Henrietta Wick April 9, 1842.

27. Lloyd was not his master. As Douglass explained, he belonged to Captain Aaron Anthony, "Lloyd's clerk and superintendent . . . the overseer of the overseers." Frederick Douglass, *Narrative of the Life of Frederick Douglass*, pp. 19–21.

28. Frederick Douglass, *Life and Times of Frederick Douglass* (Start Publishing eBook Edition, 2012), location 373–379.

29. The flirtatious Henry was also a regular visitor at the home of the notorious Peggy O'Neil Eaton, wife of Andrew Jackson's Secretary of War John Eaton, an acquaintance of William B. Foster. In her youth, Peggy was a recognized beauty and the subject of the so-called "petticoat scandal" that nearly brought down Jackson's presidency. "I visit Mrs. Eaton's frequently," Henry bragged to his brother William, "and find her and her two pretty Daughters extremely agreeable. Ex-V-Presidentess, you know."

30. Foster Family Letters, Henry Foster to William Foster Jr., March 25, 1842, C514, and Henry Foster to William Foster Jr., June 30, 1842, C519. Both letters written from Washington City.

31. Foster Family Letters, Eliza Foster to William Foster Jr., May 6, 1842, C509.

32. Foster Family Letters, Eliza Foster to William Foster Jr., May 18, 1842, C508; Eliza Foster to William Foster Jr., May 6, 1842, C509; William B. Foster to William Foster Jr., June 28, 1842, C505; William B. Foster to William Foster Jr., March 14, 1842, C515; Henry Foster to William Foster Jr., June 30, 1842, C519.

33. Foster family Letters, William B. Foster to William Foster Jr., August 25, 1842, C507.

34. Foster Family Letters, Henrietta Foster Wick to William Foster Jr., July 2, 1842, C504.

35. Foster Family Letters, William B. Foster to Morrison Foster, January 12, 1840, C685 and William B. Foster to William Foster Jr., August 25, 1842, C507.

36. The mayor's son was A. J. Cassatt, who became president of the Pennsylvania Railroad. What his relationship was to the young William B. Foster, who became vice president of the Pennsylvania Railroad, is not known. The Treasure Chest, http://www.users.totalise.co.uk/~tmd/mary-cassatt.htm.

37. Edward Baynham, "History of Music in Pittsburgh 1758–1958," unpublished manuscript, Pittsburgh: Carnegie Public Library in Oakland, p.77.

38. Evelyn Morneweck, *Chronicles*, p. 128.

39. Susan Pentland's square piano with rosewood case was built by Raven & Bacon of New York. Presently in the collection of the Foster Memorial at White Springs, Florida. Information from Calvin Elliker, *Stephen Collins Foster*, Realia #186.

40. Dan Rooney and Carol Peterson, *Allegheny City: A History of Pittsburgh's North Side* (Pittsburgh: University of Pittsburgh Press, 2013), p. 36. Allegheny's three churches were "First Wesley Church, the Third Bethel Church, and a Baptist congregation."

41. Evelyn Morneweck, *Chronicles*, p. 274.

42. Eliza Foster related a story in her journal about a favorite tree that was chopped done by mistake. The story is reminiscent of Russell's song "Woodman, Spare that Tree."

43. Evelyn Morneweck, *Chronicles*, p. 274.

44. Saunders and Root, eds., *The Music of Stephen C. Foster*, Vol. 1, pp. 9–13, 452.

45. Charles Hamm, *Music in the New World*, pp. 188–189.

46. Quoted by D. J. Rice, "Two Stephen C. Foster Songs" (New York, J. Fischer, 1931), from John Tasker Howard, *Stephen Foster: America's Troubadour*, p. 125 and William W. Austin in *"Susanna"* p. 14.

47. Letter from Stephen Collins Foster in Pittsburgh to Ann Eliza Buchanan, dated September 15, 1845, in Calvin Elliker, *Stephen Collins Foster*, Correspondence #194.

48. Morrison Foster, *My Brother Stephen*, p. 34.

49. Evelyn Morneweck, *Chronicles*, p. 288. See also "Underground Railroad," Visit Pittsburgh, www.visitpittsburgh.com/essentials/history/uggr/sites/. William Foster purchased the land for the house on the East Common or 605 Union Avenue from the Methodist Protestant Church, which stood "on the corner of Ohio Street and the East Common, now Union Avenue." The house no longer exists.

50. Ancel Henry Bassett, *A Concise History of the Methodist Protestant Church from Its Origins* (Pittsburgh: Press of Charles A. Scott, James Robinson, 1877), pp. 115–117.

51. Dorothy Sterling, *The Making of an Afro-American: Martin Robison Delany, 1812–1885* (New York: Da Capo Press, 1971), pp. 58, 59, 66.

52. Bettye Collier-Thomas, *Freedom and Community: Nineteenth-Century Black Pennsylvania* (Philadelphia: The Center, 1992).

53. Cornelius D. Scully, *Story of Old Allegheny City* (Pittsburgh: Allegheny Centennial Committee, 1941), p. 121.

54. Evelyn Morneweck, *Chronicles*, pp. 262–263.

55. Gilbert Chase, *America's Music: From the Pilgrims to the Present* (Urbana: University of Illinois Press, 1987), p. 148.

56. Pittsburgh newspaper account of May 16, 1843, quoted in Morneweck, *Chronicles*, pp. 262–263.

57. Stefan Lorant, *Pittsburgh: The Story of an American City* (Pittsburgh: Esselmont Books, 1999).

58. The explosion occurred on August 12, 1845. Ancel Henry Bassett, *A Concise History of the Methodist Protestant Church from Its Origins*, p. 127; Evelyn Morneweck, *Chronicles*, p. 288.

59. Foster Family Letters, William B. Foster to Morrison Foster, January 21, 1846, C491.

60. Foster Family Letters, William B. Foster to Morrison Foster, February 5, 1846, C490.

61. William Tasker Howard, *Stephen Foster: America's Troubadour*, p. 9. In 1846, the claim John Eaton presented to Congress for William Foster came to $4,820, including interest.

62. Letter from Stephen Collins Foster to Ann Eliza Buchanan, dated September 15, 1845, in Calvin Elliker, *Stephen Collins Foster*, Correspondence #194.

63. Foster Family Letters, P. McCormick to Marner & Philpot, Pittsburgh, April 3, 1847, C486.

64. Evelyn Morneweck, *Chronicles*, p. 302.

65. Foster Family Letters, Eliza C. Foster to William B. Foster Jr., August 7, 1840, C692.

66. Foster Family Letters, Henry Foster in Washington to Morrison Foster, March 18, 1846, C488.

67. Foster Family Letters, Edward Buchanan Jr. to Morrison Foster, March 31, 1860, C577.

68. John C. Waugh, *The Class of 1846: From West Point to Appomattox* (New York: Warner Books, 1994). The irony in store for these graduates is the theme of Waugh's book. West Point graduates commanded fifty-five of the war's sixty major battles, and a West Pointer commanded one side in the remaining five battles.

69. John Grant, James Lynch, and Ronald Bailey, *West Point: The First 200 Years* (Guilford, CT: Globe Pequot Press, 2002), p. 47.

70. Foster Family Letters, Henry Foster to Morrison Foster, March 16, 1846, C488.

71. John Grant, *West Point*, pp. 47, 75.

72. Evelyn Morneweck, *Chronicles*, p. 282.

73. Foster Family Letters, Dunning Foster to Morrison Foster, June 1846.

74. Letter from Stephen Collins Foster in Pittsburgh to Ann Eliza Buchanan dated September 15, 1845, in Calvin Elliker, *Stephen Collins Foster*, Correspondence #194.

75. Cornelius D. Scully, *Story of Old Allegheny City*.

76. See George T. Fleming, *History of Pittsburgh and Environs* for history of cotton manufacturing.

6. MUSICAL BOOKKEEPER

1. Evelyn Morneweck, *Chronicles*, p. 94.

2. Raymond Walters, *Stephen Foster, Youth's Golden Gleam* (Princeton, NJ: Princeton University Press, 1936), pp. 11–15.

3. Ashley L. Ford, "Life on the Ohio: A Captain's View," *Queen City Heritage*, 57, Summer-Fall 1999, pp. 19–26.

4. Raymond Walters, *Stephen Foster*, p. 11.

5. William Tasker Howard, *Stephen Foster: America's Troubadour*, p. 147.

6. Scene is from *Western Scenery, or Land and River, Hill and Dale, in the Mississippi Valley* by William Wells, featured in Evelyn Morneweck, *Chronicles*, p. 306.

7. Charles Dickens, *American Notes*, Vol. 3, 1843, p.130, quoted in Raymond Walters, *Stephen Foster*, p. 40.

8. Raymond Walters, *Stephen Foster*, pp. 11–15.

9. Walter Havighurst, "Travelers' Tales by Steamboat in the 1840s," *Queen City Heritage*, 57, Summer-Fall 1999, pp. 27–36.

10. Fletcher Hodges Jr., "Stephen Foster: Cincinnatian and American," *Bulletin of the Historical and Philosophical Society of Ohio*, 8, April 1950, 82–104.

11. Charles Cist, *Sketches and Statistics of Cincinnati in 1851* (Cincinnati: Wm. H. Moore), p. 163.

12. "The Cincinnati Water Front, 1848," *Bulletin of the Historical and Philosophical Society of Ohio*, 6, April 1948, pp. 28–39.

13. Foster Family Letters, Dunning Foster's Will, Cincinnati, June 9, 1847, C538.

14. Evelyn Morneweck, *Chronicles*, p. 301.

15. Evelyn Morneweck, *Chronicles* , 292, 301.

16. Morrison Foster, *My Brother Stephen*, p. 35.

17. Russell Sanjek, *American Popular Music and Its Business: The First Four Hundred Years*, Vol. 2 (New York: Oxford University Press, 1988), pp. 129–130.

18. Richard D. Wetzel, *"Oh! Sing No More That Gentle Song,"* pp. 257, 262.

19. My conclusion here is based on the opinion that Foster wrote most of the songs published in Cincinnati while he was living in that city, and that he published them not long after he wrote them. Some critics are of the opinion that Foster carried around manuscripts of songs that he had composed at an earlier date in Pittsburgh, and when he needed a song, he pulled one from an old trunk and published it. I believe Foster was actively involved with composing while he lived in Cincinnati.

20. John Tasker Howard, *Stephen Foster: America's Troubadour*, p. 147.

21. Evelyn Morneweck, *Chronicles*, p. 336.

22. Raymond Walters, *Stephen Foster*, pp. 35–36.

23. Letter from Stephen Collins Foster to Morrison Foster, April 27, 1849, quoted in Howard, *Stephen Foster: America's Troubadour*, p. 149.

24. John Tasker Raymond Walters, *Stephen Foster*, p. 62.

25. Robert Peebles Nevin, "Stephen C. Foster and Negro Minstrelsy," *The Atlantic Monthly*, November, 1867. Sometimes, these "tableaux vivant" would be sexually suggestive models, but Nevin does not mention any such display at the Eagle Saloon. See also Foster Family Letters, Robert Peebles Nevin to Morrison Foster, July 21, 1865, C473.

26. Morrison Foster, *My Brother Stephen*, p. 37.

27. Letter from Robert P. Nevin to Morrison Foster, July 21, 1865.

28. Raymond Walters, *Stephen Foster*, p. 75, from family letters in Foster Hall Collection and *Cincinnati Gazette*, April 15, 1847.

29. Letter from Stephen Collins Foster to William E. Millet, May 25, 1849, in Calvin Elliker, *Stephen Collins Foster*, Correspondence #195.

30. Raymond Walters, *Stephen Foster*, p. 62.

31. Evelyn Morneweck, *Chronicles*, pp. 337–338.

32. Jon Newsom, "Home, Sweet Home, Life in Nineteenth-Century Ohio," Library of Congress: Understanding the Music, http://memory.loc.gov/cocoon/ihas/html/ohio/ohio-newsom.html.

33. Charles Cist, *Sketches and Statistics of Cincinnati in 1851* (Cincinnati: Wm. H. Moore, 1851), p.163.

34. Letter from Stephen C. Foster to Robert P. Nevin, quoted in Evelyn Morneweck, *Chronicles*, p. 315.

35. Morrison Foster, *My Brother Stephen*, p. 35.

36. Richard D. Wetzel, *"Oh! Sing No More That Gentle Song,"* p. 266. Also letter from Steven Saunders, August 9, 1985.

37. Raymond Walters, "Stephen Collins Foster," *Cincinnati Star*, Thursday, April 25, 1940, Fine Arts, Section 10, page 2.

38. Raymond Walters, "Stephen Collins Foster," *Cincinnati Star*.

39. Raymond Walters, *Stephen Foster*, p. 92.

40. William C. Peters had various music-publishing businesses and the names changed according to his partners. Thus Foster's songs were published under W. C. Peters & Co., Peters, Field & Co., Peters and Webster, and Peters and Field, and in Cincinnati and Louisville.

41. Daniel Spillane, *History of the American Pianoforte: Its Technical Development and the Trade* (New York: D. Spillane Publishers, 1890), p. 152.

42. "Firth Pond & Co—New York Makers," Magee Flutes, www.mcgee-flutes.com/firth&c.htm; and "Firth," Antique Piano Shop, https://antiquepiano-shop.com/online-museum/firth.

43. According to William Tasker Howard, Stephen Foster never earned royalties from Firth Pond & Co. for "Nelly Was a Lady," although they did pay him later for "Brother Gum."

44. Russell Sanjec, *American Popular Music and Its Business*, p. 131.

45. John Tasker Howard, *Stephen Foster: America's Troubadour*, p. 152; Letter from Firth, Pond. & Co. to Stephen Foster, September 12, 1849.

46. John Tasker Howard, *Stephen Foster: America's Troubadour*, p. 325 and William Austin, *"Susanna," "Jeanie," and "The Old Folks at Home,"* pp. 24, 104.

47. Russell Sanjek, *American Popular Music and Its Business*, p. 131. Sheet Music from Saunders and Root, *The Music of Stephen C. Foster*, Vol. 1. pp. 64–130.

48. Letter from Stephen Collins Foster to William E. Millet, May 25, 1849, in Calvin Elliker, *Stephen Foster*, Correspondence #195.

49. William Osborne, *Music in Ohio* (Kent, OH: Kent State University Press, 2004), p. 410.

50. Richard D. Wetzel, *"Oh! Sing No More That Gentle Song,"* p. 267.

51. Foster Family Letters, Morrison Foster to I. J. Cist, February 27, 1865, C583.

52. Evelyn Morneweck, *Chronicles*, p. 353.

53. Rosemarie K. Bank, *Theatre Culture in America 1825–1860* (Cambridge: Cambridge University Press, 1997.) While early minstrelsy attracted mainly the working classes, middle-class men sneaked out of their respectable homes to find release from their repressed Victorian etiquette in a rude, masculine environment that "manufactured the allure of the low." Any white man who craved masculinity and less gentility, or who wanted to go "slumming," might have been drawn to the minstrel shows.

54. William J. Mahar, *Behind the Burnt Cork Mask* (Urbana: University of Illinois Press, 1998); Alexander Saxton, "Blackface Minstrelsy," in Annemarie Bean, James V. Hatch, and Brooks McNamara, eds., *Inside the Minstrel Mask: Readings in Nineteenth-Century Blackface Minstrelsy* (Hanover, NH.: Wesleyan University Press, 1996), p. 68; and Dale Cockrell, *Demons of Disorder: Early Blackface Minstrels and Their World* (Cambridge: Cambridge University Press, 1997), pp. 81–82, 84.

55. Eric Lott, *Love & Theft, Blackface Minstrelsy and the American Working Class* (New York: Oxford University Press, 1993), pp. 38–55. The same attraction between the racial cultures exists today when white, middle-class kids choose to wear overly large clothes and dance hip-hop and sing rap music.

And it existed a half century back, when Elvis Presley sang to white teen age girls in a rich baritone that mimicked, in tonal and musical quality, something of the black musician's voice.

56. W. T. Lhamon, *Jump Jim Crow: Lost Plays, Lyrics and Street Prose of the First Atlantic Popular Culture* (Cambridge, MA: Harvard University Press, 2003).

57. "Mel Watkins, interview for *American Experience*," Public Broadcasting Service (pbs), http://www.pbs.org/wgbh/amex/foster/sfeature/ sf_minstrelsy_5.html.

58. Fear makes people curious. After September 11, 2001, bookstores suddenly piled the tables high with books about Middle Eastern cultures and Americans wanted to know more about the people by whom they felt threatened. Pittsburgh newspapers from the 1850s mention repeatedly that white, working men would lose their jobs and what limited social status they had attained if abolition became a reality.

59. John Finch, *Notes of Travel in the United States* (London, 1844), quoted in Noel Ignatiev, *How the Irish Became White* (New York: Routledge Press, 1995), p. 97.

60. Edward Pessen, *Jacksonian America* (Urbana: University of Illinois Press, 1985), p. 42.

61. William Stanton, *The Leopard's Spots: Scientific Attitudes toward Race in America, 1815–1859* (Chicago: University of Chicago Press, 1969), pp. 97–98, 186; Louis Menand, *The Metaphysical Club* (New York: Farrar, Straus and Giroux, 2001), pp. 104–107, 145.

7. THE AWAKENING IN CINCINNATI

1. Raymond Walters, *Stephen Foster*.

2. Stephen Middleton, *Ohio and the Antislavery Activities of Attorney Salmon Portland Chase, 1830–1849* (New York: Garland Publishing, 1990), pp. 74–77.

3. John Niven, *Salmon P. Chase: A Biography* (New York: Oxford University Press, 1995), pp. 113.

4. Henry S. Ford and Kate B. Ford, *History of Cincinnati, Ohio* (Los Angeles: Williams Publishers, 1881; Cincinnati: Ohio Book Store, 1987), pp. 96–97.

5. Henry S. Ford and Kate B. Ford, *History of Cincinnati, Ohio*, pp. 96–99.

6. Henry S. Ford and Kate B. Ford, *History of Cincinnati, Ohio*, pp. 96–97.

7. Joan D. Hedrick, *Harriet Beecher Stowe: A Life* (New York: Oxford University Press, 1994).

8. Joan D. Hedrick, *Harriet Beecher Stowe*. Stowe was able to make her readers empathize with slave women by characterizing them as mothers who had lost their children through sale, if not through death, which was the white woman's experience in the nineteenth century.

9. Alexander Kinmont, *Twelve Lectures on the Natural History of Man, Cincinnati 1839*, from Joan D. Hedrick, *Harriet Beecher Stowe*, p. 218.

10. *National Anti-Slavery Standard*, January 5, 1842, quoted in George M. Frederickson, *Black Image in the White Mind* (Middletown, CT: Wesleyan University Press, 1971), p. 107.

11. Joan D. Hedrick, *Harriet Beecher Stowe*, p.97.

12. Mark Twain, *Life on the Mississippi*, in Mark Twain, *The Family Mark Twain*, p. 33, quoted in Raymond Walters, *Stephen Foster*, p. 16.

13. Carter G. Woodson, "The Negroes of Cincinnati Prior to the Civil War," in *Free Blacks in America, 1800–1860*, ed. By John H. Bracey Jr. (Belmont, CA: Wadsworth Publishing, 1971), pp. 72–77.

14. Charles H. Wesley, *Negro Labor in the United States 1850–1925* (1927; New York: Russell & Russell, 1967), p. 39.

15. Eileen Southern, *The Music of Black Americans: A History* (New York: W. W. Norton, 1971), pp. 147–148.

16. Charles H. Wesley, *Negro Labor in the United States*, p. 39.

17. Peter Quinn, *Banished Children of Eve* (New York: Viking Penguin, 1994), pp. 43–52.

18. Letter from Stephen Foster to Morrison Foster, published in *Foster Hall Bulletin*, No. 11, February 1935.

19. Raymond Walters, *Stephen Foster*, p. 90–91.

20. "Sources of Literary Regionalism in The Old Northwest, 1820–1860," http://castle.edu/localite/illinois/Literary%20Regionalism/William_Gallagher.htm; William D. Gallagher, *Facts and Conditions of Progress in the North-West* (Cincinnati, OH: H. W. Derby, 1850).

21. William D. Gallagher, *Miami Woods, A Golden Wedding, and Other Poems* (Cincinnati, OH: Robert Clarke, 1881), p. 28.

22. Edward D. Mansfield, *Personal Memories: Social, Political, and Literary with Sketches of Many Noted People 1803–1843* (Cincinnati, OH: William Clark, 1879).

23. Edward Deering Mansfield's newspapers are from the Cincinnati Historical Society Library, 1301 Western Avenue, Cincinnati, Ohio, and from the Cincinnati Public Library, Cincinnati, Ohio; Dallas Bogan, "Mansfield Was True Jack-Of-All-Trades," Warren County Ohio GenWeb, August 30, 2004, http://www.rootsweb.ancestry.com/~ohwarren/Bogan/bogan235.htm.

24. Edward Deering Mansfield, *Personal Memories*, p. 212.

25. Steven Saunders and Deane L. Root, "Nelly Was a Lady," in *The Music of Stephen C. Foster*, Vol. 1 (Washington, DC: Smithsonian Institution Press, 1990), pp. 48–51.

26. Matthew Shaftel, "Singing a New Song: Stephen Foster and the New American Minstrelsy," *Music and Politics*, Vol. 1, No. 2, 2007, pp. 1–24.

27. Charles Hamm, *Yesterdays*, pp. 138–139.

28. Matthew Shaftel, "Singing a New Song," pp. 1–24.

29. Pollard McCormick to Morrison Foster, May 11, 1848, in Evelyn Morneweck, *Chronicles*, p. 335.

30. Foster Family Letters, Ann Eliza Buchanan to Morrison Foster, July 17, 1848, C484.

31. Foster Family Letters, Dunning Foster to Morrison Foster, December 29, 1848, C483.

32. Letter, Fletcher Hodges Jr., "Stephen Foster: Cincinnatian and American," *Bulletin of the Historical and Philosophical Society of Ohio*, 8, April 1950, pp. 82–104.

33. Foster Family Letters, Dunning Foster to Morrison Foster, December 29, 1848, C483.

34. *The Atlas*, January 9, 1849, quoted in Raymond Walters, *Stephen Foster*, p. 119.

35. This figure of around 4,000 deaths was quoted in the *Memoirs of Dr. Drake*, by E. D. Mansfield, in Henry S. Ford and Kate B. Ford, *History of Cincinnati, Ohio*, p. 98. Harriet Beecher Stowe's husband, a professor at Lane Theological Seminary in Cincinnati during the 1849 cholera outbreak, wrote, "During the three months of June, July and August last, more than nine thousand persons died of cholera within three miles of my house." Lyman Beecher Stowe, *Saints, Sinners, and Beechers* (New York: Bobbs-Merrill Company, 1934).

36. Foster Family Letters, Morrison Foster to I. J. Cist, February 27, 1865, C583.

37. Foster Family Letters, Dunning Foster to Morrison Foster, December 29, 1848, C483.

38. Foster Family Letters, Dunning Foster to Morrison Foster, December 29, 1848, C483.

39. Foster Family Letters, Dunning Foster to Morrison Foster, January 13, 1849, C482.

40. Foster Family Letters, Dunning Foster to Morrison Foster, January 13, 1849, C482.

8. NON-COMPANIONATE MARRIAGE

1. Jessie Welsh Rose to William Stevenson, July 7, 1926, courtesy of Mifflin County Historical Society, Lewistown, PA.

2. For genealogy of McDowell family, see Pittsburgh collections at the Pennsylvania Room, Carnegie Library, Oakland, in Pittsburgh, PA.

3. Jessie Welsh Rose, "My Grandmother's Memories," *Pittsburgh Post*, July 4, 1926.

4. Evelyn Morneweck, *Chronicles*, pp. 365, 366. The accuracy of the description of Stephen's courtship of Martha Morse remains to be verified. Morneweck would have heard the story from her father Morrison, who did not like Jane very much.

5. Ellen K. Rothman, *Hands and Hearts: A History of Courtship in America* (New York: Basic Books, 1984), p. 103.

6. Article in *Lady's Godey's Book*, Stephen Foster Memorial Room, University of Pittsburgh, Pittsburgh, PA.

7. Steven Saunders and Deane L. Root, *The Music of Stephen C. Foster*, Vol. 1, p. 455.

8. Ellen K. Rothman, *Hands and Hearts*, p. 108.

9. Quoted in Evelyn Morneweck, *Chronicles*, p. 380.

10. Letter from Agnes McDowell to Marian McDowell Scully, July 23, 1850.

11. Ellen K. Rothman, *Hands and Hearts*, p. 108.

12. Letter from Stephen Collins Foster to Ann Eliza Buchanan, July 16, 1850.

13. Richard Storrs Willis and Augustus Morand, *Musical World*, Vol. 12, July 21, 1855; quote about Washington's residence taken from *Frank Leslie's Illustrated Newspaper*, June 7, 1856.

14. Firth, Pond and Company History, online.

15. William Tasker Howard, *Stephen Foster: America's Troubadour*, p. 166.

16. William Tasker Howard, *Stephen Foster: America's Troubadour*, pp. 166, 167.

17. Jessie Welsh Rose to William Stevenson, July 7, 1926, courtesy of Mifflin County Historical Society, Lewistown, PA.

18. Dorothy Sterling, *The Making of an Afro-American*, 1971.

19. Dorothy Sterling, *The Making of an Afro-American*, 1971.

20. Dorothy Sterling, *The Making of an Afro-American*, 1971.

21. Jessie Welsh Rose, "My Grandmother's Memories."

22. This is current historiography on a women's role in nineteenth-century marriage.

23. Evelyn Morneweck, *Chronicles*, pp. 553, 541, 514.

24. William Tasker Howard, *Stephen Foster: America's Troubadour*, p. 167.

25. Stephen Foster's Manuscript Book, Center for American Music, University of Pittsburgh, Pittsburgh, PA.

26. Stephen Foster's Manuscript Book, Center for American Music, University of Pittsburgh, Pittsburgh, PA.

27. Steven Saunders and Deane L. Root, *The Music of Stephen C. Foster*.

28. Stephen Foster's Manuscript Book, Center for American Music, University of Pittsburgh, Pittsburgh, PA.

9. "SWANEE RIVER," E. P. CHRISTY, AND SENTIMENTAL MINSTRELSY

1. Steven Saunders and Deane L. Root, eds., *The Music of Stephen C. Foster*, Vol., pp. 191–194, 78–89. The first Foster songs to be designated "Plantation Melodies" were "Dolly Day," "Gwine to Run All Night," and "Angelina Baker," all published in 1850 by F. D. Benteen of Baltimore. None of these songs have the characteristics that define "plantation songs" as some scholars use the word today.

2. Theater historian Bruce McConachie argues that the breakdown of the paternalistic family circle "found expression through the idealization of a lost home. Love of home was the truly distinguishing characteristic of American life in 1840." Bruce A. McConachie, *Melodramatic Formations: American Theater and Society, 1820–1870* (Iowa City: University of Iowa Press, 1992), p. 33.

3. Quote from Alexander Saxton, "Blackface Minstrelsy," in *Inside the Minstrel Mask*, eds. Annemarie Bean, James V. Hatch, and Brooks McNamara, p.75.

4. Leo Marx, *The Machine in the Garden: Technology and the Pastoral Ideal in America* (New York: Oxford University Press, 1964).

5. Constantine Sedikides et al., "To Nostalgize: Mixing Memory and Affect and Desire," *Advances in Experimental Social Psychology*, Vol. 51, No. 1, 2014, pp. 1–79. Online article available.

6. John Tierney, "What Is Nostalgia Good For? Quite a Bit, Research Shows," *New York Times*, July 8, 2013, Science section, http://www.nytimes.com/2013/07/09/science/what-is-nostalgia-good-for-quite-a-bit-research-shows.html?pagewanted=all. Article based on research by Dr. Constantine Sedikides, Psychology Department at University of South Hampton. Quotes are from Drs. Routledge and Hepper.

7. Constantine Sedikides et al., "To Nostalgize: Mixing Memory and Affect and Desire." Discussion about music and nostalgia from a study by Routledge et al., 2011.

8. Fyodor Dostoyevsky, *The Brothers Karamozov*, 1880.

9. Lee Glazer and Susan Key, "Carry Me Back: Nostalgia for the Old South in Nineteenth-Century Popular Culture," *Journal of American Studies*, Vol. 30, No. 1, The American Past and Popular Culture, April, 1996, pp. 1–24.

10. Bryan F. LeBeau, *Currier & Ives, America Imagined* (Washington, DC: Smithsonian Institution Press, 2001), pp. 166–169.

11. Bryan F. LeBeau, *Currier & Ives, America Imagined*. The theme of this book is emphasized in the title. Currier & Ives prints showed America as antebellumites imagined it should look—as a rural fantasy rather than as an industrializing reality.

12. Morrison Foster, *My Brother Stephen*, p. 47; John Tasker Howard, *Stephen Foster: America's Troubadour*, p. 191; Stephen Foster's Manuscript Book, Center for American Music, University of Pittsburgh, Pittsburgh, PA, p. 14.

13. Raymond Walters, *Stephen Foster*, pp. 69, 72, 78, 87.

14. Steven Saunders and Deane L. Root, eds., *The Music of Stephen C. Foster*, Vol. 1, pp. 78–89.

15. Letter from Stephen Collins Foster in Pittsburgh to E. P. Christy, February 23, 1850, in Calvin Elliker, *Stephen Collins Foster*, Correspondence #196.

16. Robert C. Toll, *On with the Show! The First Century of Show Business in America* (New York: Oxford University Press, 1976), Chapter 4.

17. Newspaper ad for Christy's Minstrels, in American Minstrel Show, Collection 1823–1947, Harvard Houghton Library, Oasis.lib.harvard.edu/oasis/deliver/~hou02063.MS Thr 556(33).

18. Robert C. Toll, *Blacking Up: The Minstrel Show in Nineteenth-Century America* (New York: Oxford University Press, 1974), p. 52; Carl Wittke, *Tambo and Bones* (New York: Greenwood Press, 1968), p. 52; Alexander Saxton, "Blackface Minstrelsy," p. 68.

19. Letter from Stephen Collins Foster in Allegheny City to E. P. Christy, June 12, 1851, in Calvin Elliker, *Stephen Collins Foster*, Correspondence #198; Conversation between the author and Deane L. Root, March 23, 2007. It is likely that Christy *would* have sung Foster's songs on the minstrel stage, without paying him for the privilege anyway. Christy felt he was giving Foster's songs publicity, which was payment in itself. If an unpublished song showed potential for popularity, Christy paid people to sit in the audience and write out the words and music while another minstrel was performing it. This type of thievery was common practice before copyright protection was well established.

20. Letter from Stephen Foster to E. P. Christy, June 20, 1851, in Calvin Elliker, *Stephen Collins Foster*.

21. Steven Saunders and Deane L. Root, eds., *The Music of Stephen C. Foster*, Vol. 1, p. 191.

22. Letter from Stephen Collins Foster to E. P. Christy, May 25, 1852, in Calvin Elliker, *Stephen Collins Foster*, Correspondence #200.

23. *The Musical World and New York Musical Times (Musical World)*, February 19, 1853, quoted in William Tasker Howard, *Stephen Foster: America's Troubadour*, p. 206.

24. Letter from Stephen C. Foster to Edwin P. Christy, May 25, 1852, in Steven Saunders and Deane L. Root, *The Music of Stephen C. Foster*, pp. 398–399; information about Firth, Pond copyright of "Old Folks at Home": Letter from Morrison Foster to Oliver Ditson & Co., April 28, 1879, in William Tasker Howard, *Stephen Foster: America's Troubadour*, p. 350.

25. Letter from Stephen Collins Foster to E. P. Christy, May 25, 1852, in Calvin Elliker, *Stephen Foster, A Guide to Research*, Correspondence #200.

26. Stephen Foster's letter to E. P. Christy, in Evelyn Morneweck, *Chronicles*, p. 400.

27. Harold Vincent Milligan, *Stephen Collins Foster*, p. 15. John Mahon gave the figure of fifteen dollars.

28. Letter from Stephen Collins Foster to E. P. Christy, February 23, 1850, in Calvin Elliker, *Stephen Collins Foster*, Correspondence #196.

29. On-line www.worldcat.org/ . . . /old-folks-at-home. See Cramer, Beale & Co., "Old Folks at Home."

30. Robert Toll, *On with the Show*, Chapter 4.

31. See images of Charles White and George and Edwin Christy from Harvard University— Houghton Library/American Minstrel Show Collection, 1823–1947: MS Thr 556 (198) Charles White images, MS Thr 556(34) George N. Christy, MS Thr 556 (33) Edwin P. Christy, oasis.lib.harvard.edu/oasis/deliver/~hou02063.

32. Carl Wittke, *Tambo and Bones*, pp. 51, 54.

33. Robert Toll, *Blacking Up*, pp. 36, 38.

34. Carl Wittke, *Tambo and Bones*, p. 37.

35. *Godey's Lady's Book*, May 1850 and August 1850.

36. Stephanie Elaine Dunson, "The Minstrel in the Parlor: Nineteenth-Century Sheet Music and the Domestication of Blackface Minstrelsy," PhD Dissertation, University of Massachusetts, May 2004, pp. 89, 125.

37. Steven Saunders and Deane L. Root, eds., *The Music of Stephen C. Foster*, Vol. 1, pp. 195–198.

38. Steven Saunders and Deane L. Root, eds., *The Music of Stephen C. Foster*, Vol. 1, pp. 18, 80, 238.

39. Note Foster sheet music covers in Steven Saunders and Deane L. Root, eds., *The Music of Stephen C. Foster*, Vols. 1 and 2.

40. Stephanie Elaine Dunson, "The Minstrel in the Parlor," Chapter 3, "Propriety and Perversion: Minstrel Sheet Music and Female Desire."

41. *New York Mirror 10,* December 29, 1832, quoted in Richard L. Butsch, *The Making of American Audiences, from Stage to Television, 1750 – 1990* (Cambridge: University of Cambridge Press, 2000), p. 50.

42. Richard Butsch, *The Making of American Audiences, from Stage to Television, 1750–1990* (Cambridge UK: University of Cambridge Press, 2000), p. 67.

43. Playbill for George Christy & Wood's Minstrels, Nov. 21, 1856, Harvard Theatre Collection, Houghton Library, Cambridge, MA.

44. *The Spirit of the Times,* quoted in Richard Butsch, *The Making of American Audiences*, pp. 90–91.

45. Richard Butsch, *The Making of American Audiences*, p. 88.

46. Larry Starr and Christopher Waterman, *American Popular Music: From Minstrelsy to MP3* (New York: Oxford University Press, 2010), pp. 22–23.

47. Dorothy Sterling, *The Making of an Afro-American*, p. 58.

48. Eric Lott, *Love and Theft*, p. 15. Douglass managed to separate the songs from the blackface performers, who were "the filthy scum of white society, who have stolen from us a complexion denied to them by nature, in which to make money, and pander to the corrupt taste of their white fellow citizens." Printed in the *North Star*, October 27, 1848.

49. Drew Gilpin Faust, *The Creation of Confederate Nationalism: Ideology and Identity in the Civil War South* (Baton Rouge: Louisiana State University, 1988), pp. 65–67.

50. *Mobile Register and Advertiser,* July 25, 1861, reprinted in Drew Gilpin Faust, *The Creation of Confederate Nationalism*, p. 67. The popular song "Darling Nelly Gray" by B. R. Hanby tells the story of a female slave who was taken away from her home and lover in Kentucky when "The white man bound her with his chain" and took "her to Georgia for to wear her life away, As she toils in the cotton and the cane."

10. SHIRAS AND THE ANTISLAVERY IMPULSE

1. Jeremy Bentham, *Introduction to the Principles of Morals and Legislation* (London, 1789), chapter 17; J. H. Burns and H. L. A. Hart, eds., *The Collected Works of Jeremy Bentham* (Oxford: Oxford University Press, 1996), p. 283.

2. William Makepeace Thackeray, "Roundabout Sketches," quoted in Edward Dickinson et al., *The American History and Encyclopedia of Music*, Vol. 4 (Toledo, OH: Irving Squire, 1908), p. 68.

3. Charles P. Shiras, *The Redemption of Labor and Other Poems* (Pittsburgh: W. H. Whitney, Third Street, 1852), p. 4.

4. Evelyn Morneweck, *Chronicles*, pp. 283, 406.

5. Ken Emerson, *Doo-Dah! Stephen Foster and the Rise of American Popular Culture*, pp. 121–122.

6. Arthur J. Larsen, *Crusader and Feminist: Letters of Jane Gray Swisshelm, 1858–1865* (Saint Paul: Minnesota Historical Society, 1934).

7. Hon. William J. Coyne of Pennsylvania [in the House of Representatives], "Celebrating African American History Month," Congressional Record, Volume 140, Number 23, March 7, 1994, Congressional Record Online through the Government Printing Office, www.gpo.gov.

8. Charles P. Shiras, *The Redemption of Labor and Other Poems*, p. 5.

9. Sally Kalson, "Along the Freedom Trail," *Pittsburgh Post-Gazette Sunday Magazine*, 1994, reprinted in Congressional Record, Volume 140, Number 23, March 7, 1994, pp. 1–7, Congressional Record Online through the Government Printing Office, www.gpo.gov.

10. Charles P. Shiras, *The Redemption of Labor and Other Poems*, pp. 64–67.

11. Evelyn Morneweck, *Chronicles* pp. 406, 431.

12. Charles P. Shiras, "The Popular Credo," in *The Redemption of Labor*, pp. 58–59.

13. Eric Foner, *Free Soil, Free Labor, Free Men: The Ideology of the Republican Party before the Civil War* (New York: Oxford University Press, 1970, 1995.) This is the theme of the book.

14. Evelyn Morneweck, *Chronicles*, p. 288.

15. Sally Kalson, "Along the Freedom Trail."

16. "Avery College Historical Marker," ExplorePAHistory.com, http://explorepahistory.com/hmarker.php?markerId=1-A-37E; "Free at Last? Slavery in Pittsburgh in the 18th and 19th Centuries," University of Pittsburgh, www.Library.Pitt.edu/freeatlast/abolition.html.

17. Frederick Douglass, *Narrative of the Life of Frederick Douglass*, pp. 23–26.

18. Frederick Douglass, *Narrative of the Life of Frederick Douglass*, pp. 23–26.

19. *The Leader*, February 23, 1879, quoted in George Shiras III, *Justice George Shiras of Pittsburgh* (Pittsburgh: University of Pittsburgh Press, 1953), p. 18.

20. *The Leader*, February 23, 1879, quoted in George Shiras III, *Justice George Shiras of Pittsburgh*, p. 18.

21. George Shiras III, *Justice George Shiras of Pittsburgh*, pp. 16–18.

22. Morrison Foster, *My Brother Stephen*.

23. Evelyn Morneweck, *Chronicles*, pp. 408–409.

24. Steven Saunders and Deane L. Root, *The Music of Stephen C. Foster*, pp. 168–172.

25. Mathew Gregory Lewis, *Journal of a West India Proprietor* (London, 1834), in *Africa, Africa, Extracts from British Travel Accounts and Journals of the Seventeenth, Eighteenth, and Nineteenth Centuries Concerning . . . the British West Indies*, ed. Roger D. Abrahams and John F. Szwed (New Haven, CT: Yale University Press, 1983), pp. 298–299.

26. Evelyn Morneweck, *Chronicles*, p. 103; Morrison Foster, *My Brother Stephen*, pp. 49–50.

27. Evelyn Morneweck, *Chronicles*, p. 409.

28. Matthew Shaftel, "Singing a New Song: Stephen Foster and the New American Minstrelsy," *Music and Politics*, Vol. 1, No. 2, 2007, p. 15.

29. Matthew Shaftel, "Singing a New Song," pp. 1–24; Steven Saunders and Deane L. Root, eds., *The Music of Stephen C. Foster*, Vol. 1, pp. 64–67, 86–89.

30. Steven Saunders and Deane L. Root, ed., *The Music of Stephen C. Foster*, Vol. 1, pp. 94–97.

31. Steven Saunders and Deane L. Root, ed., *The Music of Stephen C. Foster*, Vol. 1, pp.164–167.

32. Matthew Shaftel, "Singing a New Song," p. 18.

33. Stephen Saunders, "The Social Agenda of Stephen Foster's Plantation Melodies," *American Music*, Vol. 30, No. 3, Fall 2012, pp. 275–289.

34. Charles Hamm, *Yesterdays*, pp. 136–138, p. 215.

35. Robert B. Winans, "Early Minstrel Music 1843–1852," in *Inside the Minstrel Mask*, Annemarie Bean, James V. Hatch, and Brooks McNamara, eds., p. 152.

36. Robert B. Winans, "Early Minstrel Music, 1843–1852," p. 149.

37. Steven Saunders and Deane L. Root, *The Music of Stephen C. Foster*, Vol. 1, p. 43; "Uncle Ned" discussion in Steven Saunders and Deane L. Root, *The Music of Stephen C. Foster*, pp. 28–31.

38. Robert B. Winans, "Early Minstrel Music 1843–1852," p. 211. Stephen Foster also wrote fun-loving minstrel songs from 1848 to 1852, such as "Nelly Bly," "Oh! Lemuel!" and "Dolly Day," in which the overriding sentiment is joy and delight in life. Characters such as Nelly Bly step out of the realm of the imaginary and are brought to life as sympathetically conceived, real men and women. The jesting in the songs is gentle, and the comic elements do not overwhelmingly detract from the sympathetic traits of the song's persona. Of course, the music is lighthearted, dancing, and delightful.

39. Susan Pentland Robinson's account of Stephen Foster's trip to New Orleans, *Pittsburgh Press*, September 12, 1900, quoted in William Tasker Howard, *Stephen Foster: America's Troubadour*, pp. 169–170.

40. Letter from Richard Cowan to Morrison Foster, February 8, 1853, quoted in William Tasker Howard, *Stephen Foster: America's Troubadour*, p. 169.

41. See Stephen Foster's handwritten Manuscript Book, Center for American Music, University of Pittsburgh, Pittsburgh, PA, pp. 50–51. The words to "My Old Kentucky Home, Good Night" were altered from their original intention, which was an "Uncle Tom" song. "Poor Uncle Tom, Good Night" are the way the words appear in their first draft in his manuscript book.

42. Thomas Riis, "The Music and Musicians in Nineteenth–Century Productions of *Uncle Tom's Cabin*," *American Music*, Vol. 4, No. 3, Autumn 1986, p.272.

43. Steven Saunders and Deane L. Root, *The Music of Stephen C. Foster*, pp.235–237.

44. Evelyn Morneweck, *Chronicles*, pp. 419, 424.

45. *Musical World*, January 1853, quoted in William W. Austin, *"Susana," "Jeanie," and "The Old Folks at Home": The Songs of Stephen C. Foster from His Time to Ours* (Urbana and Chicago: University of Illinois Press, 1975) p. 204.

46. Laura Keene put on several productions of *The Invisible Prince*, one from July 11 through July 13, 1859, with a second run from May 16 through June 2, 1860, and a third run in 1867. Internet Broadway Database (IBDB), http://www.ibdb.com/person.php?id=413529.

47. Evelyn Morneweck, *Chronicles* p. 439.

48. Edward G. Fletcher, "Stephen Collins Foster, Dramatic Collaborator," *Colophon*, Vol. 1, No. 1, Summer 1935, pp. 33–37.

49. Evelyn Morneweck, *Chronicles*, pp. 433–436.

50. Evelyn Morneweck, *Chronicles*, p. 439.

51. Dale Cockrell, "Of Soundscapes and Blackface: From Fools to Foster," in *Burnt Cork: Traditions and Legacies of Blackface Minstrelsy*, ed. Stephen Johnson (Amherst: University of Massachusetts Press, 2012), pp. 51–72.

52. Thomas Riis, "The Music and Musicians in Nineteenth-Century Productions of *Uncle Tom's Cabin*," p.288.

53. Charles Hamm, *Yesterdays*, p. 139.

54. Robert C. Toll, *Blacking Up*, p. 66.

55. Mel Watkins, *On the Real Side: Laughing, Lying, and Signifying* (New York: Simon & Schuster, 1994), p. 95.

56. Mel Watkins, *On the Real Side*, p. 94.

57. Don H. Doyle, *The Cause of All Nations, An International History of the American Civil War* (New York: Basic Books, 2015), p. 36.

58. Josiah Clark Nott, contributor to *Types of Mankind or Ethnological Researches*, by Samuel George Morton, J. C. Nott, and George R. Gliddon (Philadelphia: Lippincott, Gambo. London: Trubner, 1854).

59. William W. Austin, *"Susanna," "Jeanie," and "The Old Folks at Home,"* p. 85.

60. Quotation from Mel Watkins, *On the Real Side*, p. 95; Richard Crawford, *America's Musical Life, A History* (New York: W. W. Norton, 2001), p. 219.

61. Playbills from George Christy and H. Wood's Minstrels, Harvard Theatre Library, Cambridge, MA.

62. For how Stephens Foster's songs may have been performed, author's conversation with Deane L. Root, March 23, 2007.

63. Dale Cockrell, "Nineteenth-Century Popular Music," in *The Cambridge History of Popular Music*, ed. David Nicholls (Cambridge: Cambridge University Press, 1998), pp.172–173.

11. PIANO GIRLS AND PARLOR SONGS

1. "The New York Musical World," Retrospective Index to Music Periodicals (1790–1966) (RIPM), http://www.ripm.org/?page=JournalInfo&ABB=NYM.

2. William W. Austin, *"Susanna," "Jeanie," and "The Old Folks at Home": The Songs of Stephen C. Foster from His Time to Ours* (Urbana and Chicago: University of Illinois Press, 1975), pp. 242–246.

3. *Musical World*, January 1853, quoted in William W. Austin, *"Susana," "Jeanie," and "The Old Folks at Home,"* p. 204.

4. Dale Cockrell, "Nineteenth Century Popular Music," pp. 172–173.

5. The Piano Girl is mentioned in chapter 8, "The Eternal Feminine," of James Huneker, *Overtones*, p. 286.

6. James Huneker, *Overtones*, p. 285, quoting from Judith Tick, *American Women Composers before 1870* (1979; Ann Arbor, MI: UMI Research Press, 1983), p. 218. The Center for American Music at the University of Pittsburgh has an ample collection of gold-tooled, leather volumes of sheet music. The female names on the cover are often important names for Pittsburgh, also found in the names of townships and city streets. For example, a girl with the surname Irwin had her name engraved on a beautifully bound volume of sentimental songs. This piano girl must have been related to Archibald Irwin, who was in partnership with Dunning Foster in Cincinnati, and to Judge Irwin.

7. Harold Vincent Milligan, *Stephen Collins Foster*, p. 93.

8. James A. Keene, *A History of Music Education in the United States* (Hanover, NH: University Press of New England, 1982).

9. Ronald Pearsall, *Victorian Sheet Music Covers* (Detroit, MI: Gale Research), pp. 9–11. Advertisements for "Female Seminaries" and academies appeared frequently in the *Pittsburgh Gazette* in the 1820s through 1840s. They offered such courses as mentioned above. James A. Keene, *A History of Music Education in the United States*, p. 21; Edward Baynham, "History of Music in Pittsburgh 1758–1958," pp. 40–41.

10. James A. Keene, *A History of Music Education in the United States*, p. 520.

11. Eliza Clayland Foster, "Sketches and Incidents of Pittsburgh," pp. 130–135.

12. Arthur Loesser, *Men, Women, and the Piano* (Mineola, NY: Dover Publications, 1990), pp. 282, 268.

13. Elsie Murray, *Stephen C. Foster at Athens: His First Composition, No. 222* (Athens, PA: Tioga Point Museum, 1941), p. 15.

14. For details about the Foster relatives, see Evelyn Morneweck, *Chronicles*, pp. 423, 373, 387, 328, 330, 340, 341.

15. Rather than accepting the simplicity in Foster's music as "a deliberate decision, taken in the spirit of Jacksonian democracy," as well as a mandate of the parlor style, "the extreme simplicity of melody and harmony of his most successful songs" left the composer open to charges of "musical ignorance and poverty of invention." Charles Hamm, "Review of *The Music of Stephen C. Foster: A Critical Edition*," pp. 515–526.

16. *Knickerbocker 4*, October 1834, p. 286, quoted by Karen Ahlquist in *Democracy at the Opera* (Urbana: University of Illinois Press, 1997), p.86.

17. Charles Hamm, *Yesterdays*, pp.205, 220–223.

18. Charles Hamm, *Yesterdays*, p. 219.

19. Charles Hamm, *Yesterdays*, pp. 215, 217.

20. Steven Saunders and Deane L. Root, *The Music of Stephen C. Foster*, Vol. 1, pp. 219–222.

21. Steven Saunders and Deane L. Root, *The Music of Stephen C. Foster*, Vol. 1, pp. 204–206.

22. Steven Saunders and Deane L. Root, *The Music of Stephen C. Foster*, Vol. 1, pp. 222–230.

23. Charles Hamm, *Yesterdays*, pp. 43–44, 110.

24. Walter A. McDougall, *Throes of Democracy: The American Civil War Era 1829–1877* (New York: HarperCollins, 2008), pp. 168–169.

25. Anatole France.

26. Barbara De Angelis, *How Did I Get Here? Finding Your Way to Re-newed Hope and Happiness When Life and Love Take Unexpected Turns* (New York: St. Martin's Press, 2005), pp. 154, 133.

27. Stephen C. Foster, "Ah, May the Red Rose Live Alway" (1850), described in Steven Saunders and Deane L. Root, *The Music of Stephen C. Foster*, Vol. 1. pp. 90–93.

28. Ann Douglas, *The Feminization of American Culture* (1977; New York: Anchor/Doubleday Press, 1988), p. 208.

29. Ann Douglas, "Heaven Our Home: Consolation Literature in the Northern United States, 1830–1880," in *Death in America*, ed. David E. Stannard (Philadelphia: University of Pennsylvania Press, 1975), pp. 70–80. The nineteenth century was the age of "the beautiful death," according to Philippe Ariès (Philippe Ariès, *The Hour of Our Death*); Steven Saunders and Deane L. Root, *The Music of Stephen C. Foster*, Vol. 1, pp. 90–93.

30. Barbara De Angelis, *How Did I Get Here? Finding Your Way to Re-newed Hope and Happiness When Life and Love Take Unexpected Turns*, p. 154, 133.

31. Sigmund Freud, "Mourning and Melancholia" (1917), in *General Psychological Theory* (New York: Simon & Schuster, 1997), pp. 164–179.

32. Steven Saunders and Deane L. Root, *The Music of Stephen C. Foster*, Vol. 1, pp. 130–133.

33. Steven Saunders and Deane L. Root, *The Music of Stephen C. Foster*, Vol. 1, pp. 262–265.

34. Steven Saunders and Deane L. Root, *The Music of Stephen C. Foster*, Vol. 1, pp.132–133.

35. Steven Saunders and Deane L. Root, *The Music of Stephen C. Foster*, Vol. 1, pp. 278–282.

36. Steven Saunders and Deane L. Root, *The Music of Stephen C. Foster*, Vol. 1, pp. 24–27, Vol. 2, pp. 2–9.

12. HOBOKEN AND DEATHS IN THE FAMILY

1. Foster Family Letters, Henrietta Foster Thornton to Morrison Foster, June 20, 1853.

2. Evelyn Morneweck, *Chronicles*, p. 426.

3. "The New York Musical World," Retrospective Index to Music Periodicals RIPM, Retrospective Index to Music Periodicals (1790–1966) (RIPM), http://www.ripm.org/?page=JournalInfo&ABB=NYM.

4. William W. Austin, *"Susanna," "Jeanie," and "The Old Folks at Home"*: *The Songs of Stephen C. Foster from His Time to Ours* (Urbana: University of Illinois Press, 1989; reprint of 1975), p. 205.

5. Stephen C. Foster to editor of *Musical World*, published in *Musical World*, February 26, 1853. Musicologist Stephen Saunders has shown that Foster's publishers were satisfied with his musical abilities. The only composition worked over before it went to press was his first song "Open Thy Lattice, Love," published when the composer was eighteen. Since then his publishers left his songs basically untouched, did not rewrite his accompaniments, and listened to his suggestions "concerning artistic matters." Steven Saunders, "Stephen Foster and His Publishers, Revisited," *College Music Symposium*, Vol. 28, 1988, pp. 53–69.

6. William W. Austin, *"Susanna," "Jeanie," and "The Old Folks at Home,"* p. 205.

7. Charles Hamm, "Review of *The Music of Stephen C. Foster, a Critical Edition*," pp. 515–526. Deane Root and Charles Hamm have argued that the idea that Foster was an "untutored genius" whose "writing was almost entirely instinctive" is simply untrue. They note that his songs were written in a wide variety of styles, including "piano pieces, hymns, didactic pieces for children, and instrumental arrangements," and that his musical taste extended to Italian opera and art song."

8. Stephen C. Foster to editor of *Musical World*, February 14, 1853, published in *Musical World*, February 26, 1853, reprinted in William W. Austin, *"Susanna," "Jeanie," and "The Old Folks at Home,"* p. 205, and John Tasker Howard, *Stephen Foster: America's Troubadour*, p. 220. This letter to the editor of a musical journal was not the first or the last time Foster would use literary creativity to publicly suggest inner feelings that he felt society or his family forced him to keep hidden.

9. John Tasker Howard, *Stephen Foster: America's Troubadour*, p. 237.

10. Stephen Foster, *The Social Orchestra for Flute or Violin: A Collection of Popular Melodies*, quoted from the introduction, published in Steven Saunders and Deane L. Root, *The Music of Stephen C. Foster*, Vol. 1, pp. 288–289.

11. Stephen Foster, *The Social Orchestra for Flute or Violin: A Collection of Popular Melodies*, quoted from the introduction, published in Steven Saunders and Deane L. Root, *The Music of Stephen C. Foster*, Vol. 1, pp. 288–289.

12. Letter from Stephen Collins Foster to Morrison Foster, July 8, 1853.

13. When the copyright was reissued years later, after Stephen's death, Jane and Marion Foster received royalties on the book, which had a long record of publication.

14. "Hoboken's History," Hoboken, New Jersey, www.hobokennj.org/visit/history.

15. Excerpted from the *Musical World* of February 25, 1853, quoted in William Tasker Howard, *Stephen Foster: America's Troubadour*, p. 238.

16. Manuscript Book of Stephen Foster, Center for American Music, University of Pittsburgh, Pittsburgh, PA, pp. 76–77.

17. Morrison Foster, *My Brother Stephen*, pp. 43–44.

18. Ann C. Rose, *Victorian America and the Civil War*, pp. 164–166, 170. Rose argues that strong emotional bonds between mothers and sons were commonplace in Foster's time because the relationship empowered the Victorian mother who could only reach out to the world through the male figures in the family. But Stephen would not have been the son to empower Eliza.

19. Morrison Foster, *My Brother Stephen*, p. 44.

20. Eliza Foster's relationship with her oldest son, William, a man whose success could empower a Victorian mother, is more interesting to consider. When Eliza needed money, comfort, or help getting to the East to visit her daughter, she turned to her son William. Family letters reveal she wrote to him regularly asking for advice and assistance, although the letters appear to have stopped after William married.

21. Steven Saunders and Deane L. Root, *The Music of Stephen C. Foster*, Vol. 1, p. 382.

22. Information about Jane's nickname from Evelyn Morneweck, *Chronicles*.

23. Stephen Foster's Manuscript Book, Center for American Music, University of Pittsburgh, Pittsburgh, PA, p. 84.

24. Larry Starr and Christopher Waterman, *American Popular Music*, p. 27.

25. Susan Key, "'Forever in Our Ears': Nature, Voice, and Sentiment in Stephen Foster's Parlor Style," *American Music*, Vol. 30, No. 3, Fall 2012, pp. 290–307.

26. Steven Saunders and Deane L. Root, *The Music of Stephen C. Foster*, Vol. 1, pp. 382–387.

27. Evelyn Morneweck, *Chronicles*, p. 451.

28. "Jennie," in Manuscript Book of Stephen Foster, Center for American Music, University of Pittsburgh, Pittsburgh, PA, pp. 82–84.

29. Foster Family Letters, Dunning Foster to Morrison Foster, March 1854.

30. Manuscript Book of Stephen Foster, Center for American Music, University of Pittsburgh, Pittsburgh, PA, p. 90.

31. Letter from James Buchanan Jr. to Edward Young Buchanan, October 26, 1854, quoted in Ken Emerson, *Doo-dah! Stephen Foster and the Rise of American Popular Culture*, pp. 221–222.

32. Letter from James Buchanan Jr. to Edward Young Buchanan, November 15, 1854, quoted in Ken Emerson, *Doo-dah! Stephen Foster and the Rise of American Popular Culture*, pp. 221–222.

33. Letter from James Buchanan Jr. to Edward Young Buchanan, November 15, 1854, quoted in Ken Emerson, *Doo-dah! Stephen Foster and the Rise of American Popular Culture*, pp. 221–222.

34. Foster Family Letters, Dunning Foster to Morrison Foster, December 13, 1854, C545.

35. In September 1854, Reverend Edward Buchanan had been transferred to Trinity Church, Oxford, in Philadelphia where he and his family took up residence in a new home on Church Road. Evelyn Morneweck, *Chronicles*, p. 455.

36. Foster Family Letters, James Buchanan Jr. to Morrison Foster, September 25, 1854, C541.

37. Foster Family Letters, Dunning Foster to Morrison Foster, December 13, 1854, C545.

38. Evelyn Morneweck, *Chronicles*, p. 459.

39. Letter from James Buchanan Jr. to Edward Young Buchanan, November 15, 1854, quoted in Ken Emerson, *Doo-Dah! Stephen Foster and the Rise of American Popular Culture*, p. 222.

40. Letter from Stephen Collins Foster in Allegheny City to Henrietta Foster Thornton, March 19, 1855, in Calvin Elliker, *Stephen Foster, A Guide to Research*, # 203.

41. Steven Saunders and Deane L. Root, *The Music of Stephen C. Foster*, Vol. 1, pp. 424–442.

42. Steven Saunders and Deane L. Root, *The Music of Stephen C. Foster*, Vol. 1, pp. 443–446.

43. Steven Saunders and Deane L. Root, *The Music of Stephen C. Foster*, Vol. 1, p. 450.

44. Foster Family Letters, Dunning Foster to Morrison Foster, March 17, 1856, C551.

45. Foster Family Letters, Eliza Foster to son William Foster Jr. May 14, 1832.

46. Foster Family Letters, Ann Eliza Buchanan to Morrison Foster, April 8, 1856, C552.

47. Foster Family Letters, Ann Eliza Buchanan to Morrison Foster, April 8, 1856, C552.

48. Martha Morse, once a companion of Stephen Foster, believed that "Gentle Annie" was written to commemorate the untimely death of yet another lovely young lady, a cousin of Stephen's, Annie Evans.

49. John Lair and William H. Townsend, eds., *Songs Lincoln Loved: Words and Music of Abraham Lincoln's Favorite Ballads . . . and Others* (New York: Duell, Sloan, and Pearce, 1954).

50. Ralph Waldo Emerson, "Spirit," from *Essays and Poems by Ralph Waldo Emerson*, Barnes and Nobles Classics Series (New York: Barnes and Nobles Books, 2004), pp. 41–43.

51. Stephen Foster owned a portable oak melodeon, acquired sometime between 1850 and 1860, and used it for serenading. It had detachable legs and shoulder straps so it could be carried from house to house. Calvin Elliker, *Stephen Collins Foster*, Realia, Correspondence #188.

52. From *Pittsburgh Press*, July 1895, quoted in John Tasker Howard, *Stephen Foster: America's Troubadour*, p. 255.

53. Jesse Welsh Rose, "My Grandmother's Memories," quoted in John Tasker Howard, *Stephen Foster: America's Troubadour*, p. 255.

13. THE BUCHANAN GLEE CLUB

1. The renowned historian Henry Steele Commager said that Buchanan was "by universal consent the worst president in the history of the country." From John Updike, "Buchanan Dying," quoted in Michael J. Birkner, *James Buchanan and the Political Crisis of the 1850s* (Selinsgrove, PA: Susquehanna University Press, 1996), p. 17.

2. Foster Family Letters, Henry Foster to William B. Foster Jr., March 12, 1853, C533. This letter is in part a copy of a letter of recommendation written by James Buchanan to President Franklin Pierce.

3. Evelyn Morneweck, *Chronicles*, p. 48.

4. The discussion of James Buchanan comes from Philip Shriver Klein, *President James Buchanan: A Biography* (University Park, PA: Pennsylvania State University Press, 1962) and Jean H. Baker, *James Buchanan*, The American Presidents Series (New York: Henry Holt, 2004). Klein's book is comparatively sympathetic but Baker's interpretation wounds like a knife.

5. "Rev. Edward Buchanan," Geni, www.geni.com.

6. Morrison Foster, "Morrison Foster's Scrapbook," Stephen Foster Memorial, Center for American Music, University of Pittsburgh, Pittsburgh, PA.

7. "The Bigler Boys," in Evelyn Morneweck, *Chronicles*, pp. 390–391.

8. Meade Minnigerode, *Presidential Years* (New York: G. P. Putnam's Sons, 1928).

9. William (Billy) Hamilton, *Pittsburgh Press*, July 11, 1895.

10. William (Billy) Hamilton, *Pittsburgh Press*, July 11, 1895.

11. Nineteenth-century voting practices were traditionally based on ethnic and religious affiliation rather than on policy or ideology. The Democrats in the mid-nineteenth century attracted Catholics and foreigners, while the Protestants and native-born Americans voted Whig. See Michael F. Holt's *Forging a Majority: The Formation of the Republican Party in Pittsburgh 1848–1860* (New Haven, CT: Yale University Press, 1969) for details about the voting habits of Pittsburghers.

12. Evelyn Morneweck explained the Midwesterner's distaste for Yankees: "Stephen's sarcastic reference to Ohio Yankees of Western Reserve is based on the fact that the northern section of Ohio was originally owned by the state of Connecticut and was known as the Western Reserve. This largest element among the early settlers of this reserve were the Connecticut Yankees from the mother state. They were thrifty, hard working people who gained for themselves a reputation for drawing a hard bargain. Hence, Stephen's scornful line, 'They'll fight for a six pence an hour and a half.' Moreover, the term Yankee was one of reproach to the Union Democrats of Pennsylvania or Ohio, as it was associated, in their minds, exclusively with the abolitionists of New England, and they resented most emphatically the Southern custom of lumping all Northerners under the name." From the *Chronicles*, pp. 477, 480.

13. Steven Saunders and Deane L. Root, *The Music of Stephen C. Foster*, Vol. 2, pp. 12, 13.

14. Stephen Collins Foster, "Manuscript Book," p. 131, Stephen Foster Memorial, Center for American Music, University of Pittsburgh, Pittsburgh, PA.

15. *Pittsburgh Gazette,* September 17, 1856.

16. *Pittsburgh Gazette,* September 18, 1856.

17. Steven Saunders and Deane L. Root, *The Music of Stephen C. Foster*, Vol. 2, p. 11.

18. *Pittsburgh Post*, November 1856.

19. *Pittsburgh Post,* September 16, 1856; *Pittsburgh Post,* March 1857; *Pittsburgh Post*, March 29, 1856.

20. *Pittsburgh Gazette*, November 4, 1856; "The War upon Free Labor," *Pittsburgh Gazette*, September 13, 1866; *Pittsburgh Gazette*, September 17, 1856; and *Pittsburgh Gazette*, November 4, 1856. Michael F. Holt in *Forging a Majority: The Formation of the Republican Party in Pittsburgh 1848–1860* argued that an anti-Catholic bias in Pittsburgh was the key to the victory of the Republicans in Allegheny in 1856. Catholics were associated with the Democratic vote—but contemporary newspapers point to a different factor. *Pittsburgh Morning Post*, April 3, 1856.

21. Evelyn Morneweck, *Chronicles*, p. 474.

22. Jean H. Baker, *James Buchanan.*

23. Jean H. Baker, *James Buchanan.*

24. Jean H. Baker, *James Buchanan.*

14. ROYALTIES SELLOUT

1. John B. Russell, *Cincinnati Daily Gazette*, January 22, 1857.

2. Letter from Stephen Collins Foster to J. B. Russell, January 28, 1857, in Calvin Elliker, *Stephen Collins Foster*, Correspondence #205.

3. Letter from Stephen Collins Foster to Billy Hamilton, January 16, 1857, in Calvin Elliker, *Stephen Collins Foster*, Correspondence #204.

4. Letter from Stephen Collins Foster to William Foster Jr., March 11, 1857, in Calvin Elliker, *Stephen Collins Foster*, Correspondence #206.

5. John Tasker Howard, *Stephen Foster: America's Troubadour*, p. 270.

6. John Tasker Howard, *Stephen Foster: America's Troubadour*, p. 270.

7. Foster Family Letters, William Foster Jr. to Morrison Foster, 1856.

8. Kenneth Stampp, *America in 1857: America on the Brink* (New York: Oxford University Press, 1990). Also, for depressions in the West, see Richard C. Wade, *Urban Frontier.*

9. Foster Family Letters, William Foster Jr. to Morrison Foster, 1856.

10. Stephen Foster kept a record of his finances and expenses, including rents paid, royalties received, washing and boarding, and miscellaneous expenses in a small 7 1/5" by 5 1/4" commercial ledger book. Calvin Elliker, *Stephen Collins Foster*, Realia #170.

11. John Tasker Howard, *Stephen Foster: America's Troubadour*, pp.278, 281, 284,

12. Susan Elizabeth Lyman, *The Story of New York: An Informal History of the City from the First Settlement to the Present Day* (New York: Crown Publishers, 1975), p. 185. Boarding was prevalent before New York's first apartment building, the Rutherford-Stuyvesant, was built on East 18th Street between Third Avenue and Irving Place in 1869. Lyman said it was "distinguished from tenements by such amenities as adequate space, light heat, and plumbing." Edwin G. Burrows and Mike Wallace, *Gotham*, pp. 970–971.

13. Evelyn Morneweck, *Chronicles*, pp. 387, 489.

14. John Tasker Howard, *Stephen Foster: America's Troubadour*, pp. 278, 281, 284,

15. John Tasker Howard, *Stephen Foster: America's Troubadour*, pp. 280–281.

16. Evelyn Morneweck, *Chronicles*, pp. 502–503, 494.

17. David Carlyon, *Dan Rice: The Most Famous Man You've Never Heard Of* (New York: Public Affairs, 2001).

18. David Carlyon, *Dan Rice.*

19. The piano Stephen owned was a square, six-octave model with a rose-wood case, built by Dubois & Stodart at 167 Broadway, New York. Presently at the Stephen Foster Memorial, Center for American Music, University of Pittsburgh, Pittsburgh, PA. Calvin Elliker, *Stephen Collins Foster* Realia, #185.

20. John Tasker Howard, *Stephen Foster: America's Troubadour*, p. 277.

21. Evelyn Morneweck, *Chronicles*, p. 514.

22. John Tasker Howard, *Stephen Foster: America's Troubadour*, p. 287.

23. Letter from Stephen Collins Foster in Pittsburgh to Morrison Foster, October 22, 1858, in Calvin Elliker, *Stephen Collins Foster,* Correspondence #207.

24. Letter from Stephen Collins Foster in Pittsburgh to Morrison Foster, November 2, 1858, in Calvin Elliker, *Stephen Collins Foster,* Correspondence #208.

25. Letter from Stephen Collins Foster in Pittsburgh to Morrison Foster, November 11, 1858, in Calvin Elliker, *Stephen Collins Foster,* #209.

26. *Cincinnati Gazette*, November 1858, from Raymond Walters, *Stephen Foster*, pp. 131–132.

27. Evelyn Morneweck, *Chronicles*, p. 505.

28. Morrison Foster, *My Brother Stephen*, p.39.

29. Morrison Foster, *My Brother Stephen*, p.39.

30. Ken Emerson suggested in *Doo-dah!* that Foster was the man attacked by the "two brutes."

31. Evelyn Morneweck, *Chronicles*, p. 528.

32. *Pittsburgh Post*, 1862 Advertisement.

33. Julia Murray married John V. LeMoyne and moved to the eastern United States. His father, Dr. Francis J. LeMoyne, was an avowed abolitionist whose residence in a town just south of Pittsburgh was a stop on the Underground Railroad. Today the F. Julius LeMoyne House at 49 E. Maiden Street in Washington, Pennsylvania, is a historic site open to the public. Morrison Foster's broken heart must have had a strong influence on his later Copperhead politics.

34. Evelyn Morneweck, *Chronicles*, p. 528.

35. Foster Family Letters, William Foster Jr. to Morrison Foster, 1856.

36. Evelyn Morneweck, *Chronicles,* p. 519. The success that William Foster Jr. achieved during his lifetime was made evident by the fact that William's funeral was held at the home of J. Edgar Thomson, president of the Pennsylvania Railroad. Thomson, who was appointed guardian of William's two children, was married to the sister of William's wife Elizabeth, also deceased. William left the Foster Coal & Iron Company to be operated by J. Edgar Thomson, Thomas A. Scott, and Edward C. Biddle for the benefit of his children.

37. Steven Saunders and Deane L. Root, *The Music of Stephen C. Foster*, Vol. 2, pp. 94–96.

38. *Youngstown Telegram*, February 3, 1934. The story about the Fosters' stay at Gaskill House was given to reporter Esther Hamilton by the landlord Schoenberger's daughter, Mrs. Mygatt.

39. *Youngstown Telegram*, February 3, 1934. Reported by Esther Hamilton as relayed to her by Mrs. Mygatt, Gaskill House landlord Schoenberger's daughter.

40. Letter from Stephen Collins Foster to Morrison Foster, May 31, 1860.

41. Letter from Stephen Collins Foster to Morrison Foster, April 27, 1860.

42. Letter from Stephen Collins Foster to Morrison Foster, May 31, 1860.

43. *Youngstown Telegram*, February 3, 1934. Reported by Esther Hamilton as relayed to her by Mrs. Mygatt, Gaskill House landlord Schoenberger's daughter.

44. *Youngstown Telegram*, February 3,1934. Reported by Esther Hamilton as relayed to her by Mrs. Mygatt, Gaskill House landlord Schoenberger's daughter.

15. NEW YORK "POTBOILERS"

1. Letter from Stephen C. Foster to Morrison Foster, April 27, 1860.

2. Letter from Mattie Stewart De Witt to Jane Foster, January 2, 1890. Rushanna and Mattie Stewart were the daughters of the owner of the Stewart boardinghouse on Greene Street. Mattie Stewart De Witt corresponded with Jane Foster until near the last decade of her life.

3. Jessie Welsh Rose, "My Grandmother's Memories."

4. Evelyn Morneweck, *Chronicles*, pp. 534, 556.

5. Stephen Foster's Contract with Firth, Pond & Co., February 9, 1858, Foster Hall Collection, Center for American Music, University of Pittsburgh, Pittsburgh, PA, from Ken Emerson, *Doo-Dah!, Stephen Foster and the Rise of American Popular Culture*, p. 244. Also, John Tasker Howard, "Stephen Foster and His Publishers," *Musical Quarterly* Vol. 20, No. 1, January 1934, pp. 77–95.

6. John Mahon, "The Last Years of Stephen C. Foster," *New York Clipper*, March 24, 1877, quoted in Evelyn Morneweck, *Chronicles*, p. 539.

7. Clark's *School Visitor*, April 1864, in obituary notice. Evelyn Morneweck, *Chronicles*, p. 541.

8. Steven Saunders and Deane L. Root, *The Music of Stephen C. Foster*, Vol. 2, p. 97. John Mahon, a New York friend, said that Foster had written "Jenny's Coming O'er the Green" with another girl other than his wife in mind.

"It appears that he admired a young girl named Jennie (platonic, of course), and promised to write a song for her." Mahon probably was mistaken, even if at some later date Stephen did admire a girl named Jenny. The song was published while Foster was still living with his wife, before the couple moved to New York.

9. Steven Saunders and Deane L. Root, *The Music of Stephen C. Foster*, Vol. 2, pp. 111, 429, 433.

10. Steven Saunders and Deane L. Root, *The Music of Stephen C. Foster*, Vol. 2, pp. 107–109.

11. Information about Johnny Devine from Internet sources for "Shanghai Chicken": San Francisco History, The Barbary Coast, Ch. 9, "God Help the Poor Sailor," http://www.sfgenealogy.com/sf/history/hbtbc9.htm. For the Foster boys' betting, see Evelyn Morneweck, *Chronicles*, p. 428.

12. "Political Cock Fighters," The Library of Congress, Prints and Photographs Division, LC-USZ62-1972, 1844.

13. Historian Dale Cockrell has associated ambiguity with blackface minstrelsy: "Ambiguity, even equivocation, is essential to masquerade, irony, evanescence, and the subliminal, and meanings are always slippery and multivalent—for things must never be what they seem." Dale Cockrell, "Of Soundscapes and Blackface: From Fools to Foster," in *Burnt Cork, Traditions and Legacies of Blackface Minstrelsy*, ed. Stephen Johnson, p. 69.

14. The subsequent history of John C. Breckinridge made Morrison's vote appear even more odious. Soon after the Civil War broke out, Breckinridge joined the Confederate Army and as a major general fought in such important battles as Shiloh and Chickamauga. He was appointed Secretary of War for the Confederacy by Jefferson Davis, and ran away to Europe after the South's defeat. Later, he returned to Kentucky where he practiced law until his death of natural causes.

15. *Pittsburgh Post*, November 8, 1860.

16. John Tasker Howard, *Stephen Foster: America's Troubadour*, p. 325.

17. In 1920, Harold Vincent Milligan, Stephen Foster's biographer, discussed the situation: "Among Morrison Foster's papers there are numerous statements of royalty payments to Stephen's widow and daughter made by Wm. A. Pond & Co. (the successor of Firth, Pond & Co.) on the sale of songs, up to very recent years, when the last copyright expired. There are no royalty payments from any other firm, and I have never seen anywhere a reference to royalties paid him by any other publisher." Harold Vincent Milligan, *Stephen Collins Foster*, p. 95.

18. "Our Willie Dear is Dying" was published with the words "as sung by Gustavus Geary" on the title page. Geary was a recent immigrant (1860) from England, a composer as well as a performer. In 1862 he composed the music to

"Isn't It a Wonder, or Caddy-Cadunk," with words by Henry Wood, showing that he had connections to the famous minstrel performer. Geary's British background and musical style probably influenced Henry Wood. After the war, Geary became known as a composer of sentimental ballads in the British, Scottish, and Irish tradition. Foster would have known Geary if he wrote the song for him and he already knew Henry Wood. https://jscholarship.library.jhu.edu/bitstream/handle/1774.2/31705/136.116.000.webpage.

19. Evelyn Morneweck, *Chronicles*, p. 556, for the Mahon daughter's wedding.

20. Harold Vincent Milligan, *Stephen Collins Foster*, p. 93.

21. John Mahon, "The Last Years of Stephen C. Foster," *New York Clipper*, March 24, 1877, quoted in Evelyn Morneweck, *Chronicles*, p. 539.

22. Steven Saunders and Deane L. Root, *The Music of Stephen C. Foster*, Vol. 2, pp. 134–136.

23. Letter from Jane Foster to Morrison Foster October 5, 1861, quoted in William W. Austin, *"Susanna," "Jeanie," and "The Old Folks at Home,"* p. 96.

24. Letter from Jane Foster to Morrison Foster, September 30, 1861, quoted in William W. Austin, *"Susanna," "Jeanie," and "The Old Folks at Home,"* p. 95.

25. John Tasker Howard, *Stephen Foster: America's Troubadour*, p. 311.

26. Steven Saunders and Deane L. Root, *The Music of Stephen C. Foster*, Vol. 2, p. 433.

27. Steven Saunders and Deane L. Root, *The Music of Stephen C. Foster*, Vol. 2, pp. 210–211.

28. Stephen Foster, "Tell Me of the Angels, Mother," published by Horace Waters, Athenaeum Collection of Hymns and Tunes, 1863, reprinted in Steven Saunders and Deane L. Root, *The Music of Stephen C. Foster*, Vol. 2, p. 345.

29. Drew Gilpin Faust, *The Republic of Suffering* (New York: Alfred A. Knopf, 2008), p. 194.

16. WAR SONGS AND COPPERHEAD RELATIVES

1. Edward L. Ayers, *In the Presence of Mine Enemies* (New York: W. W. Norton, 2003), pp. 215–216. Ayers points out that the Copperhead ideology among the Democrats of Franklin County in southern Pennsylvania was similar to that found in the border states during the Civil War. According to Ayers, "The Civil War simply was not popular in Pennsylvania in 1861, 'with the Democrats next to solid against coercing the South by war.'"

2. "Copperheads Once More," *Pittsburgh Post*, 1862.

3. *Pittsburgh Post*, November 1860 and February 1861; Morrison Foster, "The Uses of the Slave States," *The Plain Dealer*, February 28, 1861, Cleveland, OH; Scrapbook of Morrison Foster, Stephen Foster Memorial, University of Pittsburgh, Pittsburgh, PA.

4. Catherine Elizabeth Reiser, *Pittsburgh's Commercial Development, 1800–1850* (Harrisburg, PA: Pennsylvania Historical and Museum Commission, 1951), p. 2.

5. *Pittsburgh Post*, 1863.

6. Geoffrey R. Stone, *Perilous Times: Free Speech in Wartime* (New York: W. W. Norton, 2004), p. 98; Catherine Elizabeth Reiser, *Pittsburgh's Commercial Development, 1800–1850*, p. 39; Clement C. Vallandigham, Congressional Speech, January 14, 1863, published in the *Pittsburgh Post*, January 1863; Jennifer L. Weber, *Copperheads* (New York: Oxford University Press, 2005), pp. 98–99.

7. Morrison's daughter Evelyn Morneweck described her family as "Union Democrats," but they were in fact "Peace Democrats," which was a nice name for the Copperheads. Evelyn Morneweck, *Chronicles*, p. 548.

8. "Couldock, Charles Walter," in *American National Biography*, eds. John Arthur Garraty and Mark Christopher Carnes (New York: Oxford University Press, 1999), pp. 581–582.

9. *Pittsburgh Post*, February 1861, from Evelyn Morneweck, *Chronicles*, p. 547. Morrison Foster criticized Buchanan's politics in an article that he wrote as a parody of *Hunchback*, a play by Knowles.

10. Steven Saunders and Deane L. Root, *The Music of Stephen C. Foster*, Vol. 2, pp. 134–136.

11. Steven Saunders and Deane L. Root, *The Music of Stephen C. Foster*, Vol. 2, pp. 191–192.

12. Ernest A. McKay, *The Civil War and New York City* (Syracuse, NY: Syracuse University Press, 1990).

13. Russell Sanjek, *American Popular Music and Its Business*, p. 91.

14. Evelyn Morneweck, *Chronicles*, p. 540.

15. Evelyn Morneweck, *Chronicles*, p. 543.

16. Poem by Henrietta Foster, reprinted in Evelyn Morneweck, *Chronicles*, p. 543.

17. Letter from Martin Delany to Secretary of War Edwin Stanton, December 1863, from Dorothy Sterling, *The Making of an Afro-American*, p. 233.

18. "The Slippery Nigger" by Pell, quoted in Robert Toll, *Blacking Up*, p. 117.

19. Song was performed regularly by Bryant's Minstrels and Wood's Minstrels in New York, quoted in Robert Toll, *Blacking Up*, p. 120.

20. "Jumbo's Courage," *Negro Melodist #1*, quoted in Robert Toll, *Blacking Up*, p. 120.

21. Steven Saunders and Deane L. Root, *The Music of Stephen C. Foster*, Vol. 2, p. 286.

22. Steven Saunders and Deane L. Root, *The Music of Stephen C. Foster*, Vol. 2, pp. 284–286.

23. Steven Saunders and Deane L. Root, *The Music of Stephen C. Foster*, Vol. 2, pp. 284–286.

24. Jennie Lightweis-Goff, "'Long Time I Trabble on de Way': Stephen Foster's Conversion Narrative," *Journal of Popular Music Studies*, Vol. 20, Issue 2, August 2008, pp. 150–165. Lightweis-Goff argues that the national myth of "racial progress and progressive revelation" in America, which presumes that the society and the people's ideas about race improve over time, has been superimposed on Foster's personal story. This scholar argues that "A Soldier in the Colored Brigade" shows that Stephen Foster took two steps forward and just as many backward when it came to writing racist songs.

25. Iver Bernstein, *The New York City Draft Riots* (New York: Oxford University Press, 1990), pp. 19–20.

26. Iver Bernstein, *The New York City Draft Riots*, pp. 19, 20, 21, 36.

27. Henrietta Foster also wrote a campaign song, set to the same music, for McClellan when he ran against Lincoln in the presidential race in November of 1864. Since Stephen died in January of that year, we can conclude that he was not involved in this undertaking. After her brother's death, Henrietta felt free not only to set "Little Mac! Little Mac! You're the Very Man" to Foster's "Better Times are Coming," but also to publish the song. Henrietta gave the copyrights and royalties to Stephen's daughter Marion. If Foster had lived, it seems unlikely that he would have allowed such a travesty to his song, after he had written and dedicated songs to President Lincoln. Evelyn Morneweck quoted John Tasker Howard on the McClellan campaign song in *Chronicles*, p. 544.

28. Fletcher Hodges Jr., "Stephen Foster, Democrat," *The Lincoln Herald*, Lincoln Memorial University, Harrogate, TN, June 1945, republished by University of Pittsburgh, Pittsburgh, PA, 1946, p. 12.

29. Poem by Henrietta Foster, reprinted in Evelyn Morneweck, *Chronicles*, p. 545. When he wanted to keep Maryland on the Union side, Lincoln identified the Peace Democrats at the Baltimore polls by the color of their ballots. Lincoln's soldiers stood around, watched how the election was going, and threw out the men carrying the ballots easily identified as Peace tickets by their color. As one historian explained, "Many who attempted to vote the Peace ticket in Baltimore were arrested for carrying a ballot of the wrong color. The charge against these men was simply polluting the ballot box." Quote from

Dean Sprague, *Freedom under Lincoln* (Boston: Houghton Mifflin, 1965), p. 204, quoted in Thomas J. DiLorenzo, *The Real Lincoln: A New Look at Abraham Lincoln, His Agenda, and an Unnecessary War* (New York: Three Rivers Press, 2002), p. 143.

30. Evelyn Morneweck, *Chronicles*, pp.545, 548.

31. William Rawle, *A View of the Constitution* (1825; Simsboro, LA: Old South Books, 1993), quoted in Thomas J. DiLorenzo, *The Real Lincoln*, p. 92.

32. Thomas J. DiLorenzo, *The Real Lincoln*, pp. 140–147, 153.

33. "When This Dreadful War is Ended" is No. 15 on Foster's Melodies by Horace Water and "Oh! There's No Such Girl as Mine," copyright March 10, 1863, is No. 13. John Tasker Howard, *Stephen Foster: America's Troubadour*, p. 384.

34. The Draft Riot in July of 1863 showed the attitude of New Yorkers toward blacks after Lincoln announced the draft. Blacks in New York City were beaten and murdered.

17. THE FOSTER-COOPER "SONG FACTORY"

1. Steven Saunders and Deane L. Root, *The Music of Stephen C. Foster*, Vol. 2, pp. 266–274, 343–352.

2. John Tasker Howard, *Stephen Foster: America's Troubadour*, p. 329.

3. Steven Saunders and Deane L. Root, *The Music of Stephen C. Foster*, Vol. 2, pp. 266–274, 343–352.

4. Mrs. Parkhurst, "The New Emancipation Song," collected in *Civil War Song Book*, selected by Richard Crawford (New York: Dover Publishers, 1977), pp. 137–140. Foster's contribution to religious music has not been highly commended, but his work in the genre is an example of a popular music composer writing hymns with trendy tunes, and once again he was on the cutting edge.

5. George W. Birdseye, "A Reminiscence of the Late Stephen C. Foster," *New York Musical Gazette*, Vol. 1, No. 3, January 1867, from John Tasker Howard, *Stephen Foster: America's Troubadour*, p. 312.

6. Harold Vincent Milligan, *Stephen Collins Foster*, p. 103.

7. George W. Birdseye, "A Reminiscence of the Late Stephen C. Foster."

8. George W. Birdseye, "A Reminiscence of the Late Stephen C. Foster."

9. George W. Birdseye, "A Reminiscence of the Late Stephen C. Foster," p. 312.

10. George W. Birdseye, *Women and the War. A Poem* (New York: J. Dickson, Book and Job Printer, 1865). This collection included several war poems and an homage to Ulysses S. Grant.

11. Letter from George W. Birdseye, May 28, 1903, in the Foster Hall Collection, Center for American Music, University of Pittsburgh, Pittsburgh, PA, CAM.FHC.2011.01.

12. George W. Birdseye, "A Reminiscence of the Late Stephen C. Foster."

13. Interview with Cooper, from Harold Vincent Milligan, *Stephen Collins Foster*, p. 105. On July 1, 1863, the day before the Twenty-Second arrived in Carlisle, the Confederate General J. E. B. Stuart attacked the Pennsylvania town "with three brigades of Calvary" before he raced down to Gettysburg. George W. Wingate, *History of the Twenty-Second Regiment of the National Guard of the State of New York from Its Organization to 1895* (New York: Edwin W. Dayton, 1896; reprinted 2010), pp. 220–313.

14. Evelyn Morneweck, *Chronicles*, p. 558.

15. John Tasker Howard, *Stephen Foster: America's Troubadour*, p. 331.

16. Evelyn Morneweck, *Chronicles*, p.553, 554.

17. Gilbert Chase, *America's Music*, p. 261.

18. Edward Baynham, "History of Music in Pittsburgh 1758–1958."

19. Raymond Walters, *Stephen Foster*, pp. 135, 42.

20. Harold Vincent Milligan, *Stephen Collins Foster*, p. 96.

21. An analogy can be drawn to the 1960s and 1950s. The buying public in the 1960s did not want the songs of the previous decade, either. The generation that came of age in the 1960s witnessed terrible turmoil, the civil rights movement, car bombings, riots in the streets, and assassinations. They did not relate to the crooning of the 1950s by adolescents with broken hearts and unfulfilled sexual desire. The riotous and uncertain times of the 1960s demanded new songs, in the same way that the Civil War generation needed a new type of song.

22. Steven Saunders and Deane L. Root, *The Music of Stephen C. Foster*, Vol. 2, pp. 258–259, 300–303, 317–318

23. Steven Saunders and Deane L. Root, *The Music of Stephen C. Foster*, Vol. 2, pp. 291–292, 322–323, 355–356.

24. Steven Saunders and Deane L. Root, *The Music of Stephen C. Foster*, Vol. 2, pp.364–366, 360–362, 288–290.

25. Steven Saunders and Deane L. Root, *The Music of Stephen C. Foster*, Vol. 2, pp. 330–332.

26. Thomas Hampson, *American Dreamer: Songs of Stephen Foster*, Musical Album, released 1992.

27. Steven Saunders and Deane L. Root, *The Music of Stephen C. Foster*, Vol. 2 pp. 360–362.

28. Steven Saunders and Deane L. Root, *The Music of Stephen C. Foster*, Vol. 2, pp. 360–362.

29. Steven Saunders and Deane L. Root, *The Music of Stephen C. Foster*, Vol. 2, pp. 364–366.

30. Nicholas Tawa, *The Way to Tin Pan Alley: American Popular Song, 1866–1910* (New York: Schirmer Books, 1990), pp. 122–123.

31. Nicholas Tawa, *The Way to Tin Pan Alley*, pp. 130–133.

32. Addresses of music publishers from sheet music covers show the proximity of the publishers and the performance halls.

33. Harold Vincent Milligan, *Stephen Collins Foster*, p. 104.

34. Harold Vincent Milligan, *Stephen Collins Foster*, p. 104.

35. Harold Vincent Milligan, *Stephen Collins Foster*, p. 104.

36. Information about Wood's Minstrel Theater from Internet Broadway Database (IBDB), www.ibdb.com.

37. Henry Wood's *Songsters* contain songs by Foster and give the composer no credit. Courtesy of the Harvard Theatre Collection, Houghton Library, Cambridge, MA.

38. The words to "When the Bowl Goes 'Round" take up a small paragraph in Foster's manuscript book. Manuscript book of Stephen Collins Foster, Center for American Music, University of Pittsburgh, Pittsburgh, PA.

39. Foster probably wrote much more music that was performed but has not been preserved, or that survived without his name. It is possible that after Foster's death some people remembered the tunes, set new words to the music, and published the songs as their own. Many of Foster's songs may have been purchased for a pittance during his lifetime and interpolated onto the musical programs of the day, on the condition that the composer remain anonymous. The world shall never know.

18. CONCERT SALOONS AND VARIETY MUSIC

1. Parker R. Zellers, "The Cradle of Variety: The Concert Saloons," *Educational Theatre Journal* (Baltimore, MD: Johns Hopkins University Press, 1968), pp. 579–585.

2. *New York Post*, January 1862, from Brooks McNamara, *The New York Concert Saloon* (New York: Cambridge University Press, 2002), p. 11.

3. Brooks McNamara, *The New York Concert Saloon*, p.11.

4. Gillian M. Rodger, *Champagne Charlie and Pretty Jemima: Variety Theater in the Nineteenth Century* (Urbana: University of Illinois Press, 2010), p. 32; Parker R. Zellers, "The Cradle of Variety: The Concert Saloons," p. 585.

5. Parker R. Zellers, "The Cradle of Variety: The Concert Saloons," p. 579.

6. "The Canterbury Hall," *New York Clipper*, September 28, 1861, quoted in William L. Slout, ed., *Broadway Below the Sidewalk, Concert Saloons of Old New York* (San Bernardino, CA: R. Reginald, The Borgo Press, 1994.)

7. Gillian M. Rodger, *Champagne Charlie and Pretty Jemima*, p. 30.

8. "New York Concert Saloons," *The New York Evening Post*, January 2, 1862, quoted in Parker R. Zellers, "The Cradle of Variety: The Concert Saloons," p. 579.

9. "Changes in Vaudeville," *Chicago Chronicle*, 1899; Matthew Hale Smith, *Sunshine and Shadow in New York*, 1869, quoted in Parker R. Zellers, "Cradle of Variety: The Concert Saloons," p. 579.

10. George Birdseye, quoted in John Tasker Howard, *Stephen Foster: America's Troubadour*, p. 312.

11. "George Heydon's Melodeon," *New York Clipper*, February 6, 1864, quoted in William L. Slout, ed., *Broadway Below the Sidewalk*.

12. "Canterbury Hall," *New York Clipper*, September 28, 1861, quoted in William L. Slout, ed., *Broadway Below the Sidewalk*.

13. Information given to Harold Vincent Milligan by George Cooper, quoted in Harold Vincent Milligan, *Stephen Collins Foster*.

14. Harold Vincent Milligan, *Stephen Collins Foster*, pp. 103–105.

15. George G. Foster, *New York by Gas-Light and Other Urban Sketches* (1850), quoted in Tyler Anbinder, *Five Points* (New York: The Free Press, 2001), p.377.

16. Parker R. Zellers, "The Cradle of Variety: The Concert Saloons," p. 583.

17. Parker R. Zellers, "The Cradle of Variety: The Concert Saloons," p. 583.

18. Gillian M. Rodger, *Champagne Charlie and Pretty Jemima*, pp. 29–65.

19. Parker R. Zellers, "The Cradle of Variety: The Concert Saloons," p. 584.

20. Gillian M. Rodger, *Champagne Charlie and Pretty Jemima*, pp. 113–114.

21. Russell Sanjek, *American Popular Music and Its Business*, p. 79.

22. Edward B. Marks, *They All Sang: From Tony Pastor to Rudy Vallee* (New York: The Viking Press, 1935), pp. 3–4.

23. Playbill for George Christy & Wood's Minstrels, Nov. 21, 1856, Harvard Theatre Collection, Houghton Library, Cambridge, Massachusetts.

24. Gillian M. Rodger, *Champagne Charlie and Pretty Jemima*, pp. 99–100.

25. Armond Fields, *Tony Pastor, Father of Vaudeville* (Jefferson, NC: McFarland & Co., 2007).

26. The exact date of Pastor's birth is not known, as different information resulted from research by different historians. Armond Fields, *Tony Pastor, Father of Vaudeville*.

27. Parker Zellers, *Tony Pastor: Dean of the Vaudeville Stage* (Ypsilanti, MI: Eastern University Press, 1971), pp. 4–5.

28. *New York Herald*, April 28, 1862, advertisement, quoted in Parker Zellers, *Tony Pastor: Dean of the Vaudeville Stage*, p. 584.

29. "Concert Saloons," May 21, 1864, quoted in Parker Zellers *Tony Pastor: Dean of the Vaudeville Stage*, p. 584 .

30. Brooks McNamara, *The New York Concert Saloon*, pp. 16–17.

31. Armond Fields, *Tony Pastor, Father of Vaudeville*, p. 30.

32. *New York Clipper*, March 12, 1864, quoted in Steven Saunders and Deane L. Root, *The Music of Stephen C. Foster*, Vol. 2, p. 450.

33. *New York Clipper*, March 12, 1864, from Steven Saunders and Deane L. Root, *The Music of Stephen C. Foster*, Vol. 2, p. 450; Armond Fields, *Father of Vaudeville*, p. 51.

34. Steven Saunders and Deane L. Root, *The Music of Stephen C. Foster*, Vol. 2, pp. 340–342.

35. Armond Fields, *Father of Vaudeville*, p. 51.

36. *Bowery Autocrat*, 1874, "Interview with Tony Pastor." With Permission of Harvard Theatre Collection, Houghton Library, Cambridge, Massachusetts.

37. Tony Pastor, "Combination Song, or a Bunch of Penny Ballads . . . ." Sheet music, 1863. With Permission of Harvard Theatre Collection, Houghton Library, Cambridge, Massachusetts.

38. Tony Pastor, *Mirror Interviews*, XXXIV July 27, 1895, p. 2; *Tony Pastor's Union Songster* (New York : Dick and Fitzgerald, 1862). With Permission from Harvard Theatre Collection, Houghton Library, Cambridge, Massachusetts.

39. *Spirit of the Times, IX*, December 26, 1863, p. 261, quoted in Parker Zellers, *Tony Pastor: Dean of the Vaudeville Stage*, p. 21.

40. Tony Pastor, *Comic Songster*. Quoted with Permission from Harvard Theatre Collection, Houghton Library, Cambridge, Massachusetts.

41. Gillian M. Rodger, *Champagne Charlie and Pretty Jemima*, pp. 99, 103–106.

42. Tony Pastor, *Comic Songster*. Quoted with Permission from Harvard Theatre Collection, Houghton Library, Cambridge, Massachusetts.

43. Tony Pastor, *Comic Songster*. Quoted with Permission from Harvard Theatre Collection, Houghton Library, Cambridge, Massachusetts.

44. Tony Pastor, *Comic Songster*. Quoted with Permission from Harvard Theatre Collection, Houghton Library, Cambridge, Massachusetts.

45. Tony Pastor, *Comic Songster*. Quoted with Permission from Harvard Theatre Library, Houghton Library, Cambridge, Massachusetts.

46. Tony Pastor, *Comic Songster*. Quoted with Permission from Harvard Theatre Collection, Houghton Library, Cambridge, Massachusetts.

47. Tony Pastor, *Comic Songster*. Quoted with Permission from Harvard Theatre Collection, Houghton Library.

48. Wood's and Christy's Minstrels Playbills, ca. 1853, 1855; Tony Pastor's "American Music Hall Playbill," 1862. Used with Permission from Harvard Theatre Collection, Houghton Library, Cambridge, Massachusetts.

49. Charley White's name on the playbills at 444 Broadway should have been enough to keep Stephen Foster away. White was the minstrel who, more than a dozen years earlier, had gotten hold of a copy of Foster's "Nelly Was a Lady" and brought it to Firth, Pond and Company to be published as "Toll the Bell for Lovely Nell, or My Dark Virginia Bride," with White's name as the composer. When Firth and Pond realized the subterfuge, they copyrighted it again in July 1849 as "Nelly Was a Lady," with Foster's name as composer.

50. Gillian M. Rodger, *Champagne Charlie and Pretty Jemima*, p. 115.

51. Ben Graf Henneke, *Laura Keene*, p. 43.

52. http://boise.broadwayworld.com/bwidb/sections/theatres/index.php?var=7336; James Robin Planche, http://www-personal.umd.umich.edu/~nainjaun/.

53. IBDB Internet Broadway Database. http://www.ibdb.com/person.php?id=413529.

54. Deane L. Root, *American Popular Stage Music 1860–1880* (Ann Arbor, MI: UMI Research Press, 1977, 1981), pp. 44–45.

55. Laura Keene Playbills, with Permission from Harvard Theatre Collection, Houghton Library.

56. Steven Saunders and Deane L. Root, The *Music of Stephen C. Foster*, Vol. 2, pp. 65–68, 425.

57. "Thomas Baker," Internet Broadway Database (IBDB), http://www.ibdb.com/person.php?id=413529. See also Ben Graf Henneke, *Laura Keene*, p. 155.

58. Ben Graf Henneke, *Laura Keene*, p. 141–155.

59. Gillian M. Rodgers, *Champagne Charlie and Pretty Jemima*, endnotes to Chapter 8, #9, p. 216; song sheet from Johns Hopkins University: Lester S. Levy Sheet Music Collection, levysheetmusic.mse.jhu.edu/.

60. "You Naughty, Naughty Men," by G. Bickwell and T. Kennick, published 1866 by Dodworth & Son, New York, from Johns Hopkins University: Lester S. Levy Sheet Music Collection, levysheetmusic.mse.jhu.edu/.

61. "You Naughty, Naughty Men," by G. Bickwell and T. Kennick, published 1866 by Dodworth & Son, New York, from from Johns Hopkins University: Lester S. Levy Sheet Music, levysheetmusic.mse.jhu.edu/. Although claimed as an original, the song was rumored to have been brought over by a British soubrette who sang it in the concert saloons.

62. *Pittsburgh Post*, November 10, 1853, from Morneweck, *Chronicles*, pp. 434–435.

63. Doug Reside, "The Music of the Black Crook," New York Public Library, www.nypl.org/blob/2011.

19. LAST DAYS ON THE BOWERY

1. Walt Whitman, *Leaves of Grass*. Whitman used the more poetic sounding "Manahatta" for his city in his famous book of poems.

2. Elmer Bendiner, *The Bowery Man* (New York: Nelson, 1961), Introduction; Harold Vincent Milligan, *Stephen Collins Foster*, pp. 103–105.

3. David Isay and Stacy Abramson, *Flophouse: Life on the Bowery* (New York: Random House, 2000), p. xiv.

4. John Mahon, "The Last Years of Stephen C. Foster," *New York Clipper*, March 24, 1877, quoted in Evelyn Morneweck, *Chronicles*, p. 539.

5. E. A. Parkhurst (Composer), "Father's a Drunkard and Mother Is Dead," Johns Hopkins University: Levy Sheet Music Collection, published 1866 by John F. Ellis, JScholarship.library.jhu.edu.

6. Map of Five Points 1855–1867, Maryland Mapping & Graphics, printed in Tyler Anbinder, *Five Points*, pp. 287–289.

7. Edwin Burrows and Mike Wallace, *Gotham: A History of New York City to 1898* (New York: Oxford University Press, 1999), p. 700.

8. Eric Homberger, *Scenes from the Life of a City: Corruption and Conscience in Old New York* (New Haven, CT: Yale University Press, 1994), p. 22; Edward K. Spann, *The New Metropolis: New York City, 1840–1857* (New York: Columbia University Press, 1981), pp. 253–255.

9. Eric Ferrara, *The Bowery: A History of Grit, Graft and Grandeur* (Charleston, SC: The History Press, 2011), pp. 38–39.

10. Edward K. Spann, *Gotham at War* (Wilmington, DE: Scholarly Resources, 2002), p. 107.

11. Benedict Giamo, *On the Bowery: Confronting Homelessness in American Society* (Iowa City: University of Iowa Press, 1989), p. 8.

12. Alvin F. Harlow, *Old Bowery Days: The Chronicles of a Famous Street* (New York: D. Appleton, 1931), p.179.

13. George C. Foster, *New York by Gas-Light*, p. 420.

14. Elmer Bendiner, *The Bowery*, p. 48.

15. Walt Whitman's article "Brooklynmania" was published in *The Brooklyn Daily Standard*, p. 854.

16. Walt Whitman's article "Brooklynmania" was published in *The Brooklyn Daily Standard*, p. 854.

17. Foster Family Letters, Dunning Foster to Morrison Foster, January 13, 1849, C482.

18. *Literary World*, 1849, quoted in Edwin Burrows and Mike Wallace, *Gotham*, p. 758.

19. Charles H. Haswell, *Reminiscences of New York by an Octogenarian (1816–1860)* (New York, 1896), p. 82; George G. Foster, *New York by Gas-Light*, p. 204; Alvin F. Harlow, *Old Bowery Days*, p. 42. See "The Soap-Locks" print by Nicholas Calyo, in Alvin F. Harlow, *Old Bowery Days*, p. 179.

20. Edwin Burrows and Mike Wallace, *Gotham*, pp. 758–760.

21. Tyler Anbinder, *Five Points*, p. 195; Susan Elizabeth Lyman, *The Story of New York: An Informal History of the City*, pp. 190, 806, 816.

22. Edward K. Spann, *Gotham at War*, pp. 109, 112, 22; Marc A. Hermann and Shaun C. Grenan (compilers), Impression, 11th New York Infantry (First Fire Zouaves), http://www.myrtle-avenue.com/firezou/impression.html.

23. *New York Times*, October 20, 1862, quoted in Drew Gilpin Faust, *The Republic of Suffering*, preface, p. xvii.

24. Ambrotype of Stephen Foster and George Cooper taken in New York 1863.

25. David Llewellyn Phillips, "Photography, Modernity, and Art," in *Nineteenth Century Art, a Critical History*, ed. Stephen F. Eisenman (London: Thames & Hudson, 2002).

26. Edwin Burrows and Mike Wallace, *Gotham*, pp. 872–884.

27. Matthew Hale Smith, *Sunshine and Shadow in New York* (Hartford, CT: J. B. Burr, 1869), pp. 213–214.

28. Mathew Hale Smith, *Sunshine and Shadow in New York*, pp. 217–218.

29. Letter from Jane Foster to Morrison Foster, October 1863, quoted in John Tasker Howard, *Stephen Foster: America's Troubadour*, p. 309.

30. Evelyn Morneweck, *Chronicles*, p. 553.

31. Jesse Welsh Rose to William H. Stevenson, July 7, 1926, Mifflin County Historical Society, Lewistown, PA; Evelyn Morneweck, *Chronicles*, pp. 541–542.

32. W. J. Rorabaugh, *The Alcoholic Republic* (New York: Oxford University Press, 1979), pp. 174–176.

33. Incident related in *The House of Industry Magazine*, 1857, quoted in Tyler Anbinder, *Five Points*, p. 220.

34. George W. Birdseye, "A Reminiscence of the Late Stephen C. Foster," p. 312.

35. Harold Vincent Milligan, *Stephen Collins Foster*, pp. 103–105.

36. Robert P. Nevin, "Memoir," 1867, quoted in Harold Vincent Milligan, *Stephen Collins Foster*, pp. 98–99.

37. William L. White, *Slaying the Dragon: The History of Addiction, Treatment, and Recovery in America* (Bloomington, IL: Chestnut Health Systems/

Lighthouse Institute, 1998), pp. 64–71, 95. For Jane's paying for cures, see Evelyn Morneweck, *Chronicles*, p. 177.

38. David Reynolds, *Walt Whitman's America* (New York: Vintage Press, 1995), pp. 93–96.

39. Edwin Burrows and Mike Wallace, *Gotham*, p. 776.

40. John W. Frick, *Theater, Culture and Temperance Reform in Nineteenth-Century America* (Cambridge: Cambridge University Press, 2003), pp. 128–129, 132–133, 135.

41. Steven Saunders and Deane L. Root, *The Music of Stephen C. Foster*, pp. 276–278.

42. Jessie Welsh Rose, "My Grandmother's Memories," *Pittsburgh Post*, July 4, 1926.

43. Letter from Jessie Welsh Rose to William Stevenson of Pittsburgh, July 7, 1926, Mifflin County Historical Society, Lewistown, PA. The Foster family connections through their deceased brother William may have had something to do with Jane's securing the job. The wife of J. Edgar Thomson, the president of the Pennsylvania Railroad, was the sister of brother William's second wife Elizabeth.

44. Les Standiford, *Meet You in Hell* (New York: Three Rivers Press, 2005), p. 40.

45. Joseph Frazier Wall, *Andrew Carnegie* (Pittsburgh: University of Pittsburgh Press, 1977), p. 162.

46. Stephen and Jane's granddaughter Jessie Welsh Rose in a letter to William Stevenson of Pittsburgh, July 7, 1926, states that her grandmother Jane continued to work in the telegraph office, even after she moved back to Pittsburgh. Courtesy of the Mifflin County Historical Society, Lewistown, PA.

47. Ken Beauchamp, *History of Telegraphy*, IEE History of Technology Series 26 (London: The Institute of Electrical Engineers, 2001); Barbara Myer Worthheimer, *We Were There: The Story of Working Women in America* (New York: Pantheon Books, 1977), pp. 235–238; Helen L Sumner, *History of Women in Industry in the United States* (New York: Arno Press, 1974), pp. 241–242.

48. John Tasker Howard, *Stephen Foster: America's Troubadour*, p. 296.

49. John Tasker Howard, *Stephen Foster: America's Troubadour*, p. 296.

50. John Tasker Howard, *Stephen Foster: America's Troubadour*, pp. 296–297.

51. John Tasker Howard, *Stephen Foster: America's Troubadour*, p. 311.

52. Steven Saunders and Deane L. Root, *The Music of Stephen C. Foster*.

20. ACCIDENTAL DEATH OR SUICIDE?

1. Hans Nathan, *Dan Emmett and the Rise of Early Negro Minstrelsy* (Norman: University of Oklahoma Press, 1962), p. 117. The North American Hotel address was given as 15 Bowery and more recently as 30-36 Bowery in Eric Ferrara's *The Bowery: A History of Grit, Graft and Grandeur*, p. 49. Quoted from William Ellis Horton's *Driftwood of the Stage*.

2. Letter from Henry Foster to Mrs. Susan G. Beach, January 23, 1864, quoted in John Tasker Howard, *Stephen Foster: America's Troubadour*, pp. 339–340.

3. Letter from Henry Foster to Ann Eliza, February 4, 1864, quoted by John Tasker Howard, *Stephen Foster: America's Troubadour*, pp. 339–340.

4. Morrison Foster, *My Brother Stephen*, p. 53.

5. Harold Vincent Milligan, *Stephen Collins Foster*, pp. 103–105.

6. Harold Vincent Milligan, *Stephen Collins Foster*, pp. 103–105.

7. John Tasker Howard, *Stephen Foster: America's Troubadour*, pp. 339–340.

8. Account is found in Evelyn Morneweck's *Chronicles of Stephen Foster's Family*, p. 558.

9. Ken Emerson, *Doo-dah! Stephen Foster and the Rise of American Popular Culture*, p. 298.

10. Evelyn Morneweck, *Chronicles*, pp. 557, 558.

11. Harold Vincent Milligan, *Stephen Collins Foster*, p.100.

12. Morrison Foster, *My Brother Stephen*, p. 53.

13. Robert I. Simon, M.D., "Naked Suicide," *The Journal of the American Academy of Psychiatry and the Law*, Vol. 36, No. 2, 2008, 240–245.

14. Robert I. Simon, M.D., "Naked Suicide," 240–245.

15. "Mrs. E. A. Parkhurst (Composer) Parkhurst's first song for Horace Waters was Funeral March to the Memory of Abraham Lincoln," published in 1865, JScholarship.library.jhu.edu.

16. John Tasker Howard, *Stephen Foster: America's Troubadour*, p. 333.

17. Effie Parkhurst Duer, "Personal Recollections of the Last Days of Foster," *Etude*, 1916, quoted in John Tasker Howard, *Stephen Foster: America's Troubadour*, p. 333.

18. John Tasker Howard, *Stephen Foster*: America's *Trouba*dour. p. 315.

19. George W. Birdseye, "A Reminiscence of the Late Stephen C. Foster," *Western Musical World*, January 1867, quoted in John Tasker Howard, *Stephen Foster*: America's *Troubadour*, p. 312.

20. John Mahon, "The Last Years of Stephen C. Foster," *New York Clipper*, March 1877. Song published by *Demorest's Illustrated Monthly*, quoted in John Tasker Howard, *Stephen Foster: America's Troubadour*, pp. 330–331.

21. Michael F. Holt, *Forging a Majority*, p. 172.

22. David Reynolds, *Walt Whitman's America*, pp. 331–332.

23. "The Alarming Increase of Suicides," *New York Times*, August 3, 1859.

24. Rhodes Study, "Suicide,"1876, from Howard I. Kushner, *Self-Destruction in the Promised Land: A Psychological Biology of American Suicide* (New Brunswick, NJ: Rutgers University Press, 1989), p. 106.

25. "A Melancholy Suicide," *New York Times*, October 2, 1863.

26. "Melancholy Suicide: A Book-Keeper Hangs Himself in His Room," *New York Times*, October 29, 1863.

27. "Suicide," *New York Times*, November 4, 1863.

28. "A Horrible Case of Suicide and Probably Murder," *New York Times*, July 27, 1863.

29. "Singular Case of Suicide," *New York Times*, January 10, 1863.

30. "Suicide," *New York Times*, July 13, 1863.

31. "Suicide," *New York Times*, September 18, 1863.

32. *Journal of Insanity*, 1849, quoted in Howard I. Kushner, *Self-Destruction in the Promised Land*.

33. Dr. Redford, quoted in Evelyn Morneweck, *Chronicles*, p. 93.

34. *New York Times* articles: "The Death of E. P. Christy," May 22, 1862; "Law Reports: The E. P. Christy Will Case—Christy's Body Exhumed, and Portions of It in Court," October 16, 1863. On May 4, 1865 the Surrogate, Hon. Gideon J. Tucker, considered "it to be proven that Mr. Christy gave intelligent directions for his will to his counsel, Mr. Clark, and actually executed it with the necessary formalities." "The E. P. Christy Will: Surrogate Court—May 4," *New York Times*, May 5, 1865.

35. Peter Quinn, *Banished Children of Eve*, p. 586.

36. Morrison Foster, *My Brother Stephen*, pp. 53–54.

37. From 1861 until Foster's death in January of 1864, the names Firth, Pond & Co., Wm. A. Pond & Co., and Firth, Son & Co. are found on Foster's song sheets less frequently than the names of publishers John J. Daly, Horace Waters, and S. T. Gordon. From Steven Saunders and Deane L. Root, *The Music of Stephen C. Foster*, Vol. 2.

38. Steven Saunders and Deane L. Root, *The Music of Stephen C. Foster*, Vol. 2, pp. 414–417.

39. Eliza Clayland Foster, "Sketches and Incidents of Pittsburgh."

40. Joshua Wolf Shenk, *Lincoln's Melancholy*, pp. 74–75, from Scott Sandage, *Born Losers: A History of Failure in America* (Cambridge: Harvard University Press, 2005).

41. George H. Pollock, "Childhood Parent and Sibling Loss in Adult Patients: A Comparative Study," pp. 77–78, quoted in Howard I. Kushner, *Self-Destruction in the Promised Land*, p. 139.

42. *Illinois State Journal*, January 8, 1853, from Joshua Wolf Shenk, *Lincoln's Melancholy*, p. 73; David Reynolds, *Walt Whitman's America*, pp. 112–113.

EPILOGUE

1. Edward Marks, *They All Sang*, p. 48.

2. Parker Zellers, *Tony Pastor: Dean of the Vaudeville Stage*, p. 24.

3. Armond Fields, *Tony Pastor, Father of Vaudeville*, pp. 44, 159.

4. Brooks McNamara, *New York Concert Saloons*, p. 53.

5. *San Francisco Evening Post*, July 20, 1878, quoted in Armond Fields, *Tony Pastor, Father of Vaudeville*, p. 90.

6. Paul Antoinie Distler, "Ethnic Comedy in Vaudeville and Burlesque," in *American Popular Entertainment: Papers and Proceedings of the Conference on the History of American Entertainment*, ed. Myron Matlaw (Westport, CT: Greenwood Press, 1979), pp. 36–37.

7. Robert Toll, "Show Biz in Blackface," in *American Popular Entertainment: Papers and Proceedings of the Conference on the History of American Popular Entertainment*, ed. Myron Matlaw, pp. 27, 30–31; Richard Crawford, *America's Musical Life* (New York: W. W. Norton, 2001), p. 487.

8. Richard Crawford, *America's Musical Life*, pp. 253, 487.

9. John Kenrick, "A History of the Musical Burlesque," Musicals 101, http://www.musicals101.com/burlesque.htm; Robert C. Allen, *Horrible Prettiness, Burlesque and American Culture* (Chapel Hill: University of North Carolina Press, 1991), p. 13.

10. Deane L. Root, *American Popular Stage Music, 1860–1880* (Ann Arbor, MI: UMI Research Press, 1977, 1981), Appendix A.

11. Deane L. Root, *American Popular Stage Music, 1860–1880*, Appendix A.

12. Samuel J. Rogal, "Gospel Hymns of Stephen Collins Foster," *Hymn*, Vol. 27, 1970, pp. 7–11, from Calvin Elliker, *Stephen Collins Foster*, p. 66.

13. Ed Harrigan continued to impersonate blacks in his otherwise mostly Irish shows. According to critic William Dean Howells, his stage portrayal of blacks was racist and unsympathetic: "All the Irish aspects of life are treated affectionately by the artist, as we might expect from one of his name; but the colored aspects do not fare so well under his touch. Not all the Irish are good Irish, but all the colored people are bad colored people. They are of the gloomy, razor-bearing variety; full of short-sighted lies and prompt dishonesties, amusing always, but truculent and tricky; and the sunny sweetness which we all know in negro character is not these." William Dean Howells, "Edward

Harrigan's Comedies," from the "Editor's Study," *Harper's New Monthly Magazine*, July, 1886, reprinted in *The American Theatre as Seen by Its Critics, 1752–1934*, ed. Montrose J. Moses and John Mason Brown (New York: W. W. Norton, 1934; New York: Cooper Square Publishers, 1967), p. 134.

14. Edward B. Marks, *They All Sang*, pp. 44–45.

15. Evelyn Morneweck, *Chronicles*, p. 564.

16. Jessie Welsh Rose to William H. Stevenson, July 7, 1926, courtesy of the Mifflin County Historical Society, Lewistown, PA.

17. Fletcher Hodges, *The Swanee River and a Biographical Sketch of Stephen Collins Foster* (Pittsburgh: University of Pittsburgh Press, 1996), p. 24; John Tasker Howard, *Stephen Foster: America's Troubadour*, pp. 350–351.

18. Jessie Welsh Rose to William H. Stevenson, Pittsburgh, July 7, 1926, Pittsburgh, PA. Courtesy of the Mifflin County Historical Society, Lewistown, Pennsylvania. Jessie Welsh Rose volunteered some stories that are unflattering to her grandfather Stephen Foster. Apparently, she was defensive about the negative image presented in the 1930s about her grandmother Jane. A movie version of the life of Stephen Foster produced in 1935 portrayed Jane as a shrew whose abandonment of the composer caused him to turn to alcohol and die in misery.

19. Evelyn Morneweck, *Chronicles*, pp. 567–568.

20. Steven Saunders and Deane L. Root, *The Music of Stephen C. Foster*, Vol. 2, pp. 237–241.

21. Foster Family Letters, Morrison Foster to I. J. Cust, February 27, 1865, C583; Letter from I. J. Cust to Morrison Foster March 1, 1865, C584; Letter from Morrison Foster to Robert Nevin, July 21, 1865, C473.

22. Evelyn Morneweck, *Chronicles*, pp. 561–562.

23. Harold Vincent Milligan, *Stephen Collins Foster*, Preface.

24. Robert Nevin, "Stephen C. Foster and Negro Minstrelsy," quoted in Morrison Foster, *My Brother Stephen*, p. 55.

BIBLIOGRAPHY

BOOKS

Aaron, Daniel. *Cincinnati, Queen City of the West, 1819–1838*. Columbus: Ohio State University, 1992.

Abrahams, Roger D., and John F. Szwed. *After Africa: Extracts from British Travel Accounts and Journals of the Seventeenth, Eighteenth, and Nineteenth Centuries concerning . . . the British West Indies*. New Haven, CT: Yale University Press, 1983.

Alcott, Louisa May. *Little Women*. New York: Sterling Publishing, 2004. Reprint of 1868.

Alquist, Karen. *Democracy at the Opera*. Urbana: University of Illinois Press, 1997.

Altschuler, Glenn C., and Stuart M. Blumin. *Rude Republic: Americans and Their Politics in the Nineteenth Century*. Princeton, NJ: Princeton University Press, 2000.

Anbinder, Tyler. *Five Points*. New York: The Free Press, 2001.

Applebaum, Diana Karter. *The Glorious Fourth: An American Holiday, an American History*. New York: Facts on File, 1989.

Appleby, Joyce Oldham. *Inheriting the Revolution: The First Generation of Americans*. Cambridge, MA: Belknap Press of Harvard University Press, 2000.

Ariès, Philippe. *The Hour of Our Death*. New York: Oxford University Press.

Attig, Thomas. *How We Grieve*. New York: Oxford University Press, 1996.

Austin, William W. *"Susanna," "Jeanie," and "The Old Folks at Home": The Songs of Stephen C. Foster from His Time to Ours*. Urbana: University of Illinois Press, 1989. Reprint of 1975.

Ayers, Edward L. *In the Presence of Mine Enemies: The Civil War in the Heart of America 1859–1863*. New York: W. W. Norton, 2003.

Baker, Elizabeth Faulkner. *Technology and Woman's Work*. New York: Columbia University Press, 1964.

Baker, Jean H. *James Buchanan*. The American Presidents Series. New York: Henry Holt, 2004.

Baker, Jean H. *Mary Todd Lincoln: A Biography*. New York: W. W. Norton, 1987.

Baldwin, Leland D. *Pittsburgh: The Story of a City*. Pittsburgh: University of Pittsburgh Press, 1938.

Bank, Rosemarie K. *Theatre Culture in America, 1825–1860*. Cambridge: Cambridge University Press, 1997.

Barnes, Charles B. *The Longshoremen*. New York: Survey Associates, 1915.

Bartlett, Virginia K. *Keeping House, Women's Lives in Western Pennsylvania 1790–1850*. Pittsburgh: University of Pittsburgh Press, 1994.

Bassett, Ancel Henry. *Concise History of the Methodist Protestant Church from Its Origins.* Pittsburgh: Press of Charles A. Scott, 1877.

Baynham, Edward. "History of Music in Pittsburgh 1758–1958." Unpublished manuscript. Pittsburgh: Carnegie Public Library in Oakland.

Bean, Annemarie, James V. Hatch, and Brooks McNamara, eds. *Inside the Minstrel Mask: Readings in Nineteenth-Century Blackface Minstrelsy.* Hanover, NH: Wesleyan University Press, 1996.

Beckert, Sven. *The Monied Metropolis.* Cambridge: Cambridge University Press, 1993.

Bender, Thomas. *Community and Social Change in America.* New Brunswick, NJ: Rutgers University Press, 1978.

Bendiner, Elmer. *The Bowery Man.* New York: Nelson, 1961.

Berkner, Michael, ed. *James Buchanan and the Political Crisis of the 1850s.* Selinsgrove, PA: Susquehanna University Press, 1996.

Bernstein, Iver. *The New York City Draft Riots.* New York: Oxford University Press, 1990.

Berwanger, Eugene H. *The Frontier against Slavery: Western Anti-Negro Prejudice and the Slavery Extension Controversy.* Urbana: University of Illinois Press, 1967.

Blocker, Jack S. *American Temperance Movements: Cycles of Reform.* Boston: Twayne Publishers, 1989.

Blondheim, Menahem. *News over the Wires: The Telegraph and the Flow of Public Information in America, 1844–1897.* Cambridge, MA: Harvard University Press, 1994.

Blumin, Stuart M. *Emergence of the Middle Class: Social Experience in the American City, 1760–1900.* Cambridge: Cambridge University Press, 1989.

Bode, Carl, ed. *American Life in the 1840s.* New York: New York University Press, 1967.

Bode, Carl, ed. *Midcentury America, Life in the 1850s.* Carbondale: Southern Illinois University Press, 1972.

Booraem, Hendrik. *The Formation of the Republican Party in New York: Politics and Conscience in the Antebellum North.* New York: New York University Press, 1983.

Bordewich, Fergus M. *Bound for Canaan: The Underground Railroad and the War for the Soul of America.* New York: HarperCollins, 2005.

Brands, H. W. *The Age of Gold.* New York: Doubleday, 2002.

Browder, Clifford. *The Wickedest Woman in New York; Madame Restell, the Abortionist.* Hamden, CT: Archon Books, 1998.

Brown, Herbert Ross. *The Sentimental Novel in America 1759–1860.* New York: Pageant Books, 1959.

Burns, Debra Brubaker. "The Eclectic Piano-Forte School of William Cumming Peters." *Journal of Historical Research in Music Education* Vol. 22, No.1, October 2000, pp. 25–37.

Burrows, Edwin G., and Mike Wallace. *Gotham: A History of New York City to 1898.* New York: Oxford University Press, 1999.

Burstein, Andrew. *America's Jubilee.* New York: Alfred A. Knopf, 2001.

Bushman, Richard L. *The Refinement of America.* New York: Alfred A. Knopf, 1992.

Butsch, Richard. *The Making of American Audiences, from Stage to Television, 1750–1990.* Cambridge: University of Cambridge Press, 2000.

Capers, Gerald M. *Stephen A. Douglas: Defender of the Union.* Boston: Little, Brown Publishers, 1959.

Capps, Randall. *The Rowan Story: From Federal Hill to My Old Kentucky Home.* Bowling Green, KY: Homestead Press, 1976.

Carlyon, David. *Dan Rice: The Most Famous Man You've Never Heard Of.* New York: Public Affairs, 2001.

Carter, Edward C. *Latrobe's View of America, 1795–1820.* New Haven, CT: Yale University Press, 1985.

Cawelti, John G. *Apostles of the Self-Made Man.* Chicago: University of Chicago Press, 1965.

Chaddock, Robert E. *Ohio Before 1850: A Study of the Early Influence of Pennsylvania and Southern Populations in Ohio.* New York: AMS Press, 1967.

Chambers, Bruce W. *The World of David Gilmore Blithe (1815–1865).* Washington, DC: Smithsonian Institute Press, 1990.

Chase, Gilbert. *America's Music: From the Pilgrims to the Present.* Urbana: University of Illinois Press, 1987.

Christy, Edwin Pierce. *Christy's Plantation Melodies.* Philadelphia: Fisher & Brother, 1851.

Cist, Charles. *Sketches and Statistics of Cincinnati in 1851.* Cincinnati: Wm. H. Moore, 1851.

Cockrell, Dale. "Nineteenth-Century Popular Music." In *The Cambridge History of Popular Music,* edited by David Nicholls. Cambridge: Cambridge University Press, 1998.

Cockrell, Dale. *Demons of Disorder: Early Blackface Minstrels and Their World.* Cambridge: Cambridge University Press, 1997.

Couvares, Francis G. *The Remaking of Pittsburgh: Class and Culture in an Industrializing City 1877–1919.* Albany: State University of New York Press, 1984.

Craig, Neville B. *The History of Pittsburgh.* Pittsburgh: J. R. Weldin, 1917. Reprint of 1851.

Crawford, Richard. "Blacks, Whites, and the Minstrel Stage." In *America's Musical Life: A History.* New York: W. W. Norton, 2001.

Craven, Avery O. *Civil War in the Making 1815–1860.* Baton Rouge: Louisiana State University Press, 1959.

Curls, James Stevens. *The Victorian Celebration of Death.* Detroit: Partridge Press, 1972.

Dahlinger, Charles W. *Pittsburgh: A Sketch of Its Early Social Life.* New York: G. P. Putnam's Sons, 1916.

Davies, Sam. *Dock Workers: International Exploration in Comparative Labor History,* Vols. 1 & 2. Aldershot, UK: Ashgate, 2000.

De Angelis, Barbara. *How Did I Get Here? Finding Your Way to Renewed Hope and Happiness When Life and Love Take Unexpected Turns.* New York: St. Martin's Press, 2005.

De Tocqueville, Alexis. *Democracy in America.* New York: Bantam Books, 2000. Reprint of 1835.

DiLorenzo, Thomas J. *The Real Lincoln: A New Look at Abraham Lincoln, His Agenda, and an Unnecessary War.* New York: Three Rivers Press, 2002.

Donald, David Herbert. *Lincoln.* New York: Simon & Schuster, 1995.

Dorsey, Florence L. *Master of the Mississippi: Henry Shreve and the Conquest of the Mississippi.* Boston: Houghton Mifflin, 1941.

Douglas, Ann. *The Feminization of American Culture.* New York: Anchor/Doubleday Press, 1988. Reprint of 1977.

Douglas, Ann. "Heaven Our Home: Consolation Literature in the Northern United States, 1830–1880." In *Death in America,* edited by David E. Stannard. Philadelphia: University of Pennsylvania Press, 1975.

Dumond, Dwight Lowell. *Antislavery Origins of the Civil War in the United States.* Ann Arbor: University of Michigan Press, 1939.

Dunaway, Wayland F. *The Scotch-Irish of Colonial Pennsylvania.* Chapel Hill: University of North Carolina Press, 1944.

Dunson, Stephanie Elaine. "The Minstrel in the Parlor: Nineteenth-Century Sheet Music and the Domestication of Blackface Minstrelsy." PhD diss., University of Massachusetts, Amherst, 2004.

Elliker, Calvin. *Stephen Collins Foster: A Guide to Research.* New York: Garland Publishing, 1988.

Ellis, Joseph P. *His Excellency: George Washington.* New York: Alfred A. Knopf, 2004.

Emerson, Ken. *Doo-Dah! Stephen Foster and the Rise of American Popular Culture.* New York: Simon & Schuster, 1997.

Emerson, Ralph Waldo. *Essays and Poems by Ralph Waldo Emerson.* Barnes & Noble Classics Series. New York: Barnes & Noble Books, 2004.

Engle, Gary D. *This Grotesque Essence: Plays from the American Minstrel Stage.* Baton Rouge: Louisiana State University Press, 1978.

Epstein, Barbara Leslie. *The Politics of Domesticity: Women, Evangelism, and Temperance in Nineteenth-Century America.* Middletown, CT: Wesleyan University Press, 1981.

Epstein, Dena J. *Sinful Tunes and Spirituals, Black Folk Music to the Civil War.* Urbana: University of Illinois Press, 1977.

Faust, Drew Gilpin. *The Creation of Confederate Nationalism: Ideology and Identity in the Civil War South*. Baton Rouge: Louisiana State University Press, 1988.

Faust, Drew Gilpin. *The Republic of Suffering*. New York: Alfred A. Knopf, 2008.

Feeney, Leonard. *Mother Seton: Saint Elizabeth of New York (1774–1821)*. Cambridge, MA: Ravengate Press, 1975.

Ferguson, Eugene A. *Oliver Evans: Inventive Genius of the American Industrial Revolution*. Greenville, DE: Hagley Museum, 1980.

Filler, Louis. *Crusade against Slavery: Friends, Foes, and Reforms 1820–1860*. Algonac, MI: Reference Publications, 1986.

Finson, Jon W. *The Voices That Are Gone: Themes in 19th-Century American Popular Song*. New York: Oxford University Press, 1994.

Fleming, George Thornton. *History of Pittsburgh and Environs*. Vol. 2. New York: American Historical Society, 1922.

Foner, Eric. *Free Soil, Free Labor, Free Men: The Ideology of the Republican Party before the Civil War*. New York: Oxford University Press, 1995. Reprint of 1970.

Ford, Henry A., and Kate B. Ford. *History of Cincinnati, Ohio, with Illustrations and Biographical Sketches*. Cincinnati, OH: Ohio Book Store, 1987. Reprint of 1881.

Foster, George G. *New York by Gas-Light and Other Urban Sketches*. Edited by Stuart M. Blumin. Los Angeles: University of California Press, 1990. Reprint of 1856.

Foster, Morrison. *My Brother Stephen*. Indianapolis: privately printed, 1932.

Frederickson, George M. *The Black Image in the White Mind: The Debate on Afro-American Character and Destiny 1817–1914*. Middletown, CT: Wesleyan University Press, 1971.

Freud, Sigmund. *General Psychological Theory*. New York: Simon & Schuster, 1997.

Frick, John W. *Theater, Culture and Temperance Reform in Nineteenth-Century America*. Cambridge: Cambridge University Press, 2003.

Friedman, Lawrence M. *History of American Law*. New York: Simon & Schuster, 1985. Reprint of 1973.

Gallagher, William D. *Facts and Conditions of Progress in the North-West*. Cincinnati, OH: H. W. Derby, 1850.

Gallagher, William D. *Miami Woods, A Golden Wedding, and Other Poems*. Cincinnati, OH: Robert Clarke, 1881.

Gallant, Christine. *Keats and Romantic Celticism*. Basingstoke, UK: Palgrave MacMillan, 2005.

Giamo, Benedict. *On the Bowery: Confronting Homelessness in American Society*. Iowa City: University of Iowa Press, 1989.

Gilbert, Douglas. *American Vaudeville: Its Life and Times*. New York: Dover Publications, 1940.

Gilernter, Mark. *A History of American Architecture and Buildings in Their Cultural and Technological Context*. Hanover, NH: University Press of New England, 1999.

Glazer, Lee, and Susan Key. "Carry Me Back: Nostalgia for the Old South in Nineteenth-Century Popular Culture." *Journal of American Studies* Vol. 30, No. 1, April 1996, pp. 1–24.

Glazer, Walter Stix. *Cincinnati in 1840*. Columbus: Ohio State University Press, 1999.

Goff, Jenny Lightweis. "'Long Time I Trabble on de Way': Stephen Foster's Conversion Narrative." *Journal of Popular Music Studies* Vol. 20, No. 2, June 2008, pp. 150–65.

Goldstein, Jeffrey H., and Paul E. McGhee, eds. *The Psychology of Humor*. New York: Academic Press, 1972.

Gordon, John Steele. *An Empire of Wealth*. New York: HarpersCollins, 2004.

Grant, John, James Lynch, and Ronald Bailey. *West Point: The First 200 Years*. Guilford, CT: Globe Pequot Press, 2002.

Gray, Wood. *The Hidden Civil War: The Story of the Copperheads*. New York: Viking Press, 1942.

Hagedorn, Ann. *Beyond the River: The Untold Story of the Heroes of the Underground Railroad*. New York: Simon & Schuster, 2002.

Haight, Gordon S. *Mrs. Sigourney: The Sweet Singer of Hartford*. New Haven, CT: Yale University Press, 1930.

Haines, Kathryn Miller. "Stephen Foster's Music in Motion Pictures and Television." *American Music* Vol. 30, No. 3, Fall 2012, pp. 373–88.

Halttunen, Karen. *Confidence Men and Painted Women: A Study of Middle-Class Culture in America 1830–1870.* New Haven, CT: Yale University Press, 1982.

Hamm, Charles. "Review of *The Music of Stephen C. Foster: A Critical Edition.*" *Journal of the American Musicological Society* Vol. 45, No. 3, Autumn 1992, pp. 515–26.

Hamm, Charles. *Yesterdays: Popular Song in America.* New York: W. W. Norton, 1979.

Harlow, Alvin F. *Old Bowery Days: The Chronicles of a Famous Street.* New York: D. Appleton, 1931.

Haswell, Charles H. *Reminiscences of New York by an Octogenarian (1816–1860).* New York, 1896.

Hedrick, Joan D. *Harriet Beecher Stowe: A Life.* New York: Oxford University Press, 1994.

Heimbinder, Murray E. "Northern Men with Southern Principles: A Study of the Dough-faces of New York and New England." PhD diss., New York University, 1971.

Henneke, Ben Graf. *Laura Keene: A Biography.* Tulsa, OK: Council Oak Books, 1990.

Hershkowitz, Leo. *Tweed's New York: Another Look.* Garden City, NY: Anchor Press, 1977.

Hodge, Francis. *Yankee Theater: The Image of America on the Stage 1825–1850.* Austin: University of Texas Press, 1964.

Hodges, Fletcher. *Stephen Foster, Democrat.* Pittsburgh: University of Pittsburgh Press, 1946.

Hodges, Fletcher. *The Swanee River and a Biographical Sketch of Stephen Collins Foster.* Pittsburgh: University of Pittsburgh Press, 1996.

Holt, Michael Fitzgibbon. *Forging a Majority: The Formation of the Republican Party in Pittsburgh 1848–1860.* New Haven, CT: Yale University Press, 1969.

Homberger, Eric. *Scenes from the Life of a City: Corruption and Conscience in Old New York.* New Haven, CT: Yale University Press, 1994.

Horowitz, Helen Lefkowitz. *Rereading Sex.* New York: Alfred A. Knopf, 2002.

Horwitz, Morton. *The Transformation of American Law, 1780–1860.* New York: Oxford University Press, 1992.

Hovland, Carl I., and Robert R. Sears. "Minor Studies of Aggression: Correlation of Lynch-ings with Economic Indices." *Journal of Psychology* Vol. 9, No. 2, 1940, pp. 66–73.

Howard, John Tasker. "Newly Discovered Fosteriana." *The Musical Quarterly* Vol. 21, No.1, January 1935, pp. 17–24.

Howard, John Tasker. *Stephen Foster: America's Troubadour.* New York: Thomas Y. Crowell 1962. Reprint of 1934.

Howard, John Tasker. "Stephen Foster and His Publishers." *The Musical Quarterly* Vol. 20, No. 1, January 1934, pp. 77–95.

Hume, David. *Treatise of Human Nature.* Oxford: Clarendon Press, 1967. Reprint of 1740.

Huneker, James. *Overtones.* New York: Charles Scribner's Sons, 1904.

Hutchinson, John Wallace. *Story of the Hutchinsons (Tribe of Jess).* Boston: Da Capo Press, 1977. Reprint of 1896.

Ignatiev, Noel. *How the Irish Became White.* New York: Routledge Press, 1995.

Jackson, George Pullen. "Stephen Foster's Debt to American Folk-Song." *The Musical Quarterly* Vol. 22, No. 2, April 1936, pp. 154–69.

Jaffa, Harry V. *A New Birth of Freedom: Abraham Lincoln and the Coming of the Civil War.* Lanham, MD: Rowman & Littlefield Publishers, 2000.

Jenkins, Clare, and Judy Merry. *Relative Grief: Parents and Children, Sisters and Brothers, Husbands, Wives and Partners, Grandparents and Grandchildren Talk about Their Experience of Death and Grieving.* Philadelphia: Jessica Kingsley Publishers, 2005.

Johnson, Claudia D. "That Guilty Third Tier: Prostitution in Nineteenth-Century American Theaters." *Victorian America,* edited by Daniel Walker Howe. Philadelphia: University of Pennsylvania Press, 1976.

Johnson, Stephen, ed. *Burnt Cork: Traditions and Legacies of Blackface Minstrelsy.* Am-herst: University of Massachusetts Press, 2012.

Johnston, William G. *Life and Reminiscences from Birth to Manhood of Wm. G. Johnston.* New York: Knickerbocker Press, 1901.

Jones, Howard Mumford. *The Harp that Once—: A Chronicle of the Life of Thomas Moore.* New York: Henry Holt, 1937.

Jones, Samuel. *Pittsburgh in the Year Eighteen Hundred and Twenty-Six.* New York: Arno Press, 1970. Reprint of 1826.

Karrer, Wolfgang. "Cross-Dressing between Travesty and Parody." In *Parody: Dimensions and Perspectives,* edited by Beate Müller. Amsterdam, Netherlands: Rodopi, 1997.

Kasson, John F. *Rudeness & Civility: Manners in Nineteenth-Century Urban America.* New York: Hill and Wang, 1990.

Keene, James A. *A History of Music Education in the United States.* Hanover, NH: University Press of New England, 1982.

Kennedy, Billy. *The Scots-Irish in Pennsylvania & Kentucky.* Belfast, Northern Ireland: Ambassador Publications, 1998.

Kerber, Linda K., and Jane Sherron De Hart, eds. *Women's America: Refocusing the Past.* New York: Oxford University Press, 1991.

Kete, Mary Louise. *Sentimental Collaborations: Mourning and Middle-Class Identity in Nineteenth-Century America.* Durham, NC: Duke University Press, 2000.

Key, Susan. "'Forever in Our Ears:' Nature, Voice, and Sentiment in Stephen Foster's Parlor Style." *American Music* Vol. 30, No. 3, Fall 2012, pp. 290–307.

Kidney, Walter C. *Allegheny Cemetery: A Romantic Landscape in Pittsburgh.* Pittsburgh: Pittsburgh History and Landmarks Foundations, 1990.

Kiple, Kenneth F., ed. *Plague, Pox, & Pestilence.* London: Barnes & Noble Books, 1997.

Klammer, Martin. *Whitman, Slavery, and the Emergence of* Leaves of Grass. University Park: Pennsylvania State University Press, 1995.

Klein, Philip Shriver. *President James Buchanan: A Biography.* University Park: The Pennsylvania State University, 1962.

Klement, Frank L. *The Copperheads in the Middle West.* Chicago: University of Chicago Press, 1960.

Klement, Frank L. *The Limits of Dissent: Clement L. Vallandigham & the Civil War.* Lexington: University Press of Kentucky, 1970.

Kohn Jr., E. J. *The Merry Partners: The Age and Stage of Harrigan and Hart.* New York: Random House, 1955.

Kornblith, Gary J. "Rethinking the Coming of the Civil War: A Counterfactual Exercise." *The Journal of American History* Vol. 90, No.1, June 2003, pp. 76–105.

Krehbiel, Henry Edward. *Afro-American Folksongs: A Study in Racial and National Music.* New York: G. Schirmer, 1914.

Kushner, Howard I. *Self-Destruction in the Promised Land: A Psychological Biology of American Suicide.* New Brunswick, NJ: Rutgers University Press, 1989.

Lair, John, and William H. Townsend. *Songs Lincoln Loved: Words and Music of Abraham Lincoln's Favorite Ballads . . . and Others.* New York: Duell, Sloan, and Pearce, 1954.

Lane, Roger. *Violent Death in the City: Suicide, Accident, and Murder in Nineteenth-Century Philadelphia.* Cambridge, MA: Harvard University Press, 1979.

Lankevich, George J. *American Metropolis: A History of New York City.* New York: New York University Press, 1998.

Larsen, Arthur J. *Crusader and Feminist: Letters of Jane Gray Swisshelm, 1858–1865.* Saint Paul: Minnesota Historical Society, 1934.

LeBeau, Bryan F. *Currier & Ives: America Imagined.* Washington, DC: Smithsonian Institute Press, 2001.

Levine, Robert S. *Martin Delany, Frederick Douglass, and the Politics of Representative Identity.* Chapel Hill: University of North Carolina, 1997.

Lewis, Mathew Gregory. *Journal of a West India Proprietor* (London, 1834). In *After Africa: Extracts from British Travel Accounts and Journals of the Seventeenth, Eighteenth, and Nineteenth Centuries concerning . . . the British West Indies,* edited by Roger D. Abrahams and John F. Szwed. New Haven, CT: Yale University Press, 1983.

Lewis, Robert E., ed. *From Traveling Shows to Vaudeville.* Baltimore: Johns Hopkins University Press, 2003.

Lhamon, W. T. *Jump Jim Crow: Lost Plays, Lyrics, and Street Prose of the First Atlantic Popular Culture*. Cambridge, MA: Harvard University Press, 2003.

Licht, Walter. *Industrializing America: The Nineteenth Century*. Baltimore and London: John Hopkins University Press, 1995.

Litwack, Leon. *North of Slavery: The Negro in the Free States, 1790–1860*. Chicago: University of Chicago Press, 1961.

Loesser, Arthur. *Men, Women and Pianos*. Mineola, NY: Dover Publications, 1990.

Lorant, Stefan. *Pittsburgh: The Story of an American City*. Pittsburgh: Esselmont Books, 1999.

Lott, Eric. *Love & Theft: Blackface Minstrelsy and the American Working Class*. New York: Oxford University Press, 1995.

Lyman, Susan Elizabeth. *The Story of New York: An Informal History of the City from the First Settlement to the Present Day*. New York: Crown Publishers, 1975.

MacKenzie, Henry. *The Man of Feeling*. Introduction by Brian Vickers. New York: Oxford University Press, 1967. Reprint of 1771.

Mahar, William J. *Behind the Burnt Cork Mask*. Urbana: University of Illinois Press, 1999.

Maizlish, Stephen E., ed. *Essays on American Antebellum Politics, 1840–1860*. College Station: Texas A&M University Press, 1982.

Mansfield, Edward Deering. *Personal Memories: Social, Political, and Literary, with Sketches of Many Noted People 1803–1843*. Cincinnati, OH: William Clark, 1879.

Marks, Edward. *They All Sang: From Tony Pastor to Rudy Vallée*. New York: The Viking Press, 1935.

Martin, Scott C. *Cultural Change and the Market Revolution in America, 1789–1860*. Lanham, MD: Rowan & Littlefield Publishers, 2005.

Martin, Scott C. *Killing Time: Leisure and Culture in Southwestern Pennsylvania, 1800–1850*. Pittsburgh: University of Pittsburgh Press, 1995.

Marx, Leo. *The Machine in the Garden: Technology and the Pastoral Ideal in America*. New York: Oxford University Press, 1964.

Matlaw, Myron., ed. *Nineteenth Century American Plays*. New York: Applause Theater Books, 2001.

Mayer, Henry. *All on Fire: William Lloyd Garrison and the Abolition of Slavery*. New York: St. Martin's Press, 1998.

McCabe, James Dabney. *The Secrets of the Great City*, 1872.

McCabe, James Dabney. *Lights and Shadows of New York*, 1868.

McCall, Edith. *Conquering the Rivers: Henry Miller Shreve and the Navigation of America's Inland Waterways*. Baton Rouge: Louisiana State University Press, 1984.

McConachie, Bruce A. *Melodramatic Formations: American Theatre and Society, 1820–1870*. Iowa City: University of Iowa Press, 1992.

McDannell, Colleen, and Bernhard Land. *Heaven: A History*. New York: Yale University Press, 1988.

McDougall, Walter A. *Throes of Democracy: the American Civil War Era 1829–1877*. New York: HarperCollins Publishers, 2008.

McKay, Ernest A. *The Civil War and New York City*. Syracuse, NY: Syracuse University Press, 1990.

McNamara, Brooks. *The New York Concert Saloon*. New York: Cambridge University Press, 2002.

Mellon, Thomas. *Thomas Mellon and His Times*. Pittsburgh: University of Pittsburgh Press, 1994. Reprint of 1885.

Menand, Louis. *The Metaphysical Club*. New York: Farrar, Straus and Giroux, 2001.

Merish, Lori. *Sentimental Materialism: Gender, Commodity Culture, and Nineteenth-Century American Literature*. Durham, NC: Duke University Press, 2000.

Meserve, Walter J. *Heralds of Promise: The Drama of the American People during the Age of Jackson, 1829–1849*. Westport, CT: Greenwood Press, 1986.

Meyers, Jeffrey. *Edgar Allan Poe: His Life and Legacy*. New York: Charles Scribner's Sons, 1992.

Middleton, Stephen. *Ohio and the Antislavery Activities of Attorney Salmon Portland Chase, 1830–1849.* New York: Garland Publishing, 1990.

Milligan, Harold Vincent. *Stephen Collins Foster: A Biography of America's Folk-Song Composer.* New York: G. Schirmer, 1920.

Minois, Georges. *History of Suicide: Voluntary Death in Western Culture.* Baltimore: Johns Hopkins Press, 1999.

Morley, John. *Death, Heaven and the Victorians.* Pittsburgh: University of Pittsburgh Press, 1971.

Morneweck, Evelyn Foster. *Chronicles of Stephen Foster's Family*, Vol. 1 and 2. Pittsburgh: University of Pittsburgh Press, 1944.

Morton, Samuel George, Josiah Clark Nott, and George R. Gliddon. *Types of Mankind: Or, Ethnological Researches.* Philadelphia: Lippencott, Gambo, 1854.

Mushkat, Jerome. *Fernando Wood: A Political Biography.* Kent, OH: Kent State University Press, 1990.

Nathan, Hans. *Dan Emmett and the Rise of Early Negro Minstrelsy.* Norman: University of Oklahoma Press, 1962.

Nelson, Bruce. "Ethnicity, Race, and the Logic of Solidarity: Dock Workers in International Perspective." *Dock Workers: International Exploration in Comparative Labor History, 1790–1970.* Burlington, VT: Ashgate Publishing, 2000.

Nevin, Robert Peebles. "Stephen C. Foster and Negro Minstrelsy." *Atlantic Monthly.* November 1867.

Niven, John. *Salmon P. Chase: A Biography.* New York: Oxford University Press, 1995.

Noble, Louis Legrand. *The Life and Works of Thomas Cole.* Hensonville, NY: Black Dome Press, 1964.

Osborne, William. *Music in Ohio.* Kent, OH: Kent State University Press, 2004.

Perkin, Joan. *Victorian Women.* Washington Square, NY: New York University Press, 1993.

Pearsall, Ronald. *Victorian Sheet Music Covers.* Detroit, MI: Gale Research, 1970.

Pessen, Edward. *Jacksonian America: Society, Personality, and Politics.* Urbana: University of Illinois Press, 1985. Reprint of 1969.

Pessen, Edward, ed. *The Many-Faceted Jacksonian Era.* Westport, CT: Greenwood Press, 1977.

Phillips, David Llewellyn. "Photography, Modernity, and Art." In *Nineteenth Century Art: A Critical History*, edited by Stephen F. Eisenmann. London: Thames & Hudson, 2002.

Plante, Ellen M. *Women at Home in Victorian America: A Social History.* New York: Facts on File, 1997.

Powers, Madelon. *Faces along the Bar: Lore and Order in the Workingman's Saloon, 1870-1920.* Chicago, University of Chicago Press, 1998.

Purdy, Claire Lee. *He Heard America Sing: The Story of Stephen Foster.* New York: Julian Messner, 1940.

Quinn, Peter. *Banished Children of Eve.* New York: Viking Penguin, 1994.

Reiser, Catherine Elizabeth. *Pittsburgh's Commercial Development, 1800–1850.* Harrisburg, PA: Pennsylvania Historical and Museum Commission, 1951.

Reynolds, David. *Walt Whitman's America.* New York: Vintage Books, 1995.

Riis, Thomas L. "The Music and Musicians in Nineteenth-Century Productions of *Uncle Tom's Cabin*." *American Music Vol.* 4, No. 3, Autumn 1986, pp. 268–86.

Rice, Edward Le Roy. *Monarchs of Minstrelsy, from Daddy Rice to Date.* New York: Kenney Publishing, 1911.

Robertson, James I. *Soldiers Blue and Gray.* Columbia: University of South Carolina Press, 1988.

Rock, Howard B., and Deborah D. Moore. *City Scapes: A History of New York in Images.* New York: Columbia University Press, 2001.

Rodger, Gillian M. *Champagne Charlie and Pretty Jemima: Variety Theater in the Nineteenth Century.* Urbana: University of Illinois Press, 2010.

Rogal, Samuel J. "Gospel Hymns of Stephen Collins Foster." *Hymn* Vol. 27, 1970, pp. 7–11.

Rooney, Dan, and Carol Peterson. *Allegheny City: A History of Pittsburgh's North Side.* Pittsburgh: University of Pittsburgh Press, 2013.

Root, Deane L. *American Popular Stage Music, 1860–1880*. Ann Arbor, MI: UMI Research Press, 1977, 1981.

Root, Deane L. "Myth and Stephen Foster." *Carnegie Magazine* Vol 67, No. 7, January-February 1987.

Root, Deane L. "The 'Mythtory' of Stephen C. Foster or Why His True Story Remains Untold." *American Music Research Center Journal* Vol. 1, 1991, pp. 20–36.

Roper, Laura Wood. *FLO: A Biography of Frederick Law Olmsted*. Baltimore: Johns Hopkins University Press, 1973.

Rorabaugh, W. J. *The Alcoholic Republic*. New York: Oxford University Press, 1979.

Rosebloom, Eugene H., and Francis P. Weisenburger. *A History of Ohio*. Columbus: The Ohio State Archaeological and Historical Society, 1958.

Rosenberg, Charles E. *The Cholera Years: The United States in 1832, 1849, and 1866*. Chicago: University of Chicago Press, 1987. Reprint of 1962.

Rosenblatt, Paul C. *Parent Grief: Narratives of Loss and Relationship*. Philadelphia: Brunner/Mazel, 2000.

Rothman, Ellen K. *Hands and Hearts: A History of Courtship in America*. New York: Basic Books, 1984.

Rowson, Mrs. *The History of Charlotte Temple: A Tale of Youth*. Philadelphia, 1794.

Rubin, Lester. *The Negro in the Longshore Industry*. Philadelphia: The Wharton School, University of Pennsylvania Press, 1974.

Rudwick, Bracey Meier. *Free Blacks in America, 1800–1860*. Belmont, CA: Wadsworth Publishing, 1971.

Russell, Henry. *Cheer! Boys, Cheer!* London: John Macqueen, 1895.

Russell, Maud. *Man along the Shore*. New York: Brussel & Brussel, 1966.

Ryan, Mary P. *Cradle of the Middle Class*. Cambridge: Cambridge University Press, 1981.

Sacks, Howard L. "From the Barn to the Bowery and Back Again: Musical Routes in Rural Ohio, 1800–1929 [Phillips Barry Lecture, October 2000]." *The Journal of American Folklore* Vol. 116, No. 461, Summer 2003, pp. 314–38.

Sandage, Scott A. *Born Losers: A History of Failure in America*. Cambridge, MA: Harvard University Press, 2005.

Sanjek, Russell. *American Popular Music and Its Business: The First Four Hundred Years*. Vol. 2. New York: Oxford University Press, 1988.

Saum, Lewis O. *The Popular Mood of Pre–Civil War America*. Westport, CT: Greenwood Press, 1980.

Saunders, Steven. "The Social Agenda of Stephen Foster's Plantation Melodies." *American Music* Vol. 30, No. 3, Fall 2012, pp. 275–89.

Saunders, Steven. "Stephen Foster and His Publishers, Revisited." *College Music Symposium* Vol. 28, 1988, pp. 53–69.

Saunders, Steven, and Deane L. Root, eds. *The Music of Stephen C. Foster: A Critical Edition*. Vols. 1 and 2. Washington, DC: Smithsonian Institution Press, 1990.

Schlesinger, Arthur M. *The Age of Jackson*. Old Saybrook, CT: Konecky & Konecky, 1945, 1971.

Scully, Cornelius D. *Story of Old Allegheny City*. Pittsburgh: Allegheny City Society, 1994. Reprint of 1941.

Sedikides, Constantine, Tim Wildschut, Clay Routledge, Jamie Arndt, Erica G. Hepper, and Xinyue Zhou. "To Nostalgize: Mixing Memory and Affect and Desire." *Advances in Experimental Psychology*, Vol. 51, No. 1, 2014, pp. 1–79. Available online.

Semmes, John E. *John H. B. Latrobe and His Times, 1803–1891*. Baltimore: Norman, Remmington, 1917.

Shaftel, Matthew. "Singing a New Song: Stephen Foster and the New American Minstrelsy" [Adapted from a talk presented at the Society for Music Theory and American Musicological Society in November, 2002]. *Music and Politics* Vol. 1, No. 2, 2007, pp. 1–26.

Shenk, Joshua Wolf. *Lincoln's Melancholy*. Boston: Houghton Mifflin, 2005.

Shiras, George III. *Justice George Shiras of Pittsburgh*. Pittsburgh: University of Pittsburgh Press, 1953.

Shultz, Gladys Denny. *Jenny Lind: The Swedish Nightingale*. Philadelphia: F. B. Lippincott, 1962.

Silverman, Kenneth. *Lightning Man: The Accursed Life of Samuel F. B. Morse*. New York: Alfred A. Knopf, 2003.

Simmons, James C. *Star-Spangled Eden, 19th Century America through the Eyes of Dickens, Wilde, Frances Trollope, Frank Harris, and Other British Travelers*. New York: Carroll & Graf Publishers, 2000.

Simon, Kate. *Fifth Avenue: A Very Social History*. New York: Harcourt, Brace, Jovanovich, 1978.

Simon, Robert I. "Naked Suicide." *Journal of American Academy of Psychiatry and the Law Online* Vol. 36, No. 2, 2008, pp. 240–45. http://www.jaapl.org/cgi/content/full/36/2/240.

Sklar, Kathryn Kish. *Catherine Beecher: A Study in American Domesticity*. New York: W. W. Norton, 1976.

Slout, William L., ed. *Broadway Below the Sidewalk, Concert Saloons of Old New York*. San Bernardino, CA: R. Reginald, The Borgo Press, 1994.

Smith, Dennis. *Dennis Smith's History of Firefighting in America: 300 Years of Courage*. New York: The Dial Press, 1978.

Smith, Matthew Hale. *Sunshine and Shadow in New York*. Hartford, CT: J. B. Burr, 1869.

Sobel, Bernard. *A Pictorial History of Vaudeville*. New York: Citadel Press, 1961.

Southern, Eileen. *The Music of Black Americans: A History*. New York: W. W. Norton, 1971.

Spann, Edward K. *Gotham at War*. Wilmington, DE: Scholarly Resources, 2002.

Spann, Edward K. *The New Metropolis: New York City, 1840–1857*. New York: Columbia University Press, 1981.

Spero, Sterling D., and Abram L. Harris. *The Black Worker*. New York: Atheneum, 1968.

Spillane, Daniel. *History of the American Pianoforte: Its Technical Development and the Trade*. New York: D. Spillane Publishers, 1890.

Springhall, John. *The Genesis of Mass Culture: Show Business Live in America, 1840–1940*. New York: Palgrave Macmillan, 2008.

Stampp, Kenneth M. *America in 1857: America on the Brink*. New York: Oxford University Press, 1990.

Standiford, Les. *Meet You in Hell: Andrew Carnegie, Henry Clay Frick, and the Bitter Partnership that Transformed America*. New York: Three Rivers Press, 2005.

Stannard, David E. *Death in America*. Philadelphia: University of Pennsylvania Press, 1975.

Stanton, William. *The Leopard's Spots: Scientific Attitudes toward Race in America, 1815–59*. Chicago: The University of Chicago Press, 1960.

Starke, Catherine Juanita. *Black Portraiture in American Fiction*. New York: Basic Books, 1971.

Starr, Larry, and Christopher Waterman. *American Popular Music: From Minstrelsy to MP3*. New York: Oxford University Press, 2010.

Stauffer, John. *Giants: The Parallel Lives of Frederick Douglass and Abraham Lincoln*. New York: Twelve Hachette Book Group, 2008.

Sterling, Dorothy. *The Making of an Afro-American: Martin Robison Delany, 1812–1885*. New York: Da Capo Press, 1971.

Stone, Geoffrey R. *Perilous Times: Free Speech in Wartime—From the Sedition Act of 1798 to the War on Terrorism*. New York: W. W. Norton, 2004.

Stowe, Harriet Beecher. *Uncle Tom's Cabin*. New York: Barnes & Noble Books, 2004. Reprint of 1852.

Strong, George Templeton. *The Diary of George Temple Strong*, eds. Allan Nevins and Milton Halsey Thomas. Abridged by Thomas J. Pressly. Seattle: University of Washington Press, 1988.

Tawa, Nicholas E. *Sweet Songs for Gentle Americans: The Parlor Song in America, 1790–1860*. Bowling Green, OH: Bowling Green University Popular Press, 1980.

Tawa, Nicholas E. *The Way to Tin Pan Alley: American Popular Song 1866–1910*. New York: Schirmer Books, 1990.

Thackeray, William Makepeace. *Vanity Fair*. New York: Dodd, Meade, (reprint)1943.

Thomas, Benjamin P. *Theodore Weld: Crusader for Freedom*. New Brunswick, NJ: Rutgers University Press, 1950.

Thomas, Clarke M. *Front-Page Pittsburgh: Two Hundred Years of the Post-Gazette*. Pittsburgh: University of Pittsburgh Press, 2005.

Thoreau, Henry David. *Walden*. New York: Barnes & Noble Books, 2004. Reprint of 1847.

Tick, Judith. *American Women Composers before 1870*. Ann Arbor, MI: UMI Research Press, 1983.

Tierney, John. "What Is Nostalgia Good For? Quite a Bit, Research Shows." *New York Times*, Science, July 8, 2013. www.nytimes.com/2013/07/09/science/what-is-nostalgia-good-for-quite-a-bit-research-shows.html?pagewanted=all. Based on research by Constantine Sedikides of University of Southampton.

Toll, Robert C. *Blacking Up: The Minstrel Show in Nineteenth-Century America*. New York: Oxford University Press, 1974.

Toll, Robert C. *On with the Show! The First Century of Show Business in America*. New York: Oxford University Press, 1976.

Trollope, Frances. *Domestic Manners of the Americans*. New York: Vintage Books, 1949, reprint from 1827.

Van Deburg, William L. *Slavery & Race in American Popular Culture*. Madison: University of Wisconsin Press, 1984.

Voegeli, V. Jacque. *Free but Not Equal: The Midwest and the Negro during the Civil War*. Chicago: University of Chicago Press, 1967.

Wade, Richard C. *The Urban Frontier: The Rise of Western Cities, 1790–1930*. Urbana: University of Illinois Press, 1996.

Wall, Joseph Frazier. *Andrew Carnegie*. Pittsburgh: University of Pittsburgh Press, 1989. Reprint of 1970.

Walters, Raymond. *Stephen Foster, Youth's Golden Gleam: A Sketch of His Life and Background in Cincinnati, 1846–1850*. Princeton, NJ: Princeton University Press, 1936.

Walther, Eric H. *The Shattering of the Union: America in the 1850s*. Wilmington, DE: Scholarly Resources, 2004.

Watkins, Mel. *On the Real Side: Laughing, Lying, and Signifying*. New York: Simon & Schuster, 1994.

Waugh, John C. *The Class of 1846: From West Point to Appomattox*. New York: Warner Books, 1994.

Wesley, Charles H. *Negro Labor in the United States 1850–1925*. New York: Russell & Russell, 1967. Reprint of 1927.

Wetzel, Richard D. *"Oh! Sing No More That Gentle Song": The Musical Life and Times of William Cumming Peters (1805–66)*. Warren, MI: Harmonie Park Press, 2000.

White, William L. *Slaying the Dragon: The History of Addiction Treatment and Recovery in America*. Bloomington, IL: Chestnut Health Systems/Lighthouse Institute, 1998.

Whitmer, Mariana, and Deane Root. "Editors' Introduction." *American Music* Vol. 30, No. 3, Fall 2012, pp. 269–74.

Whitmer, Mariana. "Songs of Social Significance: An Introduction." *OAH Magazine of History* Vol. 19, No. 4, July 2005, pp. 9–16.

Williams, Raymond. *Culture and Society, 1780–1950*. New York: Columbia University Press, 1960.

Winans, Robert B. "Early Minstrel Music 1843–1852." In *Inside the Minstrel Mask: Readings in Nineteenth-Century Blackface Minstrelsy: Readings in Nineteenth-Century Blackface Minstrelsy*, edited by Annemarie Bean, James V. Hatch, and Brooks McNamara. Middletown, CT: Wesleyan University Press, 1996.

Wineapple, Brenda. *Hawthorne: A Life*. New York: Alfred A. Knopf, 2003.

Wingate, George W. *History of the Twenty-Second Regiment of the National Guard of the State of New York; from Its Organization to 1895*. New York: 2010. Reprint of 1896.

Winslow, Calvin. *The Waterfront Workers: A New Perspective on Race and Class*. Urbana: University of Illinois Press, 1998.

Wittke, Carl. *Tambo and Bones*. New York: Greenwood Press, 1968.

Woodson, Carter G. "The Negroes of Cincinnati Prior to the Civil War." In *Free Blacks in America, 1800–1860*, edited by John H. Bracey Jr. Belmont, CA: Wadsworth Publishing, 1971.

Worley, Howard V. *Pittsburgh's Vintage Firemen*. Saxonburg, PA: HowDy Productions, 1997.

Yafa, Stephen. *Big Cotton: How a Humble Fiber Created Fortunes, Wrecked Civilizations, and Put America on the Map*. New York: Viking Penguin, 2005.

Yusuba, Yasukichi. *Birth Rates of the White Population in the United States 1800–1860*. Baltimore: Johns Hopkins Press, 1962.

Zelizer, Viviana A. *Pricing the Priceless Child: The Changing Social Value of Children*. Princeton, NJ: Princeton University Press, 1994. Reprint of 1985.

Zellers, Parker. *Tony Pastor: Dean of the Vaudeville Stage*. Ypsilanti, MI: Eastern University Press, 1971.

ORIGINAL MANUSCRIPTS AND RECORDS

Birth, Death, and Marriage Records. Pennsylvania Room, Carnegie Public Library, Oakland, PA.

Foster, Eliza Clayland. Transcribed by Joanne O'Connell. *Sketches and Incidents of Pittsburgh*. Center for American Music, University of Pittsburgh, Pittsburgh, PA.

Foster Family Letters. Foster Hall Collection, Stephen Foster Memorial, Center for American Music, University of Pittsburgh, Pittsburgh, PA.

Foster, Jane McDowell. Letters and Documents, Mifflin County Historical Society, Lewistown, PA.

Foster Letters. Center for American Music, University of Pittsburgh, Pittsburgh, PA.

Manuscript book of Stephen Collins Foster. Center for American Music, University of Pittsburgh, Pittsburgh, PA.

Morrison Foster Scrapbook. Center for American Music, University of Pittsburgh, Pittsburgh, PA.

Pastor, Tony. *Comic Songsters*. American Music Hall Playbills, Harvard Theatre Collection, Houghton Library, Cambridge, MA.

Pennsylvania Railroad Men's News Vol. 9, No. 8, August 1897. Foster Collection, Center for American Music, University of Pittsburgh, Pittsburgh, PA.

"Stephen C. Foster at Athens: His First Composition." Tioga Point Museum, No. 222. Copyright 1941.

NEWSPAPERS

New York Times. 1860–1864.
Pittsburgh Gazette. September–December, 1861.
Pittsburgh Post. 1856–1863.
Saturday Evening Visiter [sic].

INDEX

ABOUT THE AUTHOR

JoAnne O'Connell has a background in history and classical vocal music. She earned her PhD at the University of Pittsburgh, where she began researching her revisionist biography of the Pittsburgh-born composer Stephen Collins Foster. She has taught at colleges and universities in Pennsylvania and Maryland and currently spends her time researching and writing.